About the Authors

Sara Naheedy has represented clients in real estate, immigration, emp
matters. She has practiced law in both the federal and state systems
several attorneys who defended individuals and business entities in an $80 million federal RICO
lawsuit in Los Angeles that eventually settled through mediation. She worked as in-house counsel
for a property management company that she represented in numerous small claims lawsuits.
Litigating small claims cases was a major influence on her view of the law as it affects ordinary
Americans. She understands the frustration that most people experience when faced with the
complexities and inefficiencies of the U.S. legal system and holds the view that it is often preferable
to mediate rather than litigate. Sara has been practicing law since 2009. She received her Juris
Doctor from Chapman University School of Law.

Tom Scott has been a litigant in approximately two dozen cases involving traffic, small claims,
criminal, divorce, jurisdictional, and other legal matters. In court he has defeated individuals who
are supposed to uphold the law—police, lawyers, and judges. He has an amazing sixteen and four
win/loss record and has won his last nine battles. The remaining matters are "ties," are ongoing, or
have another status. Although sometimes costly and mentally draining, his personal experience in
various courts in three states over more than two decades has provided him with the best means for
helping others avoid the pitfalls within the treacherous U.S. judiciary. Tom is also coauthoring *Stack
the Health Odds in Your Favor*.

Important Notice

Although the intended purpose of this book is to aid the American public in their interactions with the U.S. legal system and to help them protect themselves from it, by no means should this book be construed as a substitute for the advice or recommendations of the reader's personal attorney. The information provided herein is not legal advice or advice of any kind, and no attorney-client or confidential relationship is or should be formed by any application thereof. The authors and publisher expressly disclaim all responsibility for any detrimental or adverse effects resulting from the use or application of any of the templates, explanations, ideas, or information contained in this book.

First Edition	FEBRUARY 2016
Editor	RANDY SCHNEIDER
Cover Design	TOM SCOTT
Book Design	SARA NAHEEDY AND TOM SCOTT

Publisher   **Smart Play Publishing**

Sara Naheedy, Tom Scott

Stack the Legal Odds in Your Favor
Understand America's Corrupt Judicial System — Protect Yourself Now and Boost Chances of Winning Cases Later

www.stloiyf.com

ISBN 978-0-9965929-0-1

Dedication

This book is dedicated to individuals who have been victimized by the U.S. judicial system. In particular, it is dedicated to people who have been unjustly imprisoned and, in some cases, those who have been executed or have died in U.S. jails or prisons while serving time for crimes they did not commit. But it is also dedicated to other victims—everyone who has suffered injustices and deleterious effects at the hands of police, lawyers, judges, and other officials or entities associated with the system.

One can only speculate, but this all-inclusive group must currently number well over one million. Merely listing the subset of those who have been wrongly imprisoned would be prohibitive since it is estimated that there are literally more than a hundred thousand such persons to date. Additionally, the list is a dynamic one that is growing all the time, and every one of these people— past, present, and future—should not be forgotten. While not named explicitly on this page, we sympathize with these men, women, and children.

We have personally heard about many legal calamities from clients, family, friends, and others. The injustices they have suffered and the injustices suffered by people like them have guided us in the selection and presentation of material. We dedicate this book to all the foregoing individuals. Their tragedies have helped shape it and consequently may conceivably help others avoid becoming future victims of our country's defective legal system.

Acknowledgments

We extend our sincerest thanks and best wishes to the following individuals and businesses whose contributions were invaluable to the success of this project. It was a massive undertaking that required well over 3,000 hours of research, writing, and management. Certainly, it would not have been possible without their contributions.

Randy Schneider, editor, for his hawk-eye attention to detail, his valuable input during the entire final phase of this project, and his ultra-dry sense of humor along the way

Michael Mitroff of Casino Magic, San Diego, CA, for providing the blackjack table layout for the cover design, www.casinomagicparties.com

Zachary Barron, San Diego, CA, for photography of cover art and Sara Naheedy, www.zacharybarron.com

Robert Taliver, New York, NY, for photography of Tom Scott

Florence Chase, Tom Scott's high school English teacher, who strengthened his grasp of the English language and honed his writing skill

Table of Contents

Foreword vi

Preface viii

Introduction ix

Part I — The Legal System Is a BIG Gamble 1

    Chapter 1: The Game — Good and Bad (Mostly Bad) 3

    Chapter 2: Like Any Casino, the Legal System Is Not Your Friend 11

    Chapter 3: Behind the Scenes 25

Part II — House Rules 33

    Chapter 4: Possession Really Is Nine-Tenths of the Law 35

    Chapter 5: Rule Enforcers Are Oftentimes Rule Breakers 41

    Chapter 6: Making the Rules Work for You 49

    Chapter 7: Miscellaneous Rules 57

Part III — Playing the Game 71

    Chapter 8: Various Paths on Which to Proceed 73

    Chapter 9: Small Claims 83

    Chapter 10: Traffic Cases 107

    Chapter 11: Divorce Cases 133

    Chapter 12: Criminal Cases 145

    Chapter 13: Debt Collection 169

    Chapter 14: Residential Landlord-Tenant Law 179

    Chapter 15: Probate, Wills, and Related Law 187

    Chapter 16: Areas of Law Not Covered in Detail 197

    Appendix 207

    References 252

Foreword

While I am honored to have been asked to write the foreword to *Stack the Legal Odds in Your Favor*, I regret that this book is necessary. In a society governed by the principles of individual liberty and self-responsibility, it is easy to avoid becoming a defendant in criminal or civil litigation. All you need to do is keep your word, not take other people's property, and not initiate acts of physical violence. If you do harm another person, either intentionally or accidentally, you can still avoid litigation by accepting responsibility and fairly compensating the injured party.

In such a society, there would be no need for a book to teach those who have not committed an act of violence or fraud against their fellow citizens how to survive an encounter with the modern (in)justice system. Sadly, modern American society is neither free nor just. As a result, we live in a land where individuals are dragged into court, subjected to onerous fines, and even imprisoned for inadvertent or trivial violations of obscure laws and/or regulations. Individuals can also lose their livelihoods, property, and liberties via "civil" litigation thanks to the unholy alliance of unscrupulous lawyers and greedy plaintiffs who benefit from and contribute to our corrupt legal system.

Our legal system's transformation into a tool of oppression and redistribution shares the same origin as the American government's transformation into an imperial welfare-warfare-regulatory state: the widespread embrace of the ideologies of authoritarianism and entitlement. Calling the modern American government authoritarian may strike some as unduly harsh. But how else would you describe a society wherein government regulations control, to some degree or another, the means by which you get to work, your working conditions—including the individuals who can be hired and fired and the minimum pay they must receive, the food you can eat, or even the ways you raise and educate your children? Today, citizens of the so-called freest nation in the world are not even free of government regulations when they use the restroom.

Most of these regulations are justified as being "for our own good" or for the good of our fellow citizens. When government believes its ever-increasing control is for our benefit, it is inevitable that enforcement of laws will become increasingly draconian, with ever harsher penalties imposed for ever more trivial violations of ever more obscure regulations as clearly explained in this book.

While every authoritarian restriction on liberty is justified as being necessary for our protection, it has become increasingly common for laws to serve as little more than vehicles for legalized extortion. Civil asset forfeiture (more accurately called "civil asset theft") and laws allowing the use of red light cameras (more accurately called "red light scameras") are two of the most well-known examples of laws that exist mainly for the purpose of raising revenue. This kind of "justice system" usage is likely to escalate as the combination of growing deficits and economic decline make government officials increasingly desperate to wring more money from an already overtaxed populace.

The rise of the regulatory state has been accompanied by the rise of the welfare state. The welfare-regulatory state feeds, and is fed by, the belief that the government is not only capable of, but morally responsible for, providing all of our material needs and protecting us from all dangers and misfortunes—including those caused by our own poor life choices. The widespread embrace of the entitlement mentality has flipped the concept of rights on its head. Instead of a shield against government intrusions on our liberty, today many use rights as a sword to justify forcible redistribution either via government welfare programs or through litigation in government courts.

Just as unscrupulous politicians exploit the entitlement mentality to expand their power, unscrupulous lawyers (including judges) exploit the entitlement mentality to increase their wealth and influence. The result is a judicial system in which a business is held liable if its customers spill hot coffee on themselves. Judges, lawyers, and bureaucrats have even used the Americans with Disabilities Act to force employers to make "reasonable accommodations" for alcoholic employees.

Those of us who understand the dangers posed by the twin evils of authoritarianism and entitlement have several responsibilities. First, of course, is to do all we can to effect a change, starting with spreading the truth about the dangers of the current system and the benefits of liberty. When enough people understand the dangers of the course we are on, we can then force the politicians to change course.

While I am optimistic about the long-term prospects of the liberty movement, restoring limited government and replacing the entitlement culture with one of self-responsibility could take decades. Therefore, the second step is to ensure that we and our families are protected in the event of an economic collapse or an even further crackdown in civil liberties. It is also to ensure the same protection if we are dragged into court by the government or a predatory plaintiff.

This is why *Stack the Legal Odds in Your Favor* is such an important work. It provides an invaluable guide for laymen to survive the legal system. Some may say that it could teach those who lie, cheat, steal, and otherwise harm their fellow citizens how to avoid accountability for their actions. Unfortunately, the truth is that most of the bad actors in government and in business already know how to work the system to their benefit. It is the law-abiding citizens who would never expect to find themselves in a legal nightmare that would make Kafka blush who need the information contained in this book. *Stack the Legal Odds in Your Favor* is a must-read book for anyone who wants access to a variety of practical and not idealistic tools to help increase his chances of emerging from a run-in with our corrupt legal system with his liberty and/or property intact.

— Dr. Ron Paul
Former U.S. Representative

Preface

Thomas Jefferson warned in 1821: "...the germ of dissolution of our federal government is in the...judiciary; an irresponsible body, (for impeachment is scarcely a scare-crow) working like gravity by night and by day, gaining a little to-day & a little tomorrow, and advancing it's noiseless step like a thief, over the field of jurisdiction...it will render powerless the checks provided of one government on another, and will become as venal and oppressive as the government from which we separated."

Since the time of our country's founding centuries ago, several factors have cumulatively contributed to the government steadily eroding our constitutional rights. Corruption and the constantly expanding powers of our judicial system play major roles, thereby bringing Jefferson's cautionary tale to fruition. These problems within the system and the urgency to warn others about their consequences are specifically the driving force behind this self-help book.

Especially in criminal cases in which someone who leads a normal, everyday life is suddenly accused of a crime, having a robust plan in place could be a literal lifesaver. The following cannot be stressed strongly enough: *becoming ensnared in the criminal justice system is not some exceptionally rare occurrence that happens to someone who does not commit a crime.*

It is becoming far more commonplace for good, innocent people to fall victim to the U.S. criminal justice system. Between us we personally know at least twelve people whose lives were impacted by it through no fault of their own. Keep in mind that most people do not normally broadcast this sort of thing, nor does the subject typically arise in conversation. These individuals are merely the ones who coincidentally shared their stories with us—in actuality, we may know many others who have not. It is quite likely that you also know several such people.

Many individuals who have never interacted with the criminal justice system might believe it is fair and impartial—that only the guilty get arrested, tried, and convicted. Perhaps as law-abiding citizens, most people think there is no chance they will ever find themselves in the crosshairs of the criminal system. This complete fallacy will be debunked in the following pages.

Most attorneys would not be inclined to provide the information presented here to non-clients, and many would not be inclined to provide it to anyone under any circumstances. Doing so, most probably feel they would be giving away trade secrets by enlightening the average person about the trickery, widespread corruption, and true operation of the judiciary. In turn, they may think they would lose business by helping people make more informed decisions in order to be better prepared for a plethora of possible legal scenarios. Only an attorney with the willingness to help people outside her immediate geographic area would do so, one with altruistic motives who wants to be part of the solution instead of part of the problem. The field of potential attorneys that satisfies these criteria is miniscule indeed. Sara Naheedy is one of those attorneys.

Before our battles began with the U.S. court system, we were very much pro-death penalty. Like a good portion of the American population, we were unaware of the flaws and corruption within the system. We believed the justice system to be exactly that—a justice system—and not the "just us" system catering only to its members into which it has mostly morphed. However, after a few firsthand experiences with it, our distorted view of reality was quickly corrected to show that nothing could be further from the truth. Because of exposure to the system itself, we were, effectively speaking, tuned to the proper frequency to understand just how far we have come from the original justice system first instituted within our constitutional republic so many years ago by the Framers. We have also changed our stance on the death penalty. In short, our experiences are exactly what conceived this project in 2012.

Introduction

Since many readers might have disdain for lawyers, and justifiably so, it is noteworthy that Tom Scott is not a lawyer. It is precisely his involvement with the legal system as a non-lawyer that should resonate with many readers and his role as coauthor that should reassure readers who would otherwise discredit a book written strictly by lawyers. His experiences from outside the judicial system complement Sara's consummate experiences from inside to bring you a complete and perfect hybrid of unbiased, true, and logical information that can be used to navigate the often perilous legal waters. As far as we know, it is the only legal resource with this unique synergistic combination of authors.

Providing such a 360-degree view is optimal in helping people like you who may someday face the financial and mental strain of a civil or criminal lawsuit. Lawsuits can instantly shatter your world, especially if you are the victim of an unjust case. Furthermore, with federal, state, and local governments now in financial distress, there are other relatively minor instances when you may similarly fall victim. For example, the incentive to ticket motorists for moving and non-moving violations, quite often unjustified, and to generate income under the guise of justice directly and indirectly from other sources is soaring. With the preceding in mind, this is one of few prescriptive nonfiction books that can certainly save you money and possibly save your life.

A book such as this one is best read in its entirety *before* calamity strikes and then used later as a reference whenever the need arises. It is ideal as a preventative aid for every citizen aged eighteen and older who can unwittingly fall victim to the legal system or, worst-case, indispensable as a remedial tool for someone who needs a clearer understanding of or assistance with a current legal quagmire. Its primary suggested use derives from the notion that someone under the stress of an impending or existing legal action may not have the clarity of thought necessary to read and understand the presented material the first time through. Moreover, time is often of the essence in legal matters, so the importance of being thoroughly prepared cannot be overstated.

Whether braced for them or not, legal matters of any kind can be exhausting, financially draining, and time-consuming—and can originate through no fault of the defending party. When a legal issue suddenly arises, many people do not know where to turn. In the ensuing chapters, we will help you prepare for these battles by providing relevant information and tactics about how to fight not just the opposing party but also the legal system itself. This knowledge is critical since the system is frequently the most formidable opponent.

It is not an everyday occurrence having the police come to your door to question you about a criminal case. Neither is getting a summons to appear in court for a civil matter because of a lawsuit filed against you by a coworker, colleague, or business or being party to any life event that often mandates your participation in the judicial system, such as a death or divorce. It is ironic that the times when we are most taken by surprise are the times when we need to be most prepared. With this in mind, we uniquely provide as much background material as possible to orient you in the book's first two parts in order to set a solid foundation for understanding specific applications of law described in the third part. In essence, all the legal tools are presented for your selection.

At other times in life, it may be necessary to initiate your own lawsuit whether it is a brand new claim or some form of litigation related to previous litigation. In such cases, it is equally important to be well-informed about whatever lies ahead on the legal journey. The content in these same first two parts supplies you with the crucial provisions to sustain you on this trek.

It is fundamental to know that the U.S. judicial system has become a self-aggrandizing industry that focuses strictly on one thing—itself. Navigating it can be extraordinarily tricky and frustrating. But if you are well-equipped with the right information and right tools, it is possible for you to prevail when most others in the same circumstances would likely fail. *Knowing how to perform thorough research, get answers to important questions, and make solid arguments in a legal battle is of paramount importance and is 99 percent of good lawyering, no matter who does it.*

Our intent is to provide all the requisite data to help you every step of the way in a variety of the most common legal situations you are likely to encounter. It is our thirty-five-plus years' collective experience with the American judiciary that we wish to share in order to provide not every minute detail about how to handle every case but, at the very least, to point you in the right direction. We want to enable you to have the best possible chance of successfully handling the most prevalent legal matters.

Everything we discuss with regard to the legal system pertains to the state, federal, and Washington, D.C., court systems. However, do not forget that there are two other court systems in the United States that affect some people—the military court system for U.S. service members and the tribal court system for Native Americans. In order to provide as much information in as few pages as possible, we have focused solely on the state, federal, and D.C. systems. Nevertheless, much of the covered material could very well pertain to the other two and may prove quite helpful in situations in which individuals are facing legal issues in them.

This book is arranged with the early chapters describing a brief history of our system, why it is what it is today, where it will likely be in the future, and most of the ramifications associated with the operation of the system itself. Subsequent chapters in part III discuss specific areas of law that most people are likely to face at one time or another and present unorthodox methodologies about how to increase one's chances of successfully resolving such matters. Finally, the appendix contains links to pertinent websites, a rather broad spectrum of templates, and other valuable resources that complement the information contained within the book's body.

We have supplied the following material with the American public in mind. It is our hope to open the eyes of everyday Americans and to furnish the weaponry that will enable average citizens to defend themselves effectively against the reckless juggernaut known as the U.S. judiciary. This book is built upon a rudimentary framework of standard legal knowledge for the purpose of conveying new information. We deliberately avoided tending towards utopianism as all other known legal resources do. Instead, the material we share is presented in an atypical, exceedingly pragmatic manner.

Our objective is to provide you with every possible advantage for success in whatever legal situation you may face. In these pages, therefore, you will find fairly obscure facts about lawyers, revealing facets concerning court rules and laws, thorough discussions of both obvious and more esoteric attributes of the legal system as a whole, and detailed insights regarding many of the most common legal problems. All of this is clearly expounded to help you *stack the legal odds in your favor*!

PART I — THE LEGAL SYSTEM IS A BIG GAMBLE

Chapter 1: The Game — Good and Bad (Mostly Bad)

When the legislative or executive functionaries act unconstitutionally, they are responsible to the people in their elective capacity. The exemption of the judges from that is quite dangerous enough. I know no safe depository of the ultimate powers of the society, but the people themselves. — **Thomas Jefferson**

Chapter Sections

- The U.S. legal system has become a game
- Origin of the U.S. legal system
- Where the U.S. legal system is today
- Reasons for the system's decline
- Mass incarceration and some of its causes
- Direction the system is headed
- Few good aspects of the U.S. legal system

THE U.S. LEGAL SYSTEM HAS BECOME A GAME

First and foremost, the legal system has become a game. It benefits few individuals except the lawyers, judges, and others directly and indirectly associated with it who know how to play the game and prioritizes winning and generating revenue above all else. In civil cases, particularly divorce, the more the parties oppose each other, the more the system benefits. Such conflict produces more "work" for the lawyers, judges, courts, and corresponding parasitic entities and, therefore, more money for them.

Logic, law, justice, and truth often do not matter in a legal action and are frequently inadmissible in court. Furthermore, facts in any case can be spun. So-called experts get paid by each side to produce the desired result, namely, winning, and not necessarily to reveal the truth. Truth within the legal system is an elastic concept, and all too often, "justice" is only for those who can afford it.

ORIGIN OF THE U.S. LEGAL SYSTEM

But it was not always this way. Just after the Revolutionary War, the justice system was anything but a game. The Framers of the U.S. Constitution had studied the various forms of government exemplified by past empires, particularly ancient Rome. They knew power was something that could easily be abused and therefore implemented our constitutional republican form of government versus a traditional democracy as instituted by the ancient Greeks.

A strict democracy has various shortcomings, which will not be discussed here, but suffice it to say that the Founders had a thorough grasp of the good and bad characteristics of different types of governments. Based on their comprehensive knowledge of history, philosophy, and political theory, the Founders determined that a constitutional republic was the best form of government to safeguard individual liberty. Under the Constitution, the power of the federal government was to be shared between three coequal branches, each of which would serve as a check on the others' natural inclination to aggregate greater control to itself. In addition, the authority of the federal government was to be limited as made clear by the Tenth Amendment: "The powers not delegated to the United States by the Constitution, nor prohibited by it to the States, are reserved to the States respectively, or to the people."

The style of government the Founders created served the United States relatively well for a time—when life was simpler, when people and laws were fewer, and when people were more actively engaged in government. Fast-forward about 100 years, and the government so carefully crafted by these brilliant men gradually begins to unwind. As Thomas Jefferson warned us nearly two centuries ago, this degeneration began primarily because of the judicial branch usurping power, which continues today.

WHERE THE U.S. LEGAL SYSTEM IS TODAY

The judicial branch has transformed into a large, powerful, and far-reaching network of components and players in a metaphorical ballgame in which the American citizenry is the ball. This game is most prevalent in civil and criminal proceedings in all courts throughout America. Money and property of the average U.S. citizen are sacrificed in the former, and the citizens themselves are sacrificed in the latter.

For example, in criminal matters, prosecutors are rewarded based upon how many convictions they get, not upon how many cases in which they discover the truth. To the contrary, they sometimes try to keep the truth hidden if doing so will help secure their victory.[1] The more wins a lawyer gets, the more notoriety he gets, and correspondingly, the more quickly he moves up the ranks and likely increases his earnings. Additionally, many district attorneys use their office merely as a stepping-stone to a higher office and even greater rewards—becoming a judge or another official, for instance.

It is worthy to note the sordid state of our judicial system is not just something that happened overnight. It has morphed fairly significantly but gradually over time. In the early days of America, the intent was that a knowledgeable person could choose to represent himself, commonly called "*pro se*," in any legal matter and typically do no worse than he would with the assistance of counsel.

The term "*pro se*" is sometimes used interchangeably with "*sui juris*" or "*in propria persona*," which is frequently abbreviated "*in pro per*." It has been argued that they have legally distinct definitions, which they do, and that it might be important to use one over the other. In reality, the court will consider no distinction between them. Beating the system is accomplished by due diligence, by using its rules against it, and by various means discussed later, not by focusing on the nuances between the definitions of these or any other legal terms in an attempt to thwart a legal action as some sources might suggest.

One could proceed *pro se* much more easily in the past because our system was in a far better state than it is today. But over time and with the nearly exponential growth of the number of laws at the local, state, and federal levels, what once was simple has become an increasingly complex, confusing, and clandestine system. For the average person who has not read this book, this makes assistance of a good attorney almost a necessity in any traffic, small claims, or uncontested divorce case or in any matter that would otherwise have been straightforward. How convenient it is that the lawyers who are practicing law benefit from the lawyers in Congress legislating new laws.

REASONS FOR THE SYSTEM'S DECLINE

Lawyers of years past once covered all areas of law in their practice; however, statutes have become quite numerous and oftentimes complex. Because of this and the introduction of so many new laws every year, litigation has multiplied. Lawyers have become specialists whose practice is now limited to specific areas of law, such as divorce, landlord-tenant, criminal defense, and wills and trusts, just to name a few examples.

Other factors have contributed to the decline of our legal system. Since colonial times, many jurisdictions have quashed the right to trial by jury in some civil actions. Contemporary examples include small claims and divorce. The same holds true for certain lesser criminal actions as will be explained in chapter twelve's CRIMINAL OFFENSE CLASSIFICATIONS section. The system's partial abrogation of the right to trial by jury given to us in the U.S. Constitution has been a major detriment to the average litigant. Consider that it is far more difficult to bribe, persuade, or corrupt an uninterested party of several, a jury, than an interested party of one, a judge. Many other rights in the Bill of Rights have also been obliterated by the system, further contributing to the decline.[2] [3]

Yet another contributing factor is concealment of jury nullification power. Absolutely no entity within the legal industry today will be forthcoming with this now super-secret rule. What jury nullification power, also known as jury veto power, provides is that any jury can decide not only the facts of a particular case but also the fairness, constitutionality, and basic aspects of the laws applicable to the case itself. If the average citizen was aware of this right, which, in the United States, originated during colonial times, it would have a significant negative impact on the judicial system's business.

For example, one of the authors was a defendant in a legal matter in which a state government selectively enforced a law in an attempt to obtain a conviction. This clearly violated the equal protection clause of the Fourteenth Amendment of the U.S. Constitution, which states, "nor deny to any person within its jurisdiction the equal protection of the laws."[4] If the case had gone to jury trial, the fact that the coauthor-defendant's constitutional rights had been violated could have been revealed to the jury by the coauthor-defendant. Litigation would likely have ended much simpler and less expensively than it actually did had this happened and the jury used their nullification power. Additionally, the Fifth Amendment right of an accused person to an indictment by a grand jury prior to being formally charged in a matter such as this particular one was also completely ignored. Indeed, further investigation probably would have revealed the state's violation of other constitutional rights of the author-defendant as well.

The sheer magnitude of laws in America also cannot be overlooked as a contributing factor to the decline of our legal system. This number has likely increased well over a thousandfold since colonial times. Research for the number of statutes in any given state has yielded over 20,000 on the low end to more than 50,000 on the high end.[5][6][7][8][9][10] Someone living in just one state for his entire life would be subject to a bare minimum of 20,000 state laws and 20,000 federal laws.[11]

For 15 percent of the American population who live in four or more states during their lifetimes, this number jumps to a minimum of 100,000 state and federal statutory laws.[12] Assuming a conservative average of three minutes to read and memorize the state laws applicable in four different states and each federal law, it would take someone significantly longer than half a year of continuous reading to do this! These numbers, of course, exclude additional laws at the town, city, and county levels and thousands of new ones introduced every year at all levels.

Perhaps the most dominant—and certainly the saddest—reason for the decline of our judicial system is public apathy. Abraham Lincoln's "government of the people, by the people, for the people" is certainly not by the people anymore. Involvement in government by the average U.S. citizen today is nearly nonexistent. Americans are so obsessed with TV, media, entertainment, notoriety, and other meaningless things that they have largely ignored what has transpired within our system. It is us. We the people are mostly to blame for letting this happen. While some have certainly taken a stand against encroaching judicial tyranny, those individuals are nowhere near great enough in number to make an impact.

As bad as the legal system is today, its dysfunction has accelerated in the past few decades and continues to do so. It is our belief that the system is just as corrupt as any flagrantly corrupt judiciary in a third-world country. However, the United States is not quite so open about its corruption and continues to purvey propaganda at the highest levels of leadership that the exact opposite is true. Because of the exorbitant number of laws in existence, many of which are obscure, obsolete, confusing, and just plain idiotic, and because of other factors discussed previously, corruption is rife within the industry. The system has become a business that feeds and governs itself, no longer complying with the checks and balances instituted by the Framers nor responding to the will of the electorate.

In the same vein, the court system has become proficient at perpetuating itself and has spawned a host of subsidiaries that, in turn, feed from it. For example, if someone is charged with but not necessarily convicted of a criminal offense, there are a wide variety of parasitic feeders ready and willing to "assist" that person. Counselors, psychiatrists, probation departments, defensive driving courses, anger management classes, alcohol and drug abuse rehabilitation clinics, and community service groups, such as unpaid highway workers and cleanup crews, all exist predominantly because of the system. And by no means is this an exhaustive list.

These and other such offshoots of the system are its answer to the problems it creates through its own dysfunction, partially caused by corruption, out-of-control government, and an overwhelming number of laws. The symbiotic relationship between the legislative and judicial branches of government magnifies the problems. The system is proficient at creating the malady that requires its own "remedy." Judges, lawyers, police, and all the parasitic feeders would not exist if there were no "crimes" or litigation to be had, a fact that has become the contemporary nature of the beast. It is obviously in their best interests to add a constant source of fuel to the legal fire to keep this juggernaut industry alive and well at the public's expense.

MASS INCARCERATION AND SOME OF ITS CAUSES

Another negative aspect of the game is the overinflated incarceration rate. Currently it is just under 1 percent of the American population. The United States accounts for approximately 4.4 percent of the world's population, yet nearly 22 percent of the world's incarcerated dwell within our country's borders.[13] [14] Since it is extremely unlikely that people here are any better or worse on average than people elsewhere in the world, the number of individuals in domestic confinement is roughly five times higher than it should be even with dropping crime rates.

Various estimates of innocent people serving time range from a low of 2.3 percent to possibly even greater than 5 percent.[15] These estimates neglect inmates not yet convicted of anything—those merely awaiting trial, those languishing in protective custody, those being held for contempt of court, and others. Thus, the total of all innocent incarcerated people is sharply higher. With well over two million individuals in U.S. confinement as of 2013, 2.3 percent translates to more than 50,000 innocent persons imprisoned in the "land of the free."[16]

Put another way, this minimum number is just shy of the U.S. military casualty total for the Vietnam War. This is alarming and raises the question of why the incarceration rate is so high compared to the rest of the world. Once again, this is a relatively new development within our legal system, and the fairly recent privatization of prisons has compounded the problem.

In fact, almost two-thirds of private prison corporations have contracts requiring an 80 percent or higher occupancy rate. Taxpayers have to foot the bill for cells comprising any shortfall.[17] Augmenting the problem is the fact that prisoners manufacture many different products for various companies at an average cost of pennies per day. These include UNICOR, an arm of the U.S. Bureau of Prisons, and several private companies and corporations, with none having requirements to provide health insurance, 401(k) plans, or paid vacations. In light of these factors, it is not too difficult to see why the system demands that judges fill prisons with warm bodies.[18] [19] The confluence of the exploding U.S. inmate population, the rise of private prisons, and various businesses' utilization of inmate labor has been aptly termed the "prison-industrial complex."

Further exacerbating the situation is something commonly known as the "three-strikes law." Several states, the federal government, and Washington, D.C., have implemented this little gem. The general form of such a statute is that an individual found guilty of three felonies is punished with a prison sentence much longer than the longest sentence normally associated with any of the felonies individually. In some cases, a three-strikes conviction can result in a life sentence for the offender. The major problem with this law is that a felonious offense could be some innocuous, mundane act that just so happens to be defined as a "felony" in the particular jurisdiction where the "offender" resides. With a minimum of 20,000 state laws in any given state and a minimum of 20,000 federal laws, it is hard to believe there is any shortage of criminal laws for an overzealous or unethical prosecutor to charge whomever he so chooses.[20]

DIRECTION THE SYSTEM IS HEADED

Barring another revolution, there is no reason to believe anything in the legal industry will change for the better anytime soon. Any changes that occur will likely be for the worse. With the United States of America basically a police state after 9/11 and with the U.S. Constitution effectively being used as a doormat by those in power, an end to the decline of the U.S. judiciary appears nowhere in sight.

Therefore, citizens need to be well prepared for any legal battles that may lie ahead. The trend will probably continue with more corruption, higher costs, greater disparity, and less justice. Information in this book will be an invaluable asset to anyone who wants to have the biggest advantage when the legal system strikes. In all probability, the question is not *if* it will strike, but *when* it will strike the average person with little political power or influence.

The advent of organizations, such as The Innocence Project, whose primary function is to vindicate the wrongly convicted, which they have done in quantity, has further bolstered the fact that our system is broken. At the time of this writing, the number of exonerations resulting from these organizations via DNA testing and other means has easily eclipsed 1,500, although it may exceed 2,000 by the time this book is published.[21] With respect to the 50,000-plus innocent incarcerated people mentioned earlier, there is obviously a large gap between the number of exonerated individuals and those still rightfully awaiting freedom.

The overall dysfunction of our system is apparent in many cases in recent history. These include the Duke lacrosse criminal case involving corrupt former district attorney Michael Nifong; the case of the Korean family dry cleaner being sued for $54 million by Roy Pearson, a former judge, for mishandling his clothing; and many more.[22] [23] Some have been publicized, and some have not. But these and others exemplify the rampant cancer in our judiciary today. Such outrageous and nonsensical suits were likely nonexistent during the early days of our country.

Excluding contributing data of unjust prosecutions from the criminal side of the system and focusing strictly on frivolous tort cases, the number of such actions commenced yearly in U.S. courts must at least reach into the thousands. Projecting the data available in 2012 for eighteen states onto all fifty, the total tort claim caseload averaged about 4.2 percent of all civil claims filed in that year. With approximately 17 million incoming civil cases every year, a hypothetical 1 percent of them being deemed frivolous would translate into more than 7,000 baseless tort lawsuits annually.[24] Some of them inevitably get tossed; therefore, nobody wins—except the system, which amounts to nothing more than legalized extortion in the form of filing fees, attorney fees, and other costs.

Ridiculous rulings are now being made by judges at all levels within the system, rulings that twist and distort law, truth, and reality by sometimes making what is wrong right and making what is right wrong. This includes rulings made in our highest court that are sometimes in direct opposition to the will of the majority of Americans. There is no doubt that we are all doomed if something remedial is not done soon.

FEW GOOD ASPECTS OF THE U.S. LEGAL SYSTEM

As far as any good aspects remaining in the U.S. legal system, there really are not many. The internet is a fairly recent and valuable tool with which to fight back, and the appendix provides links to ample websites to reference for a wide assortment of information. Perhaps another advantage a litigant has today versus many years ago is more time. This is because the system has created so much work for itself that the backlog of cases allows litigants to prepare longer for their court dates, which can be many months or years in the future in some instances. Of course, this is a double-edged sword for incarcerated people awaiting their "speedy" trial.

Another possible good aspect may reside in the power of the grand jury. Although widely debated across the political spectrum, some regard the grand jury as the fourth branch of government. Grand juries are not only responsible for presenting indictments in some large, prominent criminal matters. They also serve a variety of functions, one of which is as a mechanism for ordinary citizens to obtain retribution against corrupt prosecutors, judges, and other public officials in states whose grand juries serve the function of investigating these individuals.[25] Where available for that purpose, grand juries should provide a more viable means of redress than any of the generally ineffective oversight boards discussed in the INEFFECTIVE CHECKS AND BALANCES section of chapter three.

The first clause of the Fifth Amendment of the U.S. Constitution specifically states, "No person shall be held to answer for a capital, or otherwise infamous crime, unless on a presentment or indictment of a Grand Jury..."[26] The Framers intended grand juries to serve as protection for the people from corrupt government. This right, granted us under the Bill of Rights, was one of the first to be trampled back in 1884. Since *Hurtado v. California*, fewer state criminal matters require indictment by a grand jury.[27] However, the fact that they still exist does not necessarily restrict them to usage by prosecutors for issuing indictments in criminal cases. Ordinary citizens in some states can provide them with evidence of corruption and criminal activity against public officials—even against the prosecutors and judges in the citizens' communities. This is perhaps the grand jury's most salient contemporary feature.

Keep in mind that these juries are normally comprised of ordinary people within the community but outside the legal system. Serving on them may last for much longer than a year. Therefore, they are sometimes largely composed of retirees who happen to have a genuine interest in justice, as opposed to many judges and other public officials within our courts. Since grand juries are independent of the system, they can be considered to be on your side rather than the judicial system's side. Granted, they overwhelmingly indict ordinary citizens and return "no bill" decisions against law enforcement, but this must be because of the way prosecutors present their cases to them. However, when an average person brings a complaint or evidence of corruption or criminal activity, grand juries can be most useful.

Also, unlike regular juries, also known as petit juries, with which the public is not allowed to interact or communicate during any court proceeding, grand juries that investigate public corruption are highly accessible to the citizenry. Prompting such an investigation can be accomplished in various ways, including submission of a complaint via U.S. mail or electronically or presenting evidence in person. It is even possible for everyday people to present evidence of public corruption or criminal activity to grand juries where they do not specifically have that investigative duty.

The grand jury is perhaps the best front on which to attack a public servant legally for wrongdoing. A notarized complaint, a criminal one if appropriate, should be the most that is required against a particular party when enlisting the grand jury. No special authorization should be needed from anyone, regardless of what you may be told. Entire books can be written about grand juries, but the intent of this one is to mention their prime features.

This chapter has provided a general history of the system and offered some of the many reasons why it is where it is today. The basic nature of the beast having been presented, the need to grasp many other fundamentals, learn how to protect yourself from the system, and dig deeper in order to understand it more fully is paramount before undertaking any legal matter. All of this is the subject of the following chapters in the first two parts of this book.

Chapter 2: Like Any Casino, the Legal System Is Not Your Friend

Never yield to force; never yield to the apparently overwhelming might of the enemy. — **Winston Churchill**

Chapter Sections

- Misconception held by the public
- What the legal system is
- Trust nobody
- First steps to take in any case
- Researching law and making solid arguments
- What you are up against
- "Judge shopping" to avoid bad judges
- When things go wrong
- Last resort

MISCONCEPTION HELD BY THE PUBLIC

Perhaps the biggest misconception held by the public is that the legal system is based on law, justice, and truth. People believe that if they do not commit a crime or if they have a 100 percent legitimate civil claim against an entity or individual, they have absolutely nothing to worry about. They think having facts and righteousness on their side is all that matters and will vindicate them in the end. Nothing could be further from the truth. Entire books have been written illustrating that this is not the case. In fact, it is more likely that when any right and just party prevails in court, this does not happen because of the system but *in spite* of it.

At one point in our country's history, this was not necessarily so, but in recent times, roughly in the last hundred years and particularly in the last few decades, it is a reality. In order to have the greatest chance of prevailing, the new Golden Rule applies. Its two definitions are the following:

1. Do *not* do unto others as you would have them do unto you; do unto others *before* they do unto you.
2. The person who has the gold makes the rules.

WHAT THE LEGAL SYSTEM IS

There are also fairly distinctive attributes of the legal system found in few other industries that lend it to being abysmal. It may harbor the only profession in which underperformance, if not outright failure, is generally acceptable. Of the legal actions involving two opposing parties in which both are represented by lawyers, remember that about half of the cases decided by trials are lost by those attorneys. One side wins, and the other side loses, just like any real game, barring any ties. Although some are not, there are certainly times losing attorneys are incompetent, lazy, unprepared, and unprincipled. They sometimes even do things that are illegal—yet they still get paid—and this is accepted because that is the way the system operates.

Unquestionably, the legal system is unlike almost any other industry. It is the only known one that has almost no external competition. This is perhaps the greatest contributor to its endemic corruption, high costs, and bad service and all of its other problems—most of which we might experience as consumers at our local Home Depot without a Lowe's in town, effectively speaking. If the legal industry was not a governmental business, it would be considered a monopoly and be dismantled under antitrust laws. Our largely unchallenged system is therefore a breeding ground for corruption and selective treatment.

Similar to the way a player in a casino is treated to free drinks, given other special benefits, and afforded ample attention by casino staff, all of which increase as the amount of money she places on the line increases, the legal industry panders to its own "high rollers." They receive benefits in the form of dropped criminal charges, more favorable outcomes, and the like.[1] [2] This in no way means the legal system is their friend any more than a casino is a gambler's friend, but simply means that each entity's amity is directly proportional to the amount of money involved. Regardless of the players, the system and casino ultimately want everyone to lose, that is, to contribute money in some way to their bottom line.

Keep in mind this illusion of friendship is transitory. Once a player is no longer a "high roller," she becomes less attractive to the casino or judiciary and all benefits suddenly vanish. Clearly, the casino personnel's behavior toward a gambler and the application of rules by the legal system vary for different people and entities. However, as in so many instances when there are two sets of rules, the set that applies is determined by level of wealth, and correspondingly, amount of power, and preferential treatment thus waxes or wanes accordingly.

If any flaw existed in the Framers' thinking, there may have been only one—not seeing the need for and thus having created a second, parallel judicial system, which certainly would have been better for the public. A second system would function to restrain the competing, out-of-control first system and vice versa, as would be the case in any normal competitive free market. The judicial branch is the only one of the three U.S. branches of government that directly "serves" the people on a daily basis. It is also the only one wherein having competition would be so effective in mitigating, if not completely eradicating, its malevolent and undesirable characteristics.

TRUST NOBODY

Because of a single judicial system with virtually no competition, corruption can grow and fester. Corruption can be found from top to bottom in any segment of the system in any part of the country at any time. Police officers lie, cheat, and do all sorts of illegal things. Lawyers lie, cheat, and do all sorts of illegal things. Judges lie, cheat, and do all sorts of illegal things. It is no different in any of the three groups. We are not implying all do—you may be fortunate in your legal interactions and experience only the pockets of true justice within the system. Unfortunately, they are few and far between, so this is highly unlikely and becomes more so as the number of interactions increases.

The fact that police officers, lawyers, and judges can lie, cheat, and do illegal things at any time means that ordinary people participating in the system, voluntarily or not, should trust none of its members! This is especially true when a great deal of money is on the line and even more so when someone's life is potentially on the line. It is difficult to be certain, but based upon our experience, it is likely that at least 50 percent of the police force, 25 percent of judges, and 80 percent of litigation attorneys do not fulfill their duties with complete integrity. A safe bet is to be conservative and assume these numbers are underestimated. This way, the average citizen can prepare for any legal battle in such a way as to expect the worst but to try and hope for the best.

To illustrate the point even further regarding litigation attorneys, consider the joke: "How can you tell when a lawyer is lying? When his lips move." What makes jokes funny is that they are based in truth. Whenever battling an attorney either directly as an adversary or indirectly as counsel of an opponent, contemplate *not* taking anything she says as gospel. Our experience has shown that attorneys will blatantly fabricate evidence and make false statements simply to win a case. Check all cited references in their pleadings. The fact that a reference is cited properly and otherwise looks legitimate is no indication whatsoever of its validity.

For example, attorney Francis S. Holbrook II made at least one untrue statement in a written filing while opposing one author during a Rhode Island legal matter: "See footnote 10 in *Rivera* which confirms that the Supreme Court is against rigidly applying time-of-appeal rules." However, footnote 10 actually stated, "We are reminded of the following famous observation of then-Judge Cardozo: 'Let the hardship be strong enough, and equity will find a way, though many a formula of inaction may seem to bar the path.' *Graf v. Hope Building Corp.*, 171 N.E. 884, 888 (N.Y. 1930)." This is nowhere near close enough to the attorney's statement to be considered a typographical error. What is being stressed here is the need to check *everything* any lawyer is putting forth as "facts."

Not that it is anything new, but in the last decade or so, there has been an abundance of publicized cases in which individuals in all three major divisions of the legal system—police, lawyers, and judges—were caught doing unscrupulous or illegal things. Some examples were given in chapter one in the DIRECTION THE SYSTEM IS HEADED section. At the top end of the system, there was the "kids for cash" scandal in Pennsylvania in which President Judge Mark Ciavarella and Senior Judge Michael Conahan accepted bribes from a local private prison to send juveniles there to keep the cells filled.[3]

More recently, there was the case involving Carmen Segarra, the Federal Reserve, Goldman Sachs, and U.S. District Judge Ronnie Abrams. Ms. Segarra was improperly fired by Goldman Sachs, but the judge ruled against her despite the fact that the judge's husband was representing Goldman Sachs in an advisory capacity. Judge Abrams refused to recuse herself from the case, or voluntarily remove herself. While refusal to recuse is not a criminal act as defined by law, which it probably should be, the relationship between the judge's spouse and a party to the matter was clearly a conflict of interest for the judge. Regardless of the case's legal specifics, Judge Abrams's decision to continue presiding certainly appears to have prejudiced the case against Ms. Segarra.[4]

At the bottom end of the judicial system, the police are not reluctant to commit illegal or unethical acts either. The reason for their bold behavior is probably that they are often immune to prosecution, much like lawyers and judges. Police officers have been known to file false police reports and treat the victim of a crime as the criminal. An example of this is the case wherein Florida Highway Patrol Trooper Scott Kunstmann falsely arrested several people for DUI and falsified the police reports.[5] Amazingly, he was fired from the department for these actions, but that was essentially the extent of his punishment by the system. Although the two main felony charges against him carried a combined maximum penalty of ten years in prison and a $10,000 fine, Kunstmann served no time.[6] One author knows someone personally who was similarly the victim of a false DUI arrest, albeit in another state, so this may be more common than one might think.

When police officers, lawyers, or judges are caught in wrongdoing, it is difficult to believe that they have not previously committed similar inappropriate acts. Most people in positions of power are able to conceal their crimes and gross improprieties much longer than ordinary citizens who commit the same transgressions. It is ironic that any discipline doled out to the lawbreakers in these instances is *less* severe than it is to the average person when all logic dictates that it should be *more* severe because they know the law and, criminal defense attorneys excepted, enforce it on unsuspecting citizens every day.

Federal statistics from 2010 show that the percentage of officials convicted of corruption is only slightly lower than the average conviction rate. More telling, however, they also show that the percentage of these people sentenced to prison is sharply lower than average, with far more serving lighter sentences of three years or less—74 percent versus 53 percent on average. Also, note that less than 0.4 percent of all federal criminal cases are filed against public officials for corruption.[7] If you believe the disease in our system is not widespread and corresponds to a number that low, we have a bridge to sell you in Brooklyn.[8]

It is also important to realize that when these rogues are discovered and "punished," there is an extreme lack of effort to review the perpetrator's history for further occurrences of misconduct. The reason the system does not want to investigate the police officer, lawyer, judge, or other official is strictly one of economics. If it did so and found more cases involving parties injured by these perpetrators, many would have to be re-litigated, costing the courts ample time and precious resources that could not be focused on generating fresh income from new litigants and new cases. Getting things right is of secondary importance or maybe even of no importance whatsoever. Clearing the docket while generating revenue is what matters most to the courts.

Contrast these priorities with those of a service-oriented company. Such a company—a flooring installer or plumber, for example—may be asked by its customers to redo work because it was not initially done properly. If the company does not comply with any legitimate customers' request, it will go out of business because of competition. However, the chances of the courts redoing work, or re-litigating cases, are negligible.

This book could present many more examples of corruption by police, lawyers, and judges, but we hope our point has been made. In fact, it would most likely have to become a massive series of tomes in order to cover all such cases in U.S. history. One important fact to recognize is that the publicized offenses committed by individuals in the legal system are only the ones being *reported*. It may very well be that these are only a small sampling of the true number of such misdeeds, many of which go undetected or just unreported.

Regarding state judges and prosecutors, some states afford their citizenry the advantage of being able to elect them, while in others they are appointed. In places where they are elected, the public at least has some control over who is put into these powerful positions. Unfortunately, all federal judges, including U.S. Supreme Court justices, and judges with local jurisdiction in the nation's capital are appointed. In some cases, sheriffs are elected, but ordinary police officers are not. Granted, people can choose which attorney they want to hire, but they cannot choose the individuals they want for their local police force or for various judgeships. The appointment of people to these positions is another major contributor to the problems in our legal system.

FIRST STEPS TO TAKE IN ANY CASE

For whatever reason, possibly because of the system's public relations machine, many people faced with civil and criminal cases instinctively think of contacting and hiring a good lawyer. On paper this is an elementary idea. In reality, it is not so easy. What *is* easy is creating a second problem while trying to solve the first—hiring a lawyer that will extinguish your fire with gasoline.

Hiring a Lawyer

In almost any legal battle, one of the preliminary steps is considering whether to hire a lawyer, but choosing a good and trustworthy one is a monumental task most of the time. Other than already having such an attorney, getting a referral from a friend or family member, or having a friend or family member who is an attorney, you will be faced with looking for and possibly hiring someone whom you do not know, at least indirectly. You will be expected to trust this person implicitly for a potentially important life event.

Many municipalities have lawyer referral services to help individuals find a lawyer. All that these services do is ask what particular area of law your matter entails, for example, divorce, criminal, or traffic, basically spin the wheel, and hand you an attorney that has a "check in the box" in that area of expertise and is in good standing with the bar. This might not be the optimal way to find the attorney who is best for you.

The good news is that there are several websites that rate lawyers. The bad news is that lawyers can rate other lawyers on some of them. This is similar to the fox guarding the henhouse. Having said that, if you do stumble upon such a site and find a *negative* rating of one lawyer from another, you might be better-off having Martin "Sleeps Through Trial" Zimmerman represent you if you had been considering hiring the rated attorney. Additionally, some lawyer rating sites combine factors unrelated to an attorney's track record and professionalism towards her clients when calculating a given rating, which may skew it.

Other online resources, such as Martindale-Hubble and the lawyer search feature of the Cornell law website, are somewhat useful. Websites completely outside the legal realm that specialize in rating the full spectrum of businesses including law firms and lawyers probably provide more accurate ratings than sites that use anything but the public's input. This is because everyday people have previously hired the law firms or attorneys listed on such sites and reviewed them accordingly. Similar to other businesses on these sites, a lawyer or firm having many reviews is generally more indicative of the lawyer's or firm's true rating than one with only a few.

Whenever news of a lawsuit comes as a big surprise, such as being charged with a crime or being served in a divorce or another civil matter, it is important to think carefully, clearly, and calmly. This may be easier said than done, but it is absolutely crucial. If the luxury of time exists, rushing to pick and employ any attorney, even a recommended one, is foolish. When asked, some lawyers will allow referrals from former clients by asking them to contact the potential client for a question-and-answer session. This is something to consider seriously.

Lawyers are governed by various entities in the state, federal, and Washington, D.C., court systems. Researching a lawyer through the relevant governing body may reveal a disciplinary action. If so, it is strongly suggested that you investigate the details of such action to determine if the initiating complaint was filed by a client who was harmed or by someone who was politically motivated and connected. In the latter case, it is likely a meaningless action, but the details still should be checked. Most attorneys who break their own rules of professional conduct have absolutely nothing to worry about with respect to discipline by the overseeing boards—unless, of course, they enrage a client or someone else with political power.

Nonetheless, it would be wise to avoid a lawyer with ample disciplinary actions since governing entities only discipline, at most, a miniscule fraction of lawyers for political reasons or because they have done something extremely egregious. By at least one estimate, the national total of disciplinary actions amounts to about 2 percent of all complaints received.[9] Our experience with our clients' and our own complaints is exactly two percentage points lower. Lying to a client, ineffective assistance of counsel, which includes falling asleep in the courtroom, and other such malfeasances are nowhere near severe enough for the overseeing bodies typically to intercede and discipline a lawyer.

In either civil or criminal cases, one thing to consider when searching for an attorney is the option of seeking one outside the immediate area but not so far away that her travel time to court makes hiring her prohibitive. Choosing a lawyer from a few towns or cities away, for example, is a good way to improve the chances that she will not have a strong affiliation with the court where your case will be heard and the lawyers who frequent it. Correspondingly, this may improve your chances of finding an attorney who is outside any particularly corrupt area. The potential downside of this strategy is that the outsider you hire may not be warmly received by her peers in a corrupt court, which might make working on the case more difficult for her.

More heads are better than one in any constructive project. Thus, if objective advice can be obtained from another knowledgeable person or source, hired counsel may be avoidable at least sometimes. Although fairly new, some courts allow limited assistance representation in which a lawyer and her client each do some of the work. The division of workload between an attorney and her client is agreed upon and established beforehand and should provide the benefit of having multiple heads work on the case while limiting legal expenses.

Keep in mind when talking to different lawyers about possible representation, you will likely get differing opinions about the strength of your case and the various possible tactics to pursue and get a wide range of rate quotes for their services. Sometimes you may get a seemingly different response from each lawyer with whom you speak. Just because the first lawyer says that a case has no chance does not mean anything. Furthermore, if a lawyer wants a $5,000 retainer to represent you in a legal matter that has a maximum potential total recovery of $4,500, it does not mean the case is not financially worth pursuing because you may find a lawyer willing to take it on a contingent fee basis.

Certainly, if an attorney has a monetary incentive to work on a case, she will work on it. Having said that, a contingent fee agreement, versus one based on an hourly fee and definitely versus one based on a prepaid flat fee, is the prime arrangement to maintain a lawyer's enthusiasm and effort. Certain types of cases do not allow this kind of fee agreement, such as criminal matters and domestic relations, but if the option is there, a potential litigant would be wise to consider it.[10]

On many occasions, one author has paid a lawyer a retainer, only to find that she did no or minimal work on the case afterward. Then, after firing her and attempting to recover a full or partial refund of the retainer, she had to be sued, somewhat luckily, in small claims court or sent a demand letter. A contingent or sliding-scale contingent fee agreement has no up-front costs. With either the attorney gets paid only if the client gets paid. Payment comes from any recovery upon settlement or judgment in favor of the client.

A sliding-scale contingent fee agreement has as its basic premise the following: the further along a legal matter proceeds, the higher the percentage the attorney or firm receives. For example, if a case settles after a couple of phone calls between opposing attorneys, the fee might be something like 20 percent. If it settles after one or more court appearances, the fee might become 30 percent. If the matter has to be fully litigated in the form of a trial, the fee might increase to 40 percent of the recovery. This is not only fair for the attorney who gets paid more for more hours worked but also for the client who pays less and receives more of the recovery if the case settles sooner rather than later.

Sometimes there may be alternatives to hiring a lawyer—utilizing arbitration or mediation, for example, which is often done completely outside the judicial system, or pursuing a case *pro se* in small claims and in a variety of other instances, which is partly the basis for this book. Besides juvenile criminal matters, arbitration and mediation are limited to civil cases but may be economical options compared to standard litigation. Not only that, but if the particular court of jurisdiction where the civil matter in question would be heard is corrupt, either will circumvent the possibility of any unjust outcome because of proceeding in that court. These two options will be revisited later in chapter eight.

Proceeding on Your Own

In almost any legal matter, an individual has the right to self-represent, the only known exception being class actions discussed in chapter sixteen. Section thirty-five of the Judiciary Act of 1789 as signed by President Washington stated, "in all the courts of the United States, the parties may plead and manage their own causes personally or by the assistance of . . . counsel . . . ." See *Faretta v. California*.[11] Self-representation may not always be the best choice if a litigant is not prepared to handle the case, but the decision to proceed *pro se* ultimately lies with the litigant. The choice to self-represent, however, may be overridden by a court that deems a litigant mentally incompetent or because the court contrives a reason disallowing it.

If you are an intelligent person and can check your emotions at the door, proceeding *pro se* might be a better option than hiring an attorney. Being organized, detail-oriented, and good at paperwork are requisite traits for the task. Preparing income tax returns requires similar qualities. If you file your own returns, are comfortable speaking before people and arguing a point, and are a decent writer with the ability to make a good written argument from scratch, there is probably no valid reason not to consider *pro se* representation for all but the most intricate cases. All the aforementioned skills are not prerequisites for simpler cases but might be for more complicated ones.

When determining whether proceeding *pro se* is a viable option in a complicated legal action, consider your level of intellect. If you are smarter than average, chances are your intellectual ability may surpass the majority of attorneys' capabilities. Make no mistake; there are some bright attorneys practicing law, but by and large this is the exception and not the rule. Many lawyers are fond of quoting the adage "he who represents himself has a fool for a client" in order to discourage self-representation because, of course, they are attempting to generate income. More often than not, the truth of the matter is that the person who hires a lawyer is taken for a fool. Nobody will fight harder for you than you will, but the effort and force in any legal battle have to be directed in a constructive and well-planned manner.

Also consider how much legal experience you have. If fighting a traffic violation is your first foray into the courts, it might be beneficial to proceed without counsel and get some experience. Representing yourself on a first-degree murder charge without ever having set foot into a courtroom is probably ill-advised. But if you have enough scar tissue from self-representation in traffic court, small claims, and perhaps a divorce case, accepting the challenge of a more complex matter may not be out of the question—you may do a far better job than the majority of lawyers.

To help with the analysis even further, consider the following analogous situation. Giving your sixteen-year-old child the keys to the Ferrari a week after getting her license is not necessarily the best idea. However, after ten years of driving experience, it might be reasonable, maybe even more so than giving the keys to a well-seasoned veteran, such as Grandpa, who has seventy years of experience but slower reaction times and reduced cognitive skills. Like Grandpa, attorneys with decades of experience who are elderly may also exhibit similarly slower reactions and decreased cognitive skills.

You would certainly not be alone should you choose to self-represent. In fact, the *pro se* trend has seen a steady climb over the years, from 42 percent in 1997 to 51 percent in 2014 in the U.S. courts of appeals.[12] [13] State courts nationwide have seen similar trends.[14] Reasons for this are not particularly shrouded in secrecy. Many consider the fees for representation not worth the money, and with the notoriety of attorneys in general, people feel they can do a better job themselves. In a survey taken by the American Bar Association, many people thought most lawyers are more concerned with their own self-promotion than their clients' best interests.[15]

In some instances, the choice to proceed *pro se* may be made for you. For example, if you have the intestinal fortitude to initiate a civil or criminal complaint against a judge because of a previous court proceeding or for any other reason, there is almost no chance of finding an attorney who will take the case for you. Lawyers who sue other lawyers for malpractice are rare but can be found. The ones who do this basically see it as upholding the rules of professional conduct or eliminating their competition. Alternatively, if one filed suit against a judge, she could effectively be biting the hand that feeds her. Thus, attorneys are disinclined to take such a case regardless of how much money you throw at them.

It would certainly not be good for business to file suit against a judge who would potentially be hearing and deciding future cases presented by the lawyer unless that lawyer is on the verge of retiring or moving away. Even if ruling in future cases is not a possibility, word might spread throughout the legal community labeling such a lawyer as a weasel—although with some lawyers, the title may not be without merit. When fighting a judge, you may be forced to go it alone. However, this would not necessarily be a bad thing. Just know that tackling judges in places where they are appointed is no small task—they did not magically gain the bench completely lacking in political connections.

Considering Jurisdiction and Venue

Another step to take at the beginning of any lawsuit is determining jurisdiction and venue. Jurisdiction, which refers to the power of a court to hear a case, and venue, which refers to the county where a case can be brought in a particular state, the district where a case can be brought in the federal system, or the District of Columbia for a case brought in that city, must be considered. This is true whether you are a plaintiff or defendant. If jurisdiction or venue is improper, then the case can either be dismissed or transferred to the correct court. It is important to take the time to determine proper jurisdiction and venue for the matter at hand.

If you are the plaintiff, you must ensure the initial pleadings are filed with the correct court. If you are the defendant and you realize the matter is being pursued in the wrong court, this is good for you. You can move the court, the legal terminology for asking it to do something, currently governing the lawsuit to have it dismissed or at least transferred to the proper court by filing a motion (see appendix). Jurisdiction and venue will be discussed more in chapter eight, but for now, suffice it to say that they are important parts of any court case.

RESEARCHING LAW AND MAKING SOLID ARGUMENTS

Along with being constantly vigilant for the legal system's ubiquitous corruption, possibly the most significant precept in this chapter, if not this entire book, is to research statutory and case law thoroughly whenever answers are needed and to make solid arguments in any legal battle. As mentioned in the introduction, this is 99 percent of good lawyering—the remainder being persistence. A lawyer's work should be double-checked if you have one. Even good ones are by no means infallible, and you should check their work at every given opportunity. This is also part of being thorough.

Remember that attorneys have several clients for whom they are working at any specific time and have to divide their attention among them all. However, you have to devote your attention merely to one person and one lawsuit at a time or, hopefully, not many at once. When doing legal work for yourself, it is equally important to be thorough and recheck your work several times. If you do, there is a good chance you will run circles around the vast majority of lawyers out there.

Being persistent is also important because so many people, lawyers included, get weary from battle and effectively quit. Given the nature of the judiciary, it is understandable. This is the easiest route for parties to take in lawsuits, but it is not the one that wins them. We have won many legal conflicts on thoroughness and persistence alone.

WHAT YOU ARE UP AGAINST

Besides a major misconception held by the public, the nature of the legal system itself, and other information discussed thus far in this chapter, it is critical to understand what one is up against when facing the system. In a criminal matter with a public defender, it is a three-against-one scenario with the one being the defendant and the three being the public defender, prosecutor, and judge—a rather big three, mind you. Although some public defenders are terrific, many are inundated and cannot ethically represent the overload of clients. Some public defenders have even filed suit as a result.[16] Being represented by one of them is certainly not advantageous. Besides the three-against-one scenario and being overworked, here is further reason: public defenders and prosecutors typically swap positions over the duration of their careers, often several times, and know their "adversary" well. They have to work with each other almost daily.

It is like professional wrestling. In the ring, wrestlers seemingly hate each other and will do anything to win. Behind the scenes, however, many are friends and have the complete opposite relationship of anything portrayed in the ring. The same goes for prosecutors and public defenders. They might seem to be enemies in the courtroom, but behind the scenes, they are probably all betting on how much money you will lose or whether you will look good in an orange jumpsuit. At the very least, they certainly are not the foes they appear to be in court.

Understand that judges were all lawyers at one point in their careers but have climbed the equivalent of the corporate ladder to their position as judge. They also are friends with many of the lawyers who appear in their courts since they were both prosecutors, they were once working at the same firm together, or they otherwise have some sort of common bond. Whether it is obvious or not, there is a certain amount of bias and camaraderie among most of them. Getting judges to be truly independent and objective in their capacities is unlikely.

The remaining part of the reason representation by a public defender is not ideal is that she, the judge, and the prosecutor are all paid from the same source of money, a governmental entity at the local, state, or federal level. When individuals in the private sector are paid from the same source of money, it means they work for the same company. Clearly, individuals working for the same business have the same objective in mind, which is to function as a team and generate revenue for it. The customers and others with whom they interface on a daily basis are the focus of their business.

So it is in a criminal case. The judge, prosecutor, and public defender all work for the same corporation—the judicial system. This explains the three-against-one scenario mentioned earlier in this section. Even when a defendant hires a private attorney, it is still two against two under the most favorable conditions. Under such circumstances, a private attorney is still only partially on your side. That private attorney also has to work with the prosecutors and judges on a regular basis and cannot totally alienate herself just because of your case. That would not be good business practice from her perspective.

In a civil suit, things might not be much more equitable, with all members of the court system similarly playing for the same team; however, the odds may be a little closer to 50/50 for any average non-politically connected litigant facing another such litigant. Things can still go awry for a male if the judge is female, a man-hater, and presiding in his divorce case, for example, or a litigant can have almost every weapon in her arsenal defused if the judge hates her for any reason.

There are many other things that can go wrong in a legal battle. Witnesses can die. Evidence can be lost, destroyed, concealed, or manufactured. Police officers and witnesses can lie. Judges can make mistakes or be corrupt. Bribery can occur. Clerical mistakes can be made. The statute of limitations can be a factor. Furthermore, your attorney could be incompetent or betray you, or your adversary could have a powerful legal team. Any of these or other possible problems can skew the legal landscape.

Being prepared and alert can mitigate some of these possibilities, but this would apply mostly to people who are not incarcerated and have the freedom to do their own research and keep tabs on things—once imprisoned, all bets are off, or nearly so. The last thing anyone should want is to be in confinement. This is the most vulnerable position in which to be since it not only takes away a person's freedom but it virtually destroys any chance for her to work on her case and puts her at the mercy of others for assistance.

One may not realize it initially, but there is an interesting fact about the system of which the average litigant, *pro se* or not, should be aware. A politically connected but inept opposing attorney may do far more damage in a proceeding than a skilled, non-politically connected attorney. With regard to court personnel violating statutory law and their own rules of procedure, a connected lawyer may be just the catalyst needed to enable them to take corruption to a whole new level, thereby making the seemingly impossible quite possible in a legal dispute. Although detrimental to the connected lawyer's adversary if left unchecked, some ways to overcome this problem are discussed in the INEFFECTIVE CHECKS AND BALANCES section of chapter three and the REMOVAL OF A LAWYER FROM A CASE section of chapter six.

To get more of an appreciation of what one is up against, it is important to understand the tendency of the legal system to be self-generating. Much like cancer, one single lawsuit can rapidly spawn others that, in turn, can generate even more civil or criminal litigation. One short, simple example is a false DUI arrest that results in a criminal proceeding against someone who is fortunate enough to be able to disprove the allegations and get the case dismissed or earn acquittal at trial. In an attempt to be compensated, she then files a civil suit against the police department and town or city for false arrest and possibly for other causes of action and damages.

Sometimes the lawsuit chain reaction can be longer than this relatively simple two-case instance. The system is an industry in which problems that arise because of it are addressed by that very same industry. Realize that it is designed to operate this way in order to enable its business to proliferate. It should now be apparent how the system can become the equivalent of the theoretical perpetual motion machine.

To reinforce this perpetual motion notion, it has been said the judicial system is good at metaphorically breaking someone's leg, handing her a crutch, and then saying, "See; if it wasn't for us, you wouldn't be able to walk," when it was the system that broke the person's leg in the first place. Adding insult to injury, it is also exceptional at punishing unfortunate people—the mentally ill, the unemployed, and the needy. In the overwhelming majority of states, criminal defendants can be charged for public defenders, room and board for incarceration, and other "services." In some states, they are charged for jury trials and four-figure court "costs"—some of which are used to pay for county employees' salaries and gym memberships. These burdens fall disproportionately on lower-income people.[17] Underscoring the fact that the system punishes the financially distressed, it is estimated that 66 percent of parents in state prison and 58 percent in federal prison were earning less than $24,000 per year just prior to their incarceration according to data from 2004.[18]

Targeting this group is generally done for a variety of reasons, the main one being that impoverished people are typically less educated and cannot afford the high-powered lawyers that celebrities or huge corporations can. Thus, they are easier to hunt, trap, and eat. Another reason is that the system gets more bang for its buck pursuing less wealthy people. Since lower-income individuals are much easier to convict, the time and money spent doing so is far less than it would be to convict CEOs at Goldman Sachs or pursue any of the now commonly overlooked crimes committed by others at the upper echelons of society. The system's chances of conviction are much lower with these individuals than with the impoverished; therefore, this paradigm provides a much higher return on investment for the legal industry.

"JUDGE SHOPPING" TO AVOID BAD JUDGES

One step that can be taken to avert judicial misconduct in many court battles is to do what legal professionals call "judge shopping." While it is said to be against the rules for you to pick a judge you like, the inverse of that act can be applied to many types of cases. Suppose, for example, you know that Judge Smith is rotten to the core. You know this because you have asked friends, lawyers, and others; you have researched the courthouse where she sits, ACME Courthouse; and maybe you have done some online searching to determine who the bad judges are in that court.

Some lawyers will actually give feedback about judges in their area. If you ask a few lawyers what judges they would never want presiding while representing their own mother, a judge named by most or all of them may be a good one to avoid. Remember that lawyers are trying to win lawsuits because it improves their record and marketability. If a judge is constantly ruling against them, it can put a damper on business.

You typically will not be successful when you inform the clerk of the court that you want a different court date because you do not want to take a chance of Judge Smith having anything to do with your case. However, you *can* be successful achieving the same thing via alternative means. Check the schedule for the judges sitting at ACME Courthouse over the next several weeks or months. To do this, an online search of something comparable to "court judicial assignments schedule" along with relevant county and state should reveal the judicial schedule for ACME Courthouse up to several months ahead of time. Then, note all the days when the bad judges are not scheduled to be there, or note all the days when they are scheduled to be there, whichever is easier.

Later, if the court or opposing party suggests a court date when a bad judge will be there, simply conjure up some reason why you cannot make that particular day. Have a list of several strong and believable reasons prepared as backups. A funeral for a pet turtle is not likely going to fly with the court; however, having an undisclosed medical procedure, being away on business, and other similar reasons will likely work. Using the process of elimination, there is a good chance you will eventually get offered a court date when ACME Courthouse is free of the bad judges. Unfortunately, this tactic will not work if you have the misfortune of ACME Courthouse being located where there are only horrendous judges and no relatively good ones. It also will not work if judges are assigned to cases and stay with them for their duration there, which sometimes happens for specific case types in certain states and normally happens for most, if not all, matters in the federal and Washington, D.C., systems.

Another way to avoid a bad judge is to ask her to recuse herself if it is known that her impartiality might be compromised. All American courts should have rules in place providing such disqualification. Judges may not always be aware that there is a potential conflict of interest, but if informed by either party that a conflict likely exists, she should formally recuse and allow another judge to hear the dispute.

Note that it is the judge who is usually responsible for making this decision and not any other person or entity. If the judge is corrupt enough, she may refuse to disqualify herself. If this happens, the aggrieved litigant may attempt to stymie the judge by telling her that the incident will be reported to the appropriate judicial disciplinary committee if she does not otherwise change her mind, which may or may not be enough to encourage recusal. Obviously, this is a trump card to be played only when a litigant knows the judge will stop at nothing to rule against her. Failure to recuse may also be an appealable issue.

WHEN THINGS GO WRONG

So, what can be done if something or maybe everything goes wrong? In any legal matter, appeals to higher courts, sometimes the U.S. Supreme Court, may be possible assuming the case is not already at the appellate level. However, appellate jurisdiction of the U.S. Supreme Court is limited.

Generally, it will only consider cases in which there is an important right implicated under the U.S. Constitution or that concern some matter of federal law over which there is a split among the U.S. courts of appeals. In fact, out of more than 7,000 cases in which appeal to the U.S. Supreme Court is sought annually, it will only hear about 100 to 150 of them.[19]

When things go wrong in the appellate courts, remedial options are limited. But in the trial courts, while litigation is ongoing, litigants can research case law, seek new representation, revisit the scene where an alleged incident occurred, double-check that all legal arguments have been raised, and do other such things. If a person digs deep enough, she will almost always find something on which to (re)build a case, particularly with all the statutory and case law now in existence. Just understand that the legal system is exceptionally quick to ruin people's lives but exceedingly slow to fix its mistakes, if at all. Therefore, a litigant should do whatever she can to persuade the system to adjudicate the case correctly the first time, if possible.

If more time is needed, certain delay tactics can also be used to your advantage whenever handling a case *pro se*. Informing the court that a witness is out of town, discovery requests were not answered, a clerical mistake was made, or service by the opposing party was not completed or simply asking for a continuance may provide more time to do something needed in a legal matter. However, if you have been unsuccessful trying to persuade a court to follow statutory laws and its own rules and risk losing money or property in a civil case because of corruption in that court, you do have options. You could be "sick" the morning of trial, "miss" a plane flight into town the day before, or employ any similar tactic as a last-ditch effort to postpone a trial, perhaps indefinitely. Using such tactics, you or someone else could call the court first thing in the morning on your trial day and say that you cannot make it due to sickness or a missed flight and inform the clerk that the trial needs to be rescheduled.

The opposing party or her attorney will likely try to contact you later to select possible new dates for the now deferred trial. When either one does, ensure that all contact is indirect—by email, U.S. mail, or voice mail—which will help delay things. Ponder not offering any possible dates for the trial, but instead have *your adversary* suggest a new date. This is because you may inadvertently pick a date that your opposition can accommodate, but if they pick a potential date, you can always contrive some excuse for not being able to make that day.

You could make rescheduling the trial as difficult as possible by procrastinating and then saying you never received their message or mailing—for example, waiting until any suggested court date passes before responding that you could have made the potential date but got the message too late. Other similar schemes that do not immediately betray your tactical plan could accomplish the same result as well. By doing this repeatedly and, furthermore, by making it nearly impossible for the opposing party to reach you as explained in chapter seven's REMAINING MISCELLANEOUS RULES section, you can suspend a trial nearly indefinitely. Accordingly, you may never have your day in court, but in a case wherein a judgment for either money or property will likely be issued against you because of corruption, you should be in no rush to get to the finish line anyway.

Even if you do eventually lose a monetary-based civil case in a corrupt court, there is still a failsafe available that can protect your assets. Transferring all funds you have in financial institutions out of your name and into someone else's can keep even the most tenacious judgment creditors at bay. One author has successfully shielded assets in this way from the government. With today's readily available electronic means of conducting business, managing finances in this fashion is an easy thing to do.

Think of someone who you know well and trust and who does not have a red bull's eye on her back with any sector of the legal system or creditor and will not likely have in the future. Work with this person to open a financial account in her name at an institution that provides online banking. Then ask for the username and password of the account. Other than the initial deposit to create the account, which you can later reimburse, the other person puts no money into it. Instead, have your pay or other sources of income deposited into it and conduct all your financial business from it. Come time to file income tax returns, you can resolve any liabilities with the account's true owner. Regarding your residence, if you own it and it is homesteaded, that should be enough to protect it from creditors or at least the part of it that falls under the homestead dollar limit.

LAST RESORT

Lastly, in a worst-case scenario in any criminal proceeding that has the potential for incarceration of an *innocent* defendant, it might be wise to consider having a last-resort plan in place to leave the country. Some countries have no extradition agreement with the United States. Since having or not having such an agreement can change, they will not be listed here but can easily be researched online (see appendix). They should be periodically reexamined so that possible places to live can be kept up-to-date in the event of an extreme emergency. Having funds in offshore bank accounts and an escape plan in place could be smart, especially considering the country's police-state environment, which is growing worse and shows no signs of abating.

If this is something you are considering, note that a decision should probably be made well before the onslaught of any particular criminal case since you may need to surrender your passport to the prosecutor, making it far more difficult, although not impossible, to leave the country. However, if a duplicate passport had been acquired beforehand, it can be used in place of the original. Obviously, when applying for a duplicate, stating that the original was lost or stolen is the feasible way to get another issued. It is unlikely the government will knowingly issue a second passport as an emergency means to exit the country.

There are several factors to evaluate when considering flight. Family might have to be left behind. A job or business might have to be abandoned. A lifestyle may be lost. But one has to weigh one's freedom against these and other factors. Planning should be given careful consideration, with everything properly set in place for a quick evacuation if freedom dictates the decision. For some people, a maximum penalty of thirty days in jail may be something acceptable, given the alternative. For others an even longer period might be tolerable. This is a rather personal topic and should be decided by each individual before the time comes.

In order to implement this stratagem completely, having citizenship in another country in addition to a corresponding passport for that country will further solidify the plan. The ways to acquire either are not as difficult as one might think but do require time, money, and due diligence. Doing some online research will yield the methods of accomplishing both.

The importance of having a worst-case plan in place, possibly along with a backup plan, might have an even higher priority in the grand scheme of things than having a last will and testament. One difference between the two is that the latter is for an unavoidable event, whereas the former is a glorified insurance policy for a possible event, which, hopefully, does not happen.

By now you should have a good idea of what the legal system truly is, and should be fairly well oriented regarding some basic overall tactics that can be employed and some preventative measures that can be taken in most legal situations. Other less obvious facets of the system and the clandestine things it does behind the scenes must be understood prior to any legal undertaking. The relevant material for this is presented in chapter three.

Chapter 3: Behind the Scenes

Things are not always what they seem; the first appearance deceives many. The intelligence of a few perceives what has been carefully hidden. — **Gaius Julius Phaedrus**

Chapter Sections

- Clerk of the court
- "Disappearing" evidence
- Pressure on police to meet quotas
- Militarization of police and arming of agencies
- Fighting the biggest adversary
- Bribery of officials
- Politics in the legal system
- Ineffective checks and balances
- *Mandamus* and other complaint alternatives
- Immunity and other considerations

Like a three-card monte, there is much that occurs behind the scenes in the U.S. legal system. And like the notorious three-card monte and as stated already, often many supposed adversaries are really playing for the same team and, in doing so, rigging things for you to lose. Just like this con game, what the public sees of the system is by no means representative of the true mechanism driving the whole apparatus. The average person must know what happens behind the scenes before proceeding into legal battle.

CLERK OF THE COURT

Court clerks are the point of entry for any case in U.S. courts. They are the gatekeepers, if you will, and are responsible for filing, scheduling, recording, and all other related logistics of a court matter. Like police, lawyers, and judges, they also make mistakes and break rules and laws. Two identical cases may have vastly different outcomes based merely on clerk actions alone.

For example, if a clerk deems a legal matter unworthy of court time, he will not docket it, or enter it into the system, upon attempted filing and will reject it outright. An identical matter in another clerk's hands might not get rejected but may be gladly accepted instead and bring potential litigants voluntarily or not into the contraption we call our judicial system. This is based purely on luck of the draw and court corruption and can either be beneficial or detrimental to a prospective litigant, depending upon perspective.

When clerks make errors that are later found, they generally correct them via provisional rules, reparative procedures, and any applicable statutes as if the errors had never been made. Of course, this only happens when the court decides to follow its own provisional rules, reparative procedures, and any applicable statutes, which is random or, more likely, happens less often than not based upon our experience. If the errors are not corrected, they could have a significant negative impact on future filings in the case, the direction it takes, and its outcome, which ultimately may affect other future facets of a litigant's life.

As an example of such an impact, consider a criminal record that is supposed to be sealed or expunged because of false allegations, dismissal, or any other reason. However, assume the clerk of the relevant court forgets to supply the appropriate information to the local, state, or federal authorities so that all proper actions associated with such sealing or expungement can be implemented. When the person for whom this was supposed to be done applies for a new job and a background check is performed, this irrelevant, incorrect, and potentially damaging information may be seen by those conducting the check. Therefore, information not correctly purged may improperly prevent the person from obtaining said employment.

The rules and laws that clerks break tend to be those within their purview. Because the average person may blindly accept all court-related actions from clerks as being 100 percent accurate, it is difficult to know the true number of times clerk rule- and law-breaking happen, particularly since naive individuals regard them as infallible authority figures. Furthermore, like their system member counterparts—lawyers, police, and judges—their actions have to be extremely egregious in order for them to have a chance of getting caught and punished.[1] As should be done for any lawyer's work, clerk-generated recordings, notices, and schedules and everything else clerks do related to your case should be checked for errors and verified against court rules of procedure and statutory law for validity and veracity whenever possible.

Any errors or falsities you find that are detrimental to you and are a result of clerk actions should be reported to the clerk or clerk supervisor. This may or may not resolve the issue. If it does not, you may need to take other action in the form of filing an official complaint or approaching the grand jury with evidence of corruption as discussed in the FEW GOOD ASPECTS OF THE U.S. LEGAL SYSTEM section of chapter one. You may also need to file suit against the clerk, as the situation warrants. If you find errors or falsities that are beneficial to you, there is no obligation to make this known to anyone.

"DISAPPEARING" EVIDENCE

Evidence sometimes "magically disappears" during criminal proceedings. There have been numerous cases, some publicized, some not, wherein discrepancies existed between the actual amount of drugs seized by police officials and the amount presented as evidence at trial because of theft by police.[2] [3] The fact that they sometimes steal evidence may not help the defendant but illustrates how dishonestly public officials occasionally handle it and is just one example of mischief that happens behind the scenes.[4]

PRESSURE ON POLICE TO MEET QUOTAS

Public officials, even the good ones, sometimes have pressure placed upon them to meet quotas. Ticketing quotas, stop-and-frisk quotas, and other such quotas are mandated by those at the highest levels of police authority.[5] Laws have been written in some states prohibiting the establishment of policies to meet quotas.[6] If these policies did not exist, as portrayed by some political pundits, then laws illegalizing them would never have been created in the first place.

MILITARIZATION OF POLICE AND ARMING OF AGENCIES

One of the most ominous activities happening behind the scenes is the militarization of police and arming of governmental agencies. Several typically unarmed agencies, such as NOAA and SSA, have been stockpiling ammunition for several years now, in some instances hundreds of thousands of rounds. In addition to this, there are now seventy-three federal agencies that have a significant force of armed officers.[7]

Most recently, as evidenced in the Ferguson, Missouri, unrest beginning in August of 2014, police have been given military equipment to use on unarmed U.S. citizens. This includes the use of tear gas, a weapon banned for wartime use![8] Armored vehicles, tanks, grenade launchers, and other excessive weaponry have become standard issue for various police departments throughout the country, creating a dangerous situation for the public.[9]

Basically acting as the right hand of the judicial system, the police have become a formidable enemy to the U.S. population as a whole. But in reality, the police are not the ones responsible for creating a dangerous situation; it is the controlling powers above them that are the catalyst for it all. And like most of the malaise affecting the country, we the people are ultimately to blame.

FIGHTING THE BIGGEST ADVERSARY

The revelation that the NSA has been unjustly spying on the American public, and other governmental agencies, such as the FBI, keeping records on many U.S. citizens as potential "terrorists," lend further credence to America now being a police state. Add to this, corruption at all levels of the legal system, and it is not just the opposing party in a legal proceeding that a person must fight but also the system itself. Understand that it can be a far more daunting adversary, though not an impossible one, to defeat.

Remember that the government is composed of people—people who can be lazy, careless, and irresolute. With this in mind, being thorough and persistent can benefit you. A major advantage the judiciary has is its strength in numbers, but armed with the proper knowledge, a sound approach, and some good fortune, a legal battle can be won even against this opponent.

BRIBERY OF OFFICIALS

Certainly, one thing that happens without most people knowing is bribery of public officials.[10] This has been occurring throughout human history. Today's legal system is no more immune to it than it was at its inception. If you can prove that a public official has been a party to bribery, the relevant grand jury, at a minimum, should be provided with this information if investigating public corruption is one of its functions. Since identifying everyone involved in the bribery circle may be rather arduous, addressing the problem outside the system via the grand jury might be best. If possible, reporting the issue to a district attorney, the attorney general, or any official outside the immediate vicinity of the suspects should also be considered. Because of the relative ease with which this sort of activity can go unnoticed, it may be far more commonplace than people think. It is difficult to know for sure.

Bribery does not always have to involve money either. It can occur in the form of gift giving. Essentially, its definition is giving something tangible to someone in return for him doing something. A political favor, although not technically bribery, is *doing* something for someone in hopes of him later doing something in return. While certainly not a political favor by any stretch, something comparable happens frequently and openly in many courts throughout the land every day. It is called "plea bargaining." It happens when a prosecutor does something, such as dropping or reducing one or more charges in a criminal matter, in exchange for a defendant doing something— accepting a guilty plea on the remaining charges rather than demanding a time-consuming trial on all the original charges. So, the subtle difference between the definitions makes bribery illegal but political favors and plea bargaining simply *sound* illegal.

POLITICS IN THE LEGAL SYSTEM

Possibly more closely aligned with politicking are the agreements lawyers make with each other to save themselves time, money, and aggravation. These are deals made off the record wherein an attorney may be inclined to give a little ground to opposing counsel on a lawsuit in exchange for helpful advantages later. On its face, there is nothing wrong with this. However, when such agreements cross the line of sacrificing a client's best interests for the attorney's personal gain, it may be quite a different story—not only unethical but also against the rules of professional conduct.

Of course, there are the blatant politics that occur when prosecutors or judges run for office in various states. The type of negative campaigning in which these candidates partake is basically no different from that of other political candidates. Moreover, there are times when these people will attempt to appease a certain segment of the population by dealing harshly with some legal matters, perhaps unethically, in order to win (re)election. Additional important politics of which to be aware are discussed in chapter nine's Political Connections That Negatively Influence Your Case subsection.

Although things discussed in this and foregoing sections are not just happening strictly behind the scenes anymore but are now making their way towards the forefront, they were included in order to demonstrate that there is likely much more transpiring than meets the eye. You need to be cautious when fighting any legal battle and be as prepared as possible at all times.

INEFFECTIVE CHECKS AND BALANCES

When a lawyer or judge does something wrong while performing his official duties, there are certain boards that are *supposed* to remedy this. One, for example, is the disciplinary arm of some bar associations. The basic purpose of the boards overseeing attorneys is to administer reprimands, suspensions, and disbarments when applicable. The main problem with them is that they are usually composed primarily of lawyers and judges. This is like the fox guarding the henhouse.

The boards overseeing lawyers should include one or two lawyers or judges merely to provide legal guidance for their other members. However, the majority of their members should be educated but unaffiliated lay professionals, such as engineers, doctors, business owners, and other similar individuals. Although many of these boards do have such people as members, the proportions are backwards. Rather than being predominantly lay people, they are predominantly lawyers and judges.

Note that these boards normally receive complaints, read them, and ignore them. To drive this point home and as mentioned in chapter two, we have filed many complaints in various states against lawyers who cumulatively broke dozens of their respective state's rules of professional conduct. Despite this fact, exactly zero of them were disciplined because of our complaints. On occasion, the boards will pursue a complaint against a lawyer either because he has egregiously violated a major rule of professional conduct or because he has enraged a politically connected person. But even in the rarest instances regarding punishment of an attorney because of the former, they are useless in any way of making whole the aggrieved complainant. This includes returning retainers and resurrecting any lawsuit that has been killed because of the attorney's negligence in allowing the statute of limitations to expire. These boards also do not punish attorneys for any associated criminal offenses they have committed.

Similar commissions also regulate judges. But if the ones governing lawyers are ludicrous, the ones governing judges are jokes. These boards are also ordinarily constituted mostly of lawyers and judges, although sometimes their membership includes lay people too. Ideally, it should be the other way around, with the group being a majority of educated lay people but including one or two attorneys or judges who can be consulted for legal guidance, as should the boards governing attorneys. Composing commissions such as these mainly with members outside the judicial system would be an excellent step towards legitimizing them.

If you decide to file a complaint against a judge in your legal matter while it is ongoing and notify your lawyer of such intent, you might get negative feedback. He may say that he does not recommend it because you would be "attempting to influence rulings and the outcome of your case" or something comparable. What he really means is that you are correct and proper in complaining that the judge is not following rules of procedure, statutory laws, or the U.S. Constitution. However, he cannot condone it because he will look bad in front of that judge presenting future cases as the lawyer who supported your complaint, which certainly would not be good for his business.

If he mentions that the best road to redemption is via appeal after judgment, it could be a disguised attempt at bringing more money into the legal machine. Appeal may not otherwise be necessary if you can miraculously persuade the judge to follow the rules and law *before* a decision is rendered and the damage is done. Such a miracle could be the result of action taken by the judicial oversight commission because of your complaint. Prompting his removal from the case through recusal is also a possibility, depending upon circumstances surrounding the matter.

As with the lawyer oversight groups, another major problem with the judicial oversight groups is that none negate any ramifications of wrongdoing by a judge even for the most egregious offenses. Once again, as discussed in chapter two's TRUST NOBODY section, it would be too costly for the system to fix retroactively the damage it has done. If a person is imprisoned or, worse yet, has been executed because of a lawyer's or judge's malfeasances, then that is just an unfortunate by-product of the system.

The police also have governing bodies, such as the Bureau of Internal Affairs and others. However, with strong unions and with the familiar tune heard in the above governing boards, these oversight groups are generally comprised of current or former police. As with the governing boards for lawyers and judges, this makes them inadequate control mechanisms. To underscore this fact, Chicago had approximately 12,244 total law enforcement officers as of 2013.[11] [12] An estimated thirty-one of them were disciplined in some fashion during that year, equating to one in 395 officers, or a measly quarter of a percent.[13] Even in light of the minimal amount of coverage mainstream media gives to police corruption, police brutality, and other improprieties, this number is *grossly* under-representative of what the true number of disciplinary actions should be.

All the aforementioned governing groups are discussed to inform you of their existence, not to show that they act as effective checks and balances against corruption and properly remediate any misdoings by members of the legal system. To the contrary, they are mostly useless, and our intention is to expose any myths about them being beneficial to the average citizen. Knowing this should help prepare you that, in a majority of cases, a complaint to any of these boards will not make it very far. It would be ideal not to get into a situation wherein they would be needed by applying the material covered in chapter two. Clearly, this is not always possible, but be forewarned that the probability of true success in pursuing a complaint with any of them is rather slim. Even if some marginal victory is gained in the form of a suspension, disbarment, or what have you, as stated already, it will have no direct effect on negating any damage done by the officer, lawyer, or judge on whom the complaint was levied.

MANDAMUS AND OTHER COMPLAINT ALTERNATIVES

Despite the overall futility of the above oversight groups, there are other possible paths to take for redress. Some states, the federal government, and Washington, D.C., allow petitioning for a writ of *mandamus*, or a "mandate" as it is sometimes called. This is basically an order from a higher court, usually a supreme court, instructing individuals in public positions to follow the rules and laws governing that position. Not only is the person against whom the writ is sought supposed to occupy a public position, but the duty ascribed to that position is not supposed to be discretionary in nature. In the context of this section, the person is a judge or another public official in a lower court who needs to be forced to follow court rules of procedure or law. Whenever a litigant is aggrieved by being denied a right because of the actions or inactions of a lower court official, he can normally petition a higher court for this writ if allowed by law. Also, know that there are different forms of *mandamus* in the United States, each of which has slight variations from the other.

Understand that some states, Massachusetts being one, have abolished the writ of *mandamus* and have replaced it with other "remedies."[14] The replacement used in Massachusetts is interlocutory relief. Oftentimes one criterion to be granted the order being sought in a petition for a writ of *mandamus* or the relief being sought in a petition for interlocutory relief is that no other adequate means of rectifying a problem exists in a lower court. However, statutory wording may indicate otherwise as it does in Massachusetts (see appendix).[15] Another typical requirement for either to have a chance of success is that the act of a lower court official must be clearly erroneous as a matter of law—such as a judge ruling contrary to statute—also known as corruption.

Mandamus, interlocutory relief, or any other substitute is one of few instances when a higher court can intervene during an ongoing action in a lower court. From a litigant's perspective, it can be like starting a case in the lowest court and temporarily leaping over the intermediate courts while saving time, effort, and money in the process—not beneficial for the system and perhaps why being successful with any such petition is so rare.

Some states, the federal government, and the District of Columbia may allow a lawsuit for declaratory judgment against a judge. If allowed, a judge could be sued in order to force him to follow rules of court, statutory law, or the U.S. Constitution. Declaratory judgment against judges usually excludes collection of damages since judicial immunity typically protects them from such claims. One state in particular that does not permit declaratory judgment against judges is Massachusetts, which has wisely protected itself from attack by citizens who foolishly seek justice.[16]

Another possible means of redress for a party aggrieved by a judge not fulfilling his obligations mandated by rule or law is to lodge a complaint at the next level above the judicial governing board. When a complaint with the judicial governing board falls short, another can be filed with the respective supreme court or other governing body responsible for the supervision of the judicial governing board itself. This is an option if the judicial oversight committee fails to take any action against a judge who has violated the U.S. Constitution, not followed rules of procedure, or broken canonical, state, federal, or municipal law. The same process of elevating a complaint can be followed when the governing board for attorneys does not take action against an attorney for violating the rules of professional conduct.

Lastly, if the local corruption circle is just too great, consider stepping over municipal or state government and approaching the Civil Rights Division of the FBI or contacting the DOJ to log a complaint against any public officials acting under the "color of law." As will be further explained in chapter six, acting under the "color of law" occurs when public officials, while supposed to be doing their jobs, willfully act to deprive or conspire to deprive an individual of any right protected by the U.S. Constitution or statutory law. Consult the FBI website for more information.[17]

IMMUNITY AND OTHER CONSIDERATIONS

Judicial immunity and prosecutorial immunity protect judges and prosecutors, respectively, from prosecution and many civil lawsuits, sometimes even in the most outlandish instances. Prosecutors enjoy immunity equal to or perhaps greater than that of judges. In *Connic v. Thompson*, the U.S. Supreme Court basically gave prosecutors nearly limitless power despite their wrongdoing.[18] Nothing punitive was done to any of the prosecutors after discovering their attempted murder of Thompson, the falsely charged murder suspect in the original criminal case.[19] Understand that prosecutors have attempted to murder people without penalty on many occasions.

As another shining example, it took a case that was a toxic cauldron of injustice in order for the courts finally to restrain the power of prosecutors. That specific case was the criminal one underlying *Fields v. Wharrie* in which a judge not only accepted a bribe, but prosecutors fabricated evidence and coerced witnesses into providing false testimony in order to secure a conviction and a death sentence against Fields. None of our experiences even come close to rivaling the amount of corruption in that particular case. We wonder if there were any other undiscovered forms of corruption that would truly launch it into contention for the gold medal, if not winning it outright, among contemporary miscarriages of justice. Certainly, the witch trials of colonial America in the 1600s had more integrity.

Although the lower court disgracefully ruled in favor of the prosecutors, the Court of Appeals for the Seventh Circuit reversed, rightfully stripping Wharrie of immunity. Writing for the Seventh Circuit panel majority, Judge Richard Posner said it would be absurd to allow such prosecutors to claim immunity and stated, "Wharrie is asking us to bless a breathtaking injustice."[20] Indeed it was, and oftentimes the courts do.

Judges and prosecutors have been known to commit other similarly outrageous acts, only to hide cowardly behind immunity afterward. As an aggrieved party, bringing a civil suit against a prosecutor or judge who enjoys immunity is not usually successful. Filing a criminal complaint against a judge or prosecutor may not fare much better, but if the criminal acts are committed outside his official duties, the chances are better, but not guaranteed, that he might be prosecuted.

There are times when a judge loses judicial immunity, but they are exceedingly rare. There is a two-pronged test to determine if immunity has been lost. The first prong of the test is met when a judge rules in a matter over which he has no jurisdiction. This has happened to one of the authors. The other prong of the test is met when his acts are not judicial in nature. If either prong is met, immunity is lost. Once it is lost, a lawsuit for damages that has at least some chance of success can be pursued against the judge. More on this topic will be covered in chapter sixteen.

One thing that occurs behind the scenes of which most people are likely unaware is something called "*ex parte* communication." The term "*ex parte*" has different legal applications, but the one discussed here pertains to communication between a lawyer and judge off the court record regarding a legal matter. It is uncertain how often this happens, but suffice it to say that it does happen. Frankly, when two or more attorneys and judges talk and no one else can hear, it is doubtful that the conversation is pure and good. Thus, although *ex parte* communication can be either good or bad for an average, unconnected litigant, we suspect that it is most likely bad.

An event that happened behind the scenes in a personal legal matter involving one author makes perhaps the biggest statement in this chapter. In that matter, a prosecutor effectively threw to the wolves an unfounded complainant who was opposing the author. Albeit he unknowingly made the right decision in doing so, he did it for the sole purpose of protecting the author's attorney from disciplinary action by the state's overseeing board. Written evidence proving the fact was intercepted as part of a transmission by another attorney who foolishly revealed this information in a separate case. In that case, the same author is now the plaintiff and the idiotic attorney, Joseph L. Michaud, is representing the same unfounded complainant, Alyssa L. Parent, as defendant.

The prosecutor was willing to do what he truly thought was wrong in order to protect one of his own brethren at all costs. The significance of this particular event is that corruption in the system could indeed be far greater than we have seen. As stated in chapter two's TRUST NOBODY section regarding the corruption and criminal misdeeds of public officials, the incidents being reported may represent only a tiny fraction of the true number since many go undetected or just unreported. This example supports that theory because it was only discovered by dumb luck, literally.

Hopefully, you have gained a good understanding of the basic operation of the legal system and perhaps even had some preconceived notions dispelled in this part of the book. The next part will focus on the written and spoken rules propagated by the system and how they impact the direction cases take within the courts when the system breaks them. We will explain how you can use the system's own rules to your advantage. We will also present other concepts independent of but related to system rules that you may find beneficial.

PART II — HOUSE RULES

Chapter 4: Possession Really Is Nine-Tenths of the Law

The possession of anything begins in the mind. — **Bruce Lee**

Chapter Sections

- The slow-moving system favors the possessor
- Burden of proof for recovering money or property
- Winning a civil case and enforcing the judgment
- Ways to avoid paying money or relinquishing property
- Adverse possession
- The government taking land
- Civil asset forfeiture

Possession can assume many forms as it relates to the legal system. Some of its various forms can be manifested by a thief, a neighbor, an adversary, the government, U.S. law enforcement at various levels (which some consider to be legalized thieves), and possibly others. Examples of these different kinds of possession will be examined in this chapter and discussed as they relate to legal matters.

Possession by a thief, as obvious as it sounds, is a prime example of possession being nine-tenths of the law. Suppose your car gets stolen. The thief has possession and use of it until you recover it, assuming you eventually do. To start the recovery process, you could file a police report. There is no obligation, however, to involve the police if you do not feel inclined to do so. Even if you file a report, there is no guarantee they will find your vehicle or even make the attempt. An alternative may be to look for it yourself by using social media, posting a reward, checking any surveillance video where it was last seen, or possibly hiring a private investigator. But in any event, locating your stolen car and potentially proving it is yours may be no easy task. If it is never reclaimed in whole or in part, then the thief maintains possession of it or benefits by selling it.

THE SLOW-MOVING SYSTEM FAVORS THE POSSESSOR

If you attempt to recover your property in a more conventional setting, the court system, it may be years or perhaps decades before ownership is finally resolved and your property is returned to you. Because the system moves so slowly, it is not out of the realm of possibilities for the rightful owner of property to die before a case is finally settled. In such an instance, the possessor will have deprived the owner of the property's use for the remainder of the owner's life in spite of attempted retrieval via litigation.

Even in cases in which property is finally returned to its owner, the previous possessor still had access to or use of the property in question before and during litigation. One author knows someone who was a plaintiff in a civil lawsuit wherein the defendant used the funds in dispute to pay her own attorney. This overtly defined possession as being nine-tenths of the law. A prejudgment writ of attachment, sometimes shortened to "prejudgment attachment," from a court can prevent something like this from happening and can prevent shielding of funds or property by the defendant after a judgment in favor of the plaintiff. This strictly statutory mechanism, not commonly granted by the courts, has certain limitations.

Litigation can be lengthy, causing some people to surrender whether it is because they exhaust their funds, because they tire from the whole process, or because they do both. Essentially, abandoning a lawsuit transfers the ownership of property or funds in dispute to its current possessor. This might also happen when litigation costs eventually exceed the value of the property or the amount of money, in which case it may be sensible for the non-possessing party to relent.

BURDEN OF PROOF FOR RECOVERING MONEY OR PROPERTY

The burden of proof can be a challenging hurdle to overcome when trying to recover money or property through standard litigation or by other means. Identifying a recovered stolen car via its VIN and registration and proving that it belongs to a particular person is much different and perhaps easier than identifying a recovered quantity of cash and proving that it belongs to the person from whom it was stolen. The burden can be minor or major, depending upon circumstances. In some cases, it may no longer be possible to prove ownership of something.

WINNING A CIVIL CASE AND ENFORCING THE JUDGMENT

Bear in mind that victory in a court battle regarding a dispute about money or property, no matter how long it takes, is not necessarily the end of litigation—you may have won the battle but not the war. Whether or not the losing party has a valid appealable issue, she could sequentially appeal to several increasingly higher courts before all avenues of redress have been exhausted if she is unsatisfied with the outcome of the case. Other times, the winning party does not receive the money or property in question despite the court's ruling. In such instances, a levy might have to be imposed on the losing party's bank account. Additional possible enforcement measures that may have to be undertaken include garnishing her wages or obtaining an attachment. In spite of all this, there is still no guarantee the winning party will receive whatever the judgment mandates.

WAYS TO AVOID PAYING MONEY OR RELINQUISHING PROPERTY

The losing party could also file for bankruptcy to prevent relinquishing the money or property as ordered by the court. As infuriating as this may be to a creditor, it is sometimes a legitimate way for a debtor to avoid paying her or returning her property. Once the case has been filed, it acts as a shield. It affords the debtor an automatic stay and protects her from further execution or litigation until the automatic stay is lifted or the bankruptcy is granted or denied.

In spite of a debtor filing for bankruptcy, it should be mentioned that she may not be free and clear of all debts. There are some debts that are supposedly always non-dischargeable, or not protected under bankruptcy. These include certain past due taxes, child or ex-spousal support, particular fines and penalties, and criminal restitution. While these debts do not typically require a court hearing to determine their dischargeability, some may.

Other debts such as those fraudulently incurred are not generally dischargeable to a legally responsible party if the creditor raises an objection. Raising an objection means the creditor has to take action in the proper bankruptcy court. Purchases of luxury goods, certain cash advances, and debts resulting from willful and malicious injury to another or intentional damage to the property of another also fall into the non-dischargeable category if the creditor/victim raises an objection.[1] Bankruptcy will be discussed in more detail in the DISCHARGING DEBTS THROUGH BANKRUPTCY section of chapter thirteen.

There are many other ways a losing party can evade satisfying an outstanding judgment. Some include transferring funds into someone else's name, opening an offshore account or trust and diverting funds into it, or otherwise physically taking the property at issue out of the ruling court's reach or jurisdiction. One rather obscure way is to change one's identity. Although probably illegal throughout the country, it is nonetheless quite possible.

ADVERSE POSSESSION

Along with possession of money, possession of real estate might be one of the most contentious matters in U.S. civil courts. Ownership of real estate is not absolute; just because someone has title to a property does not necessarily mean it will stay hers so long as she does not sell it or lose it through foreclosure or in a standard lawsuit. If someone cares for another person's real estate in whole or in part or lives on the premises without the owner's permission, a legal doctrine called "adverse possession" may apply, but there are also other ways it may apply. It permits the transfer of the respective portion of the property into the caretaker's or inhabitant's ownership after a certain amount of time has passed since the care or occupancy began. The period that must pass before the transfer can be requested because of adverse possession varies nationwide, but all states and the District of Columbia have established laws for it.[2] The basic premise behind this, once again, is that possession is nine-tenths of the law.

THE GOVERNMENT TAKING LAND

Not only can a neighbor or stranger occupy and eventually possess private land, given enough time, but the government can take private land without having occupied it, sometimes in relatively short order. Understand that the U.S. government already owns well over half a billion acres in the western United States. In terms of percentages, Nevada now leads the list with more than 84 percent of its land being federally owned. Over 50 percent of the acreage in many western states is owned by the U.S. government and not the states themselves.[3] The origin of federal ownership in this part of the country dates back to America's westward expansion, but despite the passing of time and the effort of some states to reclaim territory within their borders, the land remains under federal control.

Eminent domain is a classic example of the government taking private real estate rather quickly, sometimes not for a public purpose. The Fifth Amendment to the U.S. Constitution states that land can only be taken under certain circumstances, specifically, for a public purpose and after just compensation to its owner.[4] Fairly recently, however, land has been taken by local, state, and federal governments without any resulting express public use, but instead, its ownership has been transferred to private entities as it was in *Kelo v. City of New London*.[5]

"Just compensation" declared in the U.S. Constitution has become all but meaningless since compensation is widely interpretative and does not account for various losses. One such excluded loss applies to owners of businesses that are destroyed by condemnation. Future earnings of the business are often neglected as are other intrinsic benefits associated with the business itself when compensation is determined. Corresponding attorney and appraisal fees almost everywhere in America are not considered by the government as part of any compensatory package either.

In addition to property owners often being undercompensated in general, those with properties of lower value are indirectly further exploited since they may not be able to afford litigation and instead are forced to accept low offers.[6] [7] Once the government has possession of property by this means, its rightful owner could have extreme difficulty regaining possession of it, although some people have done so. See *Norwood v. Horney*.[8]

CIVIL ASSET FORFEITURE

Perhaps the biggest injustice not yet discussed that epitomizes possession being nine-tenths of the law comes at the hands of U.S. law enforcement. A relatively new wave is washing across the land. Some may have heard of it, but undoubtedly, others have already been victims of it. Unlike the government's taking of state or private land, which can simultaneously affect several people, this injustice primarily affects people on an individual basis. It is called "civil asset forfeiture," with equitable transfer or equitable sharing being the equivalent at the federal level. Civil asset forfeiture allows law enforcement officials to take personal property or money with impunity and without ever filing criminal charges against the person from whom it is taken.[9]

Just like most laws enacted to prevent certain people from doing certain things, laws, such as the ones written in support of civil asset forfeiture, that were originally enacted to stymie the illegal drug trade have backfired on the American populace. They are now predominantly used to fleece everyday citizens because it is much easier to do that than to pursue real criminals—and it is very profitable. Similar to the laws intended to trap terrorists and other criminals, the ones in support of this form of seizure are recklessly used against ordinary citizens who have committed no wrongdoing. The misuse of civil asset forfeiture laws is no different from the misuse of the USA PATRIOT Act, which was originally intended to counteract terrorism after the attacks of September 11, 2001. Instead, the act further militarized the police, stripped Americans of more rights, escalated spying on the American people, and likewise backfired. There are numerous examples of government's knee-jerk reaction effectively closing the door after the calf has already left the pen, but the point is that laws intended for one purpose are frequently misused for another.

One of the most common forms of civil asset forfeiture occurs when people are traveling on U.S. roadways and are stopped by local or state police. The officer may ask if anyone is carrying cash. Sometimes it is found during a search of the vehicle—conducted legally or illegally. In either instance, the officer takes the money under the premise that it is associated with drug dealing and that there could be no other plausible reason for a person to be carrying the amount of cash found.

The only way the victim can retrieve the seized money is through a time-consuming lawsuit, which the police know. For out-of-state drivers, this means commuting to a potentially distant court or paying a lawyer to pursue the matter for them instead. When a relatively small sum has been confiscated, $3,000 for example, attorney fees, filing fees, and other costs, such as lost wages from time out of work or travel expenses, may financially deter recovery of it. Law enforcement knows this too.

North Carolina is the only state without civil asset forfeiture laws, but by partnering with federal officials, local police agencies can pocket approximately 75 percent of the revenue generated by seizures in that state. This partnering is a convenient way for them to reap the windfall profits that can be made by swindling people traveling on North Carolina roadways.

Since 9/11 law enforcement has collected $2.5 billion from over 60,000 *known* cash seizures via equitable sharing, which excludes seizures at the local and state levels. Some states have tried to curb the activity through voter initiative, but police organizations have lobbied hard to maintain the status quo or even further it.[10] After all, the police are sometimes under no obligation to use the seized money for the war on drugs, civic improvements, or any reputable cause. Depending upon the state, some law enforcement agencies can use the money any way they want, which usually boils down to buying more lethal weapons, employing more police, and other self-serving interests. In states where the money is designated for a certain purpose, it is doubtful the funds always make it to their intended destination.

Keep in mind this money is typically being taken without the need to establish a high standard of proof and without any criminal charges ever being filed—possibly the greatest infringement of the Fourth and Fifth Amendments to the U.S. Constitution to date.[11] The moral of this story is *not* to travel on U.S. roads with a significant amount of cash. If unavoidable, a wise choice may be to refrain from admitting having such cash to any law enforcement agents and hide it well or try to keep it on someone's person where officers might be less likely to find it.

Note that people who do not drive with large amounts of money in their vehicle or carry it with them are not completely immune from this form of legalized theft. Another variation of it occurs when the government seizes a bank account because several aggregate deposits are made that exceed $10,000. When multiple smaller amounts of money are deposited into a financial account in order to avoid the governmental regulatory reporting requirements that any single deposit reaching or exceeding this level would mandate, it is termed "structuring" and is now illegal.[12] Even though money might be legitimately deposited in increments smaller than $10,000, if the total of a specific number of deposits exceeds this amount and the government perceives it to be structuring, say goodbye to your money.

Sometimes bank tellers even improperly advise customers to divide their deposits into smaller ones to avoid reporting requirements. Adding further insult to injury, bank personnel are not permitted to inform customers that their deposit habits may be illegal or to educate them about structuring laws unless they ask.[13] It is highly unlikely customers will ask about something of which they have never heard.

Civil asset forfeiture is not limited to taking money. Property can be seized, including automobiles, homes, and anything else of value. With laws as they are, someone could be living a normal middle-class lifestyle one day and be homeless the next, thanks to the government. Once again, during the time someone tries to recover her property, the law enforcement agency has possession of it. Only in a small percentage of cases is the property stolen by the government ever returned to its rightful owner—as low as 1 percent by some estimates.[14]

It is the bending of the rules that precipitated the legalized stealing of money and property by the government under civil asset forfeiture and equitable sharing. One might even argue that it is not so much the rules being bent as it is the rules being broken. Perhaps that is true, but relevant laws have opened the door for this kind of misbehavior by the government. There certainly are a myriad of other rules being broken by the legal system, particularly by people who enforce them or are undeniably aware of them, which is a separate topic and will be addressed in the next chapter.

Chapter 5: Rule Enforcers Are Oftentimes Rule Breakers

Rules are mostly made to be broken and are too often for the lazy to hide behind. — **General Douglas MacArthur**

Chapter Sections

- Hierarchy of laws applicable in the United States
- The rules defined
- How the system breaks its rules without detection
- Constitutional rights being obliterated
- More examples of rule-breaking by the system
- Rule-breakers accusing everyday people of breaking the rules

As General MacArthur once said, rules are made to be broken. That is no truer than in the U.S. legal system, which takes the blue ribbon for breaking its own. Quite often its rules do inconveniently get in the way of it trying to accomplish its objectives, but with minimal or no objection, the system can and frequently does steamroll right over its rules and thus disregards them whenever it desires. Of all organizations, countries, or other entities worldwide, there may be more rules and laws within the U.S. judicial system than anywhere else. The definitions of domestic rules and laws will be discussed in this chapter, and the ways that the system breaks them will be examined. Understanding the general hierarchy of laws is a prerequisite to this discussion and examination.

HIERARCHY OF LAWS APPLICABLE IN THE UNITED STATES

Starting at the top, the highest law of the land, as reverenced by the Founding Fathers, is natural law, which originates from Divine Providence. Natural law was the basis for the Declaration of Independence, the U.S. Constitution, the Federalist Papers, and other documents promulgated by the Founders. They had a clear understanding of the difference between right and wrong and knew there was only one absolute truth. Laws of their time were few and were written with that knowledge in mind. The contemporary U.S. judicial system, however, seems to be under the impression that more are better.

Directly under natural law is the next highest law, the U.S. Constitution, which is derived from it. The Constitution was written predominantly by James Madison and was signed by the Framers in 1787. It is based on the rights outlined in the Declaration of Independence, which states, "that all men are created equal, that they are endowed by their Creator with certain unalienable Rights," and lays the foundation for the U.S. government. The Constitution was intended to be the mother of all domestically created laws. All laws ever to be written in America were to conform to this overarching document. It was designed to withstand the test of time.

Next in the general hierarchy under the Constitution comes federal law. Federal law applies to all people and entities within U.S. borders and to U.S. citizens and American businesses abroad. The U.S. Code concerns commerce, crime, labor, maritime matters, and more. It encompasses all state and local laws.

Following federal law in the pecking order of priority is state law. States have their own constitutions and laws that are based on the U.S. Constitution and federal laws, respectively. States can create additional rights but not abridge existing federal ones with their constitutions or any laws they pass. State laws must not only conform to federal laws but also to the U.S. Constitution and their own state's constitution.

If a state law does not conform to the U.S. Constitution or its state constitution, then anyone involved in a lawsuit in that state regarding that particular law can argue that it is unconstitutional as written or applied. The jury can also be asked to use their nullification power as explained in the REASONS FOR THE SYSTEM'S DECLINE section of chapter one. Of course, imploring the jury to invoke this power assumes the litigant had the option of a jury trial and chose it should the case have made it that far. If state laws conflict with federal laws in legal matters, those state laws can similarly be challenged in court.

Sometimes states and Washington, D.C., have several laws for a federal counterpart. Sometimes there is more of a one-to-one relationship. Even though states and the nation's capital may have their own versions of a federal law, the penalties for breaking their versions may be more or less severe than the penalties for breaking the federal counterpart and may vary in severity across the nation. These variations are quite often significant.

A state usually has jurisdiction in a legal action in which all events related to it transpired entirely in-state. The federal government usually has jurisdiction in matters that occur across state boundaries. It also has jurisdiction over matters that occur in international waters and concern U.S. parties, that involve foreign diplomats or peoples on U.S. soil, and that concern events in federal buildings or on other federal property. Its jurisdiction also applies in some other matters as explained in chapter eight's FEDERAL COURTS section.

Lowest in the hierarchy of laws are local laws known as "ordinances," oftentimes constituting a code of ordinances or municipal code along with a charter. These are usually created and applicable at the town, city, or county level. Note that just like state and federal laws, ordinances must conform to all hierarchical laws above them—state laws and their state's constitution, federal laws, and the U.S. Constitution. If a person or an entity becomes party to a lawsuit in which an ordinance is its basis but the ordinance does not comply with laws above it, including the U.S. Constitution or its state constitution, its validity can also be challenged in court and it can be invalidated.

THE RULES DEFINED

As everyone knows, rules are part of any game. The laws within the hierarchy just explained, or effectively, the primary rules, are no exception and form the backbone of the legal game. The problem is that this backbone is extremely flexible like a snake's spine rather than less flexible like a typical land mammal's spine and thus can take many shapes and forms. In a legal matter, these various shapes and forms are dependent upon the litigants' identity, their political connections, the amount of power they wield, and correspondingly, the level of corruption in the particular court where their case is proceeding.

Having morphed into a twisted and perverse game as described in detail in part I of this book, the legal system has a mind-boggling number of rules. For the most part, its rules can be divided into three main categories: statutes, court rules of procedure, and *stare decisis*. All three exist within the state, federal, and District of Columbia judicial systems.

Most people know what statutes are. These are laws governments have created that define what is legal and what is illegal in a jurisdiction, among other things, and exist within the hierarchy described in the previous section. Rules of procedure are the basic blueprints for both civil and criminal proceedings, or "penal proceedings" as the latter are sometimes called, in court. These rules are supposed to govern the entire process of any legal action from start to finish. *Stare decisis* is the rule that obligates judges to follow the example of prior settled law, also known as case law, precedent, or common law, when facts of the legal matter over which they are ruling are substantively similar to the facts in the previously settled cases. Of course, any of these rules may be broken because of corruption in a given court.

Stare decisis may be relevant in some vehicular matters, for example. Suppose a driver in a particular town or city gets stopped and cited for speeding but the officer who stops him is from an adjacent town or city in that state and has crossed into the adjoining town or city to stop the driver. If the state's highest court previously ruled that jurisdiction of local officers is limited to the town or city of their employment, the driver could go to court and argue that point. In this instance, the judge should be bound by *stare decisis* and dismiss the charge for lack of jurisdiction no matter how long ago the precedential ruling had been established in the state. More on this topic will be discussed in the JURISDICTIONAL ISSUES section of chapter sixteen.

Statutes exist that define both criminal and civil offenses. As opposed to criminal statutes that can authorize both incarceration and fines, civil statutes involve law wherein the penalty is something other than jail or prison time. They ordinarily specify restitution to an opposing party or the imposition of a monetary fine for breaking the particular law, such as when a motorist receives a vehicular parking citation. Sometimes the penalty may be the loss of a medical, a legal, or another professional license. Civil statutes may also provide injunctive relief, relief in the form of a court order that compels a party to do or refrain from a specified act.

With the basic organizational structure and function of statutory laws explained, there are also rules of civil procedure and rules of criminal procedure as stated earlier in this section that should be understood.[1][2] To find them, the law library or court is a good place to look if the links in the appendix become obsolete. Searching online for rules of procedure by entering state name followed by "rules of civil procedure" or "rules of criminal procedure" or using "federal" or "Washington DC" instead of state name, as the case may be, should reveal the sought state, federal, or D.C. civil or criminal rules. Note that "penal" is used instead of the word "criminal" in some states and should be substituted accordingly. Like statutory laws and constitutions at the state level being derived from federal counterparts, state and District of Columbia rules of civil and criminal procedure share a similar relationship with their federal precursors. Thankfully, there are far fewer rules of procedure than statutes.

HOW THE SYSTEM BREAKS ITS RULES WITHOUT DETECTION

The preceding explanation of the hierarchy and definitions of the rules of the game describes all the predominant rules created by the legal system. The system is supposed to abide by these rules; however, it can and does break them on a regular basis. Although what follows in the balance of this chapter are known instances of the system breaking its own rules, these are merely our firsthand experiences and other reported examples. As sure as the sun shines, there are many other instances when public servants break their own rules, which go undetected or just unreported.

Of primary importance to the rule-breaking that will be discussed is the fact that police, prosecutors, judges, and other members of the system are very well aware of the rules that they break because they enforce them on a daily basis...whenever doing so suits them. The powerful positions they hold combined with their knowledge of the rules also make it much easier for them to evade detection while breaking them.

The average person, on the other hand, is often blindsided by the application of these rules by law enforcement and other system members and is on the wrong side of them far more frequently than those in power. In essence, the rules are nothing more than a trap for the unwary, and the system seeks to distort them while enforcing them upon unsuspecting people, including those involved in court matters. The following cannot be emphasized enough: *it is incumbent upon every litigant to read and reread the federal, state, or local rules of civil or criminal procedure and statutory laws (collectively with* stare decisis, *"the rules") that are or could be relevant to his case.*

CONSTITUTIONAL RIGHTS BEING OBLITERATED

Examples of rule-breaking by the system can be seen through the evisceration of many rights guaranteed by the U.S. Constitution. Consider civil asset forfeiture discussed in chapter four. These laws completely disintegrate our Fourth and Fifth/Fourteenth Amendment protections against unreasonable search and seizure and deprivation of property without due process of law, respectively.

The president now has the power to detain American and foreign citizens indefinitely, a clear violation of the Fifth and Sixth Amendments, if they are even remotely thought to have any connection to a terrorist group. Part of the problem lies in the definition of "terrorist," which is widely open to interpretation. Normal people would define it as someone who wants to harm individuals in the form of bombings, killings on a massive scale, or other truly terrifying acts, such as the attacks on U.S. soil perpetrated by real terrorists on September 11, 2001. The U.S. government, on the other hand, defines it as anyone deemed threatening or who could be a government dissenter—which is undoubtedly a rapidly growing segment of the American population given today's police state.

The president's authority to kill whomever he so chooses, U.S. citizens included, under this new definition is also a flagrant violation of the Fifth Amendment right of due process. Drones are thought to be the prevalent weapons of choice that fulfill this purpose, but there may be others that accomplish the same act. The president's amassing of power and the passing of laws that now violate the aforementioned rights have accelerated after 9/11.

What about other constitutional rights? Are they also being violated? Most certainly they are. Fairly recently, with the unrest that began in Ferguson, Missouri, in August of 2014, people were being assaulted and arrested by police for asserting their right to assemble peaceably, a right protected under the First Amendment.

In 2012 the Occupy movement saw many protesters lose this same right in the form of protest hours being limited, certain public areas being declared off-limits, and some of them being arrested. Others were assaulted by the police, including Scott Olsen, an Iraq War veteran in Oakland, California, who had his skull fractured.[3] Cecily McMillan in New York was groped and thrown to the ground and later convicted on trumped-up charges of assaulting the very police officer who had assaulted her.[4] In California and New York, protesters were pepper-sprayed for no reason other than for the fact that they were protesting.

In Houston, Texas, there was a clear violation of the freedom of religion clause of the same amendment. Annise Parker, the openly gay mayor, espoused the Houston Equal Rights Ordinance. Local religious ministers were opposed to the ordinance and sought its repeal. In retaliation the mayor had attorneys for the city subpoena certain sermons and writings of the ministers, a blatant violation of the First Amendment.[5] A subpoena is an order by the court for a person to appear in a legal proceeding or for documents or evidence to be given to someone by whoever possesses it.

Almost every part of the Fifth Amendment has been destroyed. Its opening sentence declares that an indictment by a grand jury is required to prosecute anyone accused of an infamous crime. Possibly because it costs the courts too much time and money, felony criminal actions brought by prosecutors only sometimes involve the grand jury in state courts. Rather dangerously, the right against self-incrimination, also known as the right to remain silent and protected under this amendment, has come under heavy fire. In *Salinas v. Texas*, the U.S. Supreme Court ruled that failing to answer questions from police officers by keeping quiet during interrogation is done at the accused's peril. Remaining completely silent when being questioned by law enforcement officers can now be used to "prove" one's guilt.[6]

But it is far worse than this. The police have multiple ways of getting around the roadblock of silence to obtain the incriminating information they want to hear. Many do not care upon *whom* they pin a crime—they just need to find a warm body to fit the bill. The due process and taking of private property for public use clauses of the Fifth Amendment have already been shown to be obsolete. Suffice it to say protections afforded under this amendment are all but officially gone.

The Sixth Amendment has also been largely eliminated. Detainees at Guantanamo Bay, Cuba, have been held there since 9/11 with no sign of a trial anywhere on the horizon.[7] Cases that have occurred on domestic soil also illustrate this amendment's demise. In *State v. Jensen*, the Supreme Court of Wisconsin ruled that some evidence is admissible in court without the accused having the right to cross-examine or to be confronted with the witnesses against him.[8] In *Michigan v. Bryant*, the highest U.S. court ruled that the police could testify on behalf of a dead witness, formally known as hearsay and formerly inadmissible, in spite of the defendant not being able to confront his accuser, the deceased witness.[9]

MORE EXAMPLES OF RULE-BREAKING BY THE SYSTEM

Other than the system violating our constitutional rights, it also breaks the law and its own rules of procedure. Innumerable known examples exist. Searching online will reveal that there are a multitude of occurrences reported by the media and in U.S. case law. Some examples of judges, lawyers, and police officers breaking the law were given in chapters one and two. There is also no shortage of rules of civil and criminal procedure being broken in U.S. courts by judges and other public officials.

Not following rules of procedure that govern the timeliness of case filings is one example of the judicial system not following its own rules. One author has an ongoing civil claim as the plaintiff in the Taunton District Court in Massachusetts. That state's rules of civil procedure require that a defendant file an answer, the legal term for "a response," within twenty days of being served the complaint. However, the court allowed the defendant's counselor, Joseph L. Michaud, to file an answer almost nine years late. In the same proceeding, the clerk of the court vacated, or set aside or canceled, a judgment originally in the author-plaintiff's favor *before* the motion to vacate was ever filed by the same attorney, a blatant violation of that state's rules of civil procedure.

In a separate traffic case in Rhode Island, the same author was the defendant in a civil action that involved jurisdictional issues. The judge of the Middletown Municipal Court, Peter B. Regan, ignored *stare decisis* by disregarding case law while making a deliberately incorrect ruling that was later overturned by a higher court. In the same case, he also broke rules of civil procedure. One rule that stated, "You will sign a notice with the new court date for your trial, with a copy retained by you," was not followed since the author-defendant was never asked to sign any notice. In spite of there being at the time a rule of civil procedure stating, "There is a no continuance policy in effect," Judge Regan also continued the matter, not once but twice.[10] He also violated the rule "A judge shall dispose of all judicial matters promptly, efficiently and fairly" by extending litigation to span well over four months and five court appearances for a simple traffic case.[11]

Mind you, these are the *known* rules of civil procedure that he violated—there could very well be more. It is almost as if these judges, magistrates, clerks, and other court officials view laws and their own rules as mere recommendations. In our experience, rules of civil and criminal procedure are broken far more often than not by court personnel. Maybe it is because they break these rules so frequently that it has become the norm and is widely accepted without a second thought, or perhaps it is because breaking them flies under the radar more easily than breaking statutory law. Possibly it is a combination of both.

Expounding on this further, at all levels of the judiciary, the system will often attempt to make the law fit the crime rather than the crime fit the law as it should do, regardless of whatever the "crime" may be. This statement holds true in civil causes of action as well, with our glorified, oftentimes unelected, lawyers in black gowns trying to make the law fit the facts. In all two dozen or so legal battles of one author, only a few come to mind in which this *did not* occur. Legislating from the bench has become far too common.

Besides our personal experiences, there is also no shortage of other known instances of judges violating the code of judicial conduct, a set of rules applicable specifically to U.S. judges.[12] The Center for Public Integrity examined the financial holdings of the circuit court judges in all thirteen U.S. circuits. They found twenty-four instances when judges owned stock in a company that was a litigant in a legal matter over which they ruled and two others when judges had financial ties to legal firms working on the cases over which they presided. Unless a complaint is filed against a judge for violating the code of judicial conduct, he faces no formal discipline. Even if a complaint is filed, it has a strong chance of being rejected as stated in chapter three's INEFFECTIVE CHECKS AND BALANCES section.

The center also found that 59 percent of federal appellate judges own stock compared to 15 percent of the average American population. The likelihood of these judges ruling over a legal matter in which they have a financial conflict of interest is certainly not zero. In fact, total reported assets including stock and other investments for the 255 appellate judges researched were between $585 million and $1.8 billion according to the center's calculations. In addition, other conflicts of these judges could still be hidden because more than 100 of the current 258 appellate judges had some information redacted from their financial disclosure reports in 2012. This includes data about gifts they received, income they earned, and investments they held.[13]

In one particular instance, Tenth Circuit Judge Bobby Baldock reported earning up to $50,000 in royalties from ConocoPhillips in 2011 and ruled on a civil action involving the company. It was sued by its workers' union for allegedly violating a collective bargaining agreement. The court's decision partially favored both the company and union. According to Tenth Circuit Clerk of Court Betsy Shumaker, the judge said the royalty payment did not require him to recuse himself.[14]

Granted, there are several appellate judges who rule over a legal cause of action in the circuit courts, but partiality to any degree is detrimental to a ruling. For such a powerful group of people to have such an overt bias in their rulings is a travesty, especially considering only a small handful of their decisions can be successfully appealed to the U.S. Supreme Court. Scariest of all, appellate judges of late have been filling vacancies in the U.S. Supreme Court. The preceding discussion clearly indicates that the center found transgressions by judges. However, as is our familiar theme, it does not mean the search was exhaustive—there may be many more undiscovered instances.

Rule-breaking is not limited solely to judges either. Plenty of lawyers break their share of statutory laws and rules of professional conduct governing legal practice. Not responding in a timely fashion to their clients and failing to provide written estimates to them when required are relatively minor violations of the rules. Other violations include not properly serving opposing parties, failing to provide certain documents to opposing parties, commingling their personal money with funds received by a client, and more. All have been seen firsthand by both authors.

As an example, one particular lawyer in a state civil matter did all but the last one of these things while representing one author. In another proceeding, an entirely different lawyer managed to commit all these violations while representing the same author. Luckily for the author, this lawyer was his *friend*—imagine what might have happened if he had been the author's enemy. Shockingly, he was actually suspended by the governing board from practicing law for a period of two years. However, it was not because of the complaint the author filed with the board. Apparently, this attorney infuriated someone with significant political power.

RULE-BREAKERS ACCUSING EVERYDAY PEOPLE OF BREAKING THE RULES

Ironically, the judicial system sometimes accuses ordinary citizens of breaking rules meant to protect the public from system members, but it instead uses them to protect its own members from the public. The Kentucky Bar Association attacked a non-lawyer for legal document preparation. Apparently, anyone who is not a licensed attorney who helps others with wills, uncontested divorces, and other simple legal matters is frowned upon in that state—especially if it undercuts lawyers who charge significantly more for the same service. In 2004 a jury's acquittal after less than a half hour of deliberation for someone criminally charged with such an offense did not seem to stop the bar from trying again by fining that person $5,000 later.[15]

     With all the rules being broken by people who enforce them, one may wonder if it is ever possible for the average person to win any legal battle in court even having irrefutable evidence. Surprisingly, it is, but there is a catch. Ordinary litigants somehow have to get the rules of the system to work in their favor. Knowledge of the system itself, its history, where it is today, and the players involved are all the prerequisites that have been covered to this point. Knowing how to use the rules so that they are most advantageous to you is the subject of the next chapter.

Chapter 6: Making the Rules Work for You

The young man knows the rules, but the old man knows the exceptions.
— **Oliver Wendell Holmes, Sr.**

Chapter Sections

- Using an abundance of laws to your advantage
- Using one of few surviving early amendments to the Constitution
- Removal of a lawyer from a case
- Appeal process
- Continuance for a "valid" reason
- Deciding not to play the game
- Demand letter
- Acting under the "color of law"
- Using rules against your adversary
- Ideas not recommended in legal proceedings

Rules in any game can be a double-edged sword—as the judicial system finds when it frequently feels the need to shred its own. Rules can work against a participant, but *if* a "team coach" can frustrate the "referee" by invoking so many rules, delaying the game, and changing the momentum, it is quite possible to win the legal game or at least create a more favorable environment for winning.

USING AN ABUNDANCE OF LAWS TO YOUR ADVANTAGE

In this chapter, we take a closer look at the ways you can make the rules work to your benefit. One of the system's weapons that can be used against it is its plethora of rules and laws. So many exist today that there is a good chance a rule of procedure, a statute, or case law can be used to solidify your case. If you even remotely suspect that there might be a rule, law, or case related to your particular legal issue, research may reveal that you are correct or on the right track. All it takes is a visit to the law library or court or a little time browsing the internet to perform the investigation. If your suspicion is not completely correct, then something fairly close might be able to be woven into the fabric of your matter.

For example, if you prevail in a civil case as a defendant and wonder if you might be entitled to reimbursement of litigation expenses from a losing plaintiff that is a governmental entity, it is quite possible in some states. See Rhode Island statute § 42-92-1.[1] In other instances, if you suspect that a party has overstepped their boundaries or has committed some procedural error while filing a motion, a brief, or another document with the court, search the relevant rules of procedure to see if they indeed have. Also remember that because there are now so many laws in America, it might be possible to use them for a wide array of purposes that benefit *you*. Like the number of such domestic laws, the possibilities are nearly endless.

Legislative errors may create glaring weaknesses in statutory law that can be exploited to fortify your case. In their zeal to keep you guessing, our legislators sometimes write or revamp laws without wording them as they intended or considering any collateral effects on other related laws. Examples include the loophole in Rhode Island law examined later in chapter ten's Reading the Law subsection and the erroneous New Hampshire statute subsequently discussed in chapter twelve's BUILDING THE DEFENSE section. Another classic concerns Massachusetts general laws chapter 89, section 9, and chapter 85, section 2.[2][3] In the first law, the maximum fine is "not to exceed $150," but in the second, it is "not exceeding twenty dollars"...for the same offenses. Apparently, when performing a search in order to increase the fines, legislators only looked for statutes containing a dollar sign and missed the latter law, which contains no dollar sign. It could easily be argued in court that in order to satisfy two statutes containing two distinct numbers, *neither* of which can be exceeded according to law, the statute referencing the lower number must prevail.

USING ONE OF FEW SURVIVING EARLY AMENDMENTS TO THE CONSTITUTION

Another way to use the rules to your advantage might lie in the equal protection clause of the Fourteenth Amendment of the U.S. Constitution. Violation of this clause occurs when some people are protected if they break certain laws, whereas others are not, or conversely, some people are prosecuted if they break certain laws, whereas others are not. Suppose a business is operating without competition in your particular community. Thinking of competing with this establishment, you open a similar company under the reasonable assumption that everything the other business is doing is legal. After all, your research revealed that the business has had no record of civil or criminal actions initiated by the legal system.

Not long after opening your new enterprise, you get attacked by the system in the form of a civil or criminal complaint. In such an instance, you could search for pertinent case law wherein the same law you are accused of breaking was selectively enforced upon another person or business. Suppose the defendant prevailed by referencing the equal protection clause of the Fourteenth Amendment in their legal argument, supported with proof of similar businesses operating without having had civil or criminal actions brought against them by the system. As part of your defense, you could use the same reasoning and arguments while citing that particular case and including the businesses it referenced to support your own case in order to invalidate the system's claim.

REMOVAL OF A LAWYER FROM A CASE

Another example of leveraging the system's rules might come into play when a member of the system can be held responsible for a major legal mistake, such as a criminal defense attorney who falls asleep during trial or does something outlandish that loses a case. Massachusetts has a rule of procedure that could be used against it to invalidate a bogus conviction resulting from such a mishap.[4] Under certain conditions, criminal procedure rule 30(b) allows someone a new trial, which comes with the benefit of the chance to obtain new counsel. In fact, obtaining new representation is supposed to be allowed at any time during any case. If the case is retried, the defendant could also be assigned a different judge if the previous one has died, has retired, or is otherwise unavailable. A different judge could further open the door for the defendant if the deciding judge was inadequate or corrupt.

Replacing your own lawyer is one thing, but removing the attorney who is representing your adversary is another. A potential way to do this is to investigate whether she has violated any rules of the governing board while pursuing the case against you. If the lawyer has, filing a complaint against her along with recommending a suspension may get her suspended and therefore removed from the case. It might be a long shot given the information presented in chapter three's INEFFECTIVE CHECKS AND BALANCES section and may take several weeks or months for any suspension to occur, but if a court date is not imminent and the luxury of time exists, then at least you have a slim chance.

If there are previous lawsuits against that attorney or any past improprieties, bringing them to the judge's attention may help strengthen your case. Although it will not get the attorney removed, it may achieve the same goal—winning your battle. In one author's experience, referencing disciplinary history by the bar against a lawyer who was pursuing a frivolous lawsuit helped shed light on the lawyer's character. The presiding judge saw through the lawyer's gamesmanship and ruled in favor of the author.

If the next potential court date against an opposing party is quite distant, you may want to consider exposing any lawsuits, disciplinary actions, or improprieties concerning your adversary's counsel on the lawyer rating websites listed in the appendix. If enough people see your reviews, it could eventually put the attorney out of business, but it certainly would be taking the long route to accomplishing that end. Keep in mind that whatever you post must be true if there is a chance disparaging comments can be traced back to you. The truth is an absolute defense against libel and slander. False statements are not.

One more way to remove an opposing attorney is to contact a federal prosecutor and file criminal charges against the attorney if she has committed any federal crimes during your case. In a civil matter in which one of the authors is involved in Massachusetts, the opposing attorney, Joseph L. Michaud, committed at least two federal felonies, perjury and conspiracy against rights, 18 U.S.

Code § 1621 and 18 U.S. Code § 241, respectively. Additionally, he committed several state felonies, obstruction of justice among others. However, he was politically connected with former U.S. Senator Scott Brown and possibly others, and the state authorities would not touch him. The only chance the author-plaintiff had was to approach officials outside his corrupt clique.

The possibility of an attorney who is opposing you similarly violating laws might not be as remote as you think. Some of these individuals become so arrogant that they break laws they believe are inferior to them because they view themselves as untouchable. As discussed later in this chapter's USING RULES AGAINST YOUR ADVERSARY section, if you think there is a chance an attorney who is your adversary has broken any laws, researching applicable statutes may reveal she indeed has.

APPEAL PROCESS

Some of the best rules to use against the system are the ones that permit appeals. If a case is lost after the first attempt at justice, take heart, especially if proceeding *pro se* since costs to appeal could only consist of filing fees, your time, and perhaps incidental expenses, all of which should make pursuing an appeal worthwhile, depending upon circumstances. This is a golden opportunity to do more research, to determine what went wrong, to get a different day in court, to have a different judge hear the case, and possibly to fight in a different court that serendipitously spins the rules more to your advantage.

CONTINUANCE FOR A "VALID" REASON

If it suits you as a litigant, consider calling the court first thing in the morning on your appointed date, saying you are sick, and asking the clerk to reschedule. Not only does this strategy significantly frustrate the opposing party by creating extra work for them and by making them waste time and money, but it also aligns itself perfectly when proceeding *pro se* since there would be no obligation to pay personal attorney fees for a missed day in court. A lawyer working on your behalf may already be there by the time you postpone the hearing or trial and would rightfully want to get paid for her time. The preceding is an excellent plan when a corrupt judge would otherwise be presiding over your case and proceedings related to it may be heard by different judges throughout its lifecycle in a particular court. Once this mission has been accomplished, that is, avoiding the corrupt judge, continue to "judge shop" as explained in chapter two.

DECIDING NOT TO PLAY THE GAME

If you truly hate the system, and you will if you have been a litigant in it long enough and stand for all that is good and just, jury duty can be quite undesirable for individuals who own businesses and may suffer loss of income if they decide to join a game that may take days, weeks, or even months to play. If the system was legitimate and also properly compensated jury members, any citizen would be proud to participate in serving justice. Since our current system is purely a dream—or purely a nightmare, depending upon perspective—it is understandable that individuals might not want to sit on a jury even though they are obligated by law.

Bringing a book about the U.S. Constitution to court with you to read during breaks is an excellent way to get released from jury duty in some jurisdictions during the selection process, if not completely run out of town by court personnel. One of the authors knows someone personally who did exactly this and was immediately released from duty because of it. Again, if the system was legitimate, he should have been the *last* person to have been released or perhaps the only person to remain. Instead, the exact opposite transpired.

Bias will also typically release you from jury duty. Your bias would be apparent if, in a criminal case, for example, you inform the attorneys during their selection process that you will likely convict a police officer, lawyer, or judge, regardless of any evidence or testimony, because of your disdain for them but will not be quite so quick to act against an ordinary citizen. Saying that you will not impose the death penalty in states where it is allowed should also relieve you from duty in a murder trial. Coincidentally, you may be against the death penalty after reading this book if you were not already.

The court often tries to brainwash prejudiced people during the jury selection process. The judge will ask certain guiding questions and make specific statements in an effort to erase any bias, at least temporarily for the trial, as ridiculous as it sounds, because judges frequently encounter this. If any openly prejudiced beliefs are maintained after questioning, they should disqualify respective potential jurors.

After receiving a summons to appear in court as a defendant and the government is the plaintiff, check it thoroughly for accuracy. Verify that the names, dates, times, and other information on it are all correct. When the summons was clearly intended for someone else or the information could not be true, the case could be dismissed. However, if the summons contains only minor errors, the courts generally will not dismiss the matter because they have given themselves the power to make corrections during case proceedings.

If the date of the alleged act indicated on the summons is one you could not have been where it says you were, then after the plaintiff rambles when presenting her charade in court, you can put forward this fact. If you have a witness or an alibi, you can disprove the allegations. Governmental plaintiffs can ask the court to change any date on a summons or complaint if the event in question allegedly happened and you are accused of doing whatever they claim you did.

However, they have to know the *correct* date. Volunteering this information will make the case much easier for them. Instead, make them guess the correct date if there even is one. If they do not, then with any luck, you will have yet another alibi. If they cannot pinpoint a date for which you do not have an alibi, the case will ultimately have to be dismissed.

As explained in the MORE EXAMPLES OF RULE-BREAKING BY THE SYSTEM section of chapter five, 59 percent of federal judges own some form of stock. Because of this and because they might ignore the rules or may not check if they are presiding over a case that may pose a potential conflict of interest, their stock ownership can be used against them. For litigants unhappy with a judge assigned to their case, they can research whether she has a financial conflict in the matter. If she does, it can be brought to her attention in hopes of recusal. If that does not work, the offended party can threaten to file a complaint against the judge at the state or federal level or in the nation's capital as appropriate.[5] [6] Of course, this is a long shot and should be a last resort when it is known there is nothing to lose; otherwise, this may have the same effect on the party as someone sticking her head into a lion's mouth.

Since many federal judges own stock, there is a chance the one newly assigned as a replacement in a federal matter may share the same financial conflict as the previous one. If this judge is satisfactory to that same party, they can simply overlook that fact and let the opposing party discover it and force them to ask for recusal. This process may take some time, but it may be worth the effort.

A possibly advantageous rule is the one requiring that a defendant in a civil matter be notified of it in person, by U.S. mail, or in any event, by some court-approved means in order to start litigation. If you suspect an upcoming lawsuit, it might be wise to screen any certified or registered mail waiting for you at the U.S. post office. There is no obligation to go get it whether it is unwanted mail or not. If you get a knock at your door and are not expecting anyone, it might be best to avoid answering it until you know who the person is or not to answer the door whatsoever. Impeding delivery of the notice for a lawsuit makes initiating it extremely difficult for a potential adversary.

Not only might the plaintiff relent, but it might give you more time to think, analyze, and prepare for the upcoming case. It is possible the server will lie and say you were served when in actuality you never were. This certainly does occur. Proper service is something that can be disputed in court; however, arguing the point once there is counterproductive since the purpose of being served is to get you to go to court in the first place.

DEMAND LETTER

Some jurisdictions mandate that a demand letter be sent to any potential defendant as a prerequisite to filing a formal civil complaint (see appendix). If this is not done, it may have detrimental effects on potential litigation up to and including dismissal. Sending a demand letter to your adversary may also be an opportunity to end a case before it even starts. Intimidate as much as you legally can in such a letter. State that legal action will ensue, the media will be contacted because of the other party's actions, and the party's business misconduct will be posted on various websites, if applicable. If the demand is made to a business, you could also say that the attorney general's office, Better Business Bureau, Federal Trade Commission, and relevant consumer protection agency will be contacted and that further actions may follow (see end of appendix). This often works quite well—even against lawyers.

Sometimes, even though the lawyer governing authority may ultimately dismiss a complaint against a lawyer, there is no reason the violation of the rules of professional conduct cannot be used in a lawsuit against her later. Hold her feet to the fire with these rules, and use breaches of them as evidence against her whenever possible. Just as rules of ethics that doctors and other professionals violate can be used against them in a court of law, rules of professional conduct that attorneys violate can also be used against them in legal proceedings.

ACTING UNDER THE "COLOR OF LAW"

Government personnel at all levels, while working in their official positions of governmental authority, sometimes will imply a law exists when none does. They may openly break the law too. Whenever either happens, such individuals are acting under the "color of law" in violation of the U.S. Code.[7] The implication here is that the government officials or officers responsible, exclusive of judges and prosecutors who normally enjoy immunity, can be held personally liable for damages as in *Monroe v. Pape*.[8] Also excluded from this group are federal officials. However, they might be liable under *Bivens* claims, which are similar to claims under 42 U.S. Code § 1983.[9]

Given that America has become a police state with an ample array of laws, the odds of the government trying to "pull one over" on an unwary citizen have undoubtedly increased. The government may go unchallenged for the law it might be breaking or for the alleged one it is attempting to enforce. The accused becomes a facilitator and enables this abuse when complying with a governmental letter or notice of a violation when no such law or legal authority exists.

Performing thorough research to establish the validity of law or legal authority in any such instance is strongly suggested.

USING RULES AGAINST YOUR ADVERSARY

Up to here, this chapter's content has mostly focused on using some of the system's own rules against it. Using those same rules against any opposing party in a legal proceeding is also possible. If you even remotely suspect that there is a law related to the opposing party's actions, research it. With well over 1,000,000 domestic laws and with the list growing all the time, there is a good chance such a law or something similar exists. The exorbitant number of laws makes it quite possible for you to find one or more to build or strengthen your case.

After finding an applicable statute, research all of its relevant case law. This is important because some laws are so terse that gleaning the true legal application of them can be difficult from the statute alone. At the other end of the spectrum and probably far more common, some laws span multiple pages and contain various sections and subsections. Learning how to apply these more complex laws to a particular legal matter is also illustrated by existing case law.

In an adversarial legal proceeding, there is an extended procedure called "discovery" during which either side is permitted to ask the other to answer interrogatories, produce specific documents, admit or deny certain facts, and participate in a deposition. Interrogatories are a set of written questions, and depositions seek oral testimony from a witness or relevant party. Throughout this process, either side can ask for bank statements, records of past employment, proof of business dealings—anything that might be associated with the case or that may uncover more evidence. Discovery is virtually a license to go on a glorified fishing expedition.

In smaller civil cases, it might make sense to inundate the opposing party with plenty of discovery requests. If you think they can be overwhelmed by the matter, whether represented by counsel or not, the strategy might be to ask for everything including the kitchen sink. If you think otherwise, it might be better not to ask for quite as much but as much relevant or even remotely relevant information as possible. That is because they could object to providing information unrelated to the case, which would defeat the whole purpose of it taking too much time and costing too much money to gather the requested data.

The other party might not respond if producing the requested information during discovery will be relatively time-consuming or may be fairly expensive. If the plaintiff does not respond, the defendant could file a motion to compel or a motion to dismiss. If the defendant does not respond, the plaintiff could file a motion to compel or a motion for default judgment. Any motion should be provided to the opposing party if required by rule and should state that the requested information is crucial for the moving party to prevail. Filing these kinds of motions after an adversary fails to respond could clinch an easy win. Granted, in a lawsuit worth millions or even thousands of dollars, this ploy probably will not work, but in matters only worth a few hundred dollars or less, such as traffic cases, it has a realistic shot.

Long before any legal battle against an adversary ensues, transferring monetary accounts into another person's name might be worth considering. Funding an offshore trust with a significant sum that may become the focus of a lawsuit might be an option. Some laws prohibit doing this once a proceeding has started or even when a party knows one is about to commence, but doing it beforehand is usually legal. The burden of proving preexisting knowledge of an impending suit would be on the opposing party, which may be difficult for them.

IDEAS NOT RECOMMENDED IN LEGAL PROCEEDINGS

With legal methodologies put forth about how to attempt to defuse the system and the opposing party, there are also certain ideas that someone might consider. These are thoughts that may happen to cross one's mind but are *not* legal in most instances. As much as one may want to try some of these things because avoiding detection would be easy, it is not recommended.

As a defendant in a traffic case for speeding, a person should not state as a defense that a speedometer or another vehicle part was defective and she was thus unable to determine her speed if untrue. If she purchased the automotive part in question, used a copy of the receipt as evidence after altering the purchase date in order to support her claim in an attempt to have the case dismissed, and then returned the part, it would be dishonest and illegal.

Email is often considered valid evidence in legal proceedings. As such, one cannot edit the source code of an email in order to make it say whatever is desired and then use a printed version of it as evidence. This is both immoral and illegal. Doing so would be at one's own peril.

Proper notice to an opposing party is required in a civil action at its various stages, including initiation of the case. One cannot falsely serve someone so that she misses a court date or arrives unprepared to respond to the particular filing that was not really served. This could waste the court's time and cost the other party attorney fees as well as cost the serving party attorney fees if not *pro se*.

Other activities that could be illegal include modifying documents provided by the court. For example, suppose you go to traffic court and listen to the decisions that are rendered prior to your matter being heard, during which time you hear fines being reduced to $X or $Y by the judge. You also see people getting notices from the court clerk in the courtroom for those two amounts afterward. They are either required to pay the fine then at court or allowed to mail the payment or make it personally at the court later. When your case is heard, you are the only one not given a reduced fine. It is not legal or ethical to reduce your own fine to $X or $Y by modifying the original notice received from the court. You might contemplate doing this perhaps by using correction fluid to cover the amount due, writing a new amount of $X or $Y over it, and photocopying the notice and then mailing the edited version to the court with a check for $X or $Y.

Some rules of the system and how they can be adapted for good use have been presented in this chapter. But there are other general rules, or more appropriately, various considerations that are relevant to thwarting litigation, fighting an opponent in a legal battle, or fighting the system itself, the largest and most imposing opponent. Before continuing to the third and final part of the book, the next chapter will cover these remaining considerations or miscellaneous rules.

Chapter 7: Miscellaneous Rules

Never write if you can speak; never speak if you can nod; never nod if you can wink. — **Martin Lomasney**

Chapter Sections

- Multiple heads are better than one
- Keep good records in many locations
- Second and third opinions
- Oral and written agreements
- Jury and bench trials
- Confident, capable, and calm in court
- New Golden Rule
- Anyone can be beaten
- Cutting losses or continuing to fight
- Long-term considerations
- Remaining miscellaneous rules

While the last chapter focused on rules that originate from the system, this one will concentrate on more pragmatic general unwritten "rules" and strategies that can help in any legal campaign. No less important than the last chapter to position someone optimally for minimizing legal risk and as part of a sound overall game plan, the miscellaneous quasi-rules discussed in this chapter should strongly be considered. What is discussed will not be found in any statute, rule of procedure, or other legal resource.

MULTIPLE HEADS ARE BETTER THAN ONE

One should try to obtain as many data points as possible from several relevant and reliable sources when attempting to formulate a solution to a problem. In line with this concept and as suggested in chapter two, more heads are better than one in any undertaking in which thought is the paramount component to success. A room filled with average minds in addition to one brilliant mind is *at least* as smart as the one brilliant mind. A legal battle is no exception to this rule, but it does not mean you must hire a platoon of attorneys or even just one in order to satisfy that criterion. There are other methods to gain access to those supplemental minds.

Using the internet is one way to get the input of another person. However, whatever information is extracted from it must be evaluated for veracity, part of which includes considering the information's source. For example, roadandtrack.com is probably a more reliable source of information about new cars than an individual's personal blog.

Avvo.com and rocketlawyer.com are websites where people can ask lawyers specific questions regarding various legal issues. Many questions about areas of law covered in this book are answered by lawyers on such sites. Some sites allow free access to answers. Some require a fee. Others provide both options. Lawguru.com is another site that features a searchable database of answers to a number of legal questions. Using its search tool enables people to get input from various lawyers in a rather short amount of time because common questions may already have several answers. Asking individual attorneys the same question successively would take longer, of course, because of the time associated with contacting each one and receiving a response.

Remember that while searching online you may see nearly as many different answers to a question as there are attorneys responding. While this can be confusing at first glance, look closer for concurrence among any of the responses. If there are a majority of answers to a particular question that sound similar, it is a good indication that the underlying content of those answers might be correct or at least partially correct.

For specific questions of law in particular states, answers may be sparse or nonexistent in databases for these and other websites—it may be hit or miss. Such gaps should fill over time as more attorneys respond. When tackling an issue that is part of a legal problem, online resources such as these and others may help you resolve it or at least steer you in the right direction. Additionally, these resources may point you towards supporting case law or legal journal articles that could provide you with other perspectives.

Websites like the ones just mentioned may come and go, but there will probably be some reputable forum or similar sites where you can get free or reasonably priced answers or legal advice without having to hire counsel directly. The internet can help you acquire the multiple inputs necessary for building a stronger legal case. For a particularly troublesome issue, using such sites is a sensible initial pursuit. Online legal forums are just one of many resources that provide input from several others as a step towards resolving a legal problem.

Having a friend or family member who is an attorney is another potential source of input for a legal issue. These people may be willing to help without requiring that you hire them. They may also be able to direct you to further resources, depending upon the type of matter at hand. For example, if you are involved in a more esoteric area of law, such as patent law, or are facing some obscure criminal charge, that friend or family member may be able to guide you to another lawyer who has experience handling those types of matters.

Another source of input to a legal problem might spring from bar associations, some of which provide free services for lower-income people. Indeed, many bar associations' governing rules suggest that their members donate a certain number of hours per month or year to lower-income clients. Contacting the pertinent bar association can clarify the kinds of services that are available and client qualifications for receiving them. Some associations only allow free guidance for home evictions, civil rights issues, and other limited areas of law, whereas others may offer guidance for a broader spectrum of matters.

Other organizations that may be related to the bar association may also provide consultation services with attorneys who answer questions free of charge on certain days and times. For instance, they might schedule lawyers to answer questions by phone on the first Wednesday of the month from 7:00 p.m. to 9:00 p.m. There may or may not be restrictions regarding scope of the questions or financial need of the questioner. Since these sessions typically occur within a relatively brief time slot during the month, it is likely that many people will be vying to get their questions answered. Therefore, prepare accordingly. Check online or contact the applicable organization directly for more information about the availability of such resources.

Finally, one more way to get legal input without hiring counsel is to search case law online or at the pertinent law library or court to learn what *pro se* litigants or attorneys did and how they fared in situations similar to yours. Remember from chapter five, *stare decisis* is the rule that obligates judges to follow the example of prior settled law. If lawsuits can be found that are markedly similar to yours in which one side prevailed by doing a certain thing or making a certain argument, it means chances are good, but not guaranteed, that you will also prevail by doing the same thing or making the same or a similar argument. Judges may not always follow case law as they should, but without an ulterior motive, their path of least resistance would be to follow it rather than to set new precedent. One of the authors has appeared before a judge who did not abide by *stare decisis* and initially lost the case as a result but eventually prevailed through the appeal process. This case will be covered in more detail in the JURISDICTIONAL ISSUES section of chapter sixteen.

Observe how *pro se* litigants or attorneys approached their problems in similar matters, how they composed written arguments, what case law they cited, and how they fared. Any case law they cited should also be researched if possibly relevant to your legal matter. In general, state actions only legitimately reference case law in that particular state, whereas federal actions generally reference case law at the federal level. Note that case law from the U.S. district court in the state where a state lawsuit is proceeding is sometimes cited in that suit to support it. Additionally, U.S. Supreme Court decisions may be cited on occasion in any matters.

To the newcomer, it might seem intimidating to be able to cite case law correctly in a legal document. The thinking might be that only a skilled lawyer knows how to cite cases properly. Nevertheless, if the format of italics for the case name, superscripting of the citation number, and all other associated information cited in the original case is replicated in your document or imitated in order to cite the original case itself, a valid citation will usually be the result. Lastly, researching case law may open a whole new door to approaching an issue otherwise unbeknownst to you. It may be somewhat time-consuming to do all the investigation, but with more information gathered, potential pathways for additional tactics and arguments might be revealed. Not only that, but the consensus of the data uncovered during your fact-finding should either point you towards or away from your initial theory.

Once your legal document is drafted, check for grammatical and other errors. Getting friends or family members to read through your work is helpful, particularly if they have some type of legal background. Proofreading is an important last step before submitting any legal document. If, as plaintiff, you are moving the court to make the defendant reimburse you for attorney's fees and you used the word "plaintiff" in the conclusion of your motion as the party liable for these fees instead of "defendant" as you intended, the consequences may be undesirable. Not only will you look stupid to the court, but your blunder could undermine your entire argument.

KEEP GOOD RECORDS IN MANY LOCATIONS

Besides utilizing the input of multiple heads in a legal undertaking, it is vital to keep good records. Most, if not all, media in digital or paper form should be valid as evidence in court and should be saved if they have possible significance to any current or future legal battle. This includes contracts, sales receipts, emails, text messages, rental agreements, bills, credit card statements, photographs, video recordings, audio recordings, and just about all other important records. Handwritten records should also be just as valid if relevant to a legal proceeding.

Keeping records without backups is pointless, however, if they get lost or destroyed. For safety it would be wise to copy all important electronic data onto multiple sources of media and keep them stored in physically different locations. Electronic file space on one of the widely available remote servers, such as Google Drive, is an option that mimics data backup on personal media but is implemented on a larger scale and is far safer with respect to recovery. At least one backup is suggested, and perhaps several may be warranted, depending on the data's importance.

For paper documents, keeping photocopies in two or more physically distinct locations is a must. If a building that contains one set of documents burns to the ground, having duplicates in another location could be crucial. All records that could similarly be destroyed by a catastrophic event should be copied and stored in multiple locations.

A precursor to the duplicative storage of important records is the quality of the records themselves. If records are of such poor quality that they will be useless for supporting a claim in a legal issue, there is no sense storing them in the first place.

When generating a contract of any kind, having one or more witnesses attest to it will strengthen its validity. Having it properly dated is also important. Ensure names are correctly spelled and that there are no typographical errors. An end date should be clearly stated on the contract if relevant.

In lieu of a mutually agreed upon contract witness, a notary public can be a sound alternative. A witness of this stature would also define the locale where the contract was signed, which could help later should it be disputed and jurisdiction need be established for pursuing legal action. Absent the services of a notary public, geographic location may be good to include on the contract anyway. Basically, a contract should state all its salient aspects in clear terms so that an outside party can determine the Who, What, When, Where, and Why of the contract.

Photographic and video records should include street name signs whenever a legal case they support is associated with a particular address or span of addresses. They should also include front or rear views of vehicles as appropriate whenever license plates identifying them are important. Likewise, parking signs in combination with street name signs or building numbers should be included in photos or video in order to establish location when contesting a parking ticket, for instance. Additionally, other landmarks identifying with certainty the location of an incident should be part of any photo or video when relevant.

Be sure that lighting is adequate when recording images. In some cases, the correct lighting may, in fact, be near or complete darkness. For example, darkness may be needed for gathering photographic evidence whenever a citation is received during a traffic stop at night for a vehicle light being out when it is really not. Recording imagery at the time of the stop with the law enforcement officer and his vehicle in the shot establishes the scene and can be used later as evidence. If the officer stopped your vehicle for the contrived reason of a faulty lighting device, it is probably a good idea to be discreet when gathering photographic or video imagery since he may not take kindly to being recorded. Equipping your vehicle with a dashboard camera might be beneficial and provides an alternative to recording overtly with a mobile phone.

Other types of records should be equally illustrative of the facts they intend to establish. When electronic receipts are printed, they should contain as much identifying information as possible, including date, time, item price and description, and other relevant data. Personally identifiable information, such as a social security number, date of birth, and whatnot, can be redacted on any copies of records to protect privacy and prevent identity theft.

SECOND AND THIRD OPINIONS

Another miscellaneous rule that applies when searching for legal representation, just as it does when searching for most other professional services, is the importance of getting a second or third opinion. People will often visit two or more doctors when faced with making an important health decision. The same approach should be considered if and when it comes time to hire legal counsel. Lawyers will sometimes shoot from the hip, giving a spontaneous analysis of a problem without having performed any due diligence researching it. Responding impulsively may help some lawyers entice new clients by creating the illusion that they have a wealth of knowledge at their fingertips.

Other lawyers simply might not have expertise in the area in which they are being consulted and openly admit it. Still others may propose a unique, beneficial strategy that no other attorney previously suggested. In addition, during this whole searching saga, it is vital that you discuss fee agreements, costs, and other terms of representation when thinking of hiring any particular attorney.

If you do ultimately decide to hire counsel, do not assume he will always give you the most accurate, unbiased advice. Lawyers interface with a great number of clients every year, some of whom lie to them. Many lie because they know lawyers lie or because they know the opposing party lied and feel that the best way to counter it is with a lie of their own. Thus, the game becomes one big circular lie. The important point here is that your attorney may not fully accept your input or evidence and may skew his advice away from what he perceives is a fabrication on your part. The translation is that your legal case may have better odds from your perspective, which you know is the truth, than from the perspective of your attorney who doubts your honesty—very ironic indeed.

ORAL AND WRITTEN AGREEMENTS

Putting oneself at minimal risk of a civil lawsuit or criminal prosecution has become increasingly difficult in the United States. Litigation has become so prolific that any person or entity in America with power and money maintains one or more attorneys on staff. Sometimes fault can be placed upon someone for being in the wrong place at the wrong time. Being as discreet as possible may reduce the chances of being falsely accused in many situations. Regarding risk of an agreement, an oral one can result in less exposure than a written one for any party who suspects its terms might sour on them at some point. Furthermore, the existence of an oral agreement is more difficult to prove than a written one.

On the other hand, sometimes a written agreement might be preferred, such as when an oral agreement's disintegration can result in greater exposure for that same party. One author knows a man who was personally involved in a situation in which a written agreement would have prevented a legal problem that resulted from the violation of a city ordinance. His first mistake was relying on a city official's word that it was legal to place remnants from a remodeling project on the sidewalk for collection. His second mistake was following the official's advice to the letter, which resulted in a hefty fine from the city.

Leaving refuse on city property was the basis for the fine. The city seemed to have developed a winning recipe for raising revenue: provide false information to citizens and then fine them for violations of an ordinance. The case was eventually resolved in the man's favor but would have ended far more quickly if he had asked the city for written approval prior to placing refuse on the sidewalk. It would be interesting to ascertain if other residents fined for doing the same thing fared as well. The bottom line is that agreements or contracts in writing will strengthen them, which may be good or bad, depending upon perspective.

Getting potentially important information in writing can also be beneficial whenever a conversation may not otherwise prompt a person to state clearly whatever he is thinking. Additionally, if relying on oral communication, keep in mind that conversation recorded without the other party's knowledge may be inadmissible in legal proceedings. Furthermore, people sometimes compose their thoughts better in writing than they do in conversation because written correspondence can be more reflective of their actual intentions. If you are dealing with someone who you feel is not being straightforward with you via oral communication, it might help to prod him subtly into an exchange by email or another electronic medium. Once discussion shifts to that format, corral him with guiding questions, and he may make frank statements in writing when his initial intent was to speak in generalities. Such electronic transmissions should be admissible in court and may prove quite useful to you if and when a dispute arises.

JURY AND BENCH TRIALS

Something else you may have to consider at some point is whether to select a bench or jury trial. Some say a bench trial, or "trial by the court" as it may be called in some states, the District of Columbia, and the federal system, is better. Others say a jury trial is the preferred option. We side with the latter.

Judges, of course, are part of the system. The system's objectives are to generate revenue for itself and settle cases by using as little of its time as possible. In a bench trial, the judge is the sole decision maker. If the judge is corrupt, dislikes a litigant for any reason, or simply has to go to the restroom, he may decide a case in complete opposition to all supporting facts.

Also, as stated in chapter one's REASONS FOR THE SYSTEM'S DECLINE section, consider that it is much more difficult to bribe an entire jury, a generally uninterested party of several, than it is to bribe a judge, a quite interested party of one. Granted, juries can be swayed, deceived by false testimony, or otherwise duped into rendering a bogus verdict, but they have the power of jury nullification, whereas judges do not. Although the judge is basically the equivalent of a referee in a sporting event and effectively makes the calls during a trial that can change the playing field before a jury even has a chance to decide your case, juries can be viewed as the lesser of two evils.

Perhaps a good understanding of both trial types can be obtained by making a comparison with world governments. Monarchy is both the best and the worst form of organized government. Monarchies have prospered and benefitted more than other countries of a contemporaneous period when benevolent monarchs have reigned. At other times throughout history, monarchies have descended into chaos when horrendous monarchs have ruled. Both extremes are possible, depending upon who is in power in the given country.

So it is with judges. Getting a good, truly impartial judge, although unlikely, certainly would be more desirable than a jury, which can be unpredictable. On the other hand, getting a corrupt or partial judge is far more likely and much less desirable than getting a potentially unpredictable jury.

For the most part, juries are composed of people from outside the system. They are members of the public, although it is possible to have lawyers, judges, and police sit on juries. Keep in mind that these individuals may not be optimal for jury selection because of potential bias against you. If any people in the jury pool happen to be amicable relatives or friends who may be biased for you whether they are members of the system or not, there is no obligation for you to reveal this information. Disqualifying potentially biased jurors is probably ideal, but the responsibility to do so falls upon the negatively affected party itself.

Another thing to note when several bench trials are held in a particular courtroom on any given day is that someone in a trial prior to yours could irritate the judge. If this happens, it may be best to devise a last-minute excuse to continue the case even if it is an apparent "slam dunk" and then go "judge shopping" as explained in chapter two's "JUDGE SHOPPING" TO AVOID BAD JUDGES section. Personal experience of one author has shown that an ultra-easy-win plaintiff's case heard by a disgruntled judge can be nearly lost and most certainly be partially lost even if the defendant fails to appear! Aggravating any single juror, a much more remote possibility than infuriating a judge, should have far less of a negative impact because there are several instead of one deciding the case.

Maybe the strongest point regarding the subject of selecting either a jury or bench trial can be made by considering the quote by Joseph Stalin: "I believe that it does not matter who in the party will vote, or how; but what is extremely important is this—who will count the votes, and how." No matter what either party does in any court proceeding in their attempt to "cast their vote" for their own cause, if the judge is the only one "counting the votes," how can there possibly be any sanity check on this? At least with a jury, there are several "counting the votes," and there is some accountability among its own members. If still not convinced, consider the following quotes by great men of the past:

- [Representative government and] tryals by juries...are as essential and fundamental, to...the preservation of...liberty [and] are the heart and lungs. — **John Adams (1766)**
- The friends and adversaries of the plan of the convention, if they agree in nothing else, concur at least in the value they set upon the trial by jury: Or if there is any difference between them it consists in this; the former regard it as a valuable safeguard to liberty, the latter represent it as the very palladium of free government. — **Alexander Hamilton (1788)**
- Trial by jury...is as essential to secure the liberty of the people as any one of the pre-existent rights of nature. — **James Madison (1789)**

- I consider [trial by jury] as the only anchor, ever yet imagined by man, by which a government can be held to the principles of it's constitution. — **Thomas Jefferson (1789)**
- The jury system has come to stand for all we mean by English justice, because so long as a case has to be scrutinized by twelve honest men, defendant and plaintiff alike have a safeguard from arbitrary perversion of the law. — **Winston Churchill (1956)**

In the highly unlikely event that a criminal case makes it to trial, it is interesting to note that federal statistics from 1990 through 2013 show that juries rendered convictions more often than judges. During that time, the average conviction rate was about 86 percent for jury trials and about 59 percent for bench trials. But these numbers may not tell the whole story. The percentage of people in this data set who opted for a jury trial versus a bench trial in U.S. district courts rose from 78 percent to 89 percent over the same period.[1]

The reason for the disproportionate conviction rates might be that some defendants chose a jury trial based upon the presumption of counsel: odds of winning without one would be minimal. Those who are truly guilty or who are factually innocent but nevertheless have a great deal of evidence—manufactured or otherwise—against them might have almost no chance of acquittal with either option, particularly with a bench trial. The relatively easier cases may have been tried without a jury and thus account for at least part of the conviction rate variation.

State statistics from Florida and California show closer conviction rates between cases decided by juries and those decided by judges. The reason for this is unknown. In Florida the conviction rate in its first circuit from 2002 through 2012 was 68 percent by jury trial and 64 percent by bench trial.[2] Data for California in 2013 showed an opposing trend, with conviction rates of approximately 84 percent and 91 percent for jury and bench trials, respectively.[3] Other states report court statistics, but none were found that report this type of data specifically.

One plausible reason is that the other states do not want defendants in criminal cases to know jury trials might be a better option. If defendants know that juries are more favorable towards them and thus choose them, it would hinder the legal machinery because of the extra time required to impanel a jury, give them instructions, allow their deliberation, and account for other related intangibles. This would not be good for the system's business.

In criminal cases, realize that the overwhelming majority of them are decided by plea bargains. In 2012 97 percent of federal criminal cases were decided this way and never made it to trial—this trend having generally risen over the last fifty years or so.[4] Plea deal acceptance rates by criminal defendants at the state level are not lagging far behind.

CONFIDENT, CAPABLE, AND CALM IN COURT

While in court, there is another unwritten rule that applies. The system can often behave like a shark. Once it smells blood or weakness, it may go for the kill. A litigant's nervousness in court is exactly the sort of weakness it senses. Many times, our experience has shown that these officiating power-trippers can fly off the handle over something as innocuous as someone inadvertently raising his left hand instead of his right when swearing to tell the truth, which has become a complete farce anyway. The judge may be in such a foul mood that no act, answer, or facial expression will be the right one from a litigant during the entire hearing or trial on that particular day.

It might be difficult, but remaining calm is paramount. A litigant must exude rock-solid confidence. If the judge fails to follow court rules of procedure or law, he should be addressed in the same manner as one would speak to an unruly child. This is accomplished by being direct and stern, not condescending or cocky, and without relenting if you feel the judge's unruliness would have detrimental effects on your case.

It may be a good idea to mention in open court that a judicial complaint might be filed with the appropriate oversight board if things are really not going your way because of malfeasance from the bench. The hearing or trial then becomes more like poker since you are implying you are holding a great hand. As explained in the INEFFECTIVE CHECKS AND BALANCES section of chapter three, complaints are almost always futile, but a less experienced judge may not know that and may thus refrain from calling or raising your bet.

Your statement may take the judge by surprise. Although it may not be completely dissuasive, it may persuade him to rethink his shenanigans and follow court rules and law instead. When mentioning your tentative complaint in court, you should be clear and brief, similar to, "Judge, I'm just asking that you follow your own court rules and the law; that's all—nothing more, nothing less." Again, the objective is to maintain a calm, authoritative demeanor just as you would if disciplining a child. If you feel you will not prevail no matter what you say or do on that day in court because of judicial misconduct, such a move could be a last resort to bring the judge in line.

If you really want to go the extra mile, one way to counteract the system rigging the odds against you is to play the game equally dirty as it does. You can perform an online background check, inquire within the community, or hire a private investigator to unearth any kind of muck in the judge's past. For example, some judges have been known to be womanizers or illegal recreational drug users. If you can gather enough solid evidence proving any improper activity that is not yet known to the public or the judge's spouse, then you, dear reader, may have just drawn a trump card from the deck.

Obviously, broadcasting your findings in open court might ruin the hand you were dealt. Once everyone knows about the judge's wrongdoings, your leverage is gone. One possible way to use the damning information to your advantage is to notify the judge quietly just prior to or on the court date by handing a letter describing your newfound dirt to the court clerk or judge's secretary. The letter could state how you are simply asking him to follow court rules and law and that the incriminating information will then be forgotten if he complies.

In fact, stating anything else may be construed as threatening and become more problematic for you. Depending upon whatever is uncovered, it may not be necessary to put anything more demanding in the letter. Let the judge draw his own conclusion. Sometimes saying less is more. There is no guarantee, but your day in court may be surprisingly pleasant.

Certainly, so many of these high and mighty glorified lawyers in black gowns view themselves as untouchable. This is arguably their weakest link. Catching them by surprise at the last possible moment before they have time to contemplate the ramifications of your accusations can have the greatest beneficial impact for you. Just as in any military campaign, the element of surprise can go a long way towards achieving victory in a legal campaign.

On your day in court, one valid and applicable rule is not to assume court personnel know what is happening. In fact, almost none of them may have a clue. This is true regardless if you are represented by counsel or are proceeding *pro se*. Different court personnel may send you from room to room, make you late for your appearance, cause you to enrage the judge, and create a multitude of problems described in the beginning of this section. Getting to court early should increase your chances of finding the correct room in time. Ask for the names of all "helpful" court personnel who instruct you where to go or what to do so you can point the finger later if necessary.

Before even going to court, it may be worthwhile checking if there is an outstanding arrest warrant issued in your name. Our experience has shown that sometimes a warrant exists without a person's knowledge. It would certainly ruin your day if you made it to court for your super-easy case only to be dragged to the Black Bar Hotel because of an outstanding warrant even if it is unjustified. Check anonymously and remotely with authorities in the jurisdiction in question, or search online just prior to any court appearance to see if the coast is clear. Just know that databases may not be up-to-date and contain new warrants. It is unknown at this time whether courts share databases between jurisdictions or between the state, federal, and Washington, D.C., judiciaries; however, if they do not now, someday they might. This means a warrant issued by one court could be known in another, perhaps the one where you are supposed to appear.

NEW GOLDEN RULE

Now, specifically regarding criminal proceedings, remember the first definition of the new Golden Rule defined in chapter two: Do *not* do unto others as you would have them do unto you; do unto others *before* they do unto you. Whenever two or more people are involved in a conflict of any kind, the first one to file a police report has an enormous advantage even if the facts of the matter are completely at odds with what that person reports. One possible reason for this is that a goal of law enforcement is to prosecute people; therefore, they and their report will go a long way towards tainting everything surrounding the matter in favor of the complainant before the true facts emerge in court—assuming they ever do.

However, before things even get that far, the police may try to guide you into confirming the other party's story during any interview or interrogation. They will likely not offer to show you the complaint so that you can see any outrageous allegations made by the complainant. This makes it seem like they are reluctant to expend any energy to change or correct the report—perhaps another reason the person filing first has the upper hand. If you have *any* suspicion that someone with whom you have recently been in conflict may contact the police and file criminal charges, doing so first can significantly tilt the scales of "justice" in your favor. The first definition of the new Golden Rule may be the most important precept in this chapter, if not this entire part of the book.

ANYONE CAN BE BEATEN

Police officers, lawyers, and judges who are parties to court proceedings can be defeated. While the chances of indicting a police officer anywhere in the country may be nearly zero, defeating one in a civil matter is quite possible.[5] New York City has fifty-five officers who have been sued ten or more times from 2002 to 2012. One leads the way with twenty-eight lawsuits. These suits have cost the city in excess of $1 billion.[6] One of the authors has defeated police several times while contesting alleged vehicular violations and may soon defeat one who has lost prosecutorial immunity.

Believe it or not, lawyers are generally easy to defeat in a non-corrupt court for savvy individuals because many are incompetent or at least not the sharpest tool in the shed. The same author has yet to lose a one-on-one case against a lawyer and has battled three thus far. These three do not include one who was sent a demand letter and returned a deposit without further legal action.

CUTTING LOSSES OR CONTINUING TO FIGHT

In any adversarial legal proceeding, be it criminal or civil, there may come a time when cashing out of the game and cutting losses might be sensible. We hope having to do this befalls no one undeserving, but in reality, there are a percentage of cases in which some blameless litigants will eventually have to consider it. Sometimes a person makes the mistake of hiring an attorney who is incompetent, skips town with a retainer, provides ineffective assistance of counsel, or fails to uphold the rules of professional conduct incumbent upon him. If so, the client might hire another attorney to sue him for malpractice in order to right whatever wrong was done. But what if the second attorney falls short of expectations while undertaking the matter to sue the first, perhaps even having been previously disciplined by the overseeing board? Where does the seemingly endless cycle of lawyer suing lawyer stop?

As unlikely as the aforementioned scenario may seem, this unfortunate chain of events is precisely what happened to one of the authors. In that instance, the statute of limitations expired on the civil infractions committed by the first lawyer before the second filed the requisite complaint in the proper court. It truly was unfair, but financially it made sense to cut the losses and learn from the experience, expensive as it was.

Sometimes litigants must pour money into the metaphorical "black hole" to keep a civil case alive. Contributing expenses include expert witness, appeal, and transcription fees; travel expenses to and from wherever the court or their attorneys' offices are located; and various other direct and indirect costs. Whenever the sum exceeds any potential return on the legal investment, it may be best to cut losses then and there unless, of course, the litigant is financially independent and wants to pursue the case based on sheer principle. At other times, when thinking of folding in a civil case because of corruption, that might be exactly the occasion to raise—just as in a real game of poker. It depends upon the situation.

There may be other, nonfinancial reasons for continuing to fight an adversary, including the legal system. Obtaining custody of children may be imperative in order to prevent them from living in an abusive or a drug-ridden environment. Elder care may have to be properly settled. Then, of course, there is the obvious example of when never to surrender—whenever you would be looking at death row if you are convicted of a crime you did not commit or are already rotting in prison for the very same reason. Sometimes, no matter what, a case must be fought without relenting, and it is an unfortunate state of affairs within our judiciary that some must pursue this painful path for a significant portion of their lives.

LONG-TERM CONSIDERATIONS

Not to be forgotten, there are long-term ramifications of a legal battle that are factors whenever considering an unrelenting fight. If any negative personal or financial consequences are possible when not continuing to brawl in a case, it may be worth persisting. For example, if one's name is not cleared through sealing or expungement because of a mistaken prosecution or for any other reason and lost future income is a legitimate concern, then fighting to the bitter end could be critical. As another example, if it would be a great loss to relinquish ownership of real estate privately known to have a rare resource or something valuable upon it, doing everything possible to prevent losing it might be worthwhile.

Depending upon the nature of a case, there may be nearly infinite odds to overcome or other obstacles that seem insurmountable. Rules of procedure or specific statutes may make it virtually impossible to win even with everything else being equitable. If a rule of procedure states that no appeal is possible in a case, then appealing it to a higher court would probably be futile.

Additionally, appeals can be costly. Cumulatively from each level of appeal, filing fees alone could run into the hundreds or perhaps thousands of dollars. Document production and mailing expenses to the courts and all parties involved add to the total. Without any viable way to recover such monies from an adversary in a civil case, it would make chasing one worth a few hundred dollars or less cost prohibitive.

Other potential costs for an appeal, besides the obvious attorney fees, are travel expenses for lodging, meals, and incidentals. Lost income from a business or job during the time required to pursue such a case is an additional indirect cost. Lastly, there are expenses associated with maintaining a home environment while away. For example, the cost of child, pet, and elder care along with a litany of other logistics must be considered when weighing the pros and cons of some appeals.

REMAINING MISCELLANEOUS RULES

A rule that will not likely be heard anywhere from any source applies when police officers or other law enforcement personnel sometimes make mistakes after arresting someone. If, by chance, they question you after being arrested and you find that your address, parents' names, birth date, or other personal information is incorrect in their database, an excellent idea is *not* volunteering to correct it most of the time. The reason for this rule is that the incorrect information may be useful in the future if you have been falsely arrested or the case otherwise gets dismissed.

Potential employers often conduct background checks on job applicants. Checks may also be performed for other reasons. Should an arrest or a criminal record be found during any check, which it will in all likelihood, then you can claim that it is probably associated with someone else with a similar name because the address, parent name(s), birth date, or other personal information does not correspond to you.

Additionally, unless absolutely necessary, think about not using full middle names, middle initials, or suffixes, such as *Jr.* or *Sr.*, or providing any other distinctive information anytime your name is requested since doing so would make it easier to identify and track you. Make it as laborious as possible for the government or anyone else to discover who you are, where you live, and everything else about you. Flying under the radar in this manner can help protect your future.

In fact, when moving to another residence, consider not informing the U.S. Postal Service of your new address for mail forwarding. For that matter, it may be worthwhile never to tell them where you are living so you can better control who can find you by U.S. mail. Notify only necessary companies about your new address—those with which you still do business and that mail you paper statements or bills. This provides two benefits: it reduces some junk mail, at least temporarily, and makes it more difficult for the government and other undesirables to ascertain where you are living.

In particular, if someone uses "Return Service Requested" on a piece of mail as a means to determine your address in order to serve you anything, it will not work if you have not provided the U.S. Postal Service with a forwarding address or its personnel do not otherwise know where you live.[7] If you pay bills completely electronically, there will be even fewer or maybe zero entities that need to know about a new residential address since you need not change a billing address in order to receive electronic statements. However, the preceding may only temporarily conceal where you are living until you register to vote, update a driver's license or vehicle registration, file your next income tax return, or file any form with the IRS that requires an address unless you can use a former address for all such events.

One rule follows on the heels of the "trust nobody" rule. When involved in any court proceeding, consider bringing an audio recording device. Absolutely nothing guarantees the record made by court officials will not get "accidentally" lost, edited, or destroyed. Ask the court ahead of time if making your own recording is allowed. Oftentimes you simply need advance approval of the court with the caveat that you use the recording strictly for personal notes of the proceedings, which, of course, is what you should say is the intended purpose.

If not allowed, it may take some creative thinking to get a recording device past TSA-style security screenings that are typical at most U.S. courthouses. Being able to turn it on and off discreetly when needed may also present a challenge, but the good news is that fairly inexpensive electronic recording devices disguised to look like pens or other everyday objects are now widely available. In the end, if your version of recorded events does not match the court's version—verbatim if theirs is also non-manually recorded—such discrepancy would be a good bomb to drop on governors outside that particular court. The attorney general or other oversight entity, such as the DOJ or FBI, and the media would make good candidates.

Very much in line with the preceding thinking is the possibility of court personnel modifying a case docket in an attempt to cover their tracks after they have broken the rules of procedure or committed any crimes. This happened starting in 2014 during a legal matter involving one author in the Taunton District Court in Massachusetts. Some states and the federal and Washington, D.C., courts maintain case dockets online.[8] If your case docket is available electronically, it might prove beneficial to download a copy to support a petition for a writ of *mandamus* or a complaint to the DOJ or FBI against court personnel acting under the "color of law" as explained in chapters three and six or for any other valid reason. Just understand that while the odds of the DOJ or FBI pursuing a complaint are higher than they are with the generally useless oversight boards discussed in the INEFFECTIVE CHECKS AND BALANCES section of chapter three, both are inefficient government agencies. As such, you cannot rely on either to take action even with mountains of evidence against the perpetrators.

Periodically downloading the docket in an ongoing case will provide you with an up-to-date copy and would be a wise thing to do in the event the online version ever gets "fixed." Not only would it be useful for catching the court manipulating a docket in order to further its own cause, but you may want physical proof that something has been filed by an opposing party without contacting the court or opposing party directly. This can be advantageous for various reasons, one of which is ascertaining information contained in the docket without alerting anyone that you are inquiring.

Another rule that can also be advantageous is to provide a paper versus an electronic copy of any particularly lengthy pleading to an adversary in a legal proceeding. Many courts now allow electronic filing, and it is usually expedient and economical to file electronically with the court. However, while it may be cheaper to do the same with your opposition, serving him with paper instead will make it much more burdensome for him to search, cross-reference, and check your document thoroughly. Therefore, he may be more inclined to make errors, including possibly even misplacing or losing a portion of your paperwork, especially if printed without page numbers and delivered unbound but, hopefully, properly ordered... Courts may eventually prevent paper filing altogether, but in the interim, the foregoing may be helpful to you.

The last remaining rule that comes to mind pertains to times when a judge says: "I will take it under advisement." In one coauthor's experience, this has always translated to: "I am going to ignore your input." Knowing this now may help with any snap decisions that need to be made later whenever you hear a judge make this statement.

Before concluding this part of the book, an important point needs to be made. Some readers may perceive the information here in part II as not being completely fair or honest. Indeed, it might not be, depending upon the situation and application, but if someone is going to try to play fair in a game that is widely corrupt, the overarching rule is that he will lose nearly every case nearly every time with few exceptions. When one is backed into a corner and is forced to go for the throat, then one should go for the throat regardless of how it is achieved, particularly when one's livelihood or life may be on the line!

Nonetheless, everything presented in this chapter needs to be evaluated on a case-by-case basis. The usage of any of the tenets proffered is neither correct nor incorrect. They are suggested to make people aware of considerations that might be important in a legal matter yet are not publicized or obtainable from standard legal channels. With this part of the book concluded, the remainder will focus on how to address various types of cases concerning the more common areas of law likely to impact the average American at some point. While reading part III, one should bear in mind the material that has been covered in parts I and II and approach it from that perspective.

PART III — PLAYING THE GAME

Chapter 8: Various Paths on Which to Proceed

Some may remember, if you have good memories, that there used to be a concept in Anglo-American law called a presumption of innocence, innocent until proven guilty in a court of law. Now that's so deep in history that there's no point even bringing it up, but it did once exist. — **Noam Chomsky**

Chapter Sections

- Background
- Alternative dispute resolution
- Arbitration
- Mediation
- Federal courts
- State courts
- Jurisdiction
- Venue
- Beginning the process

BACKGROUND

This part of the book begins with the very first question you may have when embarking upon a journey within the U.S. court system. Where do I begin? This chapter should help answer that question.

There are many types of courts in America. Their hierarchy can be confusing, and the reorganization of the court structure itself that takes place periodically compounds the confusion. We will not explain every detail about every single type of court or system of courts, but we will try to provide information that will orient readers and be most useful to those facing typical legal problems described in this book.

Nearly all Americans can travel on two possible litigation paths—the federal and state court systems. While those living in the nation's capital have the federal system available to them, they have a different path on which they can travel instead of the state court system—their own city courts. For each of these court systems, the two broad categories into which all litigation falls are civil and criminal causes of action. Before providing an overview of the two main systems, state and federal, you should know about an option that may be available to you and is discussed in various chapters throughout this text—alternative dispute resolution.

ALTERNATIVE DISPUTE RESOLUTION

In nearly all civil matters in America, arbitration and mediation, the predominant forms of alternative dispute resolution (ADR), are viable options instead of standard litigation. Unfortunately, no form of ADR is allowed in adult criminal matters, which must proceed within the court system. Additionally, collaborative law is one form predominantly used in family law, so it is mentioned in chapter eleven.

Since some arbitrators and mediators operate somewhat independently of the system, that is, their employ is in the private sector, there is market competition among them. Granted, those who reside in the courthouses might be considered parasitic feeder entities of the system as described in the REASONS FOR THE SYSTEM'S DECLINE section of chapter one if a symbiotic relationship exists between them and the courts. Their consistent presence thereat suggests it is likely, but others not normally found in that environment may lie outside this group of feeders and be relatively independent of the system.

Because of their relative independence from the system, some arbitrators and mediators—those employed in the private sector—are incentivized to do a better job than their competitors and therefore provide the best service at the best price. No such incentive exists for members of the system. ADR should be given serious consideration in a typical civil matter, but keep in mind all parties must agree to it.

Both arbitration and mediation are generally conducted in an informal setting, which means that individuals averse to fighting in court may find them more pleasant. For those concerned about possible corruption, which may abound at the particular court of jurisdiction, one of these two approaches may be a welcome alternative. If a party cannot be persuaded to try ADR, then standard litigation is the next step; however, the court may require that ADR be attempted as the first step towards resolving a civil matter. Short of any such requirement, it may be commenced at almost any time during a civil case.

When choosing ADR in a financially-based civil claim, it is wise from the creditor's viewpoint to get any settlement terms in writing and stipulate a reaffirmation agreement as part of those terms.

Doing so reaffirms the debt to the creditor and normally extends or resets the statute of limitations. To incentivize the debtor to fulfill her obligation, a clause should be written into the settlement. It should state that the debtor will be liable for the full amount of the debt along with court costs and attorney fees should she renege on the deal and the case need to be heard in court. If possible, as part of ADR, any settlement should be incorporated into a court judgment to make it presumably more enforceable than it would be as a standalone contract. Also, preparation prior to the ADR session should be just as thorough as if the case was being heard in court—which might be the next step anyway. Being successful in such a setting takes work and some strategy of its own. Entire books have been written on the subject.

ADR is a plausible option whenever the parties involved are close to reaching an agreement but need a neutral party in order to complete negotiations or whenever they must do business with each other in the future. The cost associated with ADR is almost always less than a traditional civil claim in court. One reason is that the officiator may freely offer some of her time. Her hourly rate may also be less than what attorneys normally charge.

Additionally, costs for attorneys in conventional legal proceedings are often duplicated for each party. Note also that filing fees frequently apply within the courts. Lastly, reaching an agreement outside the bloated court bureaucracy is usually more efficient. Because of this, the generally lower cost of ADR, and the less stressful environment overall, ADR might be a worthwhile consideration whenever trying to settle a civil dispute.

ARBITRATION

In arbitration the parties work with an arbitrator when trying to resolve their matter. Any party can have attorney representation if desired. An arbitrator's decision may be either binding or non-binding, depending upon circumstances. Decisions that are non-binding can legitimately be appealed in court, whereas those that are binding cannot, but for fraud, corruption, and other rare exceptions.

The typical arbitration hearing is much like a watered-down version of a court hearing, with evidence, testimony, affidavits, and everything else being presented or given in a less formal environment. An affidavit is a written statement normally made by someone under oath oftentimes for the purpose of substantiating a claim (see appendix). Similar to a mediator, an arbitrator crafts her decision based upon whatever she perceives as being fair to the parties and is not generally constrained by statutory or case law when settling disputes. But in today's courts here in America, judges and other presiding officials do not necessarily perceive themselves to be either. This means there may be no legal benefit to litigating from at least one of the parties' perspectives. Furthermore, because of this perception by many court officiators and the potential for corruption in general, there could definitely be drawbacks.

If unsatisfied with the outcome, any party can ordinarily request a trial *de novo*, a Latin expression meaning "anew," within a certain number of days after the arbitrator's decision in non-binding arbitration. The entire case is presented again but this time in court. In the event the matter has not yet been filed with the court clerk, any party can file it so that it can be placed on the docket and commence as though it had never been arbitrated. If the case has already been filed, it will continue on its course. A word of caution: if the court where the case would be reheard is corrupt, one or more of the parties may be jumping out of the frying pan and into the fire after arbitration or any form of ADR.

MEDIATION

Mediation is slightly more watered-down than arbitration. As opposed to arbitration, the mediation process has more input from the parties themselves. The mediator acts more like a facilitator than a referee, the arbitrator's role in arbitration. Decisions rendered in this fashion may have a more desired outcome for the parties rather than a decision made by an arbitrator or a judge. This is because the participants are negotiating on behalf of themselves as interested parties, whereas with an arbitrator or a judge, the decision is being made by parties who are not—and who may be biased or corrupt in the case of a judge. As in arbitration, lawyers can and sometimes do represent the parties during mediation.

Like arbitration mediation can be either binding or non-binding. Confidentiality is generally preserved in mediation such that nobody outside direct negotiations is privy to any elements of the process. In court, however, proceedings normally become public record. Mediation may incorporate issues that are indirectly related to the underlying dispute, whereas in a court of law, those same issues might be inadmissible. Another thing that distinguishes mediation from litigation is that the mediator may request confidential statements from one party and not share them with the others. This may be important in certain circumstances.

The process sometimes begins with the mediator asking the parties to sign a non-disclosure agreement to keep information exchanged during mediation private. Such information is normally restricted from release to the public by law. Some jurisdictions confer other evidentiary privileges during mediation. However, some information, particularly anything related to abuse or physical threats, is supposed to be disclosed wherever such reporting is mandated by law.

Families that want to shield private matters from public view or keep an elderly member's eccentric behavior from being in the spotlight may benefit from the privacy afforded by mediation. Parties who have agreed not to discuss the content of their mediation outside of it may speak more freely about problems that involve unpleasant relationship issues, all while developing solutions to their problems. Because of this openness, all sides may be more inclined to work through tough issues and benefit from a clearer overall understanding of each other.

Mediation gives each participant a voice and can be emotionally rewarding. Regarding disagreements among family members, money is not always the primary cause. Receiving an apology, an explanation, or a promise or being allowed to blow off steam may be more valuable to someone than a traditional settlement. Improved psychological well-being may flow from the outcome since participants have more control over it.

Because it pits parties against each other, litigation may cause more stress and trauma than mediation, and it has the propensity to escalate conflict, which is, of course, by design. The court usually fans the flames of antagonism. Furthermore, if someone suspects he will not likely prevail in a lawsuit, he may not pursue it as a possible remedy. In such an instance, the conflict precipitating the situation may persist, absent mediation or another form of ADR.

Mediation can repair, maintain, or improve familial, business, or other relationships. Since parties need to cooperate during mediation and resolve conflict, they might develop better problem-solving skills and improve communication that will help them later. Remember that litigation is more likely to drive a wedge between the parties than mediation.

Lastly, mediation lets participants formulate their own unique solution to a dispute. The process also takes into consideration interests outside law as well as legal issues. Parties to a probate matter, for example, may address the division of sentimental property better because of this benefit. Judges frequently have no idea what may or may not be most precious to people and might thus divide property based strictly on monetary value in a best-case scenario with no corruption. In familial matters involving siblings, this approach is not likely to achieve the same result that they could negotiate on their own behalf, which might be better from their perspective.

FEDERAL COURTS

The vast majority of lower federal courts are U.S. district courts, which are where many federal cases are heard. At least one district court is in every state, the District of Columbia, Puerto Rico, the U.S. Virgin Islands, Guam, and the Northern Mariana Islands.[1] There are a total of ninety-four of these courts.[2]

One of the special attributes of the federal judicial system is that it has original and exclusive jurisdiction over all U.S. bankruptcy proceedings under Title 11. Courts with original jurisdiction have the power to adjudicate a case before any appellate review. Courts with exclusive jurisdiction have the power to adjudicate a case to the exclusion of all other lower courts. Each district court maintains a bankruptcy court as an arm of itself. When looking to file a personal, a business, or any other bankruptcy petition, bankruptcy court is where to begin the process.

District courts also have original jurisdiction to hear all civil claims concerning federal eminent domain, postal matters, patents and copyrights, admiralty or maritime issues, and Native American or general matters related to the Constitution, laws, or treaties of the United States.[3] [4] [5] Certain other matters can be heard in district courts. These include some criminal cases, such as those resulting from crimes occurring across state lines, and additional civil claims.

Cases wherein a district court does not have exclusive jurisdiction can sometimes be filed in either state or federal court. As plaintiff, picking one over the other could be based on such factors as the level of corruption in a given court, its proximity to a residence, filing fees, and more. However, any claim in which a plaintiff is alleging violation of some federal law or the U.S. Constitution should be filed in the federal court system.

One special lower court, the United States Court of Federal Claims, has as one of its many functions the power to hear complaints against our government, such as those from persons injured under the mandatory administration of vaccines.[6] Another special lower federal court is the United States Court of International Trade, but this court is limited to hearing cases regarding customs and international trade law, which probably does not affect many readers, if any at all.[7]

Also within the federal system is the United States Tax Court. This lower court has jurisdiction to hear all disputes arising from issues with respect to federal income taxes assessed by the Internal Revenue Service. The court is physically located in Washington, D.C., but it is rather unusual because its judges travel to almost all states to hear tax cases.[8] Such cases are normally heard in federal courthouses or buildings.

U.S. courts of appeals, or circuit courts, are the next higher courts from the district courts and all other federal courts, including the U.S. Tax Court, the U.S. Court of International Trade, and the U.S. Court of Federal Claims but excluding the U.S. Supreme Court, the highest federal court. There are thirteen courts of appeals spread across America and its territories. Whenever appeal is sought from any lower federal court, the U.S. court of appeals for the circuit containing the lower court is typically the one in which to proceed. Note that a three-judge panel generally presides at this level instead of a jury. On rare occasion, the *en banc* court, or all judges in the court, will preside.

At the highest level of the federal judicial system is the U.S. Supreme Court, located in Washington, D.C. This is also known as the "court of last resort." There are a maximum of nine judges who decide cases at this level. Majority decision dictates the outcome for all matters heard by this court. In the case of a tie due to abstentions or absences, a lower court's opinion is affirmed without creating any supreme court precedent. Judges in the federal or a state supreme court are often called "justices." These are the only courts at either the federal or state level where this term is duly recognized.

When appeal in the federal system is sought after a decision in a U.S. court of appeals, the next and final step is the U.S. Supreme Court, which may or may not decide to hear the case. As stated in chapter two's WHEN THINGS GO WRONG section, it is rather rare that the highest court will choose to hear any cases already decided by a lower court. If you have the wherewithal and endurance as an individual to make it this far in the court system, we salute you—not just for raw fortitude but for withstanding the expenses and holding firm in your driving principles.

STATE COURTS

The state court system encompasses all courts in America outside the federal, military, District of Columbia, and Native American court systems. It includes municipal, town and city, state circuit, state district, probate, family, juvenile, land, superior, small claims, traffic, and all associated state appellate and state supreme courts and various other courts. Because there are fifty states in America that contain in excess of 35,000 municipalities and townships, there are far more courts in this category, both in type and number, than in the other court systems.[9] Chances are good that the overwhelming majority of legal matters in which you will participate will be litigated in state courts. But for bankruptcy, being involved in the federal court system as an individual is relatively rare.

Since the federal government governs the whole country, there is more uniformity within its court structure than at the state level, as confusing as it still may be. Note that the terminology used for the same type of state court varies nationwide. District court, trial court, superior court, and possibly other names can designate the same court type in different states as can other court names. Additionally, some states have more levels of judicial authority than others.

Certain states have special courts for handling specific issues. For example, Rhode Island has a special court strictly for hearing traffic cases, the Rhode Island Traffic Tribunal.[10] Other states, Florida for instance, have a special limited civil court that exists between the small claims court and full-fledged civil court. This court in Florida hears cases worth a maximum of $15,000, which is above the small claims maximum there but below the unlimited amount of a traditional civil court.[11] Our point is that many variations regarding court names and levels of court structure exist throughout the country in the state court system.

Once a case reaches its state's highest court, the decision cannot normally be appealed to the U.S. Supreme Court. Some people may be under the impression that any case can be appealed to the U.S. Supreme Court because it is the highest court in the land. While certainly true for federal cases, the only instance when a case at the state or District of Columbia level has a chance to make it into the country's highest court would be if the issue of law in the case involves interpretation of federal law or the U.S. Constitution. When this happens, the matter may then be appealed to the U.S. Supreme Court—with only a slim chance it will be heard.

JURISDICTION

Jurisdiction is the power of a court to hear a case. In order for a court to have jurisdiction, it must have authority over both the subject matter of the case and the parties involved in it. A case cannot legally proceed in a court that does not have jurisdiction to hear it. For example, a supreme court in

New York should not entertain the filing of a divorce from a couple who has never lived in that state. A county court in Florida should not accept a bankruptcy filing. A family court in Delaware should deny any small claims submitted to it.

Jurisdiction is somewhat analogous to bringing your car into an automobile dealership for service. If you own a Lexus, you cannot generally take it to the Buick dealership to have it fixed because the mechanics at each respective dealership are certified for the particular brand of cars that it sells. Where you take your car depends on its type, just like where you take your case depends on its type.

Jurisdiction is contestable if a court does not have authority to rule over a case. If, as defendant, you discover that the court where a case was filed against you does not have jurisdiction, you should petition the court to have the case dismissed. Normally, research performed at the law library or court or online should yield the name of the court that has proper jurisdiction for whatever legal problem you are facing.

Sometimes picking the right state court is simple. States that have established probate courts adjudicate all cases related to decedents' wills, estates, and the like; therefore, all such cases will initially proceed in those courts. Some states have instituted family courts that process all cases involving child support, custody, and visitation issues. Similarly, other state courts exist for the purpose of dealing with certain legal issues. If your case involves one of these areas of law, the existence of such courts in the pertinent locale could facilitate selecting the correct one in which to proceed—just as the existence of specialized courts that settle other specific legal matters could simplify selection.

Not all legal issues concern parties living in the same state. Although some state courts have the power to hear civil matters involving residents of different states, namely, some class actions, diversity jurisdiction gives U.S. district courts power to hear civil cases when the parties reside in different states, provided the amount in controversy exceeds $75,000.[12] Taking advantage of the relevant federal statute can be quite beneficial for a plaintiff who wants to file a civil lawsuit but no longer lives in the state where the cause of action occurred. If the plaintiff files the matter in her new home state, it may yield the fortuitous by-product of making it more difficult for the defendant to fight the case from a greater distance while correspondingly giving a slight tactical edge to the plaintiff. Lastly, having the option to file a matter in either state or federal court cannot hurt—for example, being able to choose the court that is more convenient or less corrupt.

VENUE

The next step that must be taken in order to begin litigation is determining the correct venue. Venue is the county or district where a case can proceed. Sometimes the same types of state cases can proceed in more than one courthouse in a given county. That is to say, multiple similar state courthouses are relatively close to each other within a geographic area. They are identical in terms of matters they adjudicate except that they are in different locations. The one selected is irrelevant except for convenience of the parties, lawyers, or witnesses or for other reasons. Initiating a case clear across the state in a county unrelated to any facts or persons in the matter, however, would be the wrong venue for it. Despite a potentially legitimate reason of trying to inconvenience the opposing party or for any other reason, filing the matter in such a court will not likely be allowed.

For criminal cases, the venue is usually the county or district where the crime was allegedly committed. With many state civil cases, it is usually the county where the defendant resides or works, where she allegedly injured the plaintiff, where she supposedly signed the contract in question, or where certain events related to the claim took place. Venue for federal civil cases can be the district where any defendant lives, where an appreciable portion of the events giving rise to the claim occurred, or where a considerable part of the property that is the subject of the action is located. It can sometimes be any district where a defendant is subject to the court's personal jurisdiction with respect to the matter. Occasionally the court will select a venue outside the geographic area where an alleged crime took place in order to try the defendant in what it views as a more neutral setting where potential jurors might not be influenced by media coverage, for example. Changing venue is possible if a party in either a civil or criminal case petitions the court.

An analogy to jurisdiction and venue combined, much in line with the underlying theme of this book, could be made by comparing them with games, specifically those played by professional baseball and football teams. A baseball team can only play on a baseball field. Likewise, a football team can only play on a football field. The officials at each respective "venue" have "jurisdiction" and can only rule over the players and plays made at the field where they are officiating. The football officiators have no power to rule over a baseball player who happens to be a spectator at the Super Bowl, nor do the baseball officiators have ruling power over a football player who happens to be a spectator at the World Series.

In fact, we can take this analogy a little further and say that either game can be played in different states, so long as the baseball game gets played on a baseball field and the football game gets played on a football field. There are minor and major leagues just like there are state and federal courts. The instant replay can loosely be likened to an appeal, with two major differences. One is that the replay, or the "appeal," in the real game is always at the same location, whereas the appeal in the fake game, the court system, is sometimes at a different location. The other difference is that the officials who review the instant replay nearly always make the correct decision in the end.

BEGINNING THE PROCESS

Finding the correct court where to proceed with your case is usually not too difficult despite the possibilities seeming nearly endless. Since legal matters are so prolific in the country, there is a good chance someone you know was involved in a lawsuit with a jurisdiction and venue that is applicable to your suit. She could tell you the name and location of the court where her case was heard, which should at least steer you in the right direction. A state statute may also direct you to the court where you need to proceed. Consider, for instance, Massachusetts general law chapter 249, section 4, which states that land court hears cases relevant to certain land issues.[13]

On occasion, rules of court provide similar indications of the proper court where you need to proceed, as in the Hawaii Family Court Rules.[14] The mere existence of rules governing family court means family matters must proceed in such a court. As explained earlier in this chapter's STATE COURTS section, the existence of specialized courts means a case regarding subject matter relevant to one of those courts should generally be heard in that respective type of court.

Know that whenever beginning almost all cases, one cannot start at the highest court. One starts at the lowest rung on the ladder, the district, probate, juvenile, or other lowest-level court that has jurisdiction over the specific claim. Once a case has commenced, however, it is possible to make a temporary jump from a lower court over the intermediate courts and into the higher courts via *mandamus* or similar such mechanisms. This was explained in the *MANDAMUS* AND OTHER COMPLAINT ALTERNATIVES section of chapter three.

Bankruptcy might be the easiest matter in which to determine jurisdiction, that being U.S. Bankruptcy Court, and venue based upon data supplied by the federal government, whereas other cases might be a little more challenging to discover jurisdiction and venue. But sometimes the discovering is done for you if you are the defendant in a legal matter. When you are the plaintiff, you or your lawyer will need to determine jurisdiction and venue. With lawyers this might be the easiest thing they do on a case. However, it is not impossible for them to select the wrong court in which to initiate a proceeding.

We are trying to impart the importance of checking that jurisdiction and venue are proper. If you need to start a legal action against a party, determine the lowest-level court that can hear your claim. In addition to being able to file some cases in either state or federal court as explained earlier in the FEDERAL COURTS section, bear in mind that overlap, also known as concurrent jurisdiction, can likewise exist within the lower state courts regarding the one in which to commence a case. See the BACKGROUND section of chapter nine for an example. Before filing, the clerk of the court may or may not accommodate you as to whether the court in question is proper for your claim. Some clerks are helpful; others are worse than Genghis Khan was on a bad day.

If you file your case in a court without the jurisdiction to hear it, it may be removed, the legal term for "transferred," to the correct one or dismissed altogether if the defendant notices your mistake and petitions the court or the court does either on its own initiative. In some matters, the statute of limitations can be quite short, and you may not have time to refile a dismissed case in the proper court. Picking the wrong court under these circumstances could result in dismissal with prejudice, meaning your case cannot normally be refiled. On the other hand, a case dismissed without prejudice can usually be refiled at any time prior to the expiration of the statute of limitations.

For most of the remaining material in this part of the book, jurisdiction for legal matters that involve you will likely fall within a state court in the state where you live, with the predominant exceptions being bankruptcy, some criminal cases, and some actions described in chapter sixteen. The court with jurisdiction in which your matter should proceed and venue can most likely be found by applying the information in this chapter. The remainder of this book will assume jurisdiction and venue have already been correctly determined and will address the most common legal problems that are likely to befall you.

Chapter 9: Small Claims

There is a higher court than courts of justice, and that is the court of conscience. It supersedes all other courts. — **Mahatma Gandhi**

Chapter Sections

- Background
- The process
- The complaint
- Serving the complaint
- Answering the complaint and filing a counterclaim
- Building the case
- The trial
- Appeals
- Enforcing a judgment

BACKGROUND

A small claim is to the judicial system what federal tax form 1040EZ is to the IRS. It is much more streamlined than a run-of-the-mill civil case in terms of filing procedures, rules, and process. Just like certain requirements must be met in order to file the 1040EZ with the IRS, certain requirements must be met in order to file a case in small claims court. Note that physical small claims courts do not exist *per se* but, rather, are part of various state courts across America and the Superior Court in Washington, D.C.

A small claim needs to be filed within a certain amount of time after an injury occurs, a loss is incurred, or a contract is broken, which varies nationwide and can be as short as six months or as long as ten years but can possibly be shorter or longer.[1] [2] This window of time is known as the statute of limitations. For some matters regarding a non-federal government agency, a claim must first be filed with the agency within a short time after the cause of the claim and then be denied by the agency. After denial it can be pursued in small claims court by filing a separate claim with the court within another short time that could be as brief as a few months or less.

Certain events will temporarily suspend the expiration of the statute of limitations. If a party, despite due diligence and after the projected expiration date dictated by the statute, discovers an injury or a loss or finds that a contract has been broken, the legal principle that generally allows filing a claim beyond the time limit set by the statute is called "equitable tolling." If any such event is known but a claim cannot be filed until after the statute's projected expiration due to circumstances beyond the affected party's control, equitable tolling can also apply. Regardless of when the tolling event happened, the tolled interval is added to the end of the statutory limitations period. Equitable tolling effectively extends the time limit by the length of time of the tolling event, however long that may be.

Some events that temporarily suspend the clock include a would-be defendant being incarcerated, living out of state, and being under legal age and a plethora of others that vary across the country. There are some exceptions to equitable tolling that apply when the adversary is a governmental entity and at certain other times. It can get quite complex; therefore, without any valid reason for delay, small claims cases should be commenced as soon as possible to preclude the dreaded expiration of the statute of limitations from ruining your day.

Sometimes a prejudgment attachment is warranted, discovery may be necessary, or something else excluded by the rules of a particular small claims court may be required in order for the plaintiff to have a reasonable chance of success. In such instances, pursuing the case in a traditional civil court might be preferable over small claims if allowed by rules of court. Just because a case *can* proceed in small claims court because it falls under the applicable maximum dollar threshold does not necessarily mean it *must* proceed there.

Conversely, a case that exceeds the monetary limit of small claims does not automatically exclude it from proceeding there either. A plaintiff may choose to pursue a case worth $5,600 in a small claims court that limits awards to $5,000 and waive, or forgo the right to collect, the $600 excess due him. This could be done for a variety of reasons. One may be for the strategic purpose of avoiding corruption in the regular civil court. Another may be as a blocking maneuver to prevent the other party from bringing a lawyer into the mix in a jurisdiction where counsel is not allowed in small claims. Yet another may be because of travel considerations to the court where the case could otherwise proceed or possibly for some other logical reason. Information in this chapter is relevant for undertaking a case in small claims court—whatever the reason may be.

One might astutely think of breaking a lawsuit that exceeds the dollar limit set by the court into pieces and pursuing them independently, perhaps in different jurisdictions, as a way to squeeze such a suit into small claims anyway, otherwise known as claim splitting. Although not legal, there are indirect lawful routes over this hurdle. An approach for events that involved only one defendant is to consider bringing multiple distinct claims against the person or business. For example, a flooring installer who replaced your carpet and linoleum in two different rooms of your home, but did it all in one continuous job over two days, might be liable for faulty installation of both floors under two separate small claims. The chances of getting this ruse to fly would be greater if you had convinced the flooring company to provide you with a separate contract and invoice for each portion of the work.

When there are multiple responsible people, the odds of successfully suing them independently are greater if the causes of action with which each person is associated are different, meaning their activities related to the underlying matter varied at least slightly. For example, suppose one person is a general contractor and another is a real estate broker. If a deposit was placed with the broker to purchase a piece of land for the purpose of building a private residence on it but the contractor committed fraud and the broker violated the contract, two small claims or a small claims/traditional civil court hybrid might offer a solution. One of the authors has had success with this approach.

Using a Credit or Debit Card Issuer to Resolve a Dispute

Before blindly marching down the small claims road, one step that can oftentimes be taken for the purpose of recovering a disputed amount of money and that can negate the legal process entirely is to exploit technology that was introduced in the mid 1900s—the credit card. Making purchases with credit cards can be particularly beneficial in today's day and age because many are completed online with companies located all across the globe and any shysters operating them are able to escape the reach of the court. Although the U.S. judicial system frequently thinks it has jurisdiction over foreign businesses or entities outside U.S. borders, it does not. With every known major credit card and more recently with debit cards, if a dispute with a domestic or an international merchant occurs, filing a complaint with the card issuer to contest the charge can yield the same result as a small claims case...or sometimes even a better result. The major difference between the two options is that the complaint process through a card issuer is much quicker, more efficient, free, and without hassle—a typical distinction between the private sector and government.[3]

A simple phone call to the card issuer or filing an online dispute form is all it takes to get the ball rolling. If you have facts on your side, the issuer basically reaches into the merchant's bank account, takes whatever is owed to you, and deposits the money back into your account. One author has prevailed in all seven complaints against merchants using this tactic. Although some national internet businesses can be sued in your local small claims court if they are headquartered out of state but do business in your state on a regular basis, case law about this is relatively new and needs to be researched in each instance. A small claim is probably best as a last resort to pursue such a business.

Suing an operating business or individual with a current income stream has a better chance of expeditious collection on a judgment, should the plaintiff prevail, than suing a destitute person, student with no income, or bankrupt company. The current financial status of such entities may be a factor when considering whether to bring a claim against them in small claims or *any* court. The many exemptions to collection specified by the system make collecting a judgment from insolvent parties much more difficult. These deadbeat weasels know this too. If, however, there is a good chance future income or assets can legally be seized to pay the debt, then a small claims case might not be futile since judgments are normally good for years or decades and can sometimes be extended—more later in this chapter's ENFORCING A JUDGMENT section.

Using a Demand Letter to Resolve a Dispute

Lastly, before filing a small claims complaint, which can also be called a "small claims petition," a "small claims affidavit," and various other things nationwide, understand that some jurisdictions require that an oral or a written demand be made prior to proceeding in any civil court. This includes small claims. Composing a demand letter is not difficult (see appendix). Once written, it can be given to the offending party electronically, in person, or by U.S. mail, but in any event, it should be delivered by some traceable means to prove that it was received. If the letter is crafted carefully enough, it may preclude any necessity for taking the plunge into small claims or the general civil court, as the case may be, and defuse any legal action before it begins. Even if not required, it is usually an excellent idea to send one to the offending party for this very reason. Avoiding the judicial system at all costs, if possible, should be your primary goal. A strong demand letter may help achieve that end.

Well before ever writing the demand letter, consider restricting all your correspondence with the noncompliant party to email or some other written form of communication. Not only will doing this provide you with physical evidence that will generally strengthen your case in court more than your testimony about any conversation, it will allow you to compose your thoughts better. It will also give your opponent a better opportunity to write something that could negatively impact him and thus solidify your position later in a demand letter. A person will sometimes make a written statement in an attempt to defend his position, but such action often backfires and strengthens his adversary's position instead. Just ask the many innocent people who are unjustly imprisoned because of the written statements they made to police in an attempt to defend their positions and prove their innocence. Other times, you have no idea what people are thinking until they inform you of it in writing.

When it comes time to create the demand letter, referring to any of a party's previously written incriminating information and quoting their words, if possible, in the body of the letter may encourage them to acquiesce. Referencing relevant statute is also a good intimidation technique as is stating that you will reveal their bad business practices or other dubious behaviors on various review or rating websites as applicable—none of which would be good if your adversary happens to be a business. Threatening to report a business to the Better Business Bureau, Federal Trade Commission, attorney general's office, pertinent consumer protection agency, and various media outlets could encourage settlement sooner rather than later (see end of appendix). A coauthor did exactly this and used the lawyer-adversary's incriminating statements he foolishly made in multiple letters, which resulted in one in the win column for the coauthor.

For foes who are individuals instead of businesses, being concise, direct, and calm but still threatening with respect to steps you will take if not made whole regarding your claim could very well get the mission accomplished. If you are firmly prepared to take them to court, people know they will have to take time out of their day to fight you. Chances are good that they might think twice before wasting time and effort in battle if you include enough damning information in the letter.

It may be beneficial to have a friend or family member who is a lawyer transfer the letter you drafted onto his law firm's letterhead before sending it. Other lawyers may also perform the same service for free or charge a minimal fee. It may be worth a few phone calls to lawyers who have been newly admitted to the bar and are seeking exposure or recognition. They may oblige you. Making such a letter look more official may have a greater intimidating effect than if merely written on ordinary paper. Some people actually fear lawyers; others eat them for breakfast.

Other Considerations

Other options to consider before firing with both barrels in small claims court are arbitration and mediation. Although similar, they differ slightly. See chapter eight for a full discussion of both. Either can be used as an alternative to small claims.

One of the niceties about small claims court is that the judicial system can sometimes be fooled into forgiving mistakes made by what it perceives as a green litigant. Even though you are reading this book, it might be best to give the impression that you are inexperienced while still being thorough in your preparation and presentation. Generally in life, it is advantageous to fly under the radar, perhaps more so in small claims cases or any legal proceeding for that matter.

The *only* reason imaginable that anyone would want to skip the options discussed in the previous subsections and in the first paragraph of this one and jump right into standard litigation is when he, for reasons unbeknownst to anyone but himself, is 100 percent certain of victory in court. Such a person may have the ulterior motive of wanting to drag an adversary through the legal mud—and enjoy every minute of it. But if that is the case, he can probably skip the rest of this chapter too. No doubt such individuals have strong political connections and corruption most likely working in their favor and almost surely would not be reading this book in the first place.

The road to small claims is fairly well-lit. Some person or entity owes you money, damaged your property, violated a contract, or did practically anything else that would warrant a civil action. If the total damage or losses fall under a certain threshold and no "fancy stuff" is needed, such as discovery or prejudgment attachments, both of which are not allowed or sometimes have limited viability, then small claims court is your oyster.

Mostly because of inflation, which causes the dollar value of all civil causes of action to rise over time, the maximum dollar threshold set by small claims courts correspondingly increases over time. The courts do not want to waste their precious resources addressing menial cases when they have bigger fish to fry in larger traditional civil cases. Big cases involving big dollars are more financially beneficial to the system but are typically more time-consuming. Such matters are sometimes adjudicated in the same courts where small claims are heard.

By increasing the dollar limits of small claims over time, the court effectively reallocates more of its caseload towards cases that are processed more quickly—an important factor to courts that handle a blend of case types including small claims. Without periodically making those adjustments, their total case throughput would fall. Serendipitously, limit increases happen to be more advantageous to an average litigant with a relatively small straightforward case since the possibility of pursuing it in small claims court keeps up with inflation, more or less.

Know that litigants in small claims cases, just as in other civil matters, can be almost any American citizen, at least in theory anyway. Lawyers, police, judges, and other officials within the legal industry can be parties to small claims. Bear in mind that in order for a case against any of them to have a reasonable chance of success, it must be brought for an act outside their official duties.

A police officer who borrows $500 to pay rent and does not pay it back after repeated attempts to collect and a lawyer who performs no work on a case for a client and then refuses to return an initial $1,000 retainer are both susceptible to suit in small claims court. If their friends work in the courthouse where your case will be heard, your chance of winning might be slim despite having rock-solid evidence against them. This aside, it is quite possible to defeat them. Suing members of the system for breaking every rule in the book while they are in uniform and on the clock is a different story and may present a far greater challenge.

One misconception some people have is that small claims cases exclusively involve damages for broken contracts, faulty repairs, and landlord-tenant issues. While these may comprise the vast majority of cases, some jurisdictions allow causes of action related to personal injury, slander, breach of warranty, health or safety hazards, malpractice, and more to proceed in small claims court. Each is handled slightly differently, but all should establish that the plaintiff has suffered an injury or a loss and that the defendant is legally responsible in order for the plaintiff to have a viable chance of success. Conversely, for the defendant to have the best chance to prevail, he should disestablish either point.

Another misconception newcomers hold is that small claims court is like *The People's Court* or *Judge Judy* TV shows. If you want to lose your case, one of the best ways to do it is to imitate some "litigants" on those shows. Judges in real life act nothing like these made-for-TV personalities. In fact, sitting in a local small claims courtroom for a day or two and observing the proceedings is perhaps the best way to get some exposure to the system's operation in preparation for your own case. These are public places, mind you, so any U.S. citizen is almost always allowed to observe. Observing is still not the same as being involved in a case of your own, but it is a way to view actual court proceedings, not televised ones that are made to increase ratings.

THE PROCESS

There are many possible combinations of plaintiffs and defendants in small claims cases. Businesses, governmental entities, people under age eighteen, class-action-like groups, dead people (their estates), and others can be litigants in certain jurisdictions and under the right conditions even if located in another part of the country in some peculiar situations. As an example of a class-action-like group, a neighborhood of people sued an entire county in small claims court because of nuisance airport noise.[4] As stated earlier, there is strength in numbers, and with the relative "speed" of a small claims proceeding versus a traditional civil proceeding, things can be accomplished in a fraction of the time and with less anguish, at least in principle anyway.

It is commonplace for just one of several members of a party to a small claim to represent the remaining members, such as just the husband of a husband and wife pair of defendants. A designee who is legally appointed to represent a business is typically the formal litigant named on the complaint and who appears in court on behalf of the business. Governmental entities also follow suit by designating their legal representatives. Note a subtle difference between small claims and class actions discussed in chapter sixteen. In small claims cases, a non-lawyer can represent other members of his party, whereas in class actions, he cannot, probably due to the closer legal relationship of a party's members in small claims and the exclusion of attorney representation in some instances.

Although lawyers might not be allowed in the applicable small claims court to represent parties, it does not mean you cannot consult with one before trial nor afterward should you decide to appeal. And they are certainly allowed in any of these courts if they happen to be witnesses or litigants—if you are suing them or if they are suing you, the latter of which we have never heard nor seen. The author who is an attorney has been called as a witness in small claims court. Her testimony added tremendous credibility that resulted in her former client's win against a party with a bogus claim. Additionally, in some small claims courts that do not allow attorney representation initially, once the case reaches the appeal stage, counsel is allowed.

For claims regarding motor vehicle accidents, sometimes the driver is liable. But sometimes the vehicle owner is liable, or both are liable, depending upon state. There could be multiple defendants in such a scenario. Applicable court rules or law would need to be consulted in order to determine the person to name on the complaint in a vehicular suit.

Suing a business has defendant-naming nuances as well. Its legal name is generally written on the complaint and may be obtained from the clerk or other court, city, or state resources, such as licensing boards and commissions. When a business is a corporation or limited liability company (LLC), it should be named the defending party. If a business is a partnership or limited partnership, the business and all partners except limited partners should be identified as defendants in the suit. For a sole proprietorship, the legal name of the owner, "DBA," which means "doing business as," and the legal name of the business should be the defendant on the complaint. Note that the legal name of the owner may not be the one by which he is widely known, nor may the legal name of the business be the one by which it is widely known. For example, Lefty's Gym might have a legal business name of Deluxe Gym and Fitness and be owned by Don Jones, not Lefty. Rules governing the naming of specific businesses and governmental entities on the complaint and the protocol for naming multiple plaintiffs and defendants can also be verified with court personnel.

Suing a minor who is not emancipated is not always worthwhile because of limited liability applicable to such minors. If a suit against an unemancipated minor is justified, at least one of the parents or legal guardians should be named in the case as in "John Smith, a minor, and William Smith, father" because there are some instances when the parents or legal guardians would be liable for their minor children's actions. Just like overestimating rather than underestimating the dollar amount of a claim, it is typically better to sue too many than too few. Defendants can be released as non-liable by the court, but adding them later might not be so easy.

One of the few entities, if not the only one, that cannot be sued in small claims court is any part of the federal government. This includes any individual performing his duties while on the job as a federal employee. Claims against the federal government are normally litigated in federal courts. Another known semi-exclusionary party to a small claim is an assignee, a person or business that acts on behalf of another, such as a collection agency. These individuals or businesses cannot bring suit in small claims court in some jurisdictions unless, for instance, an individual is acting on behalf of a minor child or some other exception applies.[5] [6] They can, however, typically be successfully sued, as opposed to the federal government.

THE COMPLAINT

The complaint, or legal form to get the process started, can usually be downloaded from the appropriate website or is available from the court of jurisdiction itself. Remember that the complaint can also be called a "petition," an "affidavit," and various other things in different parts of the country. Like the 1040EZ form, a small claims complaint is generally just one or two pages long (see appendix). It is completed by the plaintiff, or his representative in some instances, and delivered to the court. A representative is sometimes allowed when a person is homebound, serving abroad in the military, or unable to be present himself during the ensuing proceedings, or the representative is an attorney as allowed in some instances or a designee as stated earlier in THE PROCESS section. Once the court receives the completed complaint, it generates a case number, stamps or writes that number on the complaint, and sends it back to the plaintiff along with a trial date.

When completing the complaint, be sure to check relevant statutory law first. Oftentimes double or treble damages or a punitive fee is permitted, possibly limited to some maximum, which can be added to the original amount of the claim. When a bad check is intentionally passed in California, not only is the offending party liable for the amount of the check itself but, additionally, triple its value capped at $1,500.[7] For example, an issuer of a bad check for $2,000 can potentially be responsible for a $3,500 small claim. The small claims complaint will have a place on it for you to enter the total dollar amount due you. If possible, use wording that references any applicable civil rule or statute, such as "$2,000 from original check plus $1,500 damages as allowed by CAL. CIV. CODE section 1719 for a total of $3,500" for the bad check just described. Also, in some states including California, the issuer could be subject to criminal penalties irrespective of civil liabilities, and the mere threat of filing criminal charges could provide you sufficient leverage to get paid.

One consideration when completing the complaint is to estimate on the high side the amount due or cost of damage done. Understand that the legal system, taken as a whole, is quite often one big compromise, and decisions rendered by judges and juries are not always in favor of either the plaintiff or defendant but are sometimes split somewhere in between. If you ask for $1,000 in your complaint and the defendant countersues for $2,000, whether legitimate or not, the judgment might be somewhere around zero or, worse yet, state that you owe the defendant money. If you had claimed $3,000 and the case was "averaged" as many are these days, then the judgment might be in your favor and closer to the $1,000 you were actually due. Once you enter the $1,000 amount on the complaint and file it with the court, you cannot realistically just erase the figure later and replace it with $3,000 unless additional injuries are discovered during the case.

Estimating the amount sought can be difficult. If you are fairly certain there will be no counterclaim, then only a slightly high estimate might be justified. An unreasonably high figure may have a similar effect on your adversary as throwing a rock into a hornets' nest would have on the hornets. If there is absolutely nothing to lose—the judge, court personnel, and your adversary are corrupt or malevolent—then the sky is the limit. Short of corruption or malevolence, some thinking should be done so that the right balance is achieved. You do not want to be shortchanged in the event of a compromise nor appear overly greedy in the eyes of a judge, a jury, or your opponent. Remember that the judiciary has the power to reduce the amount of a claim but cannot legally inflate it by its own choosing.

Before filing the complaint, it might be worth "judge shopping" as described in chapter two in the "JUDGE SHOPPING" TO AVOID BAD JUDGES section. If you know a judge will be hearing your case, you might be able to time your complaint's submission in such a way that your case will be scheduled for trial on a day when bad judges are absent. Asking the court clerk when a matter filed today might be set for hearing may help with timing. Magistrates also hear small claims cases in various instances. They generally have less power and tend to be less corrupt than judges, based upon experience, but there is no known way to "magistrate shop." These individuals sometimes appear to be on a floating or part-time basis. Some lower court judges also float from court to court, but their schedule is publicized, whereas magistrate schedules do not seem to be readily available in the public domain.

SERVING THE COMPLAINT

The presumption for this section is that you will need to have the complaint served to the opposing party. Some states, Texas being one, have a slightly different process that begins with the issuance of a "citation," which gets served by an officer of the state or by other specified means. In most parts of the country, however, the next step should be to serve the complaint to the defendant once you have received a docketed version of it with the trial date assigned by the court. The plaintiff is not normally permitted to serve it. A friend, sheriff, constable, member of the court, or professional serving company is typically supposed to do this, the last of which is not generally recommended—be careful of the many overpriced shams out there.

Sometimes the complaint needs to be personally handed to the defendant. Other times certified or registered mail will suffice. On occasion, ordinary U.S. mail is acceptable. Still other times it can be left at a place of work or residence with someone of a specified age who is instructed to give it to the defendant. Finally, posting in a newspaper local to the courthouse or at the courthouse itself is sometimes allowed as a last-ditch means of service. This is not an exhaustive list of valid service options. Statutory laws or rules of procedure determine the allowable methods of service and the deadline by which it must be made. They vary greatly and will have to be checked for the particular court.

When required to serve the defendant in person, it may take some trickery if he senses the case coming and is elusive. If service is attempted by a court official, he may fabricate its completion if he finds it too difficult to serve the defendant. He could go so far as to state officially on the record that service was made in person even though it was not. This might be something to consider and could work in your favor if you think serving the opposing party might be difficult.

Furthermore, if the defendant claims that service never happened in order to delay the case or get it dismissed, being served by a court official would be a good blocking maneuver against that strategy. The court is equally likely to accept the presumption that proper service by a court official was made when it actually was not, as much as it would accept the presumption that valid service by an average citizen was not made when it actually was. Credibility here can be likened to that of an ordinary litigant's word against a law enforcement officer's in a legal matter. A badge somehow magically adds credibility to testimony.

Typically, a fee is required for a court officer's service of process, but if it pales in comparison to the damages sought in the suit, it may be worth the added expense. Also, most courts allow service and other fees to be added to the original dollar amount of the claim or counterclaim. These fees would then be recoverable in the event of a judgment in the claimant's favor. Just like estimating the amount of the (counter)claim, it is better to list too many than too few fees and expenses. One normally will not be able to recover babysitting, fuel, and toll costs but usually can be reimbursed for filing and service of process fees, witness expenses, and other similar costs.

Finding the Current Address of a (Potentially Elusive) Person

Unless establishments the defendant frequents are known, his current residential or work address must be found. Determining where someone lives or works can be difficult. Sometimes a person will have over a dozen aliases and move several times per year. People who are trying to evade others or who "know the ropes" of the legal system and want to avoid detection would fit this profile.

One tactic that might help locate such a person would be to subscribe to a trial membership for one of several online background check services. Sometimes the cost for a five-day trial membership is $1 or so. All you truly need is one shot to gather the information about a particular person, and then the membership can be canceled.

Utilizing online services to search for people such as our not-so-hypothetical defendant may reveal several residential addresses along with a myriad of aliases and may even show his social media picture. This, of course, is a good reason not to use your real picture on social media if you can avoid it. Remember to search for the person using any aliases you already know, perhaps a maiden name or former married name.

Once a list of potential residential addresses is obtained, the easiest but possibly slowest way to try and determine where someone is currently living is to mail a blank dummy letter to a known former address of the person. On the back of the envelope under the return address, above the delivery address, or to the left of or below the postage and below any price marking, write "Return Service Requested—Do NOT forward," the first three words of which comprise a special ancillary service provided by the U.S. Postal Service.[8] However, this method of determining a residential address may not be reliable.

Even though U.S. Postal Service rules state that its personnel will not forward a package with this particular request on it, they may erroneously attempt to forward it anyway despite the additional "Do NOT forward." A separate notification or the original letter itself, if not mistakenly forwarded, should get delivered to the sender with the new address printed on it, which, hopefully, is not a PO Box. As explained in chapter seven in the REMAINING MISCELLANEOUS RULES section, this is a good example of why supplying a forwarding or any current residential address to the U.S. Postal Service might later haunt you.

If forwarding of the letter is accidentally attempted but the recipient's current address is unknown, it should be returned with "RETURN TO SENDER," "ATTEMPTED—NOT KNOWN," and "UNABLE TO FORWARD" or something similar stamped on the envelope. Getting the returned letter or a separate notification with or without the new address can take well over a month and should be factored into the overall service time allotment. As such, this strategy may not be feasible in many instances.

Because of the potential for a processing error and forwarding of the letter anyway, it should not be sent with your return address or anything identifying you as the sender. It should be sent by someone the defendant does not know so that suspicions are not aroused. Of course, you can also send it using someone else's return address and then alert him to be on the lookout for its return or other related correspondence from the U.S. Postal Service.

If the list of potential residential addresses is rather large or geographically diverse, the above approach may be most efficient. However, if the list is more manageable, visiting each address in turn while attempting service may be quicker. In the event all potential addresses happen to be former addresses, then either the above approach using ancillary services of the U.S. Postal Service or alternatives must be considered.

When the person you are suing owns property, perhaps an apartment where you are a tenant, the tax assessor's or registrar's office personnel in the town or city where the apartment is located can search their records for the residential address of its owner. This has limited viability because the address of at least one of the person's properties must be known in order to determine his residential address as in this example. Your search may also reveal his address to be a PO Box, but it is worth a shot since it basically costs nothing. When this happens, it is not always a dead end. The U.S. Postal Service is required to provide physical address information of a PO Box customer for service of legal process under 39 CFR § 265.6(d)(4).[9] A written request citing this regulation along with a copy of the complaint that needs to be served may be required by U.S. Postal Service personnel to release the defendant's address.

Other than hiring a private investigator, the last easy way to attempt to determine someone's residential address is to use a reverse phone number search, assuming you know his phone number. An address can be obtained from a reverse telephone directory or by typing the person's number into an online search engine and sifting through the results. This will not work, of course, if the person does not have a landline phone but only has a mobile phone and uses an old address as the billing address for it.

Surprise Serving Strategies

If you wish to serve an elusive defendant without the aid of "professional" services, it can be done but will have to be carefully planned. Once the residential address of the person is known or at least reduced to a manageable set of possibilities, service can be attempted. There will generally be just one opportunity to serve the unknowing, slippery defendant unless trickery is employed. If the defendant is female, it may be helpful having flowers delivered to the residence...along with the small claims complaint. This is one creative way to shield the true intentions of the server. Women are always excited about getting flowers, so having a florist work with you on this scheme might be one worthwhile approach.

Alternatively, a friend or an associate could basically do the same thing by ordering a custom-made car door magnet from one of several online retailers and designing it for Henrietta's Flowers or whatever fabricated florist company name you prefer. He could then deliver both the flowers and complaint to the defendant...and return the flowers to you if you really like them. Male defendants might be a little more difficult to fool with this approach, so something more enticing may be in order. Perhaps Joe's Meat Service or *Gentlemen's Magazines Unlimited* would be a catchier door magnet for the bogus business. One of the preceding "companies" should certainly garner the interest of most defendants.

Have your server arrive with the flowers, meats, sample publication, or what have you at each residential address until the one is found where the defendant is living. Once the correct address is found, the defendant can be spoofed and then served, with any luck. If the server goes to a former address and the person living there does not know the defendant, then no harm, no foul.

If, however, the resident does know the defendant, someone who is his friend or family member, for example, then your server's cover is not blown if he is playing Mr. Florist, Mr. Meats, or whatever other role you have chosen. Without the disguise, the domicile's occupant might become suspicious as to why an ordinary person is inquiring about the defendant and then alert him about the incident, which he might deduce is an incoming lawsuit. Of course, if his work address is known, he could be served there using this same sham.

Once served, a special form, sometimes called a "proof of service," certifying completion may need to be filed with the court by the server. When the defendant is found but either personally rejects the complaint, throws it out, or otherwise destroys it, most courts consider all such acts to constitute valid service, in which case the serving person can still honestly file the proof of service form with the court.

Some information presented in this section may seem extreme. However, there are people who might have to resort to it or take even more drastic measures for the purpose of proceeding with their claim. Remember that if you want to play fair, you will most likely lose the legal game. There are no known laws that state you cannot pull such a hoax or any other while serving anyone anything—not yet anyway. Just give our lawmakers a little more time.

If personal service cannot be accomplished despite all attempts, sometimes substituted service will allow the serving party to deliver the complaint to a coworker, to any person over a certain age at the defendant's residence, or to other specified persons. He may then need to perform a few additional steps, which can be somewhat convoluted. Provisions for this kind of service are intended specifically for the "legal veterans" who are adept at avoiding personal service. Consult applicable small claims rules for further details. That completes this step of the small claims process unless, of course, you are the defendant.

ANSWERING THE COMPLAINT AND FILING A COUNTERCLAIM

If you are about to receive some flowers, some meats, or a complimentary magazine, you will know that someone who has also read this book could be trying to dupe you, and his trick might not be quite so successful. However, if you are reading this book after receiving a nice gift, fear not; there are ways to beat a claim if you are in the right and sometimes even if you are in the wrong but have political pull or other connections that will be explained shortly. The first step for you would typically be to file an answer to the complaint. This is not a requirement in all jurisdictions, but once again, rules of court should be consulted to determine if it is or is not.

As the defendant, if you feel you are unjustly being sued and want to contest the complaint, you should consider filing an answer in jurisdictions where one can be filed. If you do not defend at all or do so minimally in any legal matter, the system will have absolutely no remorse whatsoever mowing over you. Thus, if a defense is mounted immediately, it will put the court on notice that you are not going to go quietly or willingly. Throw enough waste material on the wall, and some of it will stick. The point here is to inundate but not annoy. If the court gets annoyed with filings it deems frivolous from any party, lawyers included, it will often turn on them.

Just like filing a complaint in small claims court is not difficult, filing an answer and a counterclaim is not either (see appendix). If you feel that the person suing you has instead committed the actual transgression by injuring you personally, financially, or in some other way and has filed suit to mask this incident, a counterclaim can be filed in conjunction with the answer to the original complaint. Note that filing an answer is normally a prerequisite to filing a counterclaim, but with small claims, the court usually combines the two on one form. Once again, the basic process is not much different from any standard civil case; it is simply much more streamlined. Some states allow an injured defendant to file an entirely separate lawsuit later as a plaintiff, so in such instances, a counterclaim may not be compulsory. Also note that sometimes the answer—and counterclaim, if filed—must be served to the plaintiff according to rules of court.

In the event your counterclaim exceeds the jurisdictional limit of a small claim, the case will likely have to be removed to the traditional civil court. This could benefit you if you think you can run circles around the plaintiff in the more formal and rule-heavy setting or if you have the opportunity to bring in a (good) lawyer and know the plaintiff cannot, assuming counsel is not allowed in the relevant small claims court. Rules about removing cases vary, but you normally first need to file a summons and complaint in the traditional civil court. You might have to bring a declaration, a request and order for consolidation, copies of the proof of service and the new complaint filed in the civil court, and possibly other documents along with the appropriate transfer fee to the small claims court clerk. The case should then be submitted to a small claims court official for removal approval.

As mentioned in chapter eight's STATE COURTS section, some states have created a branch of courts that lies between small claims and the traditional civil court. County court is the name given to these intermediate courts in Florida, but naming can vary nationally.[10] Such a court, if it exists in the pertinent state, could be the one to which you might transfer your case. Not all states have these intermediary courts, but researching online or at the law library or court should indicate if the applicable one does.

BUILDING THE CASE

Most legal battles must be built from the ground up. Small claims litigation is no exception. Gathering photographic evidence; video footage; copies of receipts, emails, invoices, deeds, leases, and demand letters; and other physical evidence to prove or bolster a case is paramount. In most instances, physical evidence is far stronger when it contains a date and time stamp. For many purchases made online, a copy of a bank card statement is helpful to substantiate them. Something to keep in mind in certain parts of the country is that documentary evidence must be provided to the court and sometimes to the opposing party before the trial date, while in others documentary evidence only need be produced at trial.[11]

When building the case, doing legal research to uncover the statutory laws that were broken by the opposing party is somewhat optional since one function of small claims court is for the judge to make that determination for the parties involved. This differs from a traditional civil setting wherein the parties themselves must identify the statutory laws that have been broken and support their complaint with corresponding settled law. There is nothing preventing any party from doing this in a small claim, but it is not a prerequisite.

However, if your investigation reveals that no statutory laws were broken or settled law is not favorable, then the likelihood of you prevailing without corruption in your favor is nil. Finding concrete proof of supporting statutes and settled law or lack thereof certainly would indicate the strength or weakness of your case beforehand. Furthermore, judges and magistrates can and do overlook or ignore applicable statutory and settled law that would otherwise help prove a case. Having such proof on hand and putting it in front of their faces makes it more difficult, though not impossible, for them to disregard law.

The next step is preparing for battle. Make sure evidence clearly shows whatever you want it to show. For instance, suppose you brought your vehicle into Schnedly's Auto for three separate automotive services—replacement of brakes, replacement of belts, and a tune-up—all with a ninety-day warranty. Also suppose you have a copy of the auto service center's receipt in the amount of $1,200. Be sure all work and the warranty are shown on it if your claim is that a belt broke seventy-five days after replacement. The receipt is nearly meaningless as evidence if the warranty or work related to replacement of the belts is not plainly visible on it. Also, keep records of all calls to the service center, any written rejection to honor the warranty, and anything else regarding the faulty repair and events surrounding it.

Conversations can become indisputable evidence by using some chicanery. If possible, phone your adversary after hours or, in any event, when you know he will not answer and leave a voicemail explaining specifically the response you want. When the call is returned, deliberately let it go to voicemail. If the message contains the supportive information you are seeking, then it can be played back while recording it to your laptop or some other secure storage device, which will make proving whatever was said a whole lot easier in court later.

It may not be mandatory to transfer the message onto other media, but some mobile phones only store messages for a certain period before they are deleted. To be safe, trust nobody, the phone company included, and make at least one backup copy. Remember that recordings of people made without their knowledge may not be admissible in court and making them may be illegal, but recordings made when they know they are being recorded, particularly when voluntarily leaving voicemail, should be admissible.

For cases concerning an oral contract wherein one or more witnesses heard its parties finalize the agreement, creating affidavits from each witness may be prudent in addition to having each one testify at trial—the more corroborating evidence and testimony, the better. In some jurisdictions, limited discovery may be permitted in small claims matters, which consists of a subset of the discovery allowed in regular civil cases. Sometimes prior court approval is needed as it is in Illinois; therefore, obtaining depositions from witnesses who might not be available for trial may or may not be possible.[12] The same may hold true for requests for production of documents or any other facet of discovery.

Depositions

Depositions are rare in small claims cases. Rules of court should be consulted in any jurisdiction where a deposition is desired to verify whether it is allowed. If allowed, the party requesting the deposition needs to contact a court reporter to arrange it. You should not be surprised that the court normally charges a fee for its own reporters. Non-government reporters might also be allowed. Before the deposition, ask the court clerk for a subpoena *duces tecum*, or a subpoena for production of evidence. This way, the deponent can be instructed to bring to the deposition whatever evidence you wish to see, such as sales receipts, deeds, surveillance video, or whatever else is related to the case at hand. Like many subpoenas, it should typically be served upon the deponent and sometimes in the same manner as the complaint.

It is possible that the deponent will not bring the requested materials to or will fail entirely to appear at the deposition. If so, like almost everything related to a legal proceeding, a multi-step process may be required to make the deponent comply. First, a motion to compel appearance or a motion to compel production of evidence might have to be filed with the court. If that does not work, then a motion for contempt might have to follow. Finally, a *capias*, also called a "writ of bodily attachment," might have to be issued, which would mean that the person could be arrested and brought before the court to answer for his refusal to comply. A worst-case scenario like this is never fast, and the only certainty is that it results in income for the courts.

At the deposition, ask the deponent probing questions about assets with significant equity and minimal liens because these are things you may want to attach later or have seized for repayment of the debt. Answers may not be forthcoming but asked from a different angle or later in the deposition may result in the desired response. If, for example, the deponent is reluctant to answer questions about the number of vehicles he owns or lies that only one is owned, ask how a family of four gets to school and work every day when three work different jobs but at similar times. If you feel an answer stating that most of the family gets rides to school and work is a fabrication, inform the deponent that you will call as witnesses at trial those persons allegedly giving the rides. Tactics such as this can make the time spent in a deposition quite productive.

Motions and Other Documents

When witnesses are reluctant to appear and testify at trial on your behalf or documentation to which you do not directly have access is needed to defend your case, a subpoena might need to be issued. As they do for other small claims filings, many courts have simple forms to be completed for this purpose. Once again, method of service, whether by plaintiff, sheriff, disinterested person, court official, or what have you, depends on locale. Checking the rules of procedure for the appropriate court should reveal the approved service methods.

Motions can be submitted by plaintiffs and defendants to dismiss claims and counterclaims, respectively, in a small claims suit, which is frequently accomplished via completing and filing specific forms provided by the court. Generally, a plaintiff's motion to dismiss his claim should not dismiss the defendant's counterclaim. Likewise, a defendant's motion to dismiss his counterclaim should not dismiss the plaintiff's claim.[13] Unlike regular civil cases, motions to dismiss the opposing party's claim or counterclaim are not allowed universally, but some localities or states permit them. Utah is one that does.[14]

If a case gets dismissed with prejudice, the plaintiff cannot legally bring it again unless the dismissal is first vacated. If it is dismissed without prejudice, then the plaintiff can refile it any time within the statute of limitations. A case may be dismissed in one of these two ways if the plaintiff fails to appear at trial, for example. To vacate a dismissal with prejudice, certain steps need to be taken and are discussed later in this chapter's APPEALS section.

There are a wide array of motions and other documents that can be filed in small claims courts throughout the country. Just a few examples are: a writ of execution, a notice of appeal, and a motion to vacate judgment. These would be filed with the court in order to enforce a judgment, to request a hearing at the next higher judicial level, and to influence the court to negate a judgment, respectively.[15] If you suspect that some element of statutory law was overlooked or case law was not followed and an unfavorable ruling for you ensued, then some of these could keep the case alive and be the first step towards changing its outcome.

Performing a Practice Trial

If you are new to the courtroom environment, you may want to practice presenting your case to a couple of friends or family members, with one playing the opposing party and one playing the judge. This can help ferret out any holes in your argument or illuminate where evidence is insufficient. Being able to present a case adequately to these people, even in an informal way, should help with presentation in the courtroom setting. Doing a dry run like this is akin to having multiple sets of eyes review a court brief. It cannot hurt, but it can certainly help and may also provide an objective opinion about the strength of your case and whether it is worth pursuing in court.

Whoever is playing the plaintiff will present his side first along with all supporting evidence. Once that person has finished and the person playing the defendant has done the same in an attempt to rebut the first player's argument, go through the scenario again. It would be a good idea to do so until it is completed smoothly and in such a way that all players think a non-corrupt judge would likely rule in your favor. If any of your actual witnesses can attend the mock trial, this should help eliminate the kinks with their testimony too.

Some states' rules of procedure, such as Vermont's, say that the judge will do most of the witness questioning.[16] Other states' rules, such as Virginia's, say that the parties can question witnesses.[17] Check rules of procedure for the relevant court to determine who does the questioning. Keep this significant difference in mind while preparing witnesses. If an important part of their testimony is overlooked at trial in a court where the judge or magistrate is supposed to do most of the questioning, be certain to direct him to ask the missed questions or ask them yourself if court rules do not state that the officiator will ask "all questions."

During practice you can even have your actor-opponent randomly interject hearsay and see if you catch it. Recall that hearsay, testifying *someone else* said something, is generally inadmissible and should provoke your immediate objection. Another mistake less experienced litigants make is, for example, testifying to facts not yet in evidence as in, "His dog jumped on me, which caused me to drop and break his $700 camera." If it has not yet been established that you owned a dog, then a statement such as this would be doing exactly that and should raise your instantaneous objection.

Have your fake opponent read the legal "script," think for a bit, and try to invent something similar and related to the facts of your case. Then, when he is testifying during the rehearsal session, he should randomly blurt his version of hearsay to see if you object.

THE TRIAL

Once all pre-trial activity is complete and the mock trial is well-rehearsed, the next step is the real deal. As discussed thoroughly in the JURY AND BENCH TRIALS section of chapter seven, the advantages of a jury trial generally outweigh the disadvantages. In states that allow juries in small claims court, it might be fruitful to request one. Costs paid in advance for juries are generally recoverable by the side that paid if judgment is in its favor. As previously stated, rules of procedure vary with jury trial requests and thus should be consulted in the applicable locale.

With respect to addressing a judge in court, once again television and film have dramatized the use of the phrase "Your Honor." In today's courts, many have not earned the title and commit acts that are in direct opposition to anything even remotely honorable. Consider an alternative if you have an aversion to bestowing upon a judge an unjust title that is expected merely because of common protocol. In a military court of law, judges can be addressed as "sir" or "ma'am" as appropriate. Personal experience has shown no judges have objected to this technically correct form of address in nonmilitary courts. If any do object, however, offer to revise addressing them as "Judge" with their last name appended.

When People Expected at Trial Do Not Appear

One thing of which to be aware that cannot be avoided is the possibility of a last-minute scratch on the ticket. Like all working people, there are times when judges and magistrates at all levels are out sick or have emergencies to tend with little notice. Their temporary replacements are called "judges *pro tempore*," or "*pro tem*" for short. At least one state, California, has a rule in place that allows small claims litigants to accept or reject such replacements.[18] All parties must agree to have their case heard by the temporary judge, or another date is given for them to return and try again.

Certainly, the more options, the better for you if embroiled in the legal system. One difficulty with the substitution, however, is not knowing if he would be better or worse for you than the absentee. As a last-minute check, consult your internet-enabled phone, and look for any lawsuits against the temporary judge. You might want to check the substitute's reputation in general, determine if he is pro-plaintiff or pro-defendant, and look for any reason why he would not be better for you than the absent judge or magistrate. After conducting such a search, it might be easier to decide whether you want the judge *pro tem* to hear your case.

There can also be a scratch when a witness you really need cannot or does not appear. If this happens or if crucial evidence will not be obtainable until after the scheduled trial date for reasons beyond your control, ask the court for a continuance. Phone the clerk as soon as possible even if it is first thing in the morning on the day of trial. If the clerk hesitates to grant your request to postpone the matter, suggest supplying an affidavit later as supporting proof. This may prevent having to drive to court and additionally missing work in order to accomplish the same thing.

If you are the plaintiff and the defendant fails to appear at trial, ask for a default judgment, a judgment given to a party when the opposing party does not appear. An exception to obtaining such a judgment would be if the defendant is on active military duty. Service members are protected by Congress. Of course, any person who is a defendant and knows this may falsely use it as an excuse not to appear at trial. If this happens and you thus know he is trying to skirt the issue, you can supply the court with a declaration of nonmilitary service, sometimes called an "affidavit of nonmilitary service" or other similarly named document, stating this fact.

Note that courts ordinarily do not allow appeals from defendants who fail to appear at the original trial. Instead, they must take an intermediate step in order to keep the case alive—more on the topic later in the APPEALS section of this chapter. If you are the defendant and the plaintiff does not appear, you should ask for the case to be decided if you filed a counterclaim or otherwise ask for dismissal with prejudice so the case cannot easily be refiled later by the plaintiff. If neither party appears at trial, the case could be dismissed without prejudice or taken off calendar, the latter of which means it is no longer scheduled to be heard and might be postponed.

Aside from not appearing, the defendant may also try stalling tactics to delay getting to trial, which might at least exploit the annoyance factor against the plaintiff. Who knows? Key witnesses may relocate. The plaintiff could die. And other events could prejudice the case against the plaintiff, given enough time. Recall from chapter four, possession would be nine-tenths of the law from the defendant's perspective the longer he can delay the trial.

Political Connections That Negatively Influence Your Case

Another fact of which to be cognizant on the day of trial, or preferably prior if possible, is that your adversary, particularly if he is the plaintiff, may be politically connected at the courthouse. One of the first forays into small claims court by one author had a most unexpected outcome for exactly this reason. By any layperson's standards, the case was a "slam dunk." The coauthor was the defendant and had written proof, video evidence, and verbal testimony heavily against the plaintiff's bogus claim. The case was heard by a judge, and the judgment arrived in the mail days later—in favor of the plaintiff. How could this have happened?

Strangely, what the coauthor-defendant noticed in court is that the plaintiff, a medium-sized business in Massachusetts named MAP Insulation, had approximately twenty-five to thirty cases scheduled that day. This was an extraordinary number for just one party since the most any other party had that same day was just a few. Apparently, dozens of other customers of the business were also defendants, prospectively totaling hundreds or perhaps thousands over the years if defendant numbers that day were representative of other days the business was in court as a plaintiff. Customers were unsatisfied enough not to pay the plaintiff for the shoddy work it had performed for them. With the plaintiff having such a poor public reputation, it should have been child's play for any defendant sued by the company to obtain a judgment in his favor.

However, the exact opposite was true. After some thought, it was simple to understand why. If the plaintiff was bad as a business in the private sector, then it was good as a customer in the legal realm. Remember that non-governmental parties except those experiencing a financial hardship and other special categories of people, individuals unlawfully detained, for instance, have to pay a fee in order to file a case in court. Doing the additive math for the cost of filing fees for the many cases brought to that particular court on that single day alone yields the obvious answer. If the court ruled against the plaintiff in all or most of those cases, what do you suppose the plaintiff would do? It certainly would not be filing many or any cases in that court, and a decent chunk of change would be reallocated to a different, more accommodating court as a result.

The moral of the story, as explained in chapter three, is that all is not as it appears in the judiciary. If your opponent, the plaintiff, has a bad reputation in the community and is in a specific court frequently contesting civil cases, you may want to reconsider expending much energy fighting in that court and focus on appeal instead. It might be sound reasoning if the appellate court happens to be one where the plaintiff might not be such a great customer. Incidentally, the plaintiff's patronage at any court would be readily apparent if it was queried in advance regarding the number of cases the plaintiff had on the docket on a given day. If the answer is more than a few, then there certainly would be reason to suspect that a symbiotic relationship exists between the plaintiff and the court. Rather than learning that your suspicion is true by going through the whole trial and then losing the battle despite having an airtight case, you might consider trying to change venue beforehand.

As it so happened in this instance, the venue should have been the county where the coauthor-defendant resided. A change of venue was not considered because the contemporaneous thinking was that the case was a sure thing, which it would have been in any non-corrupt court. Had the large volume of business the plaintiff conducted with the court been known prior to trial, a motion to change venue would have been filed in an attempt to move the plaintiff into less familiar surroundings, so to speak. Of course, the plaintiff most likely would have objected to this, which is allowed by the court; however, objections would be raised only if the plaintiff knew about the motion. It could have happened that the copy of the motion the coauthor-defendant sent by U.S. mail had inadvertently gotten lost and never reached the plaintiff...which sometimes happens to politically connected customers of a court. Granted, there is no guarantee that another court would be any less corrupt, but one thing *is* guaranteed—if you allow your case to be heard in a corrupt court where your adversary is connected, you will most certainly lose.

A Hypothetical Case—the Opening Statement

Such unfortunate circumstances of an opponent having a "business" relationship with the court aside and assuming all parties appear at trial, the normal sequence of events should begin with the litigants giving opening statements, provided they are allowed by rules of court. Even if allowed, the courts will try to steamroll right over them. They rarely, if at all, inform litigants that these statements can be made. The same holds true for closing statements.

Strategically, it may actually be more advantageous not to give an opening statement when small claims cases are heard by a single officiator since it might annoy him. Not only that, it would reveal your hand, so to speak, since it would make known that you have done your homework and understand the small claims process. However, a solid, well-thought-out opening statement in front of a jury should endear you to them and help polarize them if your evidence supports it. During an opening statement or at any juncture of case presentation, it might be best to avoid including irrelevant information or being repetitive. Doing so may bore the officiator or jury.

When giving your opening statement, quote statute if relevant. Reinforce your statement later when you present your case by providing a copy of any statute mentioned and supporting evidence to the court. Try to anticipate what your opponent will do during the trial based upon whatever has been learned prior to trial. If you state how you will counter your adversary's claim or counterclaim with solid evidence, this should go a long way towards taking the wind out of his sails. Also, make sure to stay composed while stating this with a lower tone of voice, but use more animated body language and slightly more volume and inflection when stating that there is no way the opposing party will be able to refute your evidence. If you are presenting your case to a jury, attempt to befriend them before you even begin.

Presenting Your Case

If you are the plaintiff, you will present your case first just as in other adversarial U.S. court proceedings. Make sure all your paperwork is logically sorted with tabbed folders, with binder clips, or by other means so that locating a piece of evidence, a written motion, or anything else will be much easier. Doing so will also help prevent forgetting to present something you had intended to use. Labels, such as "receipts," "court papers," "photos," and the like, can be used to organize folders in document-heavy cases. For evidence that only consists of a signed contract, a single invoice, and ample video on a smartphone or hard drive, there would obviously be no need for such labeling. Whether documentary evidence is submitted before or at trial, it is a good idea to have duplicates of it all so that when the judge is reviewing one of your documents, you can follow along and direct him if need be.

For evidence that cannot be brought into the courtroom and cannot be presented by photo or other representative way, mention early, perhaps when you first arrive, that it might be necessary to have the judge or a court officer step outside to observe the car, van, or other such object. After you give testimony and present evidence, notify the officiator that you have a witness or witnesses to support your particular claims if you do. If you are allowed to do the questioning, phrase your questions in such a way so as to enable the witness to answer them succinctly, which should demonstrably solidify your argument. Once you have finished questioning a witness, your opponent will have the opportunity to question him. This is called "cross-examination" in legal parlance. The opposing party may also ask to call him again later in the proceeding.

Presenting your hypothetical case as plaintiff against Schnedly's Auto might go something like this, assuming litigants can do the questioning:

1. Schnedly's Auto repaired the brakes, replaced the belts, and tuned the engine in your car, which consisted of replacing the spark plugs and air filter. The total fee including tax was $1,200. You state this to the court and present the date-stamped receipt marked "Exhibit A" to the judge or magistrate. Exhibits are sometimes marked starting with the letter "A" and continuing sequentially through the alphabet.
2. You state that the warranty for the work was ninety days as shown on the receipt.
3. You state that the alternator belt broke seventy-five days after servicing, and you show your phone bill indicating your call to Schnedly's reporting the incident on the day it broke.
4. Next you state that the shop manager refused to honor the warranty because his analysis of the belt indicated it was physically cut, as if by a knife. However, not only are you claiming the expense of having another repair facility replace the belt, but you are asking for reimbursement of a new battery too. You are demanding this because the previous battery no longer held a charge and had to be replaced because of the broken belt, and you present the court with receipts for belt and battery replacement from the other repair center.
5. You tell the court that the car is garaged at home and that your sister was riding with you when you heard a noise under the hood, saw the dashboard fault indicator illuminate, and noticed something on the street behind you as you began to drive away. Then you state that you stopped to retrieve what happened to be the broken belt, which you provide to the court. You then mention that your sister is with you and can testify to these facts.
6. When your sister is ready to testify, you ask if she was in the car with you on whatever day it was that the belt broke. She confirms that she was. Then you ask if she heard the noise, witnessed the dashboard fault indicator illuminate, and saw you retrieve the belt from the

street. She confirms that she did. You ask her if the car is garaged when not in use so that nobody could have cut the belt. Again, she gives a confirmative answer by saying that it is. Finally, you ask her if she was with you on the day you brought the car back to Schnedly's in order to have the belt replaced under warranty, which the shop declined. Once again, she replies confirmatively that she was there and heard the shop manager say he would not replace the belt under the warranty.

7. Once you are done, the defendant cross-examines your sister. He asks if the belt could have been partially cut by a vandal who had access to the vehicle while it was parked. Your sister testifies that it was not possible since the car was only used on five occasions during that period and was never left unattended except when garaged at night.

Once you are finished presenting your case in chief, or arguing your case as plaintiff, the defendant will have the opportunity to present his rebuttal, or argue his case as defendant. This includes giving testimony, providing evidence, calling witnesses, and questioning them himself if allowed by court rules. Pay close attention to whatever your opponent says and submits as evidence. This is no time to doze. His argument will be just as important, even if not true, as yours from the perspective of the judge, magistrate, or jury. The preceding holds true whether you are the plaintiff or the defendant.

You may find holes in your adversary's story, observe the introduction of improper evidence, or hear something that does not make sense or seems untrue. If his evidence or his or his witnesses' testimony is not immediately objectionable because of hearsay, making statements about facts not yet in evidence, or any other reason, wait until he is finished to respond. You should have a chance to refute his argument and cross-examine his witnesses if he has questioned them himself. Depending upon the number of witnesses and the amount of testimony, the whole proceeding can take about ten minutes to an hour or more, but some courts specify a fairly short time limit for each party to present their case, perhaps fifteen minutes or so.

Now, if you are the defendant and have been wronged by the plaintiff, remember that a civil case decision is not always "all or nothing" for either party. Civil cases at all levels of the judiciary are sometimes decided partially in favor of the plaintiff and partially in favor of the defendant. For instance, if you can prove two out of three claims by the plaintiff are not legally valid, then the judgment might only be partially in the plaintiff's favor and partially or mostly in your favor. It might also be at least partially in your favor if you have a counterclaim that is more legally sound than the plaintiff's claim.

Closing Statement

Closing statements can be made after the officiator asks if anyone has anything else to add. Although opening statements might not always be the best idea in small claims cases, a solid closing statement should help fortify your case and can be downplayed into something less official than what it really is. This could be done by responding with the introductory phrase "Judge, I'd just like to add…" or "If I can say just one more thing…" and remaining seated if you have done so throughout the trial. This way, you do not sound arrogant or learned about the system but still have the opportunity to recite your well-rehearsed closing statement. A few memorized summarizing sentences would be ideal.

If you have something prepared on paper that is too long to be memorized, reading it aloud should suffice. If you filed a claim or counterclaim, your statement should summarize how your evidence and witnesses proved that you sustained the injury or incurred the damage and that your adversary is responsible. Otherwise, it should simply supply the reason why you are not responsible for the plaintiff's claim. Your opponent may follow suit, but it is unlikely. In the event he does, his closing statement will undoubtedly be spontaneous and thus not as good as yours. Sometimes after a bench trial, the officiator does not give his decision orally in court like juries do after jury trials, and the judgment is instead delivered via U.S. mail.

APPEALS

If a case was lost that, without a doubt, should have been won, then an appeal should be considered. In small claims, some jurisdictions do not allow a plaintiff to appeal a judgment but only allow a defendant to do so. The typical exception might occur if the defendant filed a counterclaim against the plaintiff and won. The plaintiff can oftentimes appeal this judgment.

If a dispute with a business or people is anticipated or is a strong possibility because of a subpar product or service they provided and has a chance of escalating into litigation, it might be better to withhold paying them. This would preclude transferring possession, of money in such an instance, to the other entity, the topic of chapter four. Additionally, making them sue you rather than the other way around will almost always leave the option open for appeal as a defendant in a small claims case since just a minimal number of states do not allow appeals or only allow them under limited circumstances.[19] Such a move would basically give you two chances to win as defendant instead of one as plaintiff—the first in small claims court and the second upon appeal. Unless laws or court rules of procedure change, there is no known jurisdiction where only the plaintiff is allowed to appeal. The preceding is another reason why possession being nine-tenths of the law can be important.

It might come as a surprise to some people who are naive to the legal process that almost nothing is ever final in the judicial system. A decision or verdict can be appealed and a dismissal or judgment vacated. A case in which a defendant does not answer a small claim, fails to appear at any time in court, and does not give the plaintiff whatever is owed in accordance with a default judgment does not necessarily translate into a permanent win for the plaintiff. The defendant's case is not completely lost at that point. With the right reasons and supporting proof (or a little corruption), there is a chance the case could be reinvigorated by his motions or appeal. Not to mention, of course, laws and rules change constantly, thereby making some cases long since dead and buried now alive and well. The introduction of DNA evidence to exonerate and free the wrongly convicted is a classic example of this.

Also note that a party who has won a case without subsequent appeal or any further legal resistance whatsoever from the opposing party does not necessarily receive whatever the judgment states is due. Sometimes an attachment or a motion for contempt is necessary. At times, even this does not work. Being relentless in such instances can be helpful. This trait is not only an important one when directly fighting the legal system itself but also when fighting an adversary that is not part of the system. Persistence and powerful legal weaponry help overcome many opponents.

To the newcomer, it may seem like much nonsense must be tolerated in order to be victorious in a case. This is true. Just remember that every time a case is appealed or initially filed, there is almost always an associated fee that goes into the court's pocket. Because of the current financial instability of the government and courts themselves, courts are moving towards implementing fees for just about everything imaginable. Courts in California not only charge the public outrageous fees for making photocopies but now require a self-addressed, stamped envelope from parties expecting return U.S. mail correspondence. Other courts may soon follow.

To appeal a small claims judgment, another simple one- or two-page form is usually required along with a frequently accompanying fee. Time limits must be observed when filing an appeal. Rules of court should be consulted to determine the requisite time frame. Sometimes the appeal initiates a trial *de novo*. This means the plaintiff presents his case in chief and the defendant presents his rebuttal all over again. If any new evidence or other pertinent information is found that could effectuate a different outcome, trial *de novo* affords such an opportunity. As stated previously, attorney representation in court is usually allowed at this stage of a small claims case, regardless if allowed or not during the initial trial.

One of the potential advantages of an appeal is that a different officiator will preside over it with no known exception. However, this could be a double-edged sword if going from a less corrupt court to a more corrupt one rather than the other way around. Remember to "judge shop" if possible as discussed in chapter two's "JUDGE SHOPPING" TO AVOID BAD JUDGES section. Another potential advantage is that the prevailing party may be awarded compensation toward lost wages for time spent in court, travel and lodging expenses related to the appeal, and other relevant costs. Some jurisdictions permit further compensation of attorney fees to litigants who are victims of frivolous claims filed by the opposing party that are intended to harass, delay, or stymie them at this stage of the process. Still another potential advantage may be the opportunity for a jury trial in regions that do not allow such trials until the case is heard on appeal.

To reinforce a claim for fees and costs, having proof of said expenses at the appellate hearing or trial *de novo* should help. A sheet of itemized attorney fees and a recent pay stub along with written proof of travel and other costs are also good to have. There is no guarantee that any of these expenses will be awarded even when allowed by court rules, but it will not hurt having everything at the ready.

One thing to consider before the actual appeal in court is to read the case file. Most case files are public record, and you have a right to review yours. You might be better prepared if you know what material the appellate judge will see in the case file. Sometimes there will be information in it you may not have seen—a letter or motion by opposing counsel, for example. The trial judge may also leave notes in it that the appellate judge might see. If you know what the new judge will read, whether factual or fabricated, you may be able to tailor your case accordingly. Seeing what extraneous information is in a case file is just one example, a minute glimpse, of what occurs behind the scenes as discussed in chapter three.

Small claims courts do not normally allow a defendant to appeal a default judgment. He must file a motion to vacate the default judgment instead—another form, possibly more money for the court. If the judge denies the motion to vacate in spite of a valid medical reason or another emergency supported by affidavit or other proof, then the defendant can appeal the denial to the next higher judicial level. The plaintiff should object to this motion if a crucial witness of his will no longer be available, if the defendant failed to request a postponement prior to trial, or for any other valid reason. If the plaintiff is unsuccessful, the case could then go back to the starting line. Conversely, if the roles are reversed and the plaintiff failed to appear at trial and the case was dismissed with prejudice, the plaintiff would first usually have to file a motion to vacate the dismissal and the preceding argument would be interchanged.

ENFORCING A JUDGMENT

Without appeal judgments become enforceable after entry by the court, typically thirty days later or so. The case may or may not be officially closed at that point. Nobody forces the losing party to pay, especially the court. After all, if the system can make money by attaching property or having sheriffs seize and auction it, one can understand why. With a default judgment against an adversary, consider waiting until after the time allowed for filing a motion to vacate expires before acting to enforce it. This is because you might otherwise inadvertently alert him of an unfavorable judgment from his perspective of which he had been unaware.

If you win and are owed money, there is nothing preventing you from making arrangements with the losing party, such as agreeing to a payment plan over several months or years, particularly if you think collecting may be difficult. You can also eliminate any of the service, postage, filing, and other fees lumped onto the judgment by the court or negotiate a certain percentage less than whatever is owed if it is paid in full by a date you specify. People are inclined to take the easy way out. If they know you are willing to levy their bank accounts or seize their assets, they might much rather be done and agree to your terms. Judgments are often valid for many years and are renewable before expiration. If you make the judgment debtor aware of this and of your unrelenting resolve during subsequent negotiations, it may have the same effect as a WWE "finishing move."

Enforcing a judgment in instances when it is not financial in nature is not always easy either. Sometimes a judgment can be given for equitable relief in lieu of or in addition to a monetary-based award. Equitable relief is usually a court order to do something or to stop doing something. An example of each would be to remove waste from a piece of real estate and to stop letting runoff from a drain flow onto someone else's property, respectively. However, this type of judgment is far less common in small claims courts.

In years past, when the dollar maximum for a small claim was generally limited nationally to approximately \$2,000, few cases likely required the extremes of enforcement elaborated in this section. Litigants generally accepted the judgment, and that was the end of the matter. With monetary limits now reaching \$25,000 in one state and continuing to increase over time, the likelihood of having to resort to drastic enforcement measures is greater.[20] People are more reluctant to part with a significant sum rather than just a few hundred or a thousand dollars or so.

Wage Garnishment and Other Collection Instruments

A writ of execution, garnishment, attachment, or replevin may be necessary to encourage a judgment debtor to make good on a debt. These are special orders from the court. They direct an official to attempt to satisfy a judgment, allow seizure of a debtor's non-exempt personal property or source of money not in his custody or control, such as wages and savings, authorize seizure of his non-exempt assets, and order the return of someone's personal property in his possession, respectively. Once real and personal property are seized, they can be sold to satisfy a monetary judgment. All these orders and their associated rules of procedure vary across the nation. Relevant rules of procedure need to be consulted for definitive guidance about these and other ways to enforce a judgment.

Other than having a judgment debtor pay you directly, one of the more straightforward ways to collect a monetary judgment is through wage garnishment. However, it may sometimes be difficult to determine where a person works. One creative way to discover this information is to search court records for other judgments against the debtor. If one is found, there may be useful information that can be gleaned from the judgment creditor in that case.

For example, the creditor may be an apartment complex manager who just so happens to have evicted said debtor for nonpayment of rent. He may have previously corresponded with the debtor by email and may have saved some of those messages. Furthermore, the debtor's messages may have been sent from a work email address. If you copy and paste whatever is to the right of the email address's "@" symbol into a web browser, it may yield his employer. The human resources department could then be contacted to inquire as to whom a copy of the judgment and writ of garnishment should be sent.

When conversing with the apartment complex manager, start by saying that you were searching court records and noticed that he also had a case against the debtor. Mention that you too have been issued a judgment against the debtor and are trying to determine where he works so you can garnish his wages. When a person has the same disdain for someone that you do, he may eagerly share information that supports your cause as in this real-world example experienced by one author.

Other Considerations

Limits are set upon wage garnishment in terms of percentage of salary, with the intent of leaving the judgment debtor enough for living expenses. Existing monetary responsibilities, including child support, back taxes, and other financial burdens, further limit the amount of a wage that can be garnished. Moreover, states define a variety of property that is exempt from seizure and attachment. The addition of such exemptions onto the mandatory ones elaborated in the U.S. Code makes the list quite lengthy.[21] Beyond exemptions like these, others shield certain assets from seizure, one being residences protected under homestead.

Once a judgment has issued, know that it will sometimes create an automatic lien on the debtor's real property in the county where the judgment was entered as it does in North Carolina. In other states where the lien is not automatically created, in California, for example, the judgment creditor must record the judgment in every county where the judgment debtor owns property in order to have a lien placed on the property in each county. Needless to say, there are usually more fees associated with this endeavor.

If, as plaintiff, you had named multiple defendants in the case and one is unreachable, protected under bankruptcy, or financially insolvent, then the remaining defendants, now judgment debtors, can be pursued to fulfill the debt. Just because a judgment of $15,000 was levied against three defendants does not necessarily translate into each of them owing $5,000. Together and individually they are responsible for satisfying the obligation.

Understand that the ways to recover money or property in accordance with a judgment are not strictly limited to those discussed thus far. Other means of satisfying a legal debt in some instances include garnishing rental income, applying to the DMV to suspend the debtor's driver's license, and obtaining a till tap or keeper's levy. Check applicable rules and statutes to see if these or other avenues of redress apply to your case.

In a painstaking worst-case scenario in which a debt has not been paid in full but the statute of limitations is about to expire on the judgment, the judgment creditor should petition the court for renewal, or resetting of the expiration clock. This can usually be done by filing a motion to renew judgment before the statute of limitations expires. Also, contemporary judgments can potentially be much larger than in years past because small claims dollar limits have been pushed higher. For this reason and because it may correspondingly take longer for judgments to be satisfied, the reality is that post-judgment interest could be significant. Seeking interest as part of a judgment is a good idea in light of this fact. Some courts automatically include it; others do not.

Chapter 10: Traffic Cases

There are no traffic jams along the extra mile. — **Roger Staubach**

Chapter Sections
- Background
- Non-moving violations
- Moving violations
- Speeding
- Driving through a stop sign or red light
- Other considerations
- The process
- Building the case
- The trial
- Appeals

BACKGROUND

Without a doubt, fines from both moving and non-moving motor vehicle violations have risen drastically over the last few decades. In 2008 approximately 8.9 million U.S. drivers were ticketed of more than 17.7 million stopped by law enforcement officers. Those stopped comprised about 8.5 percent of 209 million U.S. drivers.[1] Since approximately 2008, forty-eight states have increased criminal and civil court fees, added new ones, or done both.[2] Late fees, processing fees, court costs, repeat offender insurance surcharges, and anything else the system and its parasitic feeders can concoct and add onto already exorbitant fines can easily send total vehicular fine-related expenses over $1,000 and sometimes *significantly* over. Considering that the fine for littering from a vehicle in Georgia can top $1,500, excessive costs are unmistakably apparent even before the aforementioned charges are included.[3] Of course, this fine is dwarfed by the $2,500 one Virginia now imposes for driving through a red light or reckless driving, both class one misdemeanors.[4] [5]

In the twenty-year span from 1993 to 2013, traffic fines in California have almost quadrupled, which translates to a 7.2 percent annualized increase.[6] In some areas of the state, this pales in comparison to the stunning 11 percent yearly hike.[7] Speeding fines in Georgia have leaped from $150 in 1980 to $1,000 in 2007, which equates to an annual increase of 7.3 percent.[8] [9] In Massachusetts residents have not fared any better, experiencing fines that have risen from $20 in 1992 to $150 in 2015, or 9.2 percent per year, for failing to stop at a stop sign or traffic signal.[10] [11] The average upsurge in fines for these particular violations has outpaced inflation over the last thirty years by more than *three times*. Inflation has averaged a paltry 2.7 percent per year by comparison.[12] Other localities and states are probably not far behind in terms of dramatically escalating moving vehicular fines—if they are behind at all.

Non-moving vehicular fines have seen similarly outrageous increases across the nation. In Los Angeles, expired parking meter fines have jumped from $13 in 1988 to $63 in 2014, which corresponds to an annual increase of 6.3 percent.[13] [14] In New York City, the cost of a parking ticket for blocking a driveway has risen from $35 in 1988 to $95 in 2015, which is equivalent to an average annual growth of 3.8 percent.[15] [16] That increase is not too bad considering that neighboring Nassau County has seen the cost of tickets for prohibited parking skyrocket from $15 in 1993 to $165 in 2013, a shocking 12.7 percent average yearly hike.[17] [18] Furthermore, New York City has witnessed fines for improper vehicle horn usage—there is such a thing not just in that city but in many parts of the country, believe it or not—shoot from $45 in 1989 to $350 in 2011, a whopping 9.8 percent yearly increase.[19] [20]

Comparing these non-moving violation fines with their moving violation counterparts, their average has increased not quite as rapidly but, nonetheless, also at more than three times inflation. In fact, health care and higher education, which many have deemed out of control with respect to rapidly rising costs, were the only economic sectors found that experienced increases greater than or in the vicinity of just half of these example vehicular fine increases. Health care costs rose at an average of less than 6 percent per year, and higher education costs rose at about 7 percent per year during the time frame of this analysis.[21] [22] Indeed, the preceding data show that this clandestine form of motor vehicle taxation is a lucrative multi-billion-dollar yearly industry for the government.

Contesting the Violation or Not

It should be painfully clear that the days of the $10 to $20 vehicular fines are long gone. Contesting an unjustified motor vehicle violation is therefore becoming more financially attractive to the average person. This is especially true in light of the ramifications associated with receiving moving vehicle citations, such as potentially losing a job that requires a clean driving record. The expenses mentioned earlier that the government and its parasitic feeders contrive and pile onto the heap further add to the burden and enable costs to top $5,000 or more. This makes it worthwhile to take a day or two, or perhaps even five, out of work to fight a vehicular violation, particularly if it is unjustified. Thus, the contemporary thinking might now be either to pay the fine or pay the mortgage for the next two or three months—a dire dilemma for some.

With millions of drivers cited for moving violations each year, bear in mind it is estimated that more than 95 percent of them simply pay the fine.[23] Some data for non-moving violations suggest the number of drivers not contesting them could be as high as 99 percent.[24] These two statistics happen to be beneficial for those who do. If everyone charged with a vehicular violation fought it, the system would likely implement one of two solutions to lighten the workload of the court:

1. reduce vehicular fines so that the court would not be flooded with people trying to defend themselves from being fleeced by the government and who would simply pay the smaller fine instead and then not have to be bothered with fighting the violation
2. institute sobering appeal fees to deter disputing the violation in court as the Massachusetts legislature did with its $25 to $300 fees wherein the defendant would *not* have this fee reimbursed even if she prevailed, so the system wins either way—when people pay the fine, income is generated; when people contest the violation, income is generated[25] [26]

The option the system would likely pick is not too difficult to guess. With the lack of external competition for the system as discussed in chapter two in its WHAT THE LEGAL SYSTEM IS section, extra fees are an unfortunate and unwanted by-product of its operation.

While some may still be reluctant to challenge vehicular violations, the success rate for those who do has been found to range anywhere from 58 percent to as high as 75 percent.[27] [28] With this in mind, with direct and indirect costs potentially reaching into the thousands of dollars, and specifically with the right weaponry at hand to push your chances higher than that range, it may be worthwhile to contest a vehicular violation—the very purpose of this chapter.

Furthermore, fighting vehicular violations in an already crowded court creates a bit of leverage for the defendant. Since the court's main objective is to make money processing cases and remove them from the docket, appealing violations in such an overcrowded setting motivates the judicial system to reduce fines at the very least. This is because the court weighs the cost to litigate a case against simply getting quick money outright in the form of a smaller fine payment and clearing the case from the docket. It is more profitable for the court to make a little by reducing the fine than to make nothing whatsoever if you win at trial and waste their precious time in the process. If the luck of the draw is such that a crammed court has jurisdiction over your traffic case or if you can transfer it to one that is, bear this fact in mind.

As implied earlier in this section, the two basic categories of vehicular offenses are non-moving (for example, parking violations and vehicle abandonment) and moving (for example, speeding, failure to signal when turning, and failure to stop). Some jurisdictions have decriminalized most of their moving motor vehicle laws, but others classify them as minor criminal infractions. Still others classify some as misdemeanors or felonies, depending upon their severity.

Whether laws are classified as civil or criminal can sometimes be determined by observing the title of statutory code under which they are listed. If they fall under a criminal title, they are certainly criminal laws of some type. If they do not, they could be civil laws; however, some criminal laws are part of a state's motor vehicle code, which is ordinarily a civil/criminal blend under a civil title. When referring to court rules of procedure for material presented in this chapter, refer to the civil set for civil motor vehicle violations and to the criminal set for criminal motor vehicle violations. The easiest vehicular violations procedurally to fight, non-moving ones, are discussed first.

NON-MOVING VIOLATIONS

People sometimes mistakenly think non-moving violations cannot be fought as successfully as moving violations when, in essence, it might sometimes be *easier* to fight them. The process itself is generally much simpler. Analyzing any elaborate road study meant to establish safe driving speeds is not required. None of the dynamic factors associated with moving violations are relevant. And sometimes a court appearance is not required if the process can be accomplished by U.S. mail or online as allowed in some jurisdictions. The process is also simpler because everything generally needed to fight the violation is on the citation itself or in the immediate vicinity of the "crime" scene.

Finding the Ticket in Your Mailbox

There are two ways to be informed of a non-moving violation. One is by receiving a notice in the U.S. mail stating that a fine is due or, more likely, overdue. This usually happens when the ticket either has been blown or taken off your vehicle without your knowledge. Under these conditions, it might be difficult to fight the violation if you have no recollection of its particulars. However, all is not lost. First, check that the name and address is yours on the mailing and that you have not inadvertently received someone else's mail. Next, it may be worth a phone call to the issuing authority to decipher the details of the citation. If a clerical error was made by mailing it to you instead of the correct person, the violation could be dismissed during the call.

If the ticket truly is for your vehicle, a trip to the location of the alleged violation may prove beneficial if a street view of Google Maps is neither available nor clear enough to observe if the citation is legitimate or not. A citation issued for parking outside the designated roadside parking lines—which are common on the streets in the major cities in California—where none actually exist could easily be invalidated without evidence gathered on the day and time of the alleged violation. However, a citation issued for blocking a fire hydrant will be more difficult to disprove if there is a hydrant located in the vicinity of the alleged violation and the vehicle has been moved. Fighting violations that have clearly been proved invalid might only require a follow-up call to the issuing authority asking where to send the physical proof of invalidity. In general, you should be able to have an invalid non-moving violation dismissed. Even if not invalid and dismissed, late fees might be waived if you duly inform the issuing authority that you never received the original citation.

Sometimes the information on a mailed notice may be from someone else's vehicle. For example, if the color of your vehicle is red and the notice states that the color of the offending vehicle is green, then presenting the ticketing authority with a picture of your vehicle that captures the license plate and vehicle make should suffice to get the violation dismissed. Bolstering this with a copy of the certificate of registration would be helpful if vehicle color is shown on it. Optionally, accompanying the mailing with a brief explanatory letter may clarify things on the receiver's end if she does not have a clear understanding of the situation, which is probably a safe bet. If no mailing address to send evidence for disputing the violation is specified with the delivered notice, call the records clerk to inquire how you can supply the requisite information. It may be necessary to bring such proof to a court or another designated location in order to have the case dismissed.

It is unlikely anyone would go to the great length of having a vehicle painted simply to avoid paying a fine. However, because of a recent paint job, the color of your vehicle may have coincidentally changed since the date of receiving the citation. If so, appealing perhaps even a backlog of legitimate citations under these conditions may result in their dismissal. If appeal is allowed by U.S. mail or electronically, the cited vehicle's color may even be changed in a digital image of it by using image-editing software. Not that it is recommended, but it is possible.

It may be that everything stated on the notice with respect to identifying your vehicle is correct, yet it was nowhere near the location of the alleged violation on the day stated. If possible, gather any corroborating evidence, such as dining receipts, shopping receipts, or a credit card statement showing relevant purchases, that establishes the whereabouts of you and your vehicle on the day and time in question, and submit copies as proof to discredit the citation. For a single person who owns one vehicle, this should be fairly easy to do because of the one-to-one relationship of the driver and the vehicle. For a family with multiple vehicles, it will be difficult without photographic evidence showing that the vehicle was at a location different from the one alleged. Preparing an affidavit of each person who can attest to its location may help bolster the claim (see appendix).

Finding the Ticket on Your Vehicle

The second and most ideal way to be informed of a non-moving violation is to find the ticket actually on your vehicle or to see it being placed there. Whenever this happens, the first thing to do is determine if it is legitimate. Sometimes mistakes are made ticketing vehicles that are parked legally, such as in a location where a sign states that parking is legal between the hours of 9:00 p.m. and 8:00 a.m., yet the ticket was received at 9:15 p.m. Mistakes like this might be more likely in larger U.S. cities where information on the parking signs themselves can be quite convoluted and state various exceptions and conditions under which parking is allowed in an area.

If the charge is for parking in a location where certain conditions prohibit it but no signage exists stating this, the charge should be dismissed, barring corruption. Sometimes a new ordinance becomes enacted before a town or city "has time" to install the corresponding signs, and it magically benefits from windfall profits generated from parking fines as a result. Local governments already know that only a small percentage of parking violations will be contested and thus reap huge financial gains because of missing signage. Before leaving the scene of the alleged violation, take adequate photos or video of the cited vehicle showing lack of signage if relevant, the parking meter displaying time of day if relevant, and any other supporting photographable evidence that could invalidate the citation.

All evidence gathered in still images should stand on its own. For instance, the address written on a parking citation might be different from the true address of the parked vehicle. If so and to discredit the citation, take photos that capture the cited vehicle's license plate and at least part of the cited vehicle, any location-establishing evidence, such as a street name sign or building and number, and all other distinguishing imagery. Each thing proving vehicle location should be at least partly visible in the photo or set of photos. There should also be a date and time stamp on each photo or a date and time reference in the image itself. With video footage, there is more liberty to pan and capture everything relevant in the same contiguous segment so that each piece of evidence does not have to be in every single frame of the video. A safe bet would be to obtain both still images and video in order to cover appeal methods by mail, online, or in person if unknown at the time which method of appeal is locally followed and which forms of evidence are acceptable.

Like most actions involving the courts, time limitations, which vary by jurisdiction, must be observed when fighting vehicular violations. Time constraints can typically be determined through an online, a law library, or a court search, but acting immediately may be best. Lastly, since clerical data entry errors can be made and records of dismissals can be lost, be sure to get all dismissals in writing and store multiple copies in safe locations as explained in chapter seven's KEEP GOOD RECORDS IN MANY LOCATIONS section. This is true for both non-moving and moving violations. In fact, it is true for any judgment, decision, or notice from any court clearing any person of any act from its grimy grip—one of the key precepts of this chapter, if not this entire part of the book.

MOVING VIOLATIONS

The remainder of this chapter will focus on moving violations. The basic process for fighting one is the same as it is for a non-moving violation: contesting the violation timely, gathering evidence, presenting the case at trial, appealing if necessary, and then asking for and safeguarding any written exculpating judgment from the court. Remember; trust nobody within the legal system. Once again, although the general approach is the same as it is for non-moving violations, the relevant procedures, applicable fees, and allowable time frame to fight the violation vary nationwide.

The first thing to remember when receiving a citation for a moving violation is *not* to leave an impression on any law enforcement officers who stop you, if possible, and *not* to take your eyes off them. If they draw their guns and start shooting at you as has been done in routine stops, it is certainly understandable to run for your life, but hopefully, that does not happen.[29] You should consider not raising a ruckus and not being overly polite either. The intent is to make them less inclined to take any mental or written notes after the stop, which sometimes they do. Ideally, erasing their memory of the entire incident is the goal. If a trial ensues, the officers likely will then be less able to recall events from the stop and rebut the evidence you may present or testimony you may give against them.

The second thing to remember is to think twice before offering any incriminating evidence to an officer when receiving a citation. If asked how fast you were driving when being issued a speeding citation, there are several reasonable statements you can make to the officer in order to deflect false speeding accusations. Stating that you do not drive fast, your speedometer indicated you were driving the speed limit or slower, or you were following or being passed by traffic and do not believe you were speeding all can be said without incriminating yourself. Also, it would not be a good idea to agree with an officer's assertion that you did not use your turn signal while turning or that you rolled through a stop sign. All these "confessions" will happily be used against you in court by the officer.

You do not have to state that you are certain you were not speeding or doing whatever illegal act it is of which you are accused, particularly if you can prove it in court. As appropriate and if you feel inclined, you can show the officer proof from your GPS or any physical evidence you may have on hand to repudiate her claims. She may relent. She may not. Either way, hard and fast evidence to support your case, including witnesses who are passengers, should help swing a legal fight in your favor if one ensues.

The third thing to remember is not to offer to sign the citation or remind the officer to sign it. Tickets have been dismissed for being deemed invalid because of this, but not always. If asked to sign, an issue to consider beforehand in some states, California for one, is the existence of a "county seat," the city containing the seat of government for a given county or the county's capital city.

California also has a vehicle code allowing a driver to request the court in the county seat for any moving violation case when she works or lives closer to that court than the one the officer may write on the citation—the one most convenient for the officer. See California vehicle code 40502(b).[30]

The way to make the request is orally before signing. Do not be fooled. Signing a ticket with a promise by the officer to change the court location to the county seat later may be in vain. She may try to "pull a fast one." Ensure the details of the county seat have been plainly written in the appropriate place on the citation. If the officer refuses to assign you the court located in the applicable county seat in California, write "UNDER PROTEST Vehicle Code 40502(b)" near your signature.

If you truly want your case to be heard in that court but it was not assigned by the officer, file a motion with the court to ask it to transfer the case there (see appendix). This is not a silver bullet, but the effort of driving farther to court, sometimes much farther, may make it more likely for the officer not to appear. The motive for such a maneuver, besides inconveniencing an officer in an attempt to entice a no-show, may also be to move the case from a more corrupt court to a less corrupt one or for the obvious reason of making the hearing or trial more convenient for you.

The next thing to do is gather evidence at the scene in a similar fashion to evidence collection performed for non-moving violations. If possible, doing this after the officer leaves would avoid revealing your intention of contesting the violation and make him less inclined to take notes and otherwise prepare for battle. For a speed trap where multiple drivers are stopped, it might be beneficial to exchange information with the others so that corroborating facts can be obtained and associated affidavits composed. Even if performed in the presence of officers, networking with these others may outweigh the advantage of secretively gathering physical evidence after the officers have left and your new friends have too—and are then unreachable. These other witnesses may be your greatest allies in a court challenge as you will likewise be for them.

There have been times when police officers have made faulty assumptions about speed dynamics while setting a speed trap or have been incorrectly positioned while attempting to observe traffic light violations. These mistakes are made because of their improperly chosen geographic points of reference, which have resulted in dozens of illegitimate citations being issued in one sitting. Once again, there is strength in numbers. The chance of your testimony being accepted over an officer's is nil. The testimony of many people being accepted over an officer's has a prayer.

Before leaving the scene of stops resulting from either mistake or whenever else applicable, draw a diagram of it, including the officer's original location and any relevant obstructions, roadways, and traffic signs or signals as appropriate. After receiving a citation for any moving violation, make written notes indicating whether the roadway was dry or wet and whether the traffic was light, medium, or heavy. This should be helpful for later reconstruction of the scene in court if collecting photographic evidence detailing everything at the time of the stop is simply not possible.

If taking photos or recording video is possible, doing so would generally be superior to creating handwritten drawings. If the equipment is available and conditions are safe for it, record any leaving officer's vehicle to establish the timeline. Also, capture any defaced or faded traffic sign, missing or burned-out traffic light, vegetation blocking any traffic sign or light, or potholes or other road hazards. Capturing exculpatory evidence in this way would help refute failure to stop, illegal shifting of lanes, or whatever allegations you are facing. It is important to capture everything pertinent when the citation is issued and not later because the topography may change, including street names.

SPEEDING

For this section, readers in most of Ohio can save themselves time by skipping it and just paying the speeding fine. When that state's highest court makes the ridiculous ruling that an officer can establish a vehicle's speed merely by visual estimation, it is difficult to believe anything short of the officer's retirement or death before trial can save the defendant.[31] One can only hope other states do not follow suit with this insane nonsense. In most Ohio districts, then, there is absolutely nothing to prevent an officer from stopping a motorist and citing her for driving at a contrived, arbitrary speed greater than the legal maximum or less than the legal minimum because of this high court's opinion. That reasoning is like the court saying, "We don't need to see any evidence. We know the defendant has committed murder because she *looks* like a murderer."

If you have read to this point in this section, we think we can help you, non-Ohioans. Police can now attempt to determine a vehicle's speed via various means, including VASCAR, radar, lidar or laser, pacing, aircraft, and possibly more. The important thing to remember is that all have strengths and weaknesses and can be rendered invalid under the right conditions. Regardless of the manner in which measurements are attempted, one of two different types of speed limit laws applies in different parts of the nation: absolute or presumed. Absolute limits are exactly that—absolute. Any speed greater than the posted maximum is illegal under all conditions. The same holds true for driving slower than posted speed minimums.

Alternatively, presumed limits, sometimes referred to as "*prima facie* limits," mean that speeds above maximums set by law may be legal under certain conditions. Conversely, speeds below maximums set by law may be deemed speeding under certain conditions. If it can be shown, for example, that driving on a dry, straight, lightly trafficked road during daylight hours 5 mph above the speed limit was safe but a speeding citation was issued nevertheless, the case could be dismissed. The key is that the cited driver would need to present evidence that rebuts the presumption of driving faster than the speed limit as being unsafe. However, if the roads are snowy, icy, or treacherous because of construction or for any other reason, driving slower than the speed limit can also result in a speeding ticket. Driving too fast for the conditions is also known as violating the basic speed law and applies in all fifty states and the District of Columbia.[32]

Speed Measured by Radar

Still commonly used, radar speed measuring devices can inadvertently register the speeds of vehicles close to the intended moving vehicle. As the distance between the radar device and the targeted vehicle increases, so does the width of the device's beam, thereby potentially and unintentionally registering the speed of adjacent vehicles. Large vehicles, such as tractor trailers, have many times more reflectivity than automobiles, thus increasing the chance that they might falsely attribute their speed to smaller nearby cars or motorcycles. The radar device's operator's manual should indicate its specifications regarding this issue and other limitations, as might an online search.

Environmental factors affect the reliability of most radar units used by law enforcement. Precipitation and other atmospheric phenomena, flying birds, for instance, can cause echoes and affect range of operability. Electromagnetic interference (EMI) from nearby transformers or motors, such as an operating windshield wiper motor on a rainy day, can affect readings.

Overhead roadway transformers, commonly called "pole pigs" in the trade, typically gray cylindrical objects mounted atop utility poles, and pad-mounted utility transformers can potentially interfere electromagnetically with radar speed measuring devices. You would need to show that the radar device was close enough to a transformer with sufficient power when the speed measurement was attempted to prove it faulty. The stronger the transformer's power rating, the greater the distance between the radar unit and transformer can be for it to affect the unit's readings. Power specifications of utility transformers used by electric companies are normally on the order of 10 kVA to 50 kVA but sometimes 10,000 kVA or higher, depending upon size and electrical application.[33] [34]

Power lines can also induce false readings of approximately 92 or 101 mph on radar devices.[35] This could explain things if you are stopped in a 45 mph zone when not speeding but the stopping officer says your measured speed was 92 mph. Thus, estimating speed is an important part of the process that officers must perform before trusting the reading on a radar unit. More errors can be introduced if the radar being used is "same direction radar." If an officer is using this type of radar while driving, she must guess correctly whether the vehicle she is following is moving slower or faster than her own in order for the radar device to determine speed properly.

Radar devices only capture the component of a vehicle's velocity in the direct line of the radar device. When used by law enforcement personnel in or on their moving vehicle, the cosine error introduced when both vehicles are driving towards each other at an angle because the road is curved can cause the radar unit's measurement to be greater than the targeted vehicle's actual speed. The officer would need to check her vehicle's speed displayed by its speedometer against its speed displayed by the radar unit.[36] If this is not done, the stop can be ruled invalid because of a potential discrepancy between the two speed readings of her own vehicle. Sources of radar measurement error include others not discussed in this subsection.

Speed Measured by Lidar

Lidar is becoming a more common way to estimate vehicle speed. The technology, as it applies to speed measuring devices, incorporates pulsed laser light to compute speed. The term is sometimes used interchangeably in legal parlance with the term "laser."

Lidar can more easily pinpoint a vehicle in a group because it is aimed directly at a particular vehicle, has a much narrower beam than radar, and does not have many of the common problems associated with radar, but it is also not infallible. Sweep error generated from striking various parts of a vehicle can affect speed readings significantly. At great distances, the odds of the beam striking other vehicles or objects increase because the beam widens with distance. Like radar units, laser devices also measure the component of a targeted vehicle's velocity only in the line of sight between the unit and the vehicle. When perpendicular to the vehicle's direction of travel, lidar, like radar, should measure no speed at that instant regardless of how fast the vehicle being targeted is traveling.

Because lidar uses light near or in the visible spectrum, precipitation can greatly affect its accuracy.[37] Also, if the optical sight on the unit is misaligned, it could result in an officer aiming at one vehicle and recording the speed of another. Most likely because of their relative newness, laser devices are not universally allowed for speed enforcement nationwide. Where permitted, one thing to note is that admissibility of lidar measurements in court is questionable. See *Hall v. State*.[38] Eventually, precedent may prevail across the nation, but for now, admissibility is still challengeable in some jurisdictions.

Speed Measured by VASCAR

VASCAR is another form of vehicle speed estimation used by law enforcement. It is based on the simple computation of a vehicle's speed as it passes two reference points on or near the road. Since it is strictly a visually-enabled device, accuracy decreases when used at night or during inclement weather. Additionally, since VASCAR must be triggered by an officer at both the initial and final reference points, its speed computation will be incorrect if her timing is bad. When distance between the reference points is shorter or when vehicle speed is faster, speed estimates become increasingly higher or lower than the vehicle's true speed when her timing is bad. Misidentification of vehicles is more likely in heavy traffic just like it is with radar and lidar.

Speed Measured by Pacing

Pacing is a primitive form of speed estimation. It can be done from an aircraft or a ground vehicle. If measurements are attempted from an aircraft flying into a headwind, the air speed displayed on the aircraft's speedometer will be greater than actual ground speed. So, an aircraft flying north with a true ground speed of 70 mph into a north headwind of 20 mph and pacing a ground vehicle also driving due north at 70 mph will mistakenly estimate the vehicle's speed to be 90 mph, the aircraft's own air speed as determined by its speedometer. Unless they have some way of measuring their own true ground speed or knowing the wind speed and its direction at that particular altitude and time, the aircraft's personnel have absolutely no way to avoid this error.

A ground vehicle trying to pace another ground vehicle might not be pacing it and instead may be overtaking it. This may happen when an officer is first entering a highway and decides to pace a vehicle. Obviously, the officer's vehicle would have to accelerate from a low speed while on the entry ramp to something more than posted highway speed in order to get close to the intended vehicle in a relatively short amount of time. If any "pacing" is done while driving at this faster speed, the targeted vehicle's estimated speed will be greater than it truly is.

Furthermore, speed estimation errors can be quite large when ground pacing is conducted beyond a distance of approximately 100 feet because changes in perceived vehicle range over a given time become less distinguishable. As such, an officer may not notice that she is actually closing on a vehicle when she thinks she is pacing it, thereby resulting in a high estimate of vehicle speed. Combining these two factors, pacing immediately upon highway entry and at a significant distance, would completely discredit any pacing speed estimates. If you have reason to believe that an officer was farther than 100 feet behind you or had just entered the highway at about the time she began pacing, ask for dash-cam footage during discovery. If the video verifies your suspicion, you could then argue that speed estimates are questionable at best.

Speed Measured by Aircraft

When speed is estimated by aircraft, which may not be as common as other means, at least two officers are involved when issuing a speeding citation—at least one in an aircraft and at least one in a ground vehicle. After making a speed measurement, an officer in the aircraft radios an officer in the ground vehicle to stop the motorist. If the violation is challenged in court, the officer who made the measurement in the aircraft and the one who cited the motorist from the ground vehicle would need to be present if the ground unit officer could not independently verify vehicle speed. Whenever both would need to be present, picking a trial date other than the day assigned at arraignment makes the odds more favorable to the motorist since the chances of both officers being available on the new day are lower than they would be for just one of them. This is true because the likelihood of more than one person being available for a given event decreases as the number of people who are to attend it increases.

It would be hearsay for just the ground officer to appear in court and state that the aerial officer measured your speed at X mph or for just the aerial officer to appear and state that the ground officer identified you as the driver. Both have to be present to testify legally. The aircraft officer must state the speed you were allegedly driving and how it was measured, and the ground officer must say you were identified as the driver. This is a rather expensive way for states to fill their coffers when radar, lidar, and other ground techniques offer more cost-effective solutions. In such a situation, be sure to ask that witnesses for the prosecution are not in the courtroom or within hearing distance of it whenever any one of them is testifying against you. This is because they could signal each other, corroborate their version of events, or do anything else that would help them align their stories against you.

Before your hearing or trial starts, it might be beneficial for you to send inside the court a "mole," perhaps a passenger in your vehicle at the time of the stop, who can easily identify the officers in question and "radio" back notifying you whether both are present or not before you go inside. If they are, this would be an excellent opportunity to call the courthouse and reschedule because you are "sick"—retribution in the form of using their own tag team game against them. Doing so is good for you but is a losing proposition for the money-hungry government.

An alternate way to ascertain single-handedly if both officers intend to be at court would be to make two successive phone calls to the police station prior to the start of the hearing or trial but after they would have to leave the station in order to arrive in time. Give a fake name and bogus reason for each call if you cannot dial each officer directly and another officer answers the phone. If you reach an intended officer, of course, immediately end the call when she answers. With this technique, it would be reasonable to assume they are either on their way to court or already there waiting to greet you if both are unreachable. If you have a bad feeling in the pit of your stomach, then it is time to call the court saying you need to reschedule the case due to sickness.

Recalibration of Speed Measuring Devices

Recalibration of speed measuring devices used by law enforcement along with recalibration of the speedometer in any moving land or air (or sea) vehicle used while making speed measurements is an important component of accuracy. If there are no records of recalibration, the citing officer may not have much legal standing in a speeding case. Some jurisdictions require recalibration every six months, but check relevant law to be certain since calibration requirements vary across the nation.

If the applicable jurisdiction does not mandate a recalibration interval for a speed measuring device, its manufacturer should. Check the operator's manual that should have been supplied to you by the plaintiff during discovery if you followed our template in the appendix. Worst-case, call the manufacturer to inquire. However, ask for a response by U.S. mail, email, or some other printed or printable format so that you can provide a copy of the answer to the court—and not say that someone told you the answer, which is hearsay. The most recent calibration before being cited for speeding should have occurred no more than the statutory allowed or manufacturer's recommended maximum amount of time prior to then. If that time has been exceeded, ask either orally or in a written motion for the charge to be dismissed.

Sometimes statute says the speed measuring device's calibration certificate used as evidence must be a "true copy" or the original certificate. If the officer provides you with a photocopy, it should not be valid under such statute. Ask for the certificate itself or a true copy in this instance. If anything you requested is provided to you last minute on the trial date with no time to perform whatever actions are allowed under statute or rules of procedure in order to defend the case properly, once again ask for dismissal. If your request is denied, ask for a continuance to give you more time to review the material—and give the officer another chance at a no-show.

DRIVING THROUGH A STOP SIGN OR RED LIGHT

Moving violations for driving through a stop sign or red light generally result from either direct observation or electronically via traffic light cameras. Less common than speeding, citations of this type are still a good source of revenue for the government and can also be fought successfully in court. Whenever they are given by direct observation, the ticketing officer should have a viewpoint perpendicular to the vehicle, parallel to the cross street, and near the intersection of the stop sign or traffic light in order to legitimize the citation. If the observation is made in line with the travel of the vehicle and in front of it or in back of it from a distance of approximately 100 feet or more, depth perception will be skewed with no way for the officer to obtain accurate facts relevant to where the vehicle stopped or if it even stopped at all. Other than a perpendicular viewpoint, the only other time the officer's view could be indisputable is when she is traveling directly behind you. Citations written for driving through a stop sign or red light should also be studied for errors just like all other citations.

If a stop sign is faded beyond recognition or missing, this could be evidence enough to have a case dismissed. Conversely, if a stop sign is brand new to an intersection frequented by a driver, then being cited for allegedly driving through it within the first week or so of its erection can result in successfully contesting the violation. The driver would need to prove she is a frequent traveler on the particular roadway and provide evidence that the sign was newly erected. Proving that the sign was recently installed might have to be done using witness testimony or with affidavits unless there is a time-stamped photograph available of the intersection in question taken within a week or two prior to receiving the citation and without the sign present. Another valid excuse would be driving through the stop sign well beyond such a one- or two-week window but after recently returning to the geographic area after a long absence.

It is possible that everything is in good order with the driver's actions, the stop sign, and the intersection, yet she is cited for not stopping anyway. This typically happens when the law enforcement officer has a poor view of the stop sign or stop line and the vehicle. Either the officer's view is obstructed by vegetation, a building, another vehicle, or some other object or the officer is far in front of or behind the traveling vehicle and directly in line with it or nearly so. In any event, it is important to get photographic imagery from your viewpoint of where the officer was when she allegedly made her observation. It is also important to do the same from the officer's viewpoint of where you allegedly did not stop. The evidence should show that the officer's view of your vehicle was either obstructed or that depth of field was indeterminable because she was close to being in the line of travel of your vehicle but in front of it or behind it a significant distance.

There is also the possibility you stopped your vehicle farther back than the stop sign or stop line but were out of view of the ticketing officer when you did. Having a witness testify to this fact is extremely useful but may not be possible. Ultimately, it will be your word against the officer's in court without a witness or any supporting physical evidence to the contrary, such as photographic imagery. It is certainly not rocket science to determine whom the court will back.

If the liberty of time exists when a citation for this type of moving violation is given, it may be worthwhile moving your vehicle away from the immediate intersection, stopping, and waiting to see if the officer also mistakenly cites other drivers. If so, you could approach them and exchange contact information to help each other later in court. Be sure to wait until they are being handed their citations before making your intentions known; otherwise, the ticketing officer may let them go if your plan is obvious. The officer might be satisfied having bagged a quarry of one rather than zero—a bird in the hand is worth two in the bush.

"Fake" Stop Signs

An issue that surfaces periodically should be examined—the legitimacy of citations given to motorists for driving through stop signs on private property. In some states, failure to stop at a stop sign on private property, in a mall parking lot, for example, but located away from any public roadway is not illegal. Usually, in those same states, any stop signs at exits of the private property are considered to be no different from the ones on public roads. Other states may have laws that allow enforcement of obeying stop signs anywhere within their borders.

There is some misinformation on the internet regarding this subject in certain states, so the safest bet is to research relevant statutory and case law to determine applicability. If pertinent motor vehicle statutory law does not specifically address stop sign compliance enforceability on private property, search for definitions of "way," "roadway," or whatever terms are used in the stop sign compliance law itself. Look for them either in the portion of law regarding stopping at stop signs or near the beginning of the title, the chapter, or any other similar unit. Check if private property is part of those definitions in order to determine indirectly if it is included as it is in Maine.[39] [40] If definitions cannot be found, consult *Black's Law Dictionary* or *Bouvier's Law Dictionary*, considered to be standard sources for legal definitions (see appendix). While researching statutory law, also check for statutes that relegate the authority to create ordinances and govern motorist signage compliance enforceability to local municipalities.

Regardless of enforceability, driving through a stop sign on private property is probably not the best idea when it would be unsafe to do so. However, knowing if ignoring such a sign may result in a legitimate citation or not could be helpful especially when you drive through one in a vacant shopping center parking lot during off-hours and a police officer decides to cite you for it. Based upon experience of one author who regularly disregards stop signs in private lots when conditions fully warrant, getting cited under these circumstances could be a rare occurrence.

Driving through a Red Light

Moving violations for driving through red lights are similar to the ones for failing to stop at stop signs except that traffic lights generally change color but stop signs do not. If your vehicle is already in an intersection when the traffic light changes from yellow to red, stoplight laws in some states have not been broken.[41] [42] Check applicable statutory laws to be sure. Like stop sign violations, in order to have the best viewpoint of a traffic light violation, a law enforcement officer should be situated immediately to the side of your vehicle—standing on the street corner or waiting at the same traffic light on the cross street, for instance. Besides perpendicular viewpoints, the only other time her position could be unquestionable is when she is traveling directly behind you.

One thing that should not be overlooked when being accused of driving through a red light is that the traffic lights may not be synchronized properly. If the ticketing agent was driving on the cross street and observed you driving through an apparent red light immediately after the cross street light at your intersection had turned green, the lights may be in conflict. Perhaps with the assistance of someone, watch the traffic lights closely as they change at that intersection. It is possible the cross street light is turning green while the light on the street of your travel is still yellow or has just changed to red. There should be a delay between one changing to red and the other to green in order to allow time for a vehicle that has already broached the intersection during a yellow light to clear it completely—a non-existent delay might have invited your citation.

Without assistance it may be difficult to observe traffic light behavior in the absence of low light conditions. Such conditions could allow the observation to be made alone while standing on one street corner because of the traffic lights reflecting on surrounding objects that get illuminated by them. If capturing this phenomenon during broad daylight is not possible, an option is to return later that same day when lighting conditions are sufficient to identify the intersection and to capture on video the traffic lights exhibiting the faulty behavior. However, if you plan to return to do this, the problem may be fixed by then. If a bystander is able to help identify a traffic light problem, ask if she would mind providing an affidavit or appearing in court to assist fighting the violation, perhaps for a small fee. This should be especially helpful if gathering video evidence is just not immediately possible.

The argument you should probably avoid making at trial is that the time duration of the yellow light was too short to clear the intersection or to have enough time to stop safely. It will imply that you were speeding or accelerated so you could beat the light if you cannot prove otherwise. Video footage of the light changing from green to yellow to red could help strengthen your case if, in fact, the light changed to yellow only for a moment or not at all. Unless someone is a professional with video editing software, keep in mind video footage with voice narration or background noise will be much harder to edit in order to shorten in an artificial way the time the light stayed yellow. Footage with audio should substantiate the authenticity of the video.

"Accusations" by Traffic Light Cameras

Besides being stopped by a law enforcement officer, another possible way of receiving a citation alleging that you drove through a red light is by being notified via U.S. mail—which should be one of the easiest of all traffic case types to win, in theory. Such an incident would occur when a traffic light camera captured imagery of a vehicle thought to be yours in an intersection during a red light and in the direction of travel of the red light. About half our states and the District of Columbia employ traffic light cameras for the purpose of citing motorists for traffic light violations.

Regardless of their actual validity, a ruling in 2009 by the U.S. Supreme Court in *Melendez-Diaz v. Massachusetts* has rendered these photographs and videos inadmissible in jurisdictions where the violation is criminal and not civil in nature. This is because the Sixth Amendment of the U.S. Constitution grants citizens the right to confront their accusers in criminal cases. This right would obviously be violated without scientists or other expert witnesses appearing in court and testifying as to everything associated with the traffic light camera's operation. Many such cases since this ruling have been dismissed as a result of the accused not being able to confront and question witnesses against her.

In 2010 California courts overturned red light violation convictions stemming from traffic light camera usage because of this case.[43] If a traffic light camera was the initiator of a citation in any jurisdiction where such violations are criminal, the defendant should cite this ruling in her pleadings to the court. For places where these violations are civil, applicability is not as clear. Since the case law is relatively new and the income generating stream is uncertain, the Sixth Amendment may hold for a while where the offense is criminal. However, betting on it staying this way is probably a losing wager.

For this type of case, government officials will not likely bring the video or picture of the alleged violating vehicle to court, which should result in an immediate dismissal because there would be no physical proof of any wrongdoing whatsoever in that instance, assuming you state this fact. They will be happy to find you fully responsible if you make no mention of this blunder. Even if they did bring any photographic or videographic evidence, there is no human to question other than the law enforcement officer at the court who viewed it. As soon as the officer says anything at all, object to this as hearsay. Since the officer is relying on the observations of someone else (or something else—the camera), she cannot legally give testimony to prove you committed any offense.

Added to this, a host of arguments can be raised questioning the camera's reliability. Did it capture the alleged vehicle while it was already in the midst of the intersection when the light turned red? Were the lights synchronized properly? Were there extenuating circumstances that forced the alleged vehicle to cross the intersection after the light had turned red, such as being put in a compromising position by a passing emergency vehicle? These questions and others are difficult to answer after the fact because the traffic light camera and law enforcement's corresponding delayed notification by U.S. mail of the alleged violation have effectively estopped, or prevented, the accused from defending the case. Essentially, the system has blocked her from gathering valuable evidence when the picture or video was created, which could have been done had she known there was a citation on its way to her mailbox.

Local ordinances permitting the operation of traffic light cameras may also conflict with or be preempted by state laws, and related citations issued in such communities can be nullified as a result.[44] Another consideration with purported violations recorded by traffic light cameras is that the judicial system frequently assumes the owner of the vehicle is the driver. This is a big assumption. Even if the driver is visible in any photograph or video taken by one of these cameras, there is almost no way she can be positively identified if she is wearing a hat and sunglasses. Wearing either or both while driving would make such a defense quite possible. In fact, with Big Brother and his cameras prolifically all around us *à la* the movie *Enemy of the State*, it might behoove any citizen to wear a hat and sunglasses while in public to avoid unwanted identification—just ask James "Whitey" Bulger who was hiding in plain sight for years exactly this way.[45]

Even minus the hat and glasses, there is a simple way to evade any false allegations of driving through a red light supported only by traffic light camera evidence. A receipt belonging to the vehicle owner with a date and time stamp close enough to the one shown on the citation is all that should be needed to discredit the violation if the receipt is from an in-person purchase she made far enough away from the location of said violation. If it would be physically impossible to be driving at the location and time indicated on the citation without traveling at a ridiculously excessive speed from the location shown on the receipt, the case should get tossed.

Not only should a date-stamped receipt clear the owner of any charges, but a receipt related to servicing the alleged vehicle might also have the benefit of clearing anyone else who happened to be driving the vehicle at the time and who actually may have disobeyed the traffic signal. For the most part, the vehicle owner is the person who is on the hook for the charge, but defenses include the vehicle being stolen, the owner not being the driver, and others. A small minority of states say the driver, not necessarily the owner, is the responsible party, with two requiring that the driver be identifiable.[46] Considering the amount of time and resources it would take to implement a search to identify a non-owner driver, it may not be economical for law enforcement to attempt it. Without access to mug shots of all the vehicle owner's known associates or acquaintances who could have been driving the vehicle at that time and place and without the owner identifying the driver, we say "good luck."

OTHER CONSIDERATIONS

For traffic violations not specifically discussed here, the preliminary steps to take in order to prevail when fighting them are nearly identical to the ones discussed. Be observant. Gather evidence at the scene. Research statutory and case law. And be cognizant of time limitations. Then generally follow THE PROCESS section below. Less common charges can be fought as successfully as the ones specifically scrutinized in this chapter. Just like any other legal challenge, analyzing the available data and being thorough are both part of the equation to an effective defense solution.

If possible, perhaps the best way to avoid having to pay any vehicular fines whatsoever is to get licensed and register all vehicles in a state where you will rarely drive. When fines are assessed in states other than the licensing and registering one, it becomes difficult for those states to collect them since their threat of not renewing a license or vehicle registration should not be a concern. One drawback is the potential of having your vehicle impounded during subsequent violations in the "foreign" state, but if there is no danger of this, it should not be a factor. Also, many states and Washington, D.C., are now part of a driver's license compact that provides reciprocity among its members when they try to collect fines outside their borders. The function of this network is to prevent a driver from renewing her license in her native licensing state when her license has been suspended or when she has a major outstanding moving violation on record in the foreign state. Non-moving violations associated with illegal parking, having tinted windows, and other related offenses are not supposed to be part of the information in this network.

Lastly, some states may resort to employing collection agencies for the purpose of collecting fines due. However, if a tarnished credit report is not a concern or if you feel you can successfully dispute the fine with the agency, out-of-state registration and licensing may be the most straightforward remedy for having to pay vehicular fines. Certainly, this tactic would eliminate the time lost to fighting violations in any state other than the one where your vehicle is registered and you are licensed. Many states require that you be licensed and have your vehicle registered there when you are a resident, but if you are simply visiting, even for a long time, the definition of "resident" might be subjective.

Before continuing, one point about traffic court worth mentioning is that it is probably the least painful place for you to acclimate yourself to the judicial system. It gives you practice, so to speak, in an environment less likely to have a major negative impact on your life. If you are ever involved in a more serious case, such as a divorce or criminal proceeding, without having previously experienced the courts, you would be at a *distinct* disadvantage by not knowing how the system really operates. This is why seasoned criminals sometimes fare better than the average person who fights a criminal charge for the first time—because they are much more familiar with the system's inner workings.

It is not recommended that you do something in order to receive a motor vehicle citation, but if you are issued one, it would be beneficial to fight the violation in traffic court just for the learning experience. Sitting for a day or two in a local courtroom and observing the proceedings is another way to get some exposure to the system's operation. It is still not the same as being involved in a case of your own, but it is at least a way to view court proceedings.

One thing that probably does not come to mind for most people is the strong connection between a simple civil traffic matter and a criminal case. One similarity between them is that, in either case type, the defendant is directly fighting the system itself. The judicial system is fought either directly or indirectly in all court cases, without exception, but only in these two types is the defendant fighting it directly. The number of both types of cases generated annually in U.S. courts dwarfs the number of all other types combined. In fact, in 2012 nearly three-fourths of all U.S. state and District of Columbia court cases were comprised of these top two alone, with approximately 54 percent being traffic and 20 percent being criminal.[47] While certainly quite interesting that the system generates its own work the vast majority of the time, this fact should not be at all surprising in light of what was explained about it in chapter one.

Another similarity between traffic and criminal actions is that bargaining is often part of the game in both. In criminal proceedings, something called "plea bargaining" is frequently used. This is done to minimize the courts' expenditure of time and money. In civil traffic cases, the same principle holds true. A type of bargain is often made in crowded traffic courts. Fines are generally reduced, and sometimes one or more of several charges are eliminated instead of having the case proceed to trial, also saving the courts time and money.

Deferred adjudication is a special kind of bargain wherein the accused is assigned a probationary period. If successfully completed, the charges are dropped at the end of that period. Fees and fines are sometimes still due under deferred adjudication, so this option might be one to consider when the chance to win is weak even under ideal conditions, that is, when corruption is minimal or absent. The benefit of such a deal might be to maintain a clean driving record. Having a relatively good driving record may be a prerequisite to receiving this type of disposition in some jurisdictions.

Still another similarity between traffic and criminal matters is that both support the legal system's parasitic feeder entities. In traffic cases, defensive driving courses, oftentimes called "traffic school" or something similar, are common and sometimes part of deferred adjudication as are anger management classes. The auto insurance industry also extends its hand to receive its cut in the form of surcharges levied against drivers with a certain number of moving violations regardless if any of them have resulted in accidents or not. In criminal cases, probation, parole, counseling, community service, alcohol and drug rehabilitation clinics, and a litany of other "service" providers are also fed because of the system.

THE PROCESS

Most traffic court cases follow the same general sequence of events as criminal matters. The summons, or the citation, is given by a law enforcement officer. This is then followed by an initial hearing, which is sometimes called "the arraignment," other hearings, a trial, and perhaps an appeal or appeals. At the arraignment or whatever hearing the accused is supposed to answer to the charges, personal experience of one coauthor has shown that it is not necessary to use the words "guilty" or "not guilty" when a plea is expected. If you have an aversion to either, words similar to "I'll just pay the fine" or "I'd like a trial" should suffice. Statements such as these are a little out of the ordinary and do not quite play into the system's general rules, guidelines, and expectations. The system may not stumble because of their usage instead of traditional plea words, but using them certainly does not give it any advantage either.

Some states, California for one, define the speedy trial clause mentioned in the Sixth Amendment of the U.S. Constitution to mean that a trial must occur within a certain time after initial hearing or arraignment. California sets that time at forty-five days.[48] If the case is not heard within this period, traffic violation defendants in that state should ask for the case to be dismissed. You might give kudos to California for this seemingly reasonable definition and apparently noble act, but not quite so fast.

That savvy state has cleverly concocted two exemptions as a work-around to this stumbling block. The first is that the opening phrase in the statutory code, "The court, unless good cause to the contrary is shown," is decidedly nebulous and gives the state leeway to do whatever it wants to whomever it wants. The second is due to the tight time constraint of the trial occurring within forty-five days—the stipulation that the state may threaten to deny any motion to continue that you file to obtain a respite for gathering evidence or for any other reason. An exception to the forty-five day requirement could then occur if you agree to relinquish your right to a speedy trial and allow it to take place after the time specified by law as a trade-off for allowing your motion to continue. There could be gamesmanship by either party regarding this time window, but in any event, you cannot be legally forced to waive any constitutional rights.

BUILDING THE CASE

The process of building a case as defendant has been implied earlier in the chapter with regard to taking photos, capturing video footage, making audio recordings, obtaining receipts, and collecting evidence in general. Certain documentation may be needed, depending upon the alleged violation. Zoning maps, mutual aid agreements between bordering jurisdictions, and Department of Transportation (DOT) road studies or engineering surveys of viable road speeds should all be analyzed for possible inclusion into your case as should statutory law.

Zoning maps are used to determine if zoning is residential, industrial, commercial, or otherwise for any geographic location where you get stopped for speeding. They are particularly helpful in states where presumed speed limits are the law. These speed limits generally vary by zoning type within a state. Suppose the location where you got stopped is zoned industrial. Also assume the state speeding statute is based on presumed speed limits and clearly indicates that the maximum speed in such an area is 45 mph.

If you were cited for driving 44 mph in this type of zone that had a 35 mph posted speed limit, then the DOT speed study or engineering survey should be consulted. Check to see if the posted limit of 35 mph overriding the statutory presumed speed maximum of 45 mph is justified. If neither resource indicates there is a reason for lowering the presumed limit of 45 mph to 35 mph as posted, it should be so stated in a motion to dismiss and be provided to the court or be part of your defense argument at trial. Even if the posted speed limit appears justified according to the DOT, relevant case law should be researched to see if the presumed limit trumps the posted limit.

Mutual aid agreements are common between neighboring jurisdictions. They basically give general guidance about the circumstances under which a local law enforcement officer can cross town, city, or state lines in the performance of official duties. Usually, state police have jurisdiction entirely within their state, whereas federal marshals and agents have jurisdiction everywhere in the country, and city or town police have jurisdiction only within their city or town. If a stop that resulted in a citation occurred across town, city, or state lines, both statutory law and the relevant mutual aid agreement, if any, should be checked to see if the officer had legal authority to make the stop and write the accompanying citation in the first place. Oftentimes she does not.

Reading the Law

Sometimes analyzing sentence-by-sentence the statute allegedly violated will reveal some pleasant surprises, such as not really having to stop while making a right turn at a red light in Florida at intersections where right turns on red are permissible.[49] Contrary to popular belief, some statutes are not too lengthy, especially ones relating to traffic. Some are actually single sentences. Sometimes a law may indicate that something must be done by a peace officer for it to apply. Consider the following simple single-sentence Rhode Island statute, § 12-7-19.

"Any member of a duly organized municipal peace unit of another city or town of the state who enters any city or town in close pursuit and continues within any city or town in such close pursuit of a person in order to arrest him or her on the ground that he or she has violated the motor vehicle code in the other city or town shall have the same authority to arrest and hold in custody the person as members of a duly organized municipal peace unit of any city or town have to arrest and hold in custody a person on the ground that he or she has violated the motor vehicle code in any city or town."

For a local Rhode Island law enforcement officer to have jurisdiction when crossing city or town borders, she must actually arrest the driver of the vehicle, regardless of the motor vehicle violation, in order for this statute to apply. However, an arrest for a simple speeding charge or another minor offense could warrant a lawsuit against the officer and city or town for false arrest. Once again, the rules made by government officials can be used against them. As in this instance, legislators often do a poor job of sealing everything tightly when revamping laws and introducing new ones, which they love to do quite frequently.

Therefore, following the letter of the law in Rhode Island, a case wherein a driver's speed is measured in one town but the stop is finally made in another neighboring town without any arrest of the driver might have to be dismissed for lack of jurisdiction. If the authority to cite the driver is not supported by any mutual aid agreement allowed by law, then the case should be dismissed. Mutual aid agreements can also be poorly written—and not always cover all possible scenarios for traffic stops or address all desired legal issues of importance to their parties.

Requesting Information from Law Enforcement

During discovery, a request for the operator's manual of the radar, lidar, or other device used when vehicle speed measurements were attempted should be made to the ticketing agency for speed-related citations. Calibration dates and method of calibration for the speed measuring device along with the testing certification for the calibration tool itself should also be requested. Additionally, requesting a copy of the notes made by the law enforcement officer who cited you and a host of other information regarding citations issued for moving violations should be part of your REQUEST FOR PRODUCTION OF DOCUMENTS (see appendix).

In fact, some matters can be won via the mere act of requesting information. The law enforcement agency may be too lazy to respond if the demands are arduous enough. When this happens, the prosecution might pre-dismiss the case so that on trial day when your name is called in court, the trial is over before it starts. If not pre-dismissed, the claim to make before the court as defendant is that without the requested information being supplied to you as required during discovery, you cannot properly defend the case. The plaintiff is typically given another chance to respond, or the case is dismissed outright. In the event law enforcement fails to respond, a motion to dismiss can also be filed before trial in an attempt to save the time of going to court on trial day (see appendix). One author has been successful doing this.

It is nice when law enforcement agency personnel do not respond to the informational request you made during discovery since it should lead to an easier win because of the argument presented in the previous paragraph. However, it can also be helpful when they do respond because you can then look for inconsistencies among the documents supplied by them and, furthermore, discrepancies between their evidence and yours. If you are given copies of registration and vehicle speedometer calibration certificates for the vehicle supposedly used by the citing officer but the VINs on each do not match, then that would be one example of an inconsistency. The officer's notes stating that the roads were wet, but your photographic evidence collected at the time of the stop picturing the officer's vehicle and dry road surfaces, would be an example of a discrepancy.

Subpoenas, Depositions, and Motions

There may have been other drivers stopped for the same reason as you or bystanders at the scene, but nobody in either group is able to provide a supporting affidavit because the police did not allow you to communicate with them or let the other drivers leave before you could. If so, subpoenas may need to be issued requesting their presence at trial as witnesses. It may be nearly impossible, however, to contact these people if you did not have a chance to speak with them and exchange contact information. The claim can be made that, without the others' testimony or knowing their whereabouts to subpoena or depose them, it is damaging to your defense. Proof that these unreachable witnesses exist could be presented to the court in an oral or written motion. In the case of other drivers, such proof could include their license plate numbers and vehicle descriptions you had shrewdly gathered in writing or captured by photo or video at the time of the incident. For bystanders it could simply be photographs of them.

Depositions are sometimes useful, for instance, when witnesses may not be available for trial. An affidavit can almost be considered a written form of deposition and is usually sufficient in most traffic cases. In matters handled by lawyers, there may be more of an inclination to conduct depositions for strategic reasons. Deponents may become agitated and reveal information that could normally be concealed with a simpler affidavit. If you wish to depose someone, research the relevant rules of procedure to ascertain the steps that should be followed in order to do it.

Motions can be filed for dismissal if witnesses are not available, discovery requests go unanswered, or jurisdiction is not valid or for other reasons. They can even be filed for violation of the Fourteenth Amendment's selective enforcement clause, but you will need to prove that there was a specific and improper motive to cite you. For example, suppose you are the neighbor of a law enforcement officer and happened to throw a party without extending an invite or accidentally hit her pet with your car. If you are selectively chosen from a group of "violators" driving the same speed a short time thereafter, stopped, and cited for speeding, your chance of victory with a motion to dismiss based upon selective enforcement increases. Motions can also be filed for a continuance because of sickness, medical procedures, or memorial services on the scheduled trial day or for other purposes and at just about any time during a case from its inception to its final appeal in the highest court. Rules of procedure for the particular jurisdiction need to be consulted to determine established timelines for submission of all such motions and others.

THE TRIAL

If a traffic trial is something you have never experienced, practicing with people beforehand may help. Practicing a trial was covered in the Performing a Practice Trial subsection of chapter nine. If you intelligibly present your case to someone outside court, then you should be comprehensible by the judge inside court, assuming she is not mentally challenged. Know that there is no shortage of idiots in our system.

Once all the heavy lifting is done prior to trial, the next step is the trial itself. It is usually a good idea not to go to court on the trial date assigned at the arraignment unless you are certain of a "slam dunk" victory, and there is virtually never a "slam dunk" in the legal system—at least not for the average powerless person or entity in today's day and age. Ticketing agencies inevitably arrange all their court cases so they fall on a particular day of the week or month to allow the agencies to get the biggest bang for their buck. It is not cost effective for their minions to go to court sporadically throughout the month to prosecute a smaller number of violations here and there.

If you go on the date assigned at the arraignment, it is likely the citing officer will appear unless she is sick, dead, or on vacation or had the opportunity to perform higher paying detail work. Postponing the trial to a date selected at random will increase the chances of a no-show. One benefit of civil traffic cases is that the parties sometimes do not have to agree on the date for a rescheduled trial, so this is like a "free spin" for the accused.

On occasion, the stopping officer is not present at the arraignment, and another officer is there instead representing several from the law enforcement agency. The representative has been known to agree to a day for trial that the stopping officer will not attend. This is unfortunate for the government but fortunate for you. The plaintiff may go so far as to call you later and say something like, "We need to move the trial date because Officer Beesley cannot make it on the day you chose," perhaps even incorrectly implying you chose the date. Do not fall for this trick—you can stay with the scheduled court date and are under no obligation to change it in order to assist the government.

With respect to no-shows, going to trial with your only defense being the expectation that the stopping officer will fail to appear is *not* the best-laid plan. Chances are you will be wasting your time. Many people seem to try this mundane and nearly useless tactic. Have at least one solid legitimate defense and a backup or two, if possible, to fight the violation. If one argument fails when presenting a case, another may not. All it takes is one valid argument in a set of several in order to nullify the violation. Lawyers do this all the time in their work, making a plethora of legal arguments supporting their claim in hopes that at least one will secure victory.

About half the country's states allow jury trials for simple traffic cases. Some allow jury trials from the beginning. Some allow them at a trial *de novo* following an initial "responsible" or "guilty" finding. Others allow them upon specific requests from the defendant. Some traffic courts require the ticketing officer to be present at a trial *de novo*. Others require you to file notice prior to this kind of trial asking that the citing officer be present if you want her to be. In jurisdictions where the officer is not required to appear, her testimony may be presented through her written notes and the citation itself. Of course, this would be hearsay the moment anyone but the ticketing officer testifies to either of them and would also violate the confrontation clause of the Sixth Amendment when the charge is criminal in nature. However, recall from chapter five that it is perfectly alright for the system to break its own rules.

Note that a minority of states allow a trial by declaration in which everything is accomplished in writing via U.S. mail in lieu of a trial in court. The nation's capital calls it "mail adjudication." This type of trial/adjudication is also like a "free spin." Police officers get overtime, quintuple time, or whatever ridiculous amount it may be for appearing in court, but they only get straight time for doing paperwork. Although the courts reduce their daily workload with trials by declaration and mail adjudication, an officer may be less inclined to submit documents to the court when she really has nothing financially to gain. Without any rebuttal to the forms you submit, the case should be dismissed. Even if the officer submits paperwork and the case is lost, a conventional trial, usually a trial *de novo*, or an appeal should still be an option.

Jury Composition

Just as trial preparation is a crucial factor for successful presentation of a case in court, jury selection is a crucial factor for getting a verdict in your favor. It may be obvious to some, but allowing anyone who is ex-police, a relative of police, or active police to be members of a traffic (or criminal) jury is like sitting in "the chair" and telling them to throw the switch. During the selection process, you normally want to eliminate any members of the system, including court clerks, lawyers, police, federal agents, and correctional officers, and any members of the system's parasitic feeders or associates of these members. Determining employment and relationships of members of the jury pool is part of the process.

Other people who might not be ideal as jury members for your traffic case include anyone who still believes that all law enforcement officers are always truthful. Add to this group individuals who have never faced the same charges as you, people who have never owned a vehicle or who do not drive much, and anyone who has won legal battles of her own under the same officiator or in the same court and may feel obligated to the system. Others may also include those who have a friend or relative injured by someone found at fault for the same thing with which you have been charged and anyone else who you think might be biased against you even if it is just a gut feeling. You should question jury pool members to see if they fit into any of this subsection's classifications and try to remove them if they are not disqualified by the judge or prosecutor. As a last resort, peremptory challenge allows dismissal of a potential juror for any reason. The number of allowed such challenges varies nationwide. They act as your trump card and should be used only when needed.

While in Court *Pro Se*

While in court, keep in mind that you are metaphorically a "black box" to members of the legal system. They see what goes in. They see what comes out. But they have no idea what is inside. Your view of them differs substantially. You know they are judges, clerks, police, and lawyers, and if you have read the first parts of this book, you know they can be corrupt and break laws and their own rules. You know what to expect of them. Conversely, they do not know what to expect of you. This can be yet another advantage to beat the system at its own game.

It has been said that if you proceed *pro se*, the system will hold you to the same standard as it would any lawyer representing you. This is not necessarily true. The system will normally hold you to a *higher* standard than it will a lawyer. This is because it resents outsiders encroaching upon its turf and wants to dissuade you from eating into its business revenue stream. If you are well prepared, there is no reason you should have difficulty attaining that standard—barring corruption in the given court.

Understand that choosing to self-represent can introduce some undesirable consequences for you. The system will try to discourage it in many ways. One of which is to disallow the electronic filing of documents. This privilege is extended to counsel but not to an unrepresented party in the U.S. District Court for the Central District of California under local rule 5-4.2.[50] This is just one example. Be sure to check rules of procedure in traffic court for similar restrictions.

Opening Statement

Pay attention when you are in court. When your case is called, you will most likely be entitled to an opening statement. Details about any allowable opening statements should be clarified in the appropriate rules of procedure. If you are defending in front of a jury, do not hesitate to use every second of allowable time if necessary. The court will try to mow right over opening remarks and get straight into testimony, but to hamper the system's enthusiasm and endear yourself to the jury, present your opening statement. It should be well-written and rehearsed. Have it memorized, or if you think nerves may overwhelm you on trial day, have it on hand in its entirety or in notes so that you can say exactly what you intend.

Standing is preferred when addressing a jury. A subliminal goal here is to talk and act in such a way so as to befriend the jury and paint the prosecutor and judge as Satan and Lucifer incarnate, respectively. Depending upon the judge, prosecutor, and personnel comprising the jury, this may not be too difficult to do. This is not to be done overtly but in a subtle fashion by using body language and different tones and intensities of voice at just the right times. When describing how you will supply evidence that bolsters your case, use a friendlier, lower tone and slightly less volume. When stating how the citing officer could not be correct and how you will prove it, use a slightly harsher, higher tone, more volume, and possibly more hand gestures (just none with the middle finger).

However, if the trial will be decided by a judge, you simply want to lay the foundation of your upcoming defense in your opening statement. With a jury, there is not too much to worry about, but if you portray the prosecutor as Beelzebub, this might upset the judge if they are friends and therefore hurt your chances of her ruling in your favor. Obviously, so will portraying the judge in a similar light during a bench trial. The prosecutor is also entitled to an opening statement if rules allow the defendant to give one, but unless the traffic offense is a DUI or another serious charge, there is almost no chance of this happening—unless she wants to try to one-up you. If she does try to counter yours, you should take this as a good sign or at least as a compliment. This is something she would *never* have done for a lowly traffic violation. In any event, hers will likely be spontaneous and should not sound anywhere near as good as yours if you have put the time and effort into it.

Ticketing Officer's Testimony

After any opening statements, the ticketing officer usually gives her testimony. Object immediately if the officer reads from notes she made at the time of the incident and the proper evidentiary foundation has not first been laid. The evidentiary foundation has been laid only when the officer testifies that she cannot remember all the details of the incident she recorded in her notes shortly after issuing the citation and that she needs to refer to them to refresh her memory. After such statements, the officer can legally read from notes she made when she gave the citation. Without this testimony, an officer reading directly from her notes is hearsay and should be inadmissible.

Nevertheless, objecting may still be justified even after the evidentiary foundation has been properly set. Suppose you followed the TRAFFIC REQUEST FOR PRODUCTION OF DOCUMENTS TEMPLATE in the appendix and asked for a copy of the officer's notes during discovery. If they were not provided to you, ask for them to be stricken from the court record and ruled inadmissible.

If the judge does not disallow the stopping officer's notes, ask to read them. Point to your request filed earlier to refresh anyone's memory if necessary. If the judge still does not allow you to read the notes during a bench trial, you should know by then where your case is going. Nothing you do or say will prevent a ruling against you. At that point, you may want to threaten the judge with a complaint to the judicial governing board. This almost certainly will be a fruitless act, but at least it may force the judge to respond to the complaint later. However, if the judge is lazy and anticipates having to answer a complaint, your threat may lessen her partiality towards the plaintiff.

If the judge reconsiders or obliges with the notes upon first request, take your time and read them. Look for any inconsistencies, errors, or omissions. Compare them to your notes. When done, only give them back to the citing officer if the evidentiary foundation has been laid. If not, remind the judge of your objection and ask for the officer to testify based on recollection of events and not from her notes. This may or may not induce the proper evidentiary testimony from the officer. If it does not, return the notes anyway if asked and pay close attention to the testimony.

Object if the ticketing officer attempts to assume facts not yet in evidence. Using words like "defendant's vehicle" or "defendant illegally changed lanes" should be phrased "a vehicle" or "a vehicle changed lanes." This is particularly important in the case of misidentification. If you allowed such statements without objection, you would basically be letting the officer connect you to an act that may not have been committed by you. Normally, after your objection to such phrases, a non-corrupt judge will ask the officer to rephrase her testimony or have it stricken.

Furthermore, object if "violation," "speeding," or any other incriminating term is used by anyone, including the judge, if not preceded by "alleged(ly)" any time before a decision on the case is rendered. You have not been found in violation of anything until then, so not saying "alleged violation," for instance, is assuming facts not yet in evidence. Finally, object anytime an officer or anyone else testifies that something was told to her by another person. This is hearsay and not allowed...if, of course, the system is playing by its own rules. An exception to hearsay occurs when the citing officer testifies as to what you said during the stop, which is allowed but may very well be a lie. If a lie does spew forth, this is when thinking quickly on your feet can be a lifesaver.

During cross-examination, ask how this statement you allegedly made was remembered so clearly. Also ask the citing officer if she is certain you made this statement. Take her answers with a grain of salt. Finally, ask if she has any recorded evidence of your particular statement. If the officer says she does not, which, of course, she should say, you then produce the recording you made without the officer's knowledge and play it back on your mobile device, dashboard camera, or other applicable multimedia device for the court.

You may immediately or sometime in the future face resistance from your foe by being accused of violating relatively new wiretapping laws that law enforcement officers are misusing, just as they are civil asset forfeiture, the USA PATRIOT Act, and other such laws. They are improperly trying to protect themselves with wiretapping laws rather than using them in an effort to prevent terrorism, their originally intended purpose. However, courts are ruling, at least for now anyway, that making audio recordings, even if done secretively, of police performing official duties is protected under First Amendment rights. See *Glik v. Cunniffe* and others.[51] [52] [53]

At this point, you will have proved the ticketing officer is a liar and completely invalidated her testimony in front of the judge or jury. You have not won yet but are well on your way, particularly in a jury trial. When it comes time for closing statements, mention her "amnesia" to the judge or jury. If the officer contrived statements that she said you made during the stop, her version of events regarding the whole affair is equally suspect, if not overtly false.

Presenting Your Case

Next, you will get to cross-examine the officer who stopped you, testify on your own behalf, and present evidence, generally all done in one lump sum. If you bagged her testifying perjuriously about statements you never made, she may be antsy at this point. This is the opportunity to go for the throat. Start with questions such as, "Since you can't seem to recall what was said, how can you be so sure that the vehicle you thought you saw [doing whatever it was the officer said she observed] was my vehicle?" If you found any errors in her notes, you can then magnify them and ask how she could have made yet another mistake. Bolster this with any physical evidence you may have, such as photographs, that contradicts her testimony.

Lastly, call witnesses if available. This should be a nice little surprise for the plaintiff since, in our experience, the plaintiff *never* asks for anything from the defendant during discovery in minor traffic cases, which could easily be done to identify any potential defense witnesses. This is when being the "black box" described earlier is a huge advantage. Now you call your witnesses who have been sitting across the room from you concealing the fact that you even knew each other. Better yet, they could have been waiting outside the courtroom the whole time so that if witnesses were ever ordered to leave the courtroom for any reason, your hand would not have been inadvertently revealed.

If anyone says your witnesses should have signed an attendance sheet or done anything else to make known the fact they are witnesses, just play dumb. If they do need to register upon arrival, they can simply do so as observers of court proceedings in order to maintain anonymity. Now is when you put the final nail in the coffin. Question each witness about defense testimony or evidence you want to support or plaintiff testimony or evidence you want to refute. The plaintiff will have a chance to cross-examine your witnesses, but it is highly unlikely she can do anything or pose any question at that point to discredit any witness who has already further discredited the citing officer.

Closing Statement

Once all evidence, sometimes exhibits marked starting with the letter "A" and continuing sequentially through the alphabet, has been presented and all testimony has been given, the judge may ask the parties if they have anything further to add. At that time and if allowed by court rules of procedure, you can say you would like to make a closing statement. Most likely, closing statements are allowed—but once again steamrolled by the court. Using the notes you made during trial in conjunction with the skeleton of a closing statement you made prior to trial, take some time to compose your thoughts and finalize your statement. If you have really hit it out of the park, your statement does not have to be long-winded—saying less might be better than saying more. In particular, highlighting any key points made during testimony might be all that is necessary.

Even if it takes a few minutes to finalize your statement, the worst that can happen is that your composition time is deducted from your total closing statement time. The prosecution/law enforcement officer may follow with a similar statement, but if she does, once again you will have made her do something she never would have done for a minor traffic matter. Generally, only during a trial involving a more serious traffic offense, usually a major criminal one like a hit-and-run or DUI, might the plaintiff give a closing statement. The judge normally renders a decision at the end of the trial or instructs the jury to deliberate and then render its verdict. Sometimes the judgment is delivered by U.S. mail after a bench trial instead of the judge rendering a decision in court.

APPEALS

If the case is lost, fear not; appeal may be an option. Many traffic cases have been won on appeal. An example of such a turnaround would be when a judge who is paid by the jurisdiction in which he hears traffic cases rules against the defendants 99 percent, if not 100 percent, of the time regardless of whatever case law is quoted, whatever evidence is presented, or whatever testimony is given. Such a scenario would clearly be a conflict of interest since the entity paying the judge would be the same entity benefiting from the revenue generated by the judge ruling against the defendants, but it does happen based upon experience of one coauthor. If an appeal is made to a higher court, it may not be in the same jurisdiction. In any event, it certainly should not be heard by the same judge; therefore, a solid, airtight case presented at the appellate level could have a much better shot at success.

Personal experience of the same author supports the premise that it is often possible to win a moving violation matter upon appeal. The data on this are elusive, but our suspicion is that the percentage of traffic cases won by defendants upon appeal could be higher than the percentage won at initial trial. The only drawback is that some states, such as Massachusetts, have been implementing ridiculous nonrefundable appeal fees in their attempt to curtail appellant customer flow in court—and make significant amounts of money in the process. This has benefitted Massachusetts considerably since fewer people are appealing violations than before these hefty fees were introduced.[54]

Another benefit of an appeal is that you are getting a fresh court date, possibly in a different courthouse. Since this date is sometimes set without input of the parties, you have a chance of it being one that the officer who stopped you may not desire. If the appeal is for a *de novo* trial, then a no-show by the officer should secure your default victory. However, if it is procedural wherein a higher court reviews the findings of a lower court, the ticketing officer or any of the plaintiffs are not typically required to appear since the case is reviewed strictly on the merits of law. The only requisite party in attendance is you, the defendant. The appeal will likely be dismissed if you fail to appear.

To be, or Not to Be—the Citing Officer's Presence

If the officer who cited you does not appear at the appeal hearing, the judgment may be reversed pending law, rules of procedure, and the current stage of the appeal. These factors should determine if the ticketing officer needs to be present in order for the court legally to rule against you. Some states require the officer to be present, whereas some require any officer within the same town, city, or county to be present, and some require no officer to be present—all at various stages of the case.

For example, in 2001 the Appellate Division of the Trial Court in Massachusetts ruled that the police department must send a representative to a *de novo* trial; otherwise, they lose the case. See *Boston Police Department v. Alfred M. Moughalian*, and refer to it in court if there are no officers representing the relevant police department at a Massachusetts traffic appeal immediately following an initial ruling against you.[55] The rules about forfeiture for failure of the officer to appear vary widely and should be consulted in the appropriate rules of procedure and statutory law. Some jurisdictions also have a subset of rules of procedure specifically for traffic matters. These rules supersede the standard rules of procedure normally applicable to a given type of case, be it civil or criminal as appropriate.

Some states (miraculously) have enacted laws that allow a defendant to be reimbursed litigation expenses incurred while fighting an unjust legal battle against a governmental entity. For example, see Rhode Island statute § 42-92-1.[56] If you finally prevail in your traffic case, much more could thus be gained than a mere dismissal. This is why keeping track of all your legal expenses could be important for a later motion for costs and fees supported by a statutory law like this one and its corresponding case law. Additionally, under certain conditions, you may be one of the rare individuals to *earn* money from a judge after litigating a motor vehicle violation or other types of cases! Accomplishing this notable feat will be discussed in the JURISDICTIONAL ISSUES section of chapter sixteen.

Chapter 11: Divorce Cases

Divorce is a game played by lawyers. — **Cary Grant**.

Chapter Sections

- Background
- The process
- Arbitration, mediation, and collaborative law
- The complaint
- Serving the complaint
- Answering the complaint and filing a counterclaim
- Building the case
- The trial
- Settlement agreement
- Appeals

BACKGROUND

Divorces are rather distinct among civil cases. It seems that either they are super-easy and painless or they are dogfights to the death, with nothing in between—occurring at either end of the spectrum. Most other types of civil cases, however, run the full gamut. The system prefers the latter, much more adversarial divorce for the obvious reason of drafting far more money into the legal industrial machinery. From the system's perspective, a long, bitter divorce is preferable to one in which a simple form is completed by both amicable parties and filed with the court for a minimal fee. It is not uncommon for a party's legal folder to be literally several inches thick when a messy, unpleasant, standard divorce is at hand and lawyers are involved—this is by design, of course.

One relevant point to be made is that many of the so-called divorce myth busters found on the internet are themselves perpetuating myths or at least revealing only partial truths because of the way they present statistics. One coauthor has repeatedly said that statistics are made to show whatever people want them to show. This is no truer than in the realm of divorce. Other sources of reliable data countering misinformation on such websites must be considered as does the sources' gender for many of these "myth busters."

Divorces in court are *supposed* to proceed according to law just like all other kinds of litigation. However, as shown many times throughout this book in its first two parts and with various case types here in part three, the system quite often does the opposite of its legal duties by breaking statutory law and not following case law, rules of procedure, and the U.S. Constitution. Divorce is no different. The system regularly operates this way, which is a valid reason to consider the alternatives described later in the ARBITRATION, MEDIATION, AND COLLABORATIVE LAW section. Such alternatives are certainly not the cure-all but are exactly that—alternatives.

Many states impose a mandatory minimum waiting period after initially filing the complaint, or "petition" as it is sometimes called, before their courts allow a divorce to proceed in them.[1] The original intent of such a requirement might have been to allow the plaintiff a "cooling off" period in case he might have second thoughts. Unfortunately for many people, this time is typically viewed by lawyers as an excellent opportunity to generate more business for themselves, which is akin to the way laws intended to protect the public are misused by law enforcement for their own benefit as explained in previous chapters.

Possible Paths on Which a Case Will Proceed

Notice that from a purely mathematical perspective, there are four possible paths for a divorcing couple to travel upon during their marriage dissolution in a standard court proceeding:

- Both spouses are logical and agreeable—litigants get through the system unscathed.
- One spouse is logical and agreeable, but the other is not (two possible permutations of/paths for these)—litigants get burned by the system.
- Neither spouse is logical and agreeable—litigants get burned by the system.

So, in terms of probability, there is only a 25 percent chance of smooth sailing and getting through the entire process without being fleeced by the legal system. Only the first option yields the pleasant path. In the remaining three options, at least one party drags the other down the path of pain, which will be the focus of the analysis in this chapter. Therefore, projecting the approximated

75 percent of adversarial breakups onto the 50 percent of U.S. marriages ending in divorce means the system hits the metaphorical lottery about 38 percent of the time.[2] With the average price tag of divorce being about $20,000 as of 2013, or the cost of getting unmarried approaching the cost of getting married, this is a huge payday for the system nationwide.[3]

The high cost may be mitigated if one or both parties in a messy divorce proceed *pro se*. However, concern for minimizing expenses is not always top priority, particularly when blood boils and one spouse wants to punish the other. Lawyers absolutely love this. Certainly, it may be the most difficult type of case in which to represent oneself since keeping emotions at bay in order to ensure equitable settlement is a monumental task for the mere mortal. For those with intestinal fortitude, it can be done, perhaps unpleasantly.

Disguised Alimony

When children are involved, disguised alimony in the form of excessive court-ordered child support is a genuine possibility. If the parent responsible for these payments, typically the father, can convince an irrational spouse to utilize alternative dispute resolution (ADR), it could redirect such costs and attorney's fees towards future educational expenses for the children. As just explained in the last subsection, the more likely scenario is that money will be poured into the legal "black hole" roughly 75 percent of the time because of illogical or disagreeable behavior by one or both of the parents. ADR was covered in chapter eight.

In almost all states, the cost of mandated child support is much higher than the true cost of raising a child. This is clear from the fact that more than $110 billion has accumulated in arrearages nationwide through 2010.[4] It is clear from the fact that the governmental cost estimate to raise children and, therefore, the average support payment can be significantly higher than actual expenses.[5][6] Finally, it is also clear from the fact that the vast majority of states effectively double-charge the non-custodial parent by not reducing the computed annual support by the percentage of time the child spends with that parent, with the notable exception being Minnesota.[7] Although a full proportionate credit is not given in that state, about a 12 percent reduction in support is prescribed when the child spends up to 45 percent of the time with the non-custodial parent—a partial step in the right direction.

Most states, however, arbitrarily base their figures on the non-custodial parent's income, whatever it may be. Obviously, this is a nonsensical thing to do because it costs $X to raise a child in America, regardless of parental income, plus or minus a small amount, depending upon the cost of living in various parts of the country. The main reason the courts oftentimes gouge the non-custodial parent for support is practically to guarantee that no custodial parent/child combination will ever need financial assistance from the government. The twisted logic of it all is that most non-custodial parents, overwhelmingly fathers, are labeled "deadbeats" when they cannot continue making excessively high payments and are expected to bear the financial burden without governmental assistance. On the other hand, families with married parents or unwed mothers receive such aid when they fail to make ends meet.

It is also nonsensical, or at least adds insult to injury, when the custodial parent effectively gets paid for the privilege of raising the children. Many would argue it should be one or the other—a parent either gets the money or the children but not both. Additionally, the child support process is sometimes structured in such a way that allows the custodial parent to influence the children to dislike the non-custodial parent by telling them that support payments are insufficient to buy whatever is wanted or needed. So, it is lose, lose, and lose for the unfortunate non-custodial parent.

Prenuptial and Postnuptial Agreements

Not much will be discussed about prenuptial and postnuptial agreements because information about them can be found elsewhere. Nevertheless, suffice it to say that any rational couple getting married or already married should strongly consider one if they want to improve their chances of channeling money into better investment vehicles than potentially parasitic attorneys' bank accounts should they ever divorce. One author made the error of not being party to a protective marital agreement and regretfully defaulted into the latter option. Beware of making the same mistake. Of course, such an agreement may very well lose traction or be entirely disregarded in corrupt courts.

Other Considerations

The fact of the matter in most U.S. divorces is that the husband gets raked over the coals. There are the famed Hollywood types and other husbands rumored to have taken their elite wives to the cleaners, but if these cases are not urban legend, they certainly are few and far between. Not getting married in the first place, avoiding service of the divorce complaint, and untimely passing of the spouse are extreme and unrealistic options to prevent this unpleasantry from unfolding.

Understand that women are incentivized to divorce, which probably accounts for the fact that over two-thirds of all U.S. marital dissolutions are initiated by the wife.[8] There are several reasons behind this. As of 2007, 82.6 percent of all custodial parents were the mothers.[9] Because the underlying assumption is that mothers will get custody of the children of the marriage and get paid besides, clearly, the incentive is rather strong. If custody was automatically 50/50 as it should be without atypical circumstances, this prime motivator might be eliminated. Another reason women may be incentivized to end their marriages is the relatively new introduction of no-fault divorce, which is a rather oxymoronic concept since *all* other known civil case types require that one party be at least partially at fault in order to begin or at least legitimize a case. It now makes divorce unique among civil lawsuits.

The term "no-fault" means that no fault need be established against the defendant of a marital dissolution. It also means that the behavior or contribution of the parties during the marriage no longer has to be considered when dividing the marital property. No-fault's liberally biased ramifications are such that a cheating husband, for example, would not be penalized by the courts. Conversely, a wicked wife could get half or more of her husband's assets even though she contributed almost nothing throughout the entire marriage. Just as plea bargaining unjustly levels the playing field in criminal actions, no-fault divorce uniquely does so in civil actions. The other dubious distinction of divorce is that most states and the District of Columbia do not allow jury trials, which is one of the many erosions of our constitutional rights as stated in chapter one.

Arguably, divorce may be one of the most mentally exhausting types of legal battles for a person to handle *pro se*—perhaps only being eclipsed by a criminal proceeding. If one spouse is in love with the other who suddenly decides to end the marriage, it may be quite traumatizing for the loving spouse. Alternatively, divorce can provide a great sense of relief by finally breaking the chains of enslavement for some individuals. It all depends on the circumstances.

Jurisdiction is an important component of divorce. Just because people get married in a particular state or in the nation's capital does not mean the divorce must proceed there. Like any other type of case, laws for divorce vary nationwide, and the location where it is to begin should be carefully considered by both spouses. This is especially true if they have been living apart from each other in different states until the beginning of the process. Bear in mind that some parts of the country may have laws that are more beneficial to the husband, while others may have laws that are more beneficial to the wife.

The overwhelming majority of states and the District of Columbia require residency for some period, which can vary greatly across the nation, prior to filing for divorce.[10] People who move frequently, those in the military, for instance, should keep this fact in mind. It should be understood, however, that future modifications to any settlement agreement, judgment, or decree would likely have to be done where the divorce proceeded. This could be a factor if relocation is planned.

Logically, it makes sense that whoever contributes more in a marriage should walk away with more, just as in any civil suit concerning a business venture among partners. It is not necessarily this way with divorce, however. As an example, Massachusetts general law chapter 208, section 34, states, "The court may also consider the contribution of each of the parties in the acquisition, preservation or appreciation in value of their respective estates and the contribution of each of the parties as a homemaker to the family unit."[11] Contributing more than 50 percent in a marriage, including the raising of any children, theoretically should be beneficial for the contributor during Massachusetts divorce proceedings in light of this sentence. For the stalwarts who did the most for the family, sadly, it may only prove relevant during a trial if the case even makes it that far and sufficient witnesses can testify to the fact. With bench trials being the only option in Massachusetts, there is probably far less of a chance that the preceding statutory wording will factor into the ruling.

Regarding health insurance, the above Massachusetts law also states, "When the court makes an order for alimony on behalf of a spouse...said court shall include in the support order a requirement that the obligor...obtain [health] coverage for the spouse." In one author's experience, the court will require one spouse to carry health insurance for the other—even after the divorce is final—absent alimony obligations upon either party. Amazingly, insurance companies have to comply with this outrageous demand. Clearly, and shown yet again, the court breaks the law and its own rules unless, of course, it considers child support a form of disguised alimony that it partially is.

THE PROCESS

Like many civil proceedings, a divorce usually begins when a complaint is filed in court. Once begun, the case winds its way through the state or Washington, D.C., family court system during which time documents are filed and hearings are held, but it rarely ends in trial. Instead of trudging along the well-worn litigation path, the parties may try common forms of ADR, such as mediation, arbitration, or collaborative law. Regardless, the case is eventually disposed and gets filed in the court as a settlement agreement or judgment, with either typically being part of a decree.

Without appeal the matter remains closed until the spouse with custody of the children decides that two to three times the cost of raising them is still not enough money and moves the court to amend the child support order. While some custodial parents may wisely save excess child support for the children's future benefit, others may take a more wasteful approach, effectively sharing in the same lottery winnings as the system, and view the support period as an opportunity for an extended shopping spree.

The process of divorce through the courts is generally neither quick nor inexpensive. For obvious reasons, there is no incentive for the system to hurry a divorce. As part of the whole proceeding, the system may require "parent training," offer counseling, and involve many of its parasitic feeder entities, further bleeding at least one of the parents, if not both, when minor children are involved. It may go so far as to assess child support to the non-custodial parent for children who are not even that parent's children.[12] [13]

ARBITRATION, MEDIATION, AND COLLABORATIVE LAW

Divorcing couples should consider the more common forms of ADR, arbitration and mediation, if they want to minimize financial losses and perhaps minimize stress during the dissolution process. From a purely business perspective, recall from chapter two in the WHAT THE LEGAL SYSTEM IS section that there is almost no external competition for the system. The roles of arbitrators and mediators are somewhat of a small variation to that norm. Even in the absence of children or other dependents, it generally makes much more sense to follow an alternate course of action rather than to try and navigate around the pitfalls of the family court system. In fact, the argument can be made that of all battles in American courts, the legal system's involvement in family issues is where it belongs the least. Logically thinking, how could an entity that has no clue whatsoever about our familial relationships have any clue about fairly breaking families apart?

The other option relevant to this section, collaborative law, covers a broader range of topics besides divorce, such as prenuptial and postnuptial agreements. Next to an amicable, single-form, one-day-in-court, no-kids-involved divorce, mediation may be the optimal path to follow, but generally, arbitration and collaborative law are still preferred alternatives to the court system even though attorneys can be involved in any of them. With ADR a divorcing couple should experience better financial welfare, higher efficiency of process, less stress, and possibly other benefits as well— not to mention the bonus of avoiding any corruption in their local family court.

For the sake of brevity, we will not discuss all the intricacies of arbitration, mediation, or collaborative law. The first two were covered in chapter eight, and entire books have been written on all three subjects. The purpose of this terse section, as is the format in much of this book, is to summarize information that is not quite so obvious or is non-existent in other resources.

THE COMPLAINT

Like many U.S. civil cases, one party starts the divorce process by filing a complaint, also known as a petition, or by seeking ADR services. If the path most trodden is followed, that is, the one through the U.S. court system, a complaint gets filed, and the case begins. As in small claims cases, a divorce complaint is sometimes supplied by the court as a one- or two-page form of the "canned" variety that contains numbered items to be completed with specifics by the complainant. It is not known for certain, but the reason for this simpler mechanism over lengthier, more standard, self-generated complaints may be to allow spouses entry into the game sooner rather than later and facilitate contention between them. After all, the longer the game goes and the more confusing it gets, the more money can be made by members of the system. Some states and the nation's capital allow these simpler forms to start all divorces. Other states only allow them for divorces in which no minor children are involved. The remainder may not allow them whatsoever.

The numbered items on the complaint generally include names of spouses, date and location of the marriage, minor children of the marriage, and date of marriage breakdown. If there are minor children of the marriage, the complaint usually has a provision seeking their custody. Other claims that may be listed include those for payment of the mortgage, conveyance of the primary residence, possession and use of one or more vehicles, and financial support for the minor children and spouse. Add to this anything one would want that is owned or may have been purchased by the other spouse, perhaps even prior to the marriage, and division of the remaining marital assets. Any of the preceding may be allowed by the court, at least temporarily, in the form of temporary orders.

Normally, temporary orders are issued during the initial phase of a divorce, possibly when filing the case in court, which makes divorce fairly unusual among civil actions. Infrequently does a court issue a prejudgment attachment or another similar order in civil cases; however, temporary orders are basically the equivalent in a divorce. The court may ask the plaintiff for a financial statement as a requirement for issuing temporary orders. The (potentially untruthful) statement may be used as the basis to estimate payments the defendant is to make to the plaintiff or vice versa. Note that temporary orders can heavily favor the plaintiff and include not only the previously stated expenses but health insurance and other costs, which may be wildly excessive based on the input of that spouse alone. This becomes likely if the defendant is not present to object when such orders are issued, which is quite possible since most defendants do not know that the spouse is proceeding with a divorce and they are sometimes given before the defendant is served with the complaint.

SERVING THE COMPLAINT

If the standard divorce course is driven, service of the complaint must be completed by a court-approved method where the couple is proceeding with the dissolution. Like other civil cases, how and when service can be completed vary nationwide. Service at a place of employment might be possible except when the party to be served works on a U.S. military base or at another facility where special access is required for entry. If this is so, then he will have to be served elsewhere.

In some divorces and as explained in the SERVING THE COMPLAINT section in chapter nine, a hired court official who is supposed to serve a complaint may never do it if he finds it too difficult and instead side with the plaintiff by falsifying court documents saying that he did. Remember that court rules and statutory laws are often treated as mere recommendations by members of the system. If the defendant-spouse never gets served yet the official states that he was, the court will proceed full steam ahead. A lopsided default judgment can then be entered against the defendant. To begin reversing the damage, he must go to court and state that he was never served, which is somewhat meaningless because the intention was to bring him into court in the first place.

ANSWERING THE COMPLAINT AND FILING A COUNTERCLAIM

As typically done in other civil cases, an answer to the complaint should be filed by the defendant with the court of jurisdiction. Time limits for filing vary. The answer should address all numbered items listed on the complaint, with each response either confirming or denying each of these items. There is no need to get too fancy here.

A counterclaim can be filed against the plaintiff as well. Nothing elaborate need be claimed here either. In fact, experience of one author has shown that answering each item in the claim and then restating each of these same items in a counterclaim can certainly hinder the opposing party. Reversing these very same issues upon the plaintiff should have no more or less weight than they should upon the defendant. After all, if it is valid for the plaintiff to ask for something in the complaint, such as requesting the marital residence or custody of the children, then it should be equally valid for the defendant to ask for the same thing in a counterclaim.

Items listed in a counterclaim do not have to be limited to those in the original complaint; there can be special circumstances that dictate the inclusion of elements not specifically addressed. For instance, suppose your spouse had recently bought expensive jewelry under a business name or funneled funds into an offshore bank account while planning the upcoming divorce. You can state in the counterclaim that these acts were performed strictly to avoid inclusion of such assets into the division of the marital estate.

In a best-case scenario with minimal or no corruption, the judicial system's *modus operandi* in divorce is generally to divide things in what it perceives as down the middle between opposing parties. If your spouse asks for the world and you do not significantly oppose this, he may ultimately get half of the world. If he asks for the world and you ask for the universe in your counterclaim, it puts a whole new spin on things. Not many of your requests may be legitimate, but several of his may not be either. At the end of the day, the eventual middle ground will at least be closer to reality than to fantasy if this approach is taken. This is the same principle explained in chapter twelve's THE PROCESS section regarding plea bargains.

BUILDING THE CASE

If you are initiating the case and still living in the marital residence, it could be relatively easy since you should have access to all tax records, bank statements, and other data pertinent to the marriage. Getting access to this data may be more difficult, however, if you are the one served and subsequently evicted from the dwelling. If there is a time when you know your spouse will not be home and only older children will be present, it would be advantageous to go there and get whatever you need before any restrictions set by the court take effect. They will undoubtedly be excited to see you and let you into the home if the doors are locked and you do not have the key or the locks have been changed.

Once important records have been obtained, building the case is a matter of objectively looking for anything that will help present it to an arbitrator, a mediator, a judge, or a jury. For example, look for all evidence that supports your claim of cooking most of the meals, cleaning and maintaining the home, repairing the cars or other vehicles, caring for your children 75 percent of the time, and doing anything else that would prove your case.

Because you and your adversary know each other well, discovery can take a long time. Whatever your spouse's attorney requests during this procedure should encourage you to consider asking for the same in return and more. If he asks for federal tax records from 2012 to 2015, ask for federal and state records from 2010 to 2015, for example. If he asks for copies of appraisals of your gun collection, ask to see copies of appraisals of your spouse's rare coin and stamp collections from two or three different appraisers. Raising the stakes this way may make the other side think twice. It is not necessarily a disadvantage if your spouse has an attorney and you do not. In fact, following this suggestion is basically learning by example. Whatever action one party takes in the case, the court should allow of the other—barring corruption.

A divorce proceeding is actually rather narrow in scope because of the defining characteristics of marriage. For instance, only two litigants are involved in divorce, whereas several can be involved in other civil cases. Also, many civil actions pertain to motorized vehicles, personal injury, business dealings in a multitude of environments, and a litany of additional matters across different states. Because of their rather narrow nature, appellate or supreme court divorce rulings in the applicable jurisdiction should be considered potential resources. The finite characteristics of marriage minimize the variety of case law and maximize the chances that some of it will apply to your marital breakup, so researching it may prove especially helpful in litigating your own divorce.

As part of the preliminary work, doing some research on the judge or possible judges who may hear your case and reviewing their prior decisions would help determine if any may be biased. Bias may originate from experiences in their own divorces. Research may also reveal the likelihood of a judge awarding child custody to either the mother or father and reveal whether everything seems in excellent order with respect to his track record of following civil or family court rules of procedure and statutory law. If nothing disadvantageous to you is immediately found but you are assigned a judge who you later find has a conflict of interest, ask him to recuse himself. For example, a conflict may become apparent if you somehow discover that the judge plays poker with your spouse on Thursday nights. Be at the ready to threaten the judge with a judicial complaint if recusal is warranted but nevertheless refused.

THE TRIAL

As explained in chapter seven's JURY AND BENCH TRIALS section, criminal trials in the U.S. court systems are a rather rare bird. This is also true for civil cases, including divorce. Only 5 percent or less of divorces end in a trial.[14] [15] For the relatively fortunate individuals divorcing in Georgia, Texas, and a few other states, the possibility exists of the case proceeding to a jury trial.[16] [17]

Of all places in the U.S. judiciary where bias can live, family court makes the ideal home for it. Bias is a difficult thing to prove or disprove in legal matters. It is also difficult to avoid. If a judge is male and has been the victim of a lopsided divorce or is female and harbors hatred for all men for the very same reason, there is no way on God's green earth that these individuals will put aside their feelings towards the opposite sex and rule impartially in a marital dispute. Something in a case over which the judge is presiding may even trigger certain feelings that produce uncontrollable subconscious prejudice.

Ruling with bias of which they are aware is particularly likely when judges believe that they can do so unchallenged. With the exception of a jury trial—an available but limited option in Georgia, Texas, and a few other states—the biggest gamble in a divorce trial is that your ultimate fate typically rests in the hands of an undoubtedly prejudiced judge. One author has seen time and time again just how unfair divorce rulings can be in California because judges legislate from the bench, a far too common contemporary event. The division of marital assets in these instances was decided based upon how the parties presented their case and what the judge perceived to be "fair" under the circumstances in court, not upon the facts of the matter.

Even though jury trials are allowed in some states as previously explained, they all restrict what juries can decide. However, if you are a male and are certain your soon-to-be ex-wife is not forthcoming with all the facts during a divorce, opting for a jury trial where one is permitted and trying to include as many divorced men as possible should help even the odds despite any potentially biased female judge. Keep in mind that the opposing party will try to eliminate those men from the jury just as you should try to remove any bitter divorced women.

Once a jury is selected, the trial should progress as any would in other civil matters. The plaintiff and defendant may give opening statements if allowed by rule, present evidence, call witnesses, and finish with closing arguments. If represented, you should not rely solely upon your lawyer to catch everything and do whatever he is supposed to do. The more learned you are about the legal process beforehand, the better-off you should be. Take notes, and nudge your lawyer to object or object yourself if *pro se* whenever the opposition alleges facts not yet in evidence, testifies about anything someone else said, which should be inadmissible hearsay, or does anything else worthy of an objection.

One characteristic most likely unique to a divorce is that you know your adversary exceedingly well—probably better than in any other type of legal matter. You undoubtedly also know with near 100 percent certainty all the facts of the case, while nobody else does except for your spouse. Therefore, if you are somewhat knowledgeable about the system, it may be ideal to handle the case yourself *if* you can check your emotions at the door and proceed like a machine, which may be easier said than done.

As an example of factual knowledge, maybe your spouse owns a business in which you know certain dealings have not been completely clean. You might know that he spent $X under his business's name on a brand new luxury vehicle just to hide revenue from taxing authorities. If so, use this type of information as leverage to prevent a trial or as ammunition during one to woo the jury or judge. Just keep in mind that your adversary probably knows the facts of the case with the same level of certainty as you do, which is important to remember when thinking of putting any spin on them.

If forced to accept a bench trial as is so overwhelmingly common in America, be on the lookout for rule- and law-breaking judges. They will likely have been identifiable prior to trial, perhaps during related hearings, since judges usually do not go from uncorrupt judge to corrupt judge with the flip of a switch. Thus, you should have seen the corruption coming and have tried to prevent it. As described in the CONFIDENT, CAPABLE, AND CALM IN COURT section of chapter seven, attacking the power source of corruption directly is one of the best ways to stymie or neutralize it.

Recall from earlier in this chapter in the Other Considerations subsection of the BACKGROUND section, spouses in a divorce do not have many of the theorized advantages available to litigants in other civil matters, and no-fault divorce further flattens the playing field. Short of any marital agreement between the parties intended to alleviate that problem, the assets of the couple are basically divided in half from the court's viewpoint after a bench trial in a best-case scenario for the husband as previously stated. Keep in mind that real estate; pensions; retirement accounts; investments; land, air, and sea vehicles; or anything else of value obtained by either party or both is considered fair game for "equal" division—with the possible exception of bequests and other special items. No-fault divorce is possible in all states and the nation's capital.

SETTLEMENT AGREEMENT

In lieu of a trial, most divorces end with some form of settlement agreement, sometimes called a "separation agreement" or "separation and property settlement agreement," among other things, along with the divorce decree. The agreement will likely bear the date of the marriage, any children from the marriage, and other pertinent information in a brief section. If written by a lawyer, the agreement will typically be long-winded and replete with legalese spanning dozens of pages even for non-wealthy couples or the relatively straightforward divorce. It is reasonable to believe this is partly done for the purpose of making later modifications more costly for either party since legal complexity equals legal dollars. The intent and understanding of the parties and their property rights will most likely be part of the document. Other stipulations may appear in the introductory sections, such as each party having had the opportunity to be represented by counsel, the acts of each party being voluntary, and each party having had a chance to speak with a tax advisor.

As explained earlier in this chapter's BUILDING THE CASE section, divorces are narrow in scope, which means differences between settlement agreements from case to case should be minimal. Therefore, many lawyers do not draft these documents from scratch but simply cut and paste from a template or modify a previous client's agreement. If you have an attorney, be sure to check for any prior clients' "leftovers" that do not apply specifically to your case in any settlement agreement or documents you receive from him. If such errors are not corrected after enlightening him about them or new ones later arise, it might be time to hire another lawyer.

The agreement might cover the acquisition of future property, its independence of the agreement, and the indemnification of each party from future claims against each other for anything related to terms specified in the agreement. The division of the marital estate and any ramifications of breach of the agreement may likewise be included. It might also include relevant exhibits, explain exclusive terms of the split, define a breach of terms clause, and specify independence of the agreement with respect to other matters. Like most contracts or legal agreements, there is generally a severability clause allowing the remainder of the agreement to stay in force if a portion is later deemed invalid. Sometimes governing law, attorney's fees, absorption of existing debt, maintenance of a life insurance policy with the (ex)spouse listed as beneficiary, and various other provisions are elaborated in the agreement.

Children of the Marriage

Custody and visitation are usually defined in the settlement agreement if there are children of the marriage. A tough decision generally for the non-custodial parent is to decide whether to keep pouring money into the legal "black hole" and fighting for custody. The alternative is to relinquish custody of the children to a potentially lesser qualified parent and redirect whatever funds remain to better causes. Some of the content in the agreement's custody and visitation section may be completely ludicrous. For instance, being respectful of the other parent could be included; however, this and similar considerations can in no way be verified or enforced when children are mainly in the presence of one parent at a time.

The system likes to use the term "visitation" to designate how and when children will spend time with the non-custodial parent. This makes it sound as if spending time with them is a special privilege—similar to visiting incarcerated people. It might not do much, but you can send a subtle message to the system by replacing the term "visitation" with "co-parenting time" in all court documents before signing them. Time spent on an ongoing basis, during holidays, and on vacation should be clearly elaborated in the agreement and perhaps annotated with your new term.

A potential sore spot that may trigger a fierce battle is the one regarding the custodial parent attempting to relocate with the children outside the residing state of the non-custodial parent. If you are the non-custodial parent, beware of this possibility and address it in the appropriate section of the agreement, perhaps by ensuring that your written consent would be needed to make the move. Some states allow relocation of children out of state via a typically nebulous clause of law that basically gives the court the prerogative to do whatever it wants.[18] Child support, emancipation, education, and related issues should be addressed in the same section where other matters related to the children are addressed. Handling of emergencies and defining who will be claimed as tax exemptions by each parent should be included too.

Other Considerations

The remainder of the agreement may address miscellaneous issues concerning every subject imaginable. The court may require one party to carry health insurance for a new spouse and the ex-spouse, as ridiculous as it sounds. Alimony for either party or its exclusion should be clearly stated in the agreement. Tax-related issues, such as those regarding indemnification of penalties incurred from past due taxes, may be included as well.

Beware in any final copy of an agreement composed by the other party that your desired changes might not always be replicated one-for-one from the draft version. The opposing party may also try to make changes for that spouse's benefit in the final copy without redlining them and without informing you of them. Check for these kinds of differences between versions—digital copies will make comparison easiest. In fact, it would behoove you to check for such gamesmanship in any final version of any legal document prepared by an opposing party.

Modifications to the agreement can be made at just about any time post-settlement for issues related to child custody, support, or visitation or for any matters relating to minor children. As an example regarding support, the non-custodial parent may want to reduce the amount due because of the loss of a job, and the custodial parent may want an increase when the non-custodial parent hits the lottery. The court may allow a revision whenever the paying parent experiences a change in income. Another plausible reason for modification surfaces when custody should be changed because it has been delegated to an unfit parent who gets arrested frequently, has substance abuse problems, or beats the children, for example. Finally, understand that corruption is not out of the realm of possibilities as a reason for the court to change the agreement. Absent corruption, a motion to modify can be filed with the court to initiate the update.

APPEALS

Just because a divorce is "final" does not necessarily mean litigation is finished. It may not be common, but appeal is possible after a divorce trial. Remember that divorce trials are one of many types of civil trials, all of which are appealable provided certain criteria are met. If the reason for appeal is legitimate, the case could proceed to the appellate court. "Legitimacy" is defined as a mistake of law wherein a lower court misapplied law that materially affected the trial's outcome, a definition that is quite subjective. Misconduct and other issues can also legitimize appeal.

If the particular court where your divorce trial occurred is notoriously corrupt, proceeding onto the next step may provide relief if legal grounds allow it. Conversely, appealing may be suicide for an appellant who is jumping out of the frying pan and into the fire of corruption. Doing research before the need arises should shed some light and help you choose the optimal path.

When settlements are reached, appeal can be difficult, the reason being that both parties allegedly agreed to the terms. An exception may exist under special circumstances or if either party committed fraud in part or all of the agreement. Like most other appeals, new evidence cannot normally be introduced at this stage. Be aware of any time limits when filing an appeal. A thirty-day window may not be uncommon. Other time restrictions might apply to filing briefs after filing the notice of appeal and to responding to the opposing party's brief. Consult relevant rules for all time requirements.

Attorney's fees can be requested in an appeal, but one of the main drawbacks of a marital dissolution through the courts is that it places such a heavy financial burden upon a family because funds are drained from *both* parents if they are represented by paid counsel. In most other civil matters in which lawyers are involved, however, they are derived only from the family member who is a party to the case or from the family as a whole if more than one member happens to be a litigant. In either instance, legal expenses are not doubled for the family. Besides the initial divorce proceeding, which can be extremely costly because expenses *are* usually doubled when both spouses are represented, an appeal generally will make things at least *twice* as expensive as that. All things considered, divorce might be the only type of legal battle you might win but still lose.

Chapter 12: Criminal Cases

The only power any government has is the power to crack down on criminals. Well, when there aren't enough criminals, one makes them. One declares so many things to be a crime that it becomes impossible for men to live without breaking laws. — **Ayn Rand**

Chapter Sections

- Background
- Criminal offense classifications
- *Mens rea* and strict liability
- *Scienter*
- Entrapment and estoppel
- The process
- The complaint/indictment/ information
- Service of summons/process
- Arraignment
- Plea bargains
- Building the defense
- The trial
- Sentencing
- Probation
- Parole
- Appeals
- Clearing one's name

BACKGROUND

Statistically speaking, the average U.S. citizen has greater than a 6 percent chance of becoming a defendant in the U.S. criminal justice system based upon a population of 315 million people and 19.3 million criminal cases entering the state and Washington, D.C., trial courts in 2012.[1][2] Although this percentage is closer to zero than 100, more than one in seventeen is still an uncomfortably high ratio of people who have their destiny determined by a judge, jury, or prosecutor every year. These numbers disregard the fact that many criminal cases involve the same repeat "customers" and offsetting facts that some criminal cases involve more than one defendant and that the smaller contribution of federal data has been omitted. Also, the data are presented assuming an even distribution and complete randomness simply to illustrate the prevalence of the second most common case type being processed in U.S. courts.[3]

An analogy to our criminal system can be made with a swimmer, water, and fish. Suppose a skilled swimmer with open cuts is forced across a piranha-infested body of water. Normally, this person would have no problem, but with the cuts and piranha, prospects are bleak. If the swimmer could afford to purchase and use a protective suit or cage, the likelihood of success would be greater. The fact that she could wait until winter before crossing and simply walk across the frozen surface of the water is not disclosed. Additionally, nobody bothers to tell her that there is a walking bridge over the water a few hundred yards away.

In this analogy, the piranha are the legal system. The swimmer is a criminal defendant. The protective suit or cage is an excellent private attorney for affluent defendants. Not apprising the swimmer that she can wait until winter before crossing is the evidence sometimes concealed by prosecutors. And the walking bridge entirely negating the problem is jury nullification power. Of course, subsequent passes are much easier for the seasoned swimmer or repeat defendant in a real-world criminal case once she understands the predicament. Thus, being a novice can certainly be disadvantageous to the average first-timer.

Although criminal acts are sometimes planned, all criminal cases, at least from the defendant's perspective, are not. For those individuals who knowingly commit a heinous crime, being criminally charged certainly should fall into the realm of future possibilities for them, but understand that there is not a one-to-one relationship between the people who commit crimes and criminal cases in the courts. Quite often, real crimes go unsolved—more than 37 percent of murders and 59 percent of rapes according to the FBI.[4] Conversely, people are sometimes accused and convicted of crimes they did not commit. But in the event you are ever falsely accused of a crime and have the misfortune of seeing firsthand the very bowels of the judiciary, this chapter is intended to help you protect yourself from the reckless juggernaut otherwise known as the U.S. criminal justice system.

Many times, the system is not as concerned with apprehending the true perpetrator of a crime as it is with finding a person who can instead be held accountable, a scapegoat, if the evidence can be manipulated to convict her. It is not done this way all the time or maybe even a majority of the time, but it does happen frequently—possibly much more than most people think. Some substantiating proof of this fact is the large number of people who have been exonerated and released from prison and the projected number of currently incarcerated innocent people as presented in chapter one in the MASS INCARCERATION AND SOME OF ITS CAUSES section.

Contributing to the injustice is the contemporary need in our litigious society to hold someone accountable for every accident that occurs. For instance, if there is a vehicle rollover on a highway where someone gets killed, then something in the asphalt surfacing has to be to blame or, more specifically, the poor slob who laid it must be criminally charged and tried. The large corporation that manufactures the surfacing circumvents criminal penalties unscathed. Perhaps a private road inspector hired by the Department of Transportation or by another government agency gets crucified, while the agency and its agents easily deflect blame. This all occurs, of course, assuming the deceased driver of the aforementioned vehicle or the driver of another vehicle was not to blame, which may not be the case.

Unfounded criminal prosecutions can ruin people's lives beyond just the repercussions of the prosecution itself. A criminal case is sometimes used as a springboard to obtain a huge monetary settlement via a subsequent civil claim. Prosecuting the defendant is perceived as an unfortunate by-product of the process in that instance. A multitude of parties may be directly and indirectly involved in the latter civil action.

Although many life events are certainly quite tragic, it is not uncommon for the poor, hapless souls who are trying to earn a living to be criminally charged and punished, while the rich, large corporations are left with only paying the plaintiffs in any resulting civil claims.[5] Data from 2012 reveal that federal criminal cases involve business entities such as corporations and partnerships approximately 0.2 percent of the time, or once in every 450 cases, while the remaining cases involve individuals.[6]

Corruption in the criminal justice system is a major catalyst that makes prosecutions against individuals much easier, likely contributing to this lopsided data. Corruption can literally have a lethal effect on a person's future.[7] Therefore, this sector of the system is the least desirable place for it.

About This Chapter

When reading this chapter, remember that the system will break its own rules of procedure and laws in order to enforce a law or set of laws upon you. This probably happens quite frequently but goes undetected by the average person because she is unaware of the rules of procedure and laws or is misinformed by her lawyer as to how the rules and laws are "interpreted" by the system when no interpretation is necessary or should be done. Attorneys may consciously or subconsciously defend the system's actions and justify them with partial truths or complete nonsense. Thus, either through ignorance of the defendant or because misinformation has been introduced by her attorney, the system simply breaks the rules and laws without detection. Add to this the fact that the Bill of Rights has mostly been eviscerated, with any remnant rights having largely become a fairytale, and the system is now breaking the rules and laws it has overtly given itself permission to break in addition to the ones it covertly breaks.

The message is to beware of any nefarious activity by the system. Leeway and leverage to defend your case may depend upon who or what part of the system is doing the rule- or law-breaking. Two illustrations follow. A prosecutor hiding exculpatory evidence could be reported to the attorney general in hopes of getting her reprimanded or at least removed from your case. A motion for a new trial or another appropriate motion could be filed if your own lawyer has an illegal gambling habit or drug addiction, has broken other laws, or is simply incompetent because personal problems are interfering or have interfered with proper defense of your case. Of course, she should be fired for any of these reasons.

Obviously, with a tremendous number of criminal laws in America and with an exorbitant amount of case law, nobody can fully explain nor understand everything there is to know about criminal law in just one chapter. However, what *can* be explained and understood is the manner in which the criminal system truly operates and how to beat it at its own game. Keep in mind the intent of this chapter is not to help true criminals escape justice, which is probably a relatively small minority of people anyway. It is to help individuals who are falsely accused and those who break ridiculous, obscure, or unconstitutional laws that are designed strictly to generate business for the system or prestige for those who are a part of it. Protecting the citizenry from overzealous slimeball police and prosecutors who are trying to destroy people's lives for their own personal gain is the primary goal.

With the preceding in mind, atypical concepts and tactics in criminal law are presented in order to achieve that objective. The overarching tenet of this chapter is to *trust nobody* in the system during any criminal proceeding, and to repeat what was first stated in chapter two's aptly named section, trusting system members at any time is not recommended. Also, as explained in chapter ten, there are strong similarities between a criminal prosecution and a simple civil traffic matter. They are the only two types of legal battles wherein a person fights the judicial system directly. Furthermore, both have a form of bargaining associated with them, and both support the system's parasitic feeders. See the OTHER CONSIDERATIONS section of chapter ten for a deeper explanation and rationale about the benefit of getting practice in the system via traffic court, particularly as a precautionary measure for unforeseen criminal matters.

The Illusion of Legality

Finally, before delving into the crux of this chapter, know that criminal laws can sneak up on you. This is partly because of the wildly excessive number of laws in America as discussed in the REASONS FOR THE SYSTEM'S DECLINE section of chapter one. It is also partly because laws passed in recent decades do not require prosecutors to show criminal intent of the laws' violators. Read this to mean that you can be prosecuted for laws you had absolutely no clue you were breaking—even those you may have diligently tried *not* to break.

A study by the National Association of Criminal Defense Lawyers and the Heritage Foundation confirmed that legislators have been passing federal laws that increasingly lack any requirement whatsoever for violators to show criminal intent.[8][9] The study also found that any such intent included in relatively new laws tends to be vague and widely interpretative by prosecutors, thereby giving them more abusive power and opening the door to corruption even further.

The impact of these underhanded actions by our legislature and by others in power can manifest itself when starting a business, for example. You could easily find yourself and your venture embroiled in a criminal matter for violation of any such vaguely written or counterintuitive laws. Just because another business sells the same product, performs the same service, or does the same marketing as your new business does not at all mean any of it is lawful. Although it is completely immoral and illegal, remember that the system has multiple sets of rules that it applies to different people and entities. To minimize the possibility of being criminally charged, be sure to check all local, state, and federal laws prior to launching your fledgling enterprise to ensure that no facet of it is illegal. Doing so *should* virtually eliminate all chances of becoming victimized by the system when opening the doors to a start-up.

In exceptionally rare instances, an obscure criminal law will state that a warning shall be issued to anyone who violates it for the first time.[10] As much as this completely makes perfect sense to the average person who could unknowingly break one of many esoteric laws, understand that it limits some prospective income to the legal industrial machine. We do not know why the system extends this form of courtesy, but perhaps the income-limiting effect of a warning makes laws allowing the issuance of one so rare. Only a single statute was found that mentioned such a warning.

There is a strong similarity between our current U.S. criminal justice system and ancient Rome under Gaius Julius Caesar Augustus Germanicus, better known as Caligula. He would write laws in such small print and post them so high above the ground that none of the Roman citizenry could read them.[11] Then, when laws were broken, he took great pride in trapping and prosecuting his unwitting quarry. He certainly had the winning formula, unmatched by any government, until our contemporary U.S. criminal justice system decided to take it a step further.

Not only does the exorbitant number of criminal laws make the prevention of breaking some of them a near impossibility, but because of selective enforcement, our system creates the illusion that some illegal acts are legal. This is particularly true when criminal law does not reflect prevailing moral code or intuition and is not limited to conduct that is inherently malicious—certainly conditions under which the conduct itself might alert a potential offender that she may be violating the law. The discussion in this subsection certainly makes one of the most prominent points of this chapter and in this part of the book.

CRIMINAL OFFENSE CLASSIFICATIONS

Criminal offenses basically fall into three categories: felonies, misdemeanors, and infractions. Some are subdivided further, depending upon jurisdiction. For felonies and misdemeanors, some states and the federal government categorize them into subclasses using letters or numbers, such as "A" through "E" or "1" through "6."[12] [13] Felonies are considered to be the most serious offenses and are the most traumatizing to people charged with them. They are also offenses for which the clearest thinking is critical to defend the case successfully—not a trivial task even with the assistance of a good lawyer. But make no mistake; some felonies pertain to acts that are either innocuous or not that appalling and are felonious only by definition.

Consider the following gems from two randomly selected states. In Michigan it is a felony to commit adultery.[14] The lunacy of this law goes further, however. It defines the man guilty whether married or not, but the woman must be married in order to be guilty of this "crime." Wyoming has made it a felony to cut half or more of a sheep's ear.[15] It seems just as wrong, but to do this to less than half the animal's ear is quite legal. And who does the measuring? Furthermore, is the damage calculated by length, area, volume, or some wacky government-contrived capricious unit? We would not even venture to guess the number of such domestic laws in existence or the number of similarly outlandish new ones enacted every year.

Felonies also include murder, rape, robbery, and other real crimes that apparently do not seem to comprise a large enough segment of the legal business to keep the prosecutors happy and the courts busy. However, some felony statutes, such as the two preceding preposterous laws in Michigan and Wyoming, are created simply as a luxury for prosecutors to pursue good people, label them as criminals by putting them through the legal grinder, and keep the legal industry thriving by doing so.

Some may find it doubtful such ridiculous laws would ever possibly be used to criminalize someone, but rest assured that there are plenty of prosecutors out there who have no reservations doing exactly that. A Michigan man was charged with reading his wife's email, a felony that carried a five-year maximum sentence. More than two years later, the charges were dropped only because his ex-wife, who correspondingly had also read his messages, was the key witness in the case. The Fifth Amendment to the U.S. Constitution prevents self-incrimination, which clearly would have happened during cross-examination had she testified and would have led to her being charged with the same offense.[16] If prosecutors could have discovered a way to charge, prosecute, and convict them both, you can bet your bottom dollar they would have done so without remorse.

With so many nonsensical cases on record, albeit some not felonies, it is difficult to determine the one that takes the cake. The twelve-year-old New York City girl who doodled on her school desk and was handcuffed, arrested, and dragged to the police station is certainly in the running.[17] The arrest of the boy farting in class or the boy who opened Christmas presents early are also contenders for the blue ribbon.[18] [19] These all might seem quite humorous, but when the system has drawn a bead on your forehead, it is highly unlikely you will find anything funny about it then.

Misdemeanors are considered to be less serious than felonies but more severe than infractions. While sentences for felonies often vary from any term of about one year imprisonment up to and including the death penalty, misdemeanors usually carry sentences of anything longer than five days up to one year. Writing a bad check, public intoxication, and other such "atrocities" are crimes that are generally classified as misdemeanors.

Infractions are the newest category of laws. The first known related charges brought against someone in America occurred just over 100 years ago. Criminal acts of this sort are supposed to be the most mundane offenses and normally carry maximum sentences of five days but routinely result in fines only. Certain traffic-related offenses, attempting to purchase alcohol as a minor, and fishing without a license are sometimes considered infractions. Infraction convictions may appear on a criminal record just like misdemeanors and felonies. If they do, it is possible for them to have similar negative future consequences as felony and misdemeanor convictions regarding employment, adopting children, obtaining security clearances, and other important life events. Not getting convicted in the first place is top priority. Clearing a criminal record would be the second priority, which will be discussed later in the CLEARING ONE'S NAME section of this chapter.

At the federal level, "petty offenses" are defined as a group of criminal offense classifications composed of infractions and the lesser misdemeanors.[20] Obstructing the mail and trespassing, which are oftentimes misdemeanors and infractions, respectively, and other federal crimes that carry a maximum penalty of six months of incarceration usually are petty offenses. The U.S. Supreme Court has ruled in *Lewis v. United States* that defendants in matters of this type are not entitled to a jury trial—not even if the aggregate penalty of multiple individual charges themselves exceeds the six-month maximum.[21]

This means that someone could be incarcerated for well over a year, perhaps much longer, if she is prosecuted and convicted on three or more petty counts after a bench trial by some renegade judge. Under this newer classification of criminal laws, a conviction would result *without* the defendant ever having had a jury trial. Petty crimes now make it convenient for the system to process cases quickly by further stripping individuals of rights, particularly the right to a jury trial, finding defendants guilty, and generating revenue expeditiously without the nuisance of the U.S. Constitution getting in the way. It may seem as though we are being flippant with our discourse here, but rest assured that we are being quite factual.

In addition to laws created at the federal, state, and District of Columbia levels, ordinances are laws that are enacted at the town, city, or county level. They can be classified as either civil or criminal. Things get a little murky with ordinance offenses since they are not normally considered crimes, but in certain jurisdictions, some are, such as feeding the homeless in parts of Florida or growing vegetables on your own property in many parts of the country.[22] [23] Committing these and other similar "crimes" could land someone in jail who would and should never have otherwise seen the inside of one.

Ordinance transgressions that are not criminal should not appear during background checks, but those that are might. Understand that anything is possible in the legal system, even the seemingly impossible, depending upon who is doing the prosecuting, judging, recording, sentencing, checking, or filing—it just depends on what rules or laws are interpreted, twisted, broken, or created out of thin air at the time.

New criminal laws are enacted annually, but the supporting data found were quite limited and indicate that their numbers seem to be somewhat evenly split between felonies and misdemeanors. If the average of about thirty-four criminal laws enacted yearly in North Carolina from 2008 to 2013 is extrapolated to all fifty states and the District of Columbia, the result yields over 1,700 new criminal laws every year.[24] Considering the new criminal laws at the federal and local levels and the number of all non-criminal new laws, the grand total of fresh laws we are burdened with annually easily reaches into the thousands as speculated in the REASONS FOR THE SYSTEM'S DECLINE section of chapter one.

MENS REA AND STRICT LIABILITY

Based upon experience of one author, attorneys might not tell their clients the meaning of *mens rea* and strict liability. Both should be understood and are of prime importance in any criminal matter. "*Mens rea*," Latin for "guilty mind," in law means that people should normally be culpable for breaking criminal laws only if they have a guilty state of mind and awareness of their misconduct. People are supposed to exhibit this mental state when breaking severe criminal laws in order for them to be successfully prosecuted, although knowledge that a given act is illegal is not necessary for conviction of it.

Minor crimes, however, do not require an element of blame upon the offender and are therefore classified as strict liability laws. When a person breaks a strict liability law, a conviction can result despite not having a guilty state of mind. This means that the act of breaking the law itself is sufficient for someone to be found guilty of the crime. Some felonies and misdemeanors and most, if not all, infractions are strict liability laws.

The original purpose of *mens rea* and strict liability seems logical. One who is publicly intoxicated, a minor misdemeanor or an infraction, clearly has no guilty state of mind, whereas one who kidnaps another, a felonious act, certainly must. More serious crimes that have severe penalties should require a higher level of culpability on the part of the accused. However, relatively minor crimes for which the penalties are usually fines or community service, crimes like smoking or spitting in a public area, can result in a conviction with no knowledge of wrongdoing on the part of the offender.

Unfortunately, the guilty mind criterion required for obtaining some criminal convictions is now being largely ignored. Should you be charged with any obscure or insidious offense that you believe might deem some element of culpability on the part of the offender, research statutory and case law thoroughly to find supporting arguments in your defense if you certainly were unaware your behavior was wrong. Anyone charged with a non-strict liability crime who did not have a guilty mind could be found not guilty if the case was decided by a jury. Using this now bygone rule of the system against it may improve your chances of acquittal, particularly during a jury trial when jurors may not be so apt to brush *mens rea* aside.

A defense using *mens rea* might be possible for a known criminal act, such as murder, that truly was the result of an unfortunate accident. For example, someone could have been pruning a tree with a chainsaw while standing on a ladder and tried to hand the saw to an assistant, but the saw slipped and cut a major artery of the helper who later died from the wound. The pruner obviously had no intention to kill the helper; therefore, lack of *mens rea* could result in acquittal. Another example of a criminal case that should also be defendable under this principle could be one in which someone commits an obscure felony while trying to help someone else perform a routine task. Remember that no good deed goes unpunished.

SCIENTER

"*Scienter,*" Latin for "knowingly," is another term of which some lawyers might be unaware or keep hidden from their clients. It is similar to *mens rea* but has a broader application that can include civil litigation. For purposes of this chapter, *scienter* is required to be written into a criminal law that authorizes harsh punishment. It should be incorporated into many felony statutes. At least for obscenity statutes, absence of *scienter* would violate the due process clause of the Fourteenth Amendment during state prosecutions and thus render such statutes unconstitutional according to the U.S. Supreme Court in *Smith v. California*.[25] *United States v. Wulff* made absence of *scienter* in criminal laws that authorize harsh punishment a violation of the same clause of the Fifth Amendment during federal prosecutions regarding these laws.[26]

For criminal laws with severe penalties, their statutory wording needs to have some provision stating that breaking them must be done willfully, knowingly, intentionally, or recklessly as implied above. Regarding many prosecutions, including those based on alleged violations of obscenity laws, the government has become penny-wise but pound-foolish. For example, small or individual adult material retailers are sometimes prosecuted, while large distributors are completely ignored. If someone is charged with breaking a criminal law carrying a severe penalty but absent wording that says doing so must be done willfully, knowingly, intentionally, or recklessly, she accordingly has a chance of beating the charge.

A case concerning statutory rape could involve *scienter*. If it is omitted from the law the defendant has been charged with breaking, she might prevail by claiming the law is unconstitutional. In some states, she may also be able to defend herself by saying she did not know her partner was underage. Of course, that defense should become stronger the smaller the difference in the couple's age becomes. Technically, the two could be within a couple of days in age difference if one is of the age of consent plus one day and the other is one day younger than the age of consent, further illustrating the lunacy of statutory rape laws.

In fact, any law, exclusive of speed laws, that contains a specific age or measurement, such as the one about cutting half a sheep's ear in Wyoming, in which an infinitesimally small bufferless separation exists between what is legal and what is illegal is, by definition, a poorly written law. These kinds of laws open the door for absurd outcomes whenever they are enforced. As another example, successfully defending accusations of having pornographic content on your mobile phone because an obscene text was sent to you without your knowledge could strongly hinge on the decision rendered in *Smith v. California* based on *scienter*.

ENTRAPMENT AND ESTOPPEL

It is not known for certain, but with the level of corruption in the system, entrapment may be a common occurrence. It can be loosely defined as luring a person to violate some criminal code so she can be prosecuted for it. If you are the victim of a rigged criminal prosecution, be on the lookout for this and do more research if it is relevant to your case.

Estoppel is a little more esoteric but can be relevant in criminal cases based upon the experience of one coauthor. It can be basically defined as a set of legal doctrines that prevents an individual from asserting a fact or right, from doing or not doing a certain thing, and more. In one form of it, an individual's actions are constrained based upon the actions or inactions of another party thereby preventing the individual from doing something she would normally do. Conversely, an individual's actions might be dictated based upon the actions or inactions of another party thereby provoking the individual to do something she would not normally do. The reference to it in chapter ten in the "Accusations" by Traffic Light Cameras subsection is one example of the many forms of it. Neither of the two terms in this section is typically mentioned by lawyers in criminal proceedings, but either can be of extreme importance, depending upon the facts of the case.

THE PROCESS

Initially in a criminal proceeding, law enforcement will contact potential victims, witnesses, and suspects and investigate. Many sources say that rule number one is *never* talk to police without an excellent lawyer present during formal interrogation, general questioning, or any other communication even if you are 100 percent innocent—it will not help you and instead may harm you.[27] [28] There are scores of resources explaining why you should heed this warning, which will not be repeated here. Furthermore, a competent attorney not only acts as a legal advocate but also as a witness during these discussions.

It is critical to understand that simply *remaining silent is no longer invoking the right to remain silent* when police speak to you. The courts have now ruled that, in order to assert this right, a person must verbally state that she is unequivocally remaining silent, a ridiculous contradiction.[29] *Miranda v. Arizona* has now been somewhat abridged by a newer U.S. Supreme Court ruling and will remain so until the judicial system opts to quash this right even further.

Additionally, as unbelievable as it may sound, false confessions are a genuine danger when talking to police alone. Keep in mind that when they have someone isolated in an interrogation room, there is basically an endless stream of officers who effectively tag into the ring and continue the conversation for the parting officer. They are on the clock and getting paid to swap places every hour or two. You as the accused, on the other hand, have to sit there for four, eight, or twelve hours or until they decide to let you go. People have made self-incriminating statements, including false confessions, either inadvertently because of fatigue or deliberately just to get out of there, only to learn later that it will be like trying to un-ring a bell to reverse the damage.

If there comes a point in any legal proceeding when it is your word alone against a law enforcement officer's regarding whatever was said or done during any interview process, rest assured that the court will favor her word over yours. Even if you have a criminal defense attorney with you, her testimony to the contrary or recorded video or audio evidence obtained during your interview may not be enough to guarantee that the legal system will not side with law enforcement. However, a knowledgeable lawyer should vehemently oppose questions that cannot legally be asked during any examination session. Criminal proceedings may be the only type of legal case in which having an excellent private attorney is practicable and warranted. The operative word in the previous sentence is "excellent."

Depending upon the charges, the system may impose a restraining order against you at the request of alleged victims in the case, which may precipitate another legal action outside the criminal matter. This is not uncommon and is the cancer of the system metastasizing. The more accusations and charges the system can throw at you, the more it will make you look like a criminal, even if you are not, and increase the system's chances of getting something to stick. It is best to resist as much as possible anything that the system tries to pin on you because doing so should put a damper on its negotiating power later.

When all is said and done, the case will most likely end in a negotiation phase. If you provide the system with as few bargaining chips as possible, you should receive a better deal when it comes time for a plea bargain. If you give the system the world initially, it will leave you with a more costly uphill battle to get an equitable settlement or win your innocence and clear your name.

Once you have been formally charged, it means the wheels of "justice" have been set into motion to begin grinding your future into a fine pulp. The sooner you can stop these wheels, the better-off you should be. This is by no means an easy task and may take all your reserve, willpower, and focus and perhaps much money—and like stopping a car, the longer you let either accelerate, the more it will take when applying the brakes to bring either to a complete stop.

THE COMPLAINT/INDICTMENT/INFORMATION

Commencing many criminal cases, law enforcement agents file a criminal complaint or an information in court and sometimes arrest the accused and hold her in custody. Complaints and informations can be written against known or unknown parties. Complaints can be initiated by the police, the prosecutor, the alleged victim or victims, or another interested party, depending upon circumstances. An information can generally be filed only by a prosecutor or another duly authorized public official and is similar to an indictment except that a public official rather than a grand jury presents it to the court.[30]

In the federal system, an indictment by a grand jury is one way that felony criminal cases can get off the ground. In the state system and Washington, D.C., an indictment can also begin the process. However, only in the District of Columbia, the federal system, and fourteen states is an indictment by a grand jury a requisite first step, unless waived by the defendant, to begin all felony prosecutions in spite of the existence of such juries nationwide.[31] [32] In fact, at least as early as 1983, Pennsylvania and Connecticut were no longer using grand juries for indictments to initiate criminal charges.[33] Of the representative data found for two jurisdictions that do, indictments were only used about two-thirds of the time or far less.[34] [35] Indictment statistics are elusive, but hypothesizing and extrapolating the data found to the entire country mean that indictments are used no more than half of the time for felony prosecutions.

Keep in mind that indictments are normally reserved for felonies, which comprise only one of the few types of criminal cases as explained earlier. Also note that although federal grand juries indict ordinary citizens over 99 percent of the time, a returned "no bill" means the prosecutor must resubmit evidence to a different grand jury in order to continue pursuing the indictment legally against the accused.[36] [37] Criminal proceedings that begin with an information or a complaint outside the employment of the grand jury and its corresponding indictment include those for infractions, most misdemeanors, and some felonies. Felony cases begin this way whenever an indictment by a grand jury is not required or a defendant waives her constitutional right to one in instances when it otherwise would be.

At the federal level, only the government may file a criminal complaint with the court.[38] Some states, however, permit private prosecutions. They allow a criminal complaint to be filed by the purported victim of an alleged crime or her counsel against an individual without having to file a police report or having a state prosecutor initiate the case. Laws regarding this vary wherein some states have no statutory laws governing the process but have case law that does. Other states define the specifics in their rules of criminal procedure.

In New Hampshire, a private party cannot start a criminal prosecution that could result in imprisonment. See *State v. Martineau*.[39] This takes the wind out of the sails for many of that state's residents who could otherwise file private criminal complaints whenever any of that state's criminal laws have been violated. However, at least the potential for some retribution exists, especially when the perpetrator is politically connected with the district attorney's office or local or state police, all of whom refuse to take any action against the offender. In some states, unfortunately, the public prosecutor reserves the right to dismiss private prosecutions, which will likely happen in the aforementioned instance.

Some states allow a private prosecution to be initiated with an affidavit or other requisite form that needs to be filed with the court. If the affidavit or form is later reviewed by a judge or another court official and found to have substantive merit, then an arrest warrant could be issued in the event of a serious criminal accusation. The case should then proceed as it would if it had been started through standard law enforcement channels.

Lastly, in states that allow private prosecutions, the clerk of the court may tell you that you need to file a complaint with the local police department to initiate the process instead of letting you file anything directly with the court. If you have done your research and are certain you can personally submit whatever needs to be filed, be persistent and ask for the required form from the clerk so you can complete it and file it yourself. Direct her attention to the statute, case law, or rule of procedure if necessary and as appropriate.

If you do not have a good relationship with the police in the town or city where you live, or anywhere in the country for that matter, there is a decent chance they will not lift a finger to help you at any time under any circumstances. This would probably include filing a criminal complaint on your behalf, regardless of its severity. You may also live in a jurisdiction where law enforcement is just plain lazy and will only eagerly respond to detail work or court duty because of the overtime pay, or will happily give speeding tickets as if they were candy instead of "protecting and serving" its citizens. The more you can short-circuit various segments of the legal system by stepping around them as in this private prosecution example, the better chance you will have at circumventing corruption and increasing the odds of success in your legal matter.

A criminal complaint or information, along with any corresponding incident report, filed by a law enforcement official can contain errors, be heavily one-sided, or be completely bogus. If any of these are ever filed against you, understand that the police and prosecution will most likely not be forthcoming with regard to providing you copies unless specifically requested. But it is imperative that you see whatever is stated by the alleged victims and witnesses so you can begin to build your defense.

The complaint or information and incident report should be reviewed thoroughly for incorrect dates, false witnesses to the alleged crime, and other untruths and for hearsay in any narrative portion. These documents will be the fulcrum upon which the prosecutor will attempt to obtain as much leverage as possible for the case. She will do this by talking with victims and witnesses identified in the documents and gathering or manufacturing evidence, which will probably be used to strengthen later plea bargaining. Knowing what is true and what is false on the documents will at least provide you with the most basic input needed to build your defense.

In order for a crime to have occurred against a victim, there must, of course, be a victim. The people listed as victims on the complaint, indictment, or information should ordinarily be unwilling participants in the act precipitating the charges against the accused. Rape and consensual sex are the same physical act—the distinction between the two is that the person who gets raped is an unwilling participant. In fact, consent is a popular defense in many rape cases.

The incident report may state that the complainant was reluctant or refused or rejected some particular act or service. If there is clear evidence to the contrary, consider yourself most fortunate because your case could be over before it starts. If not dismissed by the prosecutor, a jury trial might be a far better option than a plea bargain in disposing of the matter. Of course, for victimless crimes, such as illegal drug use, public intoxication, and gambling, the majority of the analysis here does not apply, and only the narrative by the reporting officer will need to be analyzed for inaccuracies.

SERVICE OF SUMMONS/PROCESS

If the accused is not arrested and then jailed, the complaint, information, indictment, or summons is typically served to her by personal delivery via a law enforcement officer or another official, by leaving it with someone at her last known address, or in any event, by an approved method. The allowable forms of service should be defined in applicable statutes or rules of criminal procedure. In state criminal cases, service can only be legally performed within the confines of the named state. If the accused leaves that state with the intention never to return, then the court system must extradite her across state lines in order to bring her back to the complaining state to answer the charges. For major felonies, this is commonly done, but for infractions and other lesser crimes, the chances of extradition are much lower or nearly zero.

ARRAIGNMENT

The first court appearance for the accused is usually the arraignment. A more appropriate term would be "arrangement" because that is what it truly is—an arrangement between the government and the accused to begin a process that will, in all probability, end with a plea bargain of some sort. The arraignment is the hearing at which the accused is supposed to be read the charges against her. This is also the time when she is supposed to enter a plea. Charges are not always properly read to the accused as they should be, which could open the door for a later appeal or legal challenge. Once this phase is accomplished by the system, the person just charged will have a permanent stain on her previously clean criminal record unless it is later removed by expungement.

If you have been recently surprised by a criminal accusation, reading the relevant statutes and rules of criminal procedure, particularly sections regarding arraignments and pleas, would be an excellent initial step to take prior to your first court date. In an effort to speed through the arraignment, the court may skip some or most of the rules governing this process just like it will do at other points along the way. To make it ultra-easy for the system, pleading guilty to whatever crimes of which you are being accused will set in motion sentencing, typically done then or at the next and usually last court date, and the case will be closed. Rules of court normally state that the consent of the court is required for acceptance of a guilty plea. The likelihood of any judge disallowing such a plea is about the same as a blizzard hitting Guam before the next ice age. If an entered plea is one that leads to a trial, as several listed below can, the court will generally set a date for a pre-trial hearing or trial.

Besides the two obvious, well-known pleas, guilty and not guilty, there are others that the system does not openly reveal to accused individuals, possibly to save time. One such plea is *nolo contendere*, which is called "no contest" in English, and requires consent of the court. Another is a conditional plea, which requires the consent of both the court and prosecution. In the federal system, a defendant may enter conditional pleas of *nolo contendere* or guilty and reserve in writing the right for review by an appellate court of any adverse determination of a specified pre-trial motion. If successful with this appeal, a defendant may then withdraw the plea.[40]

If no plea is entered by the accused, the court is supposed to enter a not-guilty plea for her. In addition to informing the defendant about a dozen or so different rights she is waiving and rules that apply when she enters a guilty or no-contest plea in the federal system, the court is supposed to ensure that the plea is voluntary and has a factual basis. Some state courts significantly shorten the list by not informing the defendant of all applicable rules and waived rights, probably to save time at her expense.

Pleas that apply in any given jurisdiction are dictated by relevant rules of criminal procedure or statute. Between the federal and state systems, the following pleas are known to exist, but there may be others:

- guilty
- not guilty
- no contest/*nolo contendere*
- conditional plea of *nolo contendere*, guilty, or guilty but mentally ill
- not guilty by reason of insanity
- guilty but mentally ill
- a former judgment of conviction or acquittal of the offense charged
- once in jeopardy
- Alford plea
- no plea whatsoever (wherein the court is supposed to enter "not guilty")

At the arraignment, a defendant charged with more serious crimes will normally be assigned a public defender if she cannot afford a private attorney and will be billed for the public defender's services in some instances. As early as the arraignment, she may also be offered the "opportunity" to agree to a plea bargain with Satan's right hand, the prosecutor. By the end of the hearing, the defendant will be released on her own recognizance, will be informed of the amount of bail that must be posted in order to be released until trial, or will be incarcerated without bail until trial.

Usually, a defendant waives her right to appeal a plea or conviction as part of the plea agreement. Later appeal would then be allowed only if the plea agreement was made involuntarily, unknowingly, or without knowledge of the consequences of the plea, including the waiving of constitutional rights. Such agreements made under any of these circumstances might have the best chance of un-ringing the proverbial bell even after sentencing. For example, if it can be proved that the court ignored or omitted certain important statements to the accused during proceedings, her unintentional waiving of constitutional rights can come into play. An analysis to determine that the court did so could begin by examining the court record and then researching appropriate case law to see what arguments and citations from it should be included in filings to begin undoing the damage. Other than this, there are no known silver bullets to fire at the system in order to change the ramifications of the arraignment except for what was explained in chapter two's LAST RESORT section.

PLEA BARGAINS

Plea bargains, sometimes called "plea agreements" or "plea deals," are a mechanism to reduce the workload of the courts and gathered steam in the United States in the late nineteenth century.[41] People accused of a crime in jurisdictions where these deals are offered are faced with making a decision—an unpleasant one based on their perception of which option is the lesser of two evils. One option is to go to trial and gamble that the outcome will be favorable; however, prosecutors often add or threaten to add as many charges as possible, with some carrying long mandatory minimum sentences, in an attempt to discourage a trial. The other option is to accept an offer of lesser charges and plead guilty to them and, in return, to be given a shorter jail or prison sentence or be sentenced to probation instead of being imprisoned, all while being spared from the agony of a trial and avoiding risk altogether. The best analogy that comes to mind is a perverse version of the game show *Let's Make a Deal*, but instead of a prize behind any of the doors, there is a torture rack behind one and water boarding behind the other two.

The Ugly Truth

There are various opinions about the advantages and disadvantages of plea bargains. In reality, they are an extremely liberal tool of the judicial system, leveling the playing field for all defendants by reducing penalties on the guilty and burdening the innocent with criminal records and potential incarceration. Thus, plea bargains serve no beneficial value to society and truly only benefit the system.

Recall from chapter seven's JURY AND BENCH TRIALS section that the overwhelming majority of criminal defendants accept plea agreements instead of going to trial. Many result from false guilty pleas. By one conservative estimate, 0.5 percent of all criminal defendants falsely plead guilty, which translates to approximately 11,000 people currently incarcerated in America for crimes they did not commit.[42] This number, of course, neglects those wrongly convicted by a judge or jury, propelling it significantly higher. Of the approximated 19 million criminal cases entering state and Washington, D.C., trial courts every year, in excess of 86,000 defendants are pleading guilty annually to crimes they did not commit. This number is derived by subtracting the dismissals, estimated to be 8.5 percent of all incoming cases, similarly projecting the 0.5 percent false guilty plea rate onto the remainder, and conservatively assuming that there is only one defendant per case. Federal court data further add to the total.

Many of these people are given probation instead of being imprisoned. This fact and some of the formerly incarcerated being paroled help explain why more than 86,000 new "criminals" are generated every year from false guilty pleas alone but the jails and prisons are not bursting at their seams. By some estimates, the number of innocent individuals pleading guilty in U.S. criminal cases could be far greater and lie between 2 and 8 percent.[43] The relatively large spread might be due to data scarcity or other uncertainty. However, assuming the actual tally is on the low end of that estimate, it would translate into a mind-boggling number of more than 347,000 criminal defendants pleading guilty every year to crimes they did not commit and approximately 44,000 currently incarcerated for the same reason.

The explanation for this alarmingly high number of innocent people imprisoned, on probation or parole, and having criminal records is partly because of the plea bargaining process. It is sometimes used to force innocent people into pleading guilty to criminal charges in exchange for lighter sentences. If facing the threat of a death sentence for a murder charge, life in prison might not look so bad. This is obviously a worst-case scenario, but experience of one of the authors has shown that the pressure with far lesser charges is still overwhelming, particularly for people with much to lose. Reading this material makes it easy to armchair quarterback. But believe us; it will almost certainly be much more difficult than you think to make such a decision if and when the time comes. The pressure will likely be intense from the prosecutor and possibly from your own lawyer if you have one.

Alternatively, destitute innocent people sometimes feel they will not have the resources to win their acquittal at trial and therefore agree to make a "deal." Still others face the strong incentive of reduced incarceration, which is nearly impossible to resist. This frequently happens when the accused is held in jail awaiting her "speedy" trial because she cannot afford bail or because it has been denied. If the time already served is greater than or equal to the time offered in the deal, then the risk of a trial ending in a guilty verdict or decision that could add even more incarceration for the defendant could easily induce her to accept the deal, get out of jail, and eliminate risk.

Plea bargains are also bad for the innocent because others accused of being part of the same crime, particularly the guilty, can be incentivized to testify against them. Another major force propelling innocent people into accepting plea deals is the fact that severe sentences are sometimes imposed for minor crimes. With three-strikes laws, mandatory minimum sentencing, a wildly excessive number of laws, and other dangerous tools at prosecutors' fingertips, the immense power they now wield intimidates many into accepting deals that avoid a trial and potential incarceration or longer incarceration. Prosecutorial power gives the system an enormous advantage.

Unite and Beat the Entire Criminal System

One of the simplest ways to counteract prosecutorial power and instead empower everyday Americans is via a plan that has been contemplated previously by others but, to our knowledge, not yet been put into action. Petty and similar minor offenses aside, if every person accused of a crime demanded a jury trial as allowed by the Sixth Amendment rather than accepting a plea bargain, the corresponding overload would put the entire system into a tailspin. There is absolutely no way that the courts could handle the inundation.[44]

One judge has stated openly, "Properly administered, it [plea bargains] is to be encouraged. If every criminal charge were subjected to a full-scale trial, the States and the Federal Government would need to multiply by many times the number of judges and court facilities."[45] The only thing missing from the end of this statement is, "Or our government would need to eradicate about 95 percent of its laws, and the judiciary would need to reinstate true checks and balances—and the system in general would need a major overhaul to eliminate corruption." Like any revolutionary change, however, it takes a multitude of people, possibly as little as 15 percent of those criminally charged, or about five times as many defendants currently opting for a trial, to stand firm and unify to effect such an alteration. If people did unite and demand jury trials, it would bring the current U.S. criminal justice system to a grinding halt.

On a small scale, a scheme like this could easily be implemented at the local court level. If you are ever fighting criminal charges, check the relevant court's docket to see who else is fighting criminal charges. Make a list of ten to twenty or more of these people. Nobody should legally be able to object because court proceedings are normally a matter of public record. Next, try to use social media to contact the people on your list. If you and most of them unite and insist on a jury trial rather than accepting a plea deal, that particular court would certainly feel the impact of trying to schedule an abundance of trials in between its other business. Think of this tactic as "legal sabotage."

If some people are unreachable, several trips to the courthouse may be required in order to catch them there or to contact others instead. As time-consuming as this might be, it may be better than the alternative of facing charges for a crime you did not commit. If the prosecutor does not sweeten her deal or relent entirely, make your circle of court friends larger by recruiting even more people. As stated previously, there is strength in numbers. Eventually, that particular court will have to do something to avoid all these trials, or else it will quickly have to build another courthouse!

Fight Fire with Fire

As explained in chapter seven in the CONFIDENT, CAPABLE, AND CALM IN COURT section, another way to negate the odds being in the system's favor is basically to fight fire with fire. Check the prosecutor's past by searching online, inquiring within the community, or hiring a private investigator. Any unpublicized inappropriate or illegal activity in her past may contribute tremendously towards calling off the dogs. Not all prosecutors have a sordid past, but in our experience, certainly some do. There is no shortage of media reports regarding improprieties by such individuals either. One example concerns former Texas District Attorney Chuck Rosenthal. He was involved in a prescription drug and pornographic email scandal that prompted his resignation in 2008.[46]

Another more recent example in 2015 was the Ashley Madison website hacker's revelation that one of the site's members was Jeff Ashton, the prosecutor in the Casey Anthony murder trial.[47] Finding any such unpublicized improprieties about a prosecutor may make her attitude much more malleable toward your cause or at least certainly encourage her to play by the system's own rules and laws. Once you confront her quietly about your findings, she may offer a reasonable plea bargain. She might also drop the charges altogether, depending upon how serious they are, the magnitude of the wrongdoing you have uncovered against her, and the strength of the evidence she *thinks* she has against you.

Another prosecutor may replace the current one because she will not be able to continue without personal risk, but if you can defeat the replacement or any prosecutor assigned to your case, even one at a time if necessary, then you are making progress. There is also a chance these vermin will circle the wagons to protect each other; therefore, finding filth on any of them may be enough to entice the district attorney's office as a whole to release its grip. Remember that they are the energy source in any criminal case. If you can cut off the power fueling it at the source by defeating the prosecutor via this or any other means, you will basically be pulling the plug on the entire operation.

Deal on Your Own Terms

Keep in mind that the system will try to get everything done as quickly as possible when it comes time to process your case. This means that the offer of a plea bargain might come as a complete surprise in the form of an unexpected proposal but with an immediately expected answer. Accepting a plea bargain is a major decision that should not be made lightly by an innocent individual. If inclined to take the deal, its long-term effects should be considered. A mark on someone's otherwise perfect record could mean the loss of a job, rejection from housing, the loss of custody of one's children, and a litany of other unforeseen negative ramifications. Of course, any of these events may later engage other "services" offered by the parasitic feeders and possibly even begin an endless cycle for the individual thereby forcing her to become a repeat "customer" of the system. This is not a pleasant prospect for anyone except for associates of the legal meat grinder itself who benefit from it.

If such a surprise deal is offered to you, ask for some time to consider it. Try to negotiate it more in your favor if the prosecution has a weak case. If you have an attorney, ask her for input, but ultimately the decision is yours. What makes the decision so difficult is not knowing the case's result should it go to trial. One thing for certain, there is no jury nullification power with a plea bargain, but with a jury trial, there most definitely is. If you or your attorney thinks there are constitutional issues regarding the laws you are accused of breaking or how they were wrongly or selectively applied in your case, a jury trial may be a better option. A jury can be informed of the government's wrongdoing and thus use nullification power to acquit you.

There is no single reference that can guide someone about choosing the best path to follow when offered a plea deal. It may be helpful to have others provide their input if panic overwhelms you during this time. If friends, family members, or others who have been in the same position give their opinion, it might make the decision easier.

Know that in some jurisdictions, even if a plea deal is taken, it is still possible to have a record repaired later by various means. Possibilities include vacating a judgment, having a trial, sealing a record, obtaining a pardon or an expungement, and potentially more. However, none of these are guaranteed, and most do not happen overnight. The bottom line is that anything that undermines the U.S. Constitution cannot be considered a good thing. With plea bargaining eradicating at least three different constitutional rights protected by the Fifth and Sixth Amendments—the right against self-incrimination, the right to a jury trial, and the right to confront hostile witnesses—it certainly can be considered a bad thing.

BUILDING THE DEFENSE

A logical first step in building the defense of a criminal case might actually be to look at the law or laws allegedly violated. In their haste to criminalize as many U.S. citizens as possible, our legislators sometimes enact criminal laws that say something entirely different from their intended meaning. Consider New Hampshire statute 570-A:2 Interception and Disclosure of Telecommunication or Oral Communications Prohibited.[48] It begins:

"I. A person is guilty of a class B felony if, except as otherwise specifically provided in this chapter or without the consent of all parties to the communication, the person:

(a) Wilfully intercepts, endeavors to intercept, or procures any other person to intercept or endeavor to intercept, any telecommunication or oral communication;..."

Do you see the problem? Clearly, the intention of the first phrase is to provide some exceptions to the law and exclude people who give their consent. However, in this same first phrase, the word "without" is used *instead* of "with." This gives the law a whole new meaning, much to the dismay of our politicians. To convey their desired meaning, that first phrase could have been written as follows:

- "A person is guilty of a class B felony if, except as otherwise specifically provided in this chapter or with the consent of all parties to the communication, the person:"
- "Without the consent of all parties to the communication, a person is guilty of a class B felony if, except as otherwise specifically provided in this chapter, the person:"
- "Except as otherwise specifically provided in this chapter, a person is guilty of a class B felony if, without the consent of all parties to the communication, the person:"

As written, it is perfectly legal to do everything in the chapter without the consent of all parties to the communication. We wonder if anyone who has been accused of violating this law has noticed that fact. The point here is to pore over whatever law it is that you are charged with violating. You might find an exceptionally pleasant surprise and a simple solution to your quagmire! Since it is legislators who write laws, it is not anyone else's fault that they are not written to say what they were meant to say. Other statutes use the phrase "except as otherwise specifically provided in this chapter or" much more clearly and with its intended meaning.[49] [50]

Similar to civil cases, there is discovery in criminal proceedings. Both the prosecutor and the defendant or her attorney can request certain information from each other. This is when being vigilant is paramount. If the prosecutor is known to be using manufactured evidence—for example, a bag of cocaine allegedly found at your residence but the video from your hidden surveillance camera clearly showing it was planted there—ask for fingerprints from it to see if any match yours. Regardless, consider making the government waste all the time and energy on a trial and bursting its bubble then by showing the video footage to the jury.

If the prosecutor is known to be withholding evidence, this would be another opportune time to pull the rug out from under her. An example could be verbal communication secretly recorded by a friend or family member when investigators spoke with that person and admitted something was found at the scene clearing you of all allegations, but the fact that it did so was unbeknownst to the interviewee at the time. Recording such conversations and using them as evidence may be legal according to 18 U.S. Code § 2511(2)(d).[51]

As discussed in chapter ten's Ticketing Officer's Testimony subsection, recent rulings have overcome charges of illegality in cases involving the recording of law enforcement officers of any type while performing their official duties. It might be wise to ask any potential witnesses for your defense or other suspects or defendants to record their conversations with investigators secretly in the event that something the authorities say can be used to obliterate their case later. The NSA has been illegally wiretapping the U.S. public for years.[52] [53] It is time to turn the tables.

There could be other things that investigators overlook, forget, disregard, or conceal in their zeal to build their case against an innocent person. It may take significant time and effort to poke holes in their theories. It may also take multiple overlapping pieces of evidence to pinpoint an alibi clearing someone of all charges.

For instance, if you made a credit card purchase at a certain department store at a certain time, it would establish your whereabouts when your transaction was completed. Video surveillance recordings from the store might identify you wearing blue cotton shorts and a white T-shirt. Suppose a coroner's report substantiates the murder of which you are being accused taking place one hour after the time you made your purchase. If the store is 200 miles from the crime scene where fibers from the perpetrator's clothing were identified as red polyester, it would be impossible for you to change into any other clothes and drive 200 miles per hour in order to commit said crime. All evidence taken together would create your "get out of jail free" card.

Also, for evidence that is subject to the exclusionary rule, the court should be petitioned to have it deemed inadmissible. Ruling this way is what the court *should* do, not necessarily what it *will* do. This is one reason why no person within the system or any contingent of it should be trusted. Evidence that can stand on its own or be used in combination with other evidence clearing you of all charges and that can be shown to a jury should be much more reliable in vindicating you.

If you can personally inspect evidence anytime before trial, it would be wise to do so. Recall from chapter two in the WHAT YOU ARE UP AGAINST section that evidence can be lost, destroyed, concealed, or manufactured. Before trial would be the best time to discover manufactured or tainted evidence, not during or after trial. The prosecutor may try to hide as much from you as possible and not offer any exculpatory evidence or information known only to her unless specifically requested by defense during discovery—and even then there is no guarantee she will comply. However, having knowledge of facts and access to evidence in the case should go a long way towards dispelling that secrecy.

Lastly, it might be a good idea to rehearse the trial whether you have an attorney or not. Gathering witnesses and a mock judge in order to perform a dry run would be an excellent idea so that you (and your attorney, if you have one) can ensure everyone is cognizant of hearsay, leading of witnesses, testifying about facts not yet in evidence, and all other objectionable activities. If you are represented by a lawyer, it will afford you the opportunity to make sure that she is prepared and not shooting from the hip, which attorneys have been known to do. It will also allow you to peer into her strategy. If you have questions, it is better to ask them then and resolve any confusion rather than asking in court when there may be plenty of confusion and disorder already. Exchanging questions and answers may reveal new trains of thought that could lead to improved tactics and is yet another example of why more heads are better than one.

THE TRIAL

If you have caught the prosecutor red-handed breaking rules, violating laws, or tampering with evidence or witnesses and have forgone a plea bargain or have decided to take your chances anyway, it will eventually be time for the trial. As in all trials in U.S. courts, the plaintiff, or specifically the prosecutor in criminal matters, will present her case first. If represented, it could be a mistake to rely solely on your lawyer to pay attention and take notes of everything that transpires. You should come prepared with a notebook of your own and remain razor-sharp during the whole proceeding as if you were *pro se*. Keep track of everything said.

If any government witness says something objectionable and your lawyer does not object, prod her to do so. If it happens again later in the proceeding, it may be time to get another lawyer. Stand and interrupt the court if it does and you want to replace your lawyer. Request a recess to allow you time to find new counsel, or state that you are firing your attorney and taking the case yourself. Your choice would depend largely on the situation and gravity of the charges.

If you have decided to be a witness on your own behalf, make sure that you and your attorney have determined whatever is to be said beforehand. When it comes time for you to take the witness stand, answering your lawyer's questions should be the easy part. The hard part is when the prosecutor cross-examines you after your attorney is through. You may have no idea what raw sewage is going to spew forth from the prosecutor's mouth. Listen carefully and answer slowly.

If you are represented by a lawyer, pausing briefly before answering the prosecutor's questions will provide time for your lawyer to raise an objection if necessary. This tactic could be important in front of a jury. They would not hear your answer if the objection is sustained before you speak, instead of hearing your answer and having it be stricken from the record but not from their ears. If the answer to a question can be given by a simple "yes" or "no," responding in that manner is usually better than saying something such as, "Yes, but my prints were on the gun because I had just taken it out of the murderer's hand at the scene and cannot recall in the slightest what she looked like." There can be many twists and turns during a trial, and it is difficult to predict where it will go. If a disputable or an uncomfortable question is asked during cross-examination, your attorney should have more questions for you oriented towards clarifying any ambiguities once the prosecutor is done.

Regarding a *pro se* defendant who chooses to testify on her own behalf, the court may require her to phrase testimony in a question-and-answer format in order to allow the prosecutor an opening to object to a question if she so desires. Narrative testimony may not be allowed. See *United States v. Beckton*.[54] As awkward as it may be for the defendant, the requirement will likely be upheld since Federal Rule of Evidence 611(a) and a corresponding rule in many, if not all, states and the nation's capital give the court broad control over examining witnesses and presenting evidence.[55] However, if narrative testimony has been allowed by the court until that point for other witnesses, the *pro se* defendant should object to its discontinued use strictly for her since this would be prejudicial by the court.

SENTENCING

A presentence report is usually prepared in the federal and Washington, D.C., court systems and in some state systems for people about to be imprisoned. It outlines the individual's criminal record, the perceived facts of a case, and other pertinent information. The judge should use the report to determine sentence length. If there are any mistakes in this report that are to your benefit, you may want to think twice before making them known.

Sentencing is sometimes done in U.S. courts on a day following the trial. For minor offenses, it is sometimes done immediately after the trial on the same day. If you have considered the information put forth in the LAST RESORT section in chapter two but are willing to go to jail or prison instead, then you should appear at the sentencing hearing. If you were incarcerated before trial, this time should count towards the total sentence. For relatively minor offenses, the time already served may even eclipse the sentence as it sometimes does for poorer individuals who cannot afford bail and wait jailed for their "speedy" trial.

Jurisdictions have guidelines for sentencing. If you have the misfortune of reaching this point in your case, consult these guidelines for the specific crime of which you have been convicted or pled guilty. You may find the prosecutor is pushing for a sentence well beyond the guidelines. If she has no valid reason for this, which is a good possibility, research you should have done of case law for similar situations might contradict her recommendation and support your claim for a reduced sentence or no incarceration whatsoever. You may be able to reduce any potential incarceration to probation in spite of the prosecutor's wishes. Judges may nonetheless choose to prescribe sentences that fall outside the recommended length since guidelines are exactly that—guidelines.

The wildcard here is the newer mandatory minimum sentencing laws that govern the absolute minimum amount of time to which a judge can sentence a person. There are two known federal exceptions that allow for sentences shorter than the mandatory minimum. One is if the prosecutor requests the court for a reduced sentence in exchange for your cooperation in investigating or prosecuting someone else in the case. The other applies only to federal drug offenses. See 18 U.S. Code § 3553(e) and (f).[56]

If you experience the calamity of having prior false convictions on your record before the current tragedy strikes, consider not volunteering this information during sentencing if the judge is unaware of them. She will perceive any prior convictions as being valid, which will not help to reduce your sentence but can certainly increase it. A judge may still lengthen your sentence if you were acquitted through a jury trial of an unrelated previous charge and she thinks you were guilty, as disturbing as this sounds.

For federal sentences of one year or slightly shorter, you or your attorney should consider asking for a sentence of a year and a day. This would take advantage of the "good time" statutory clause wherein you can actually serve much less than one year with a sentence slightly longer than one year. You can earn credit toward service, or a maximum reduction of fifty-four days per year of the imposed sentence, provided it is longer than one year. So, a year and a day sentence could be reduced substantially.[57] States and Washington, D.C., also have incarceration reduction laws.

PROBATION

The nation's capital, the federal government, and states use the probationary system. Probation differs from parole in that it can be part or all a sentence, whereas parole *follows* part or all of a sentence, jail or prison. Someone might be sentenced to one year of probation or thirty days in jail and eleven months of probation rather than one year in jail. Probation can be designated as supervised or unsupervised. The supervision can range from daily to monthly, more or less. Typically, one of its conditions is that the probationer remains employed while on probation. Having to report to a probation officer every day or even once a week is an excellent way for the system to generate more business for itself since it is highly unlikely anyone who is not self-employed will keep her job if she has to waste time reporting to court that frequently.

Unsupervised probation is basically the same thing as the supervised form except reporting to a probation officer is not required. Adding insult to injury, sometimes the probationer must pay a fee for this "service." When probation is completed, the case is generally closed and only reopened in the future if the individual attempts to clear her name through one of the processes described later in the CLEARING ONE'S NAME section. Rules about probation vary across the nation.

PAROLE

Parole is usually supervised early release of a prisoner and is not a sentence or part of one, unlike probation discussed above, but in some states, Colorado for one, parole is mandatory under certain circumstances after completing a sentence. While most states and Washington, D.C., still use parole, the federal system has abolished it for people convicted of crimes after November 1, 1987.[58] The "good time" clause mentioned in the SENTENCING section above and halfway houses have taken its place. Individuals who violate the conditions of their parole are often sent back to prison since the two are basically interchangeable. Some statutes do not allow parole, while others do. Several other factors determine parole eligibility, including particular state, type of crime, parole board's opinion, criminal history of the detainee, and more.

APPEALS

If there is one saving grace—and the expression is being used extremely loosely—about the criminal system, it is the fact that all known U.S. jurisdictions permit appeals. Although not a fully redeeming quality, appeals allow some people to request that higher courts revisit their case. It might not be the only reason, but perhaps appeals exist because more money gets poured into and feeds the legal monster during the process.

The U.S. Constitution has no explicit requirement that appeals are necessary for due process of law. It was not until 1879 that U.S. circuit courts were given the power to review federal criminal cases.[59] This power later extended to state courts and those in the nation's capital. Just because someone is convicted of a crime and does not like the outcome does not mean the judgment will be appealable. Appeals generally can be successful only when they concern errors of law; ineffective assistance of counsel; juror, prosecutorial, or judicial misconduct; or extraordinary issues.

As an example, hearsay during trial that was not ruled inadmissible is a question of law and should meet the error of law criterion. Additionally, any legal errors made by the trial judge must be "preserved" so the appellant can object to the trial court's ruling and explain so in her appeal. Finally, any errors made must have been prejudicial and should have likely affected the outcome of the case. If all three elements are satisfied, the appellate court can order a new trial by remanding the case back to the lower court, order a hearing related to sentencing or something else trial-related in the lower court, or vacate the conviction entirely.

There are other types of appeal-like proceedings that can be performed in state courts. Some pertain to revising or revoking the sentencing portion of a conviction. For example, see Massachusetts criminal procedure rule 29.[60] Others essentially pertain to sending the case back to the starting line if proper court procedures were not followed during litigation. See Massachusetts criminal procedure rule 30(b), for example.[61] Errors of law, ineffective assistance of counsel, and a judge failing to warn the accused about rights she would be waiving in a plea bargain or guilty plea would pertain to the application of this particular rule.

Motions to commence these kinds of proceedings would be filed in the court originally deciding the case, as opposed to an actual appeal, which would be filed in an appellate court. Personal experience of one coauthor has shown that these types of proceedings can be successful. New evidence can be introduced. Different witnesses can be called. And everything about the case can be revisited, unlike an appeal in which only issues stated three paragraphs prior can legally be addressed.

CLEARING ONE'S NAME

Other than successfully avoiding a wrongful conviction in the first place, perhaps the most important step in the criminal process for wrongly convicted individuals is clearing their names. Even though the U.S. criminal justice system is largely a total, complete joke, and an extremely bad one at that, people who make decisions in your life might not know it. Such decisions could be related to employment, adopting children, security clearances, and other important things. Decision makers may instead think that if you have a mark on your record, it must be factual and you should be feared or avoided. Therefore, clearing your name could bring paramount future benefits. Doing so can theoretically be accomplished in a variety of ways: expungement, or "expunction" as it is sometimes called, sealing, or pardon.

Expungement

Expungement is the ideal way to restore one's good name. It completely erases all traces of a particular crime within the system's records as though it never existed—if done correctly. This may not prevent the information from being found during internet searches since online databases may contain the initial conviction but are not updated despite the subsequent court order to remove it. The reason for this is that database administrators are unaware of the court order. Police and court records, governmental database entries, and everything associated with the case under the judicial system's control are supposed to be destroyed with a standard expungement. The process can require multiple steps. A person might have to write to a probation department, have a hearing before a judge, or conduct other business in order to receive expungement—all of which likely bring money into the system.

Afterward for state cases, a notice of expungement from the state is supposed to be supplied to its state police and probation departments to clear information from those databases. Additionally, the expungement for the crime being erased must be reported to the FBI on form R-84 in order to clear the federal criminal history record of any associated arrest of the person from the FBI database.[62] Relying on governmental authorities to complete all these steps for you is certainly risky. If they were quick to destroy your life in the first place, rest assured they will not be quick to fix it, and even if by some miracle they are, they may make mistakes in the process.

To ensure they have finally rectified everything, personally contact all relevant local, state, and federal agencies. As a final check, ask for written proof from the government. You are allowed to ask for a copy of your own criminal record. In the case of an expungement, your criminal record should appear as a blank sheet of paper except for your personally identifiable information and governmental header or logo. It should be no surprise, but you normally must pay a fee to obtain a copy of your record.

Expungements in some states, one being Delaware, are mandatory for those whose misdemeanor or infraction cases have been terminated in their favor.[63] We have no plausible explanation of why any state would help someone in this way, particularly when it makes perfect sense, other than for the fact that the state financially benefits from "a reasonable fee" paid when the application is filed.

Sealing

In other states and for most crimes in the District of Columbia and at the federal level, expungement is not allowed, and sealing is the inferior alternative. With sealing all data about the crime still exist; however, the government makes it inaccessible to some potential employers and non-law enforcement entities. For anyone holding a security clearance, sealing a record is useless since government officials conducting a background check punch through any sealing as if it was not even there—the same way any law enforcement officials would. This is extremely prejudicial by the government whenever expungement is not allowed but sealing is; some people are fully protected by sealing, whereas those who need government clearances are not.

Pardons

Receiving a simple pardon, similar to sealing, is an inferior method of clearing one's name. It generally makes no attempt to conceal or erase convictions or pleas but instead notes in specific criminal record databases that charges have been pardoned, with some states potentially removing all traces of a crime from an individual's record on rare occasions.[64] A pardon should also restore voting rights, allow an individual to acquire a firearm license in some instances, and not jeopardize future employment because of the conviction's existence, but pardon particulars vary greatly across the nation.[65] At the federal level, pardons are granted by the president. At the state level, they are granted by the governor. In the District of Columbia, they are granted by the mayor.

Sometimes a pardon specifically authorizes expungement. Anything relating to the name-clearing process that includes an expungement would be ideal. Note that there may be a mandatory waiting period before pursuing any of the above name-clearing mechanisms. This also varies by crime and jurisdiction.

Other Considerations

It may also be wise to have criminal records expunged or sealed or offenses pardoned because in some jurisdictions such records cannot *legally* be used in court proceedings thereafter.[66] This could be beneficial if the reason for the original criminal charge stemmed from a party having something to gain in an associated future civil case and you want to block admissibility of the records. In addition, if you want to file a civil suit later against the initiator of the criminal charges for an unrelated event, then you may have a stronger case if any such unrelated criminal charges are inadmissible in court, barring any corruption, of course. Experience of one author has shown that corrupt judges will knowingly break the law—not only a common theme in this book but also in courts nationwide—and allow such records to be used in other court cases anyway.

Lastly, if, for some reason, expungement, sealing, pardoning, or any other name-clearing process available via the government fails you, a remote possibility might help you. Recall from chapter seven in the REMAINING MISCELLANEOUS RULES section that sometimes incorrect information about you exists in the records or databases maintained by the legal system. Also understand that confusion often abounds within the courts themselves. These two aspects of the system can be used to your advantage.

If addresses, parents' names, or other personally identifiable information stored by the government is incorrect or partially incorrect, any investigative report later produced using these records or databases as its source can be disputed. Resulting bogus claims against you can be deflected by stating that the person named in the report is not you because you have never lived at said addresses, because you do not have said parents, or because of other reasons supported by the incorrect data. The confusion within the courts also helps fog the cockpit further and makes pinpointing the misidentification more difficult.

As part of the name-clearing process or independent of it, one piece of information should be conveyed before concluding this chapter. Laws exist prescribing monetary compensation for victims of prosecutorial and other governmental misconduct. The Hyde Amendment in the federal system and possibly state and local laws were created to mandate that all such victims be compensated by the government, but with nebulous terminology in statutory and case law, these laws have largely proved toothless for several would-be recipients.[67]

Chapter 13: Debt Collection

Rather go to bed supperless, than run in debt for a Breakfast. — **Benjamin Franklin**

Chapter Sections

- Background
- The Fair Debt Collection Practices Act
- Enforcement of the FDCPA
- Alternative dispute resolution
- Defenses to debt collection
- Types of credit and the statute of limitations
- Disputing a debt
- Discharging debts through bankruptcy

BACKGROUND

Debt collection has become more prolific since the most recent financial crisis that peaked in 2008. As a result, debt collection actions via debt collection attorneys and agencies have increased accordingly. The average American likely has experienced or will experience an attorney, agency, or other entity pursuing him to collect some type of debt.

Debt collection agencies abound in America. Some conduct business in certain cities or states, while others operate in specific business sectors. Because the United States is geographically large and has a population of more than 320 million, it is conducive to a wide variety and large number of collection agencies.

Most collection agencies in America work for a fee that is contingent upon successfully recovering a debt. The fee is usually a percentage to which the collection agency and creditor have mutually agreed and is obtained from the recovered debt. Contingency fee arrangements can vary widely across agencies.

If a suit is filed by a lawyer on behalf of a creditor, the lawyer is normally entitled to court costs in addition to a base fee. The base fee may be entirely contingent, partially contingent, or not contingent whatsoever. Whenever the base fee is not entirely contingent, it is partially or fully paid by the creditor. Court costs vary across the nation. The responsibility of paying them generally falls on the creditor.

The United States enables far greater access to credit information for individuals and businesses than many other countries do. Sophisticated databases of credit information are operated by various reporting agencies, which allow creditors to determine at the outset whether a person or business is a credit risk. These same databases also provide a variety of information that is helpful for maintaining credit records and determining whether to pursue a debt.[1]

The operation of collection agencies in America is governed by law, and agency collection efforts are generally limited to telephone and written correspondence as a result. Typically, collection agencies will conduct a background check on a person or business in order to determine if either has assets and, therefore, the probability of recovering debt. When a collection agency determines that legal action might result in successful recovery, it will usually refer the case to a debt collection attorney.

Debt collection attorneys in America do not have the most pristine reputation. In one author's experience, they are some of the most unsavory characters to battle because they often do not play by the rules. But by this same token, not following the law or court rules of procedure can be used against them by challenging their questionable tactics directly to the judge when in court. In one particular collection lawsuit, the same author was able to obtain a dismissal for failure to prosecute because the debt collection attorney failed to appear in court for two consecutive hearings.

The average American is probably not aware of the fact that, under certain federal, state, and District of Columbia laws, he may be entitled to recover his attorney's fees from litigation related to a debt collector using unfair practices while trying to recover a debt from him whether it is valid or not. There are countless free educational resources available to anyone facing a debt collector. A short internet search can point you in the right direction and help educate you about debtor rights, including your potential right to recover attorney's fees for prosecuting or defending a case against a debt collection agency.

Private companies are not the only clients of debt collection agencies and lawyers. Government agencies across the nation are using private debt collection services to pursue millions of Americans for unpaid taxes, age-old parking tickets, and even ridiculously small tolls—sometimes unjustly. This provides a great revenue stream for cash-strapped states, cities, and local governments. By outsourcing the dirty work and letting debt collectors charge debtors sky-high fees, an excellent deal for debt collectors, government agencies can get collection services free of charge. In an industry already known for bad behavior, debt collectors that work for government agencies usually do not have to operate within the confines of consumer protection laws, which opens the door for higher fees and even more aggressive, unscrupulous tactics.[2]

THE FAIR DEBT COLLECTION PRACTICES ACT

The Fair Debt Collection Practices Act (FDCPA), codified as 15 U.S. Code § 1692 to 1692p, is a consumer protection law. Its intended purpose is to eliminate abusive practices during attempted collection of alleged consumer debts and to provide consumers with an avenue for disputing them. The act defines rights of afflicted consumers, creates guidelines under which debt collectors may conduct business, and prescribes penalties and remedies for violations of the act.[3]

The FDCPA broadly defines a debt collector as "any person who uses any instrumentality of interstate commerce or the mails in any business the principal purpose of which is the collection of any debts, or who regularly collects or attempts to collect, directly or indirectly, debts owed or due or asserted to be owed or due another." See 15 U.S. Code § 1692a.[4] While the FDCPA normally applies to third party debt collectors and not in-house collectors for an original creditor, some states, California being one, have consumer protection laws that emulate the FDCPA and regulate collection by original creditors. Additionally, some federal courts have ruled under the FDCPA that while a creditor can collect its own debts, a creditor cannot be a "debt collector" nor can it be any entity that "receives an assignment or transfer of a debt in default solely for the purpose of facilitating collection of such debt for another." See *Holmes v. Telecredit Service Corp.*[5]

The definitions of and distinction between "creditor" and "debt collector" and their applicability have changed over time. The FDCPA itself contains numerous exclusions regarding the definition of a debt collector. However, attorneys originally exempted from this definition have been included so that they now meet it. The definition of "debt" in the FDCPA restricts the coverage of the act to personal, familial, or household transactions. Therefore, debts from businesses or individuals for business purposes do not fall under the FDCPA.

ENFORCEMENT OF THE FDCPA

Under the Federal Trade Commission Act per 15 U.S. Code § 1692l, the Federal Trade Commission (FTC) and the relatively new Consumer Financial Protection Bureau (CFPB) have authority to enforce and administer the FDCPA, with the latter agency now handling consumer complaints.[6] Besides intervention by these government agencies, aggrieved consumers may also file private lawsuits as described in the following subsections to collect actual and statutory damages, attorney's fees, and court costs from third-party debt collectors.

The FDCPA is a strict liability law. This means consumers need not prove an actual injury occurred in order to claim statutory damages of $1,000 or less plus reasonable attorney's fees and costs. A person only need prove that a debt collector has violated the FDCPA during attempted collection. However, the collector may evade penalty under 15 U.S. Code § 1692k(c) if it shows that the violation was unintentional and resulted from a "bona fide error" in spite of procedures put in place to avoid the error at issue. Furthermore, if the court determines that the consumer filed the case in bad faith and for the purpose of harassment, it may rule that the collector is due the debt in addition to awarding it attorney's fees and costs.

Keep in mind the following with the FTC and CFPB: we do not want to paint an overly rosy picture of either of them. Remember that both are government agencies and both are brimming with bureaucracy, and it may take significant persistence to get anywhere with either agency. If your complaint is not successful with the CFPB, it might get referred to the FTC. In that case, the FTC may inform you that their standard operating procedure requires that they get several complaints against a debt collector before they decide to take any action. This means that you may not get the help you seek if you are one of the first persons to file a complaint against the collector.

Sue Debt Collector in Regular Civil Court

As a consumer, you can bring a civil lawsuit against a debt collector in state or federal court or in the appropriate city court in the nation's capital as applicable. In the suit, you must prove the debt collector violated the FDCPA. You may be able to collect actual damages and possibly punitive damages if you suffered harm from the violation and you are successful with the suit.

Consumers are usually represented by counsel in such suits. Although a consumer could proceed *pro se*, there may be no significant advantage in doing so if the monetary claim in the suit includes the consumer's attorney fees as are allowed in most jurisdictions as are costs. Suing in state court is often the most time-consuming and lengthy avenue of redress because these courts are usually more overburdened than other courts.

Sue Debt Collector in Small Claims Court

Small claims court is an option for consumers who may prefer to proceed *pro se* or who may not want to expend the time and effort necessary for a standard full-fledged lawsuit. Small claims court provides individuals and businesses or other entities with an expedited process for pursuing civil cases that fall under a certain maximum dollar threshold, which varies nationwide. These courts generally offer litigants one relatively short trial in order to argue the case in front of a judge, some other officiator, or a jury. Usually, completing and filing a simple pre-printed court form is all that is needed to start the case. Trials are usually held within three months after lawsuits are filed. Chapter nine covered small claims cases in detail.

Consider Class Action Lawsuit

Statutory laws allow members of a class action to recover both actual damages and penalties. Uniting with a group of people who have experienced similar transgressions can be a great way to fight a collection agency or creditor that has violated your consumer rights. Class actions are an option for debt collection violations and are discussed in chapter sixteen.

Notify Government Oversight Agency

Since the CFPB now handles complaints against debt collectors, consumers can contact its agents to report related problems. The CFPB receives complaints from consumers, provides them to collectors that are registered with the agency, and then works with both parties in order to try to find an amicable solution. Complaints to the CFPB can be submitted online.[7] Note that a complaint will reach a dead end with the agency if the collector is not registered, that is, not in its database, and will likely be referred to the FTC as stated above in the ENFORCEMENT OF THE FDCPA section.

Notify Attorney General

A debt collector may also have violated state or local laws irrespective of the FDCPA. You could contact an attorney general's office to get information about filing an FDCPA lawsuit or to pursue any viable local sanctions against the debt collector. If these offices get enough complaints against one collector, they might prosecute the collector on behalf of the complainants. To find an office, see the National Association of Attorneys General.[8] If you are trying to determine which attorney general's office to contact, you can begin with contacting either the one in the state where you became a party to the contract or the one in the state where a party to it resides. It could be that a state may not be applicable, and the District of Columbia may be instead, which also has an attorney general.

Leverage Violations during Debt Settlement Negotiations

You can oftentimes use a debt collector's FDCPA violations as leverage when attempting to settle a debt. This can be successful since collectors know an FDCPA lawsuit could result in a judgment against them in addition to incurring the expense of defending it. The amount of leverage you get from threatening with a lawsuit should depend on the amount of evidence you have against the collector. Solid evidence proving any violation—for example, documentation of phone calls being received after 9:00 p.m., confirmation from coworkers who received phone calls, and other such records—should afford much more leverage during debt settlement negotiations. So should the collector failing to inform you that you have thirty days from the required written notice to dispute the debt.

ALTERNATIVE DISPUTE RESOLUTION

Some debts may be governed by a contract between the respective parties that dictates alternative dispute resolution (ADR) be pursued for any resulting conflicts. If you are obligated to settle a debt dispute by this avenue, then your first step will probably be to contact the other party to initiate the process. It has become widespread practice for many companies to put into written contracts language requiring ADR for resolving potential disputes. As such, there is much debate as to whether this practice is against public policy because it effectively takes away a person's day in court to challenge the contract. For more information about ADR, consult chapter eight.

DEFENSES TO DEBT COLLECTION

It is a good idea to get a copy of your credit report at least yearly to check that you do not have outstanding debts of which you are unaware. Unexpected debts, perhaps illegally attributed to you by identity theft, may have negatively impacted your credit score and should then appear on your credit report. If you have incurred debts from identity theft, you should not be legally responsible for them.

If you have an old debt, you may escape liability for it too. This is because a creditor or debt collector has a limited time to file suit in order to recover a debt. The time limit is known as the statute of limitations and is set by law. The allotted time varies greatly nationwide and for different kinds of debts. Under certain circumstances, this period can be extended or restarted. So, be careful when communicating with a debt collector about an old debt because you could unintentionally increase the length of time that you can legally be held liable and sued for it—not pleasant, particularly for invalid or fraudulent debts. More on this topic can be found in the Waiving, Extending, and Reviving the Statute of Limitations subsection later in this chapter.

TYPES OF CREDIT AND THE STATUTE OF LIMITATIONS

You can ascertain if your debt is time-barred, meaning that it is too old for a collector or creditor to file a legitimate lawsuit.[9] First, determine the type of debt it is. Is it the result of an oral contract, a written contract, or a promissory note, a written promise to pay money to somebody? The statute of limitations for written contracts and promissory notes generally lies between three and ten years. For oral contracts, it ordinarily ranges between two and ten years.

Second, determine the specifics of any associated account. Is the debt from a credit account? If so, determine whether the account is open-end or closed-end. This is not always easy. Generally, if you can use the account repeatedly, it is open-end credit, or revolving credit. The amount of credit you use in a certain period determines the size of your payments. A credit card account is the classic example of open-end credit.

Closed-end credit typically involves a single transaction, for example, the purchase of a home or vehicle. The amount and number of payments are fixed, or the amount can change only at periodic intervals in the case of an adjustable-rate mortgage. Some accounts fall somewhere in between open- and closed-end credit. An example of this might be a person whom you employ for recurring services and with whom a contract was never signed, but you have an open-ended relationship with that person to call upon him on an as-needed basis. Also, many creditors try to characterize a closed-end account as open-end either to take advantage of a longer statute of limitations or to avoid providing the more extensive disclosures required for closed-end credit that may more fully inform the consumer.

As just implied, the statute of limitations for open- and closed-end accounts often differs. To complicate matters further, the statute for an open-end account is not always obvious. Some states have a special statute of limitations for open-end credit. Others apply the one for written or oral contracts to open-end credit.

Third, determine the applicable statute of limitations. Statutes of limitations for debt collection are set by law as explained earlier in this section. To determine their specifics for debts relevant to your matter, you can easily access this information online, consult with a lawyer, conduct research at a law library or court, or contact a consumer protection agency (see last entry in appendix).

Fourth, determine when the statute of limitations started running. For open-end accounts, it usually starts to run on the day the first due payment is missed. If the account is closed-end, it will generally begin to run on the date the account's contract is breached.

Using the Statute of Limitations

If a creditor files a collection suit against you after expiration of the statute of limitations, you should raise this as a defense in the answer you file to the lawsuit. You should not have to repay the debt if you can prove that it is defendable under the statute of limitations. If the debt collector knows time has expired for collecting the debt and sues you anyway, it may have violated the FDCPA.

Expiration of the statute of limitations does not nullify a debt, however. It simply limits the legal remedies available to the creditor or a collection agency after a specified period. Even though you cannot be legally forced to repay a debt for which the statute has expired, the creditor or a third party debt collector can still seek voluntary payment of it. Despite any resolution to a debt dispute, outstanding debt can be reported by either to a credit reporting agency.

Attempting to Collect Time-Barred Debts

Fairly recently, debt collectors have been attempting to recover debts for which the statute of limitations has expired. They buy them from original creditors at a fraction of their value and can make large profits if they collect anything from the debtor. They sometimes use pushy tactics when trying to collect time-barred debts. Debt collectors can and do harass people and try to trick them into reaffirming debts in order to increase the amount of time they have to collect under the statute of limitations. If they are successful, the expiration clock is reset or its time is extended.

Whenever communication is verbal, whatever you say can sometimes be recorded and used against you in court. Legality and admissibility depend upon several factors, which vary widely by jurisdiction. One factor is that you could need to be informed the conversation is being recorded and consent to it. Another is that certain requirements may also have to be met in order to use recorded conversation as evidence.

Waiving, Extending, and Reviving the Statute of Limitations

If you claim that the expiration of the statute of limitations absolves you of a debt, the collector or creditor might argue that you waived, extended, or revived it in your earlier correspondence. When you waive the protections afforded you under the statute of limitations for a debt, it means you relinquish your right to assert them as a defense later. The law makes it difficult for a consumer to waive these protections accidentally. A court should uphold a claim of waiver only if you knew what you were doing when you agreed to waive them. Under certain conditions, a waiver might be unenforceable. Even if you think you may have waived your protections, you should still consider raising not having done so as a defense and make the collector or creditor prove you did.

Tolling temporarily stops the expiration clock of the statute of limitations for a specific reason—when the creditor or collector extends your time to pay, for example. Suppose you owe Schnedly's Auto $1,200. Assume that the place of business is in a location where the statute of limitations for this type of debt is six years. Normally, the statute would begin to run when payment for services was due. Also assume that Schnedly's gave you an additional six months to pay and therefore tolled, or extended, the statute for six months. If you still cannot repay the debt after six months, then the six-year statute of limitations begins to run at that point.

Reviving a statute of limitations means that the entire period for which you can be held liable for a debt resets. Depending upon location, you can extend or revive the statute of limitations if you make a partial payment on a debt or otherwise acknowledge that you are responsible for one or promise to repay one that you have not been paying. In many jurisdictions, the acknowledgement or promise must be in writing and sometimes signed by the debtor.

For example, suppose that you have an outstanding $5,000 balance on an open-end account with a health care provider, that you stopped making payments in 2006, and that the statute of limitations for medical debts in the jurisdiction in question is four years. The four-year statute began to run on the date you missed the next due payment. In 2009 suppose you made a $500 payment and then stopped making payments again. Also suppose the partial payment revived the statute of limitations. The provider has at least four years from the date of your $500 payment to file a lawsuit against you for the remainder of the debt in order to have a viable chance of collecting.

Note that at the federal level, section 14219 of the Food, Conservation, and Energy Act of 2008 eliminated the statute of limitations for nearly all federal debts, so any reviving or extending typically does not apply.[10] Since then, income tax refunds of many people have been seized by the government to cover alleged federal debts that are oftentimes many decades old. A simple way to prevent this form of theft is to do what one author does, which is to ensure that the government is always owed money every tax year rather than the other way around. Provided the amount owed is kept under the penalty threshold, doing this can also be considered getting an interest-free loan from the government.

DISPUTING A DEBT

You should understand that you can lose valuable rights if you fail to dispute a debt in writing within thirty days of receiving written notice of it. Sample letters that you could use to respond to a debt collector and helpful tips can be found on the CFPB website. The sample letters could help you obtain information, avoid losing important rights, and define the specifics regarding further communication.[11]

If you dispute a debt or part of one within thirty days of reception of the required initial written correspondence from the debt collector, it cannot legally continue collection activities or contact you until after your dispute has been properly investigated. The required information that is supposed to be sent to you within five days of the collector's first contact, commonly called the "validation notice," should contain the following:

- amount of the debt
- name of the party to whom the debt is allegedly owed
- statement that you have thirty days to dispute the debt, or it will be assumed valid
- statement that the debt collector must provide written verification of the debt if you dispute it in writing within thirty days
- statement that the debt collector will provide the name and address of the original creditor, if different from the current creditor, if you make a written request within thirty days

If you dispute the debt after those thirty days have passed, the debt collector can legally continue to contact you while it investigates your dispute. However, if the collector reports information about the debt to an entity such as a credit reporting agency, it must also report that the debt is being contested. If investigation reveals the debt is not yours or it is invalid for some reason, the debt collector may not legally continue collection activities against you. You also may personally have to contact the credit reporting agency to correct any incorrect information that they now have on record because of the unfounded claim by the collector. Remember that there is an agency to which you can turn for help if you cannot single-handedly defeat a debt collector that is pursuing you. If you are having trouble with a debt collection entity, you can submit a complaint to the CFPB online or by calling the agency directly. As stated earlier in this chapter's ENFORCEMENT OF THE FDCPA section, there is no guarantee you will receive the help you seek, but there is a chance.

If you acknowledge that you owe a debt to a creditor and want to resolve the issue, one option is to request a payment plan. This can reduce your burden by allowing you to make smaller payments over time and may help resolve the ongoing dispute. A payment plan may also mitigate damages if the creditor is thinking of suing you. If you agree to a payment plan, it may prevent legal action by the creditor. However, if you default on making payments, then the creditor has the right to pursue the matter in court or seek any other available legal remedies. When in doubt, research applicable laws, or consult an experienced attorney.

DISCHARGING DEBTS THROUGH BANKRUPTCY

Bankruptcy can offer a fresh start when you find yourself overwhelmed by debts and unable to repay them. People turn to bankruptcy for many reasons, and sometimes bankruptcy is a legitimate option. For reasons beyond your control, you may find yourself in a tough financial situation—after losing a job, incurring exorbitant medical bills, or experiencing some unforeseen catastrophe, for instance. Sometimes bad decisions and being financially irresponsible are behind a bankruptcy. Other times it is just plain bad luck. The law tries to balance the need for a fresh start with creditors' interests.

Many people do not realize that bankruptcy does not erase all debts. Bankruptcy law recognizes that some debts must be repaid. You will not normally receive relief from non-dischargeable debts in a bankruptcy case. Some non-dischargeable debts were discussed in chapter four's WAYS TO AVOID PAYING MONEY OR RELINQUISHING PROPERTY section.

There are four common types of bankruptcy: chapter 7, chapter 11, chapter 12, and chapter 13. Under Title 11 of the U.S. Code and immediately upon filing, a bankruptcy proceeding provides protection from certain debts and obligations, at least temporarily. It does this via an automatic stay, which prevents evictions, stalls foreclosure proceedings, and stops collection activities from creditors. Note that someone may file a bankruptcy petition that might not be legitimate, and the act of doing so could be purely for this reason.

Chapter 7 bankruptcy is intended for debtors under financial strain who do not have the ability to repay their existing debt. It is best suited to cases in which the majority of debt is unsecured—credit card debt, for example. Debtors can protect certain assets up to a predetermined amount. Chapter 7 is the most common form of bankruptcy.

Chapter 11 bankruptcy petitions can be filed by companies or individuals. Unlike chapter 13, chapter 11 has no limits on debt or time frame for repayment. Its intent is to restructure the terms of debt. It is probably the most complex form of bankruptcy.

Chapter 12 bankruptcy caters to family fishermen or family farmers in financial trouble who have regular annual income. It enables them to suggest and implement a plan to repay all or part of their debt over time. Debtors make installments to creditors over three to five years under this chapter. It also provides a simpler, more streamlined, less expensive way to file for bankruptcy for those who qualify.

Chapter 13 bankruptcy is a total reorganization of debt. The goal for the debtor is to resume regular payments of non-dischargeable debt and pay the arrearages over time. As with chapter 12, the U.S. Bankruptcy Code gives the debtor three to five years to repay creditors under this chapter. A chapter 13 bankruptcy is completed under the supervision of the government.

Filing for bankruptcy is a big decision that should not be taken lightly. Although bankruptcy can alleviate some short-term problems of being unable to repay debts, it can and does have a negative impact on your credit score. As a result, it also affects your ability to qualify for loans, credit cards, and jobs in the financial industry. Due to bankruptcy's complicated codes and procedures, you may want to consult with an attorney when considering whether to proceed with it.

If you are not ready or willing to consider bankruptcy as an option, a good alternative might be debt consolidation. Debt consolidation companies have become increasingly popular after the most recent economic collapse of 2008. They typically offer to consolidate your debts under one lower interest rate. If this is something you might consider, research the legitimacy of these companies because plenty of them exist that scam consumers. To help minimize abuse, laws have been written that forbid them from charging fees in advance. Consolidation of debt may be a better alternative than filing for bankruptcy or trying to arrange a payment plan with your creditors.

Chapter 14: Residential Landlord-Tenant Law

We are but tenants...for shortly the great Landlord will give us notice that our lease has expired. — **Joseph Jefferson**

Chapter Sections

- Background
- Landlord duties
- Tenant remedies
- Tenant duties
- Landlord remedies
- Resolving ongoing disputes

BACKGROUND

For the vast majority of Americans, being a residential renter and subsequently under the umbrella of residential landlord-tenant law is something they will experience. This area of law is one in which dramatic *Judge Mathis* episodes come to mind. "Litigants" on the show are often landlords and tenants fighting over landlord-tenant issues.

A leasehold estate gives a tenant the temporary right to occupy someone else's property. In American residential landlord-tenant law, many duties and rights of landlords and tenants have been codified into the Uniform Residential Landlord and Tenant Act. As a rule of thumb across America, matters related to real property must be in writing in order to be valid. Consequently, it is best for landlords and tenants to have any type of rental living arrangement in writing so that they can protect themselves and their rights. The lease or other written rental agreement might be crucial when resolving any legal issues that may arise between the parties. While a lease usually encompasses a longer term than a rental agreement and they can differ in other ways, the language used throughout this chapter is intended to mean either one in general; therefore, only the word "lease" will be used.

Residential leases are contracts applicable to individuals or families who will live in a leased space (see appendix). Because residential landlords and tenants are considered to be on a less level playing field than commercial landlords and tenants, residential tenants are generally afforded more rights. They are normally more protected under the law for this same reason.

Being a landlord in places such as southern California and New York City is big business due to the ever-increasing cost of rent. Recent data show that rent is more expensive in various cities than the cost of a mortgage.[1] Because of the potential return on investment being so favorable in many booming markets, some landlords tend to cheat the system and cut corners. As much as landlords can acquire the reputation for being "slumlords," cities also can and do, for political or financial reasons, target certain landlords who own several residential apartment buildings.

When it comes to renting residential properties, many people hold a common misconception. They think it is better to rent to a single female than a single male. From the landlord's perspective, it might actually be better to rent to a single, responsible male. If renting to a single female with children, it may be virtually impossible in some jurisdictions to have them evicted. The landlord would be perceived as a heartless magnate trying to put a helpless woman and her children outside on the cold, unsafe streets, regardless if she has not paid rent for months or has destroyed the property.

Also, if something breaks in the rental unit, a handyman is more capable of making repairs. This is especially pertinent if the prospective tenant happens to be a tradesman. Lastly, when renting to a single female, a landlord is not privy to her future boyfriend selection. A five-star apartment could quickly become a drug den if she chooses the wrong type. Of course, should someone decide not to rent to a female for any of these reasons, she would need to state that she found a more financially qualified applicant or give some other nondiscriminatory reason in order to avoid legal action by the prospective tenant.

Finding good, responsible tenants is often desirable for a landlord. To incentivize them to care for her rental property, a landlord may benefit from proposing that she and they split the costs of certain repairs and write such a clause into the lease if allowed by law and amenable to both parties. In return, rent could be discounted by a small amount to compensate her tenants for possible future repair costs. The likelihood of appliances and heating and air conditioning units breaking and requiring service or replacement is minimal when a rental is new, so the incentive for them to agree to such terms should be even greater in this instance.

This kind of proposal in a lease may slightly limit rental income to a landlord but may offset headaches associated with having to repair fairly new furnishings because of misuse by tenants. It also benefits tenants who want to save money on rent—and perhaps even more money if they are handymen or tradesmen and are quite capable of making many repairs. Under the right conditions, such an agreement could be win-win. Lastly, to incentivize conservation, writing into the lease that tenants will be responsible for all usage-based expenses, such as utilities, water, and sewage, should not only accomplish that end but minimize landlord costs as well.

LANDLORD DUTIES

Renting property with the intent of earning income from it without regard for tenants' well-being or safety is not commonly permitted by law. Landlords of residential properties have specific duties incumbent upon them. In order to offer a residential property for rent, the landlord must comply with relevant laws and codes.

Implied Warranty of Habitability

One of the most common issues at the root of landlord-tenant disputes is the landlord's failure to provide habitable conditions. The basic premise of the implied warranty of habitability is that a rental unit must be fit to house people. In legal terms, "habitable" means the rental unit is suitable for occupation by human beings and that it substantially complies with applicable building codes as well as health and safety codes that materially affect tenants' health and safety.[2] It is important to note that almost every jurisdiction requires a landlord to provide basics, such as electricity, heating, operational plumbing, hot and cold running water, and other necessities.

Residential leases in most states and in the nation's capital contain an implied warranty of habitability, which was established by the U.S. Court of Appeals for the District of Columbia case *Javins v. First National Realty Corp.*[3] A landlord must keep her rental habitable under the implied warranty even if the lease does not explicitly require her to do so. Since a tenant's duty to pay rent is conditioned upon her landlord providing habitable living conditions under this warranty, absence of habitability would then relieve the tenant of the duty to pay rent. The implied warranty of habitability makes it easier for tenants to hold landlords accountable for repairs. This warranty is usually coupled with rules prohibiting landlords from retaliating against tenants who complain about housing code violations.

The warranty of habitability is controversial. Supporters argue that it protects lower-income tenants from callous landlords. Opponents argue that it inflates rental prices and promotes abandonment of older buildings by landlords. Sometimes a tenant has the right to cancel a lease and leave the premises if defects are severe enough and the landlord has not made repairs in a reasonable amount of time. A tenant who wants to cancel her lease can seek assistance of counsel or a government agency that is in the business of addressing landlord-tenant issues. Or, if she is capable, she can do some research on her own to determine if conditions are severe enough to break the lease and how to go about it.

A rental may be considered uninhabitable if it contains a lead hazard that endangers the occupants or public. A building with a structural hazard, inadequate sanitation, or something else that endangers the health, life, safety, or property of the occupants or public may also be deemed uninhabitable. In California see Civil Code Section 1941.1 paragraph 1 and Health and Safety Code Sections 17920.3 and 17920.10 as applicable.[4] [5] Keep in mind that a rental unit not in perfect, aesthetically pleasing condition does not necessarily violate the implied warranty of habitability. Any minor housing code violations, which by themselves do not affect habitability, also do not violate the warranty. See *Hinson v. Delis.*[6]

There are also other ways the implied warranty of habitability may be violated. One is the presence of mold in the rental unit that affects its livability. Another in California results from a 2006 law that mandates a property be vacated when it is contaminated by methamphetamine. The following reference book suggests that a tenant who is harmed by this kind of contamination may be able to claim a breach of the implied warranty of habitability: Moskovitz et al., *California Landlord-Tenant Practice*, section 3.11B.

Many free legal services are available to both landlords and tenants and can be found with just a little bit of research. In most jurisdictions, there are nonprofit legal aid organizations that offer no-cost legal assistance. In addition, many state courts and the Superior Court of the District of Columbia offer free self-help in a designated location within their courthouses during specific times to people with landlord-tenant matters. Most free legal services offered to the public are just a short drive, internet search, or phone call away.

Implied Covenant of Quiet Enjoyment

A covenant is an agreement or a promise concerning two or more parties regarding the performance or restriction of an action. Normally included in residential leases in the United States is an implied covenant of quiet enjoyment. By virtue of this covenant, a landlord is not supposed to bother or disrupt her tenant during the tenancy of the rental unit. However, a landlord may enter her property without prior notice during emergencies. If a situation arises that should have reasonably been anticipated by the landlord, it does not eliminate her need to notify her tenant that she wants to enter her property. Therefore, just because a landlord must take quick action to enter her property does not necessarily constitute an emergency according to the doctrine of imminent peril, which excludes peril as a result of negligence or poor planning on the part of the landlord.

Also, most leases have provisions for a landlord to enter her rental unit for an inspection or to show it to a prospective tenant provided advance notification is given to the current occupants. In California, for example, a landlord must give her tenant a minimum of twenty-four-hour and forty-eight-hour notice before entering her unit to show it to prospective tenants and to inspect it, respectively.

Deliver Possession

Under common law, a landlord has to deliver legal possession of her rental unit to her tenant at the commencement of the lease. Wherever a landlord is also required to deliver physical possession, the reasoning behind placing this duty upon her is that she is presumed to have greater resources than the new tenants to pursue legal remedies against holdover tenants, occupants who will not relinquish possession of the property.

Make Repairs

An issue that frequently arises in landlord-tenant disputes is one identifying the responsible party for making and paying for repairs. In many jurisdictions, the law states that landlords have the affirmative duty to make repairs for basic living conditions. But in several states, including California, the law makes landlords and tenants each responsible for certain kinds of repairs, although landlords ultimately are legally responsible for assuring that their rental units are habitable. Regarding repairs, a landlord must make a unit livable before renting it to a tenant. Additionally, while a unit is being rented, the landlord must make necessary repairs that continue to keep it livable.

In California landlords have the duty to make major repairs because of California Court of Appeal case *Hinson v. Delis* requiring that all residential leases contain an implied warranty of habitability. Whether landlords or tenants are responsible for making minor repairs is usually governed by the lease. When in doubt, consult your lease or speak with your landlord before issues arise. If a landlord does not comply with her tenant's request to make certain repairs, oftentimes the tenant can make the repairs herself and then deduct the expenses associated with them from rent the following month.

TENANT REMEDIES

Landlord-tenant laws in most parts of the country include various protections for tenants. Such laws provide tenants with specific remedies for landlords with cavalier attitudes towards them. Remedies involve constructive eviction, retaliatory eviction, breach of covenant, and damages.

Constructive Eviction

In a legal action for unpaid rent brought by a landlord against her tenant, the tenant may be able to offer constructive eviction as an affirmative defense against having to pay any outstanding rent under the lease. "Constructive eviction" means that the tenant is unable to occupy the property because of something her landlord has done or failed to do, not that she was actually evicted by her landlord. A defense such as this is often used in conjunction with a breach of the implied warranty of habitability.

Retaliatory Eviction

A tenant can use retaliatory eviction both as an affirmative defense against an eviction and as a cause of action in a counterclaim or separate lawsuit against her landlord. See landmark case *Edwards v. Habib*.[7] California Civil Code Section 1942.5 defines the legal aspects of retaliatory eviction in that state and furthermore prohibits evictions occurring within 180 days after a series of triggering events. Some form of protection for tenants against retaliatory eviction for reporting health and safety code violations is available in the vast majority of states and the District of Columbia.

Breach of Covenant

Leases include dependent covenants. The implied covenant of quiet enjoyment and the implied warranty of habitability are two dependant covenants that were discussed in their own subsections earlier in this chapter. Yet another is the covenant to repair, an agreement to which a landlord is implicitly bound to keep a rental property in good condition. These three dependent covenants apply in various parts of the country. The breach of such covenants by a landlord can be used, for example, as an affirmative defense by her tenant in a lawsuit for eviction brought by the landlord because of unpaid rent.

Damages

In some states, Wisconsin for instance, a tenant can be monetarily compensated for a loss or an injury when her landlord violates administrative codes or state statutes. In order for this to happen, a tenant must prove that her landlord owes her damages associated with the tenancy and be fortunate not to have her case heard in a corrupt court where her landlord is politically connected. The Wisconsin Department of Agriculture, Trade and Consumer Protection regulates unfair and deceptive business practices, which include the protection of tenants from unfair rental practices by landlords. If a tenant can prove a violation by her landlord, she should be entitled to double the amount of damages under Wisconsin law.[8]

TENANT DUTIES

A tenant has several duties to her landlord. Notwithstanding the duties of a tenant set forth in the lease itself, common law imposes three obligations. A tenant's first duty is to pay the rent. Her second duty is to preserve the premises. Her third is not to use the premises for an illegal purpose.

Duty to Pay Rent

Formerly under common law, a tenant's duty to pay rent was considered an independent covenant. This means that a tenant was still required to pay rent irrespective of whether her landlord fulfilled her obligations or not. Now, the duty of a tenant to pay rent is considered to be a dependent covenant. A tenant can be freed from having to pay rent if her landlord breaches the covenant of quiet enjoyment, the covenant to repair, or the warranty of habitability and possibly because of other breaches. The only known exception to the foregoing exists in Arkansas where it is also a crime to pay rent late. See Arkansas code § 18-16-101.[9]

Duty to Preserve the Premises

Tenants must refrain from committing waste, otherwise known as damaging a rented property. Under common law, they are required to take reasonable care of their rental units and common areas, including hallways and outside spaces. Tenants must keep the aforementioned clean and undamaged. They are also responsible for repair of all damage resulting from their neglect or abuse, from pets, and from anyone for whom they are responsible, such as family or guests. Most of the relevant statutes require premises to be returned to a landlord in the same or better condition than they were at move-in; otherwise, the tenant will be liable for damage. If a tenant expects to get her security deposit returned in full after move-out, she must preserve the premises and return them to her landlord in no worse condition than they were at move-in.

LANDLORD REMEDIES

Although predicting problematic tenants can be difficult, it is a great idea for a landlord to screen rental applicants as rigorously as the law allows in order to alleviate future headaches and potential legal issues. Typically, a landlord will run a credit check for an applicant and obtain references. If you are a landlord looking for a reference from a landlord of a potential tenant, it might be wise to speak with a prior landlord of the tenant and not the current one, if possible. The current landlord may not be completely honest about a tenant with another landlord if she wants to remove an undesirable tenant from her rental property and thus might give an overly positive recommendation. Landlords have several remedies at their disposal to reclaim possession of their rental units and collect unpaid rent if these or other preventative measures fail them.

Eviction

Eviction, "unlawful detainer" or "ejectment" as it is called in some parts of the country, refers to the process of attempting to remove persons occupying a property who allegedly do not have legal right to it. The term "unlawful detainer" ordinarily refers to the conduct of a tenant who is in possession of leased property and refuses to leave it upon expiration or termination of the lease. Typically, a tenant gets evicted for not paying rent, for endangering other tenants, or for damaging or performing illegal acts on the rented property but remains there nevertheless.

In years past, a landlord was personally permitted to remove a tenant by force for nonpayment of rent or violation of the lease. Current U.S. laws, however, require a landlord to file an eviction lawsuit to begin the process of removing an unwanted tenant. Of course, this is another moneymaker for the system. A tenant who faces eviction may successfully fight it if the landlord is not following law or because a violation of her right to due process guaranteed under the Fifth or Fourteenth Amendments to the U.S. Constitution occurs.

Eviction processes vary nationally and are similar to procedures for other civil lawsuits in whatever part of the country in which the eviction occurs. A landlord must file a lawsuit and have the tenants served the complaint according to court rules of procedure. The tenants are then given time to answer the lawsuit, and the case continues through the court system as other civil suits do. Alternative dispute resolution (ADR), such as arbitration or mediation, can also be used for resolving evictions instead of litigating. Furthermore, some jurisdictions or leases may require it as a first attempt at resolution. ADR was covered in chapter eight.

If a tenant is facing the unpleasant prospect of being unfairly evicted from her rental unit, one option is to seek help from a non-profit that educates tenants about their rights and another is to consult an attorney. Most jurisdictions, either directly through the court or a non-profit, offer free legal aid to such people who cannot afford to hire an attorney.

Damages

Landlords can also be compensated in the form of damages for unpaid rent. The methods of obtaining past due rent and the amount acquirable are dictated by law. In most instances, a landlord has to go through the eviction process, obtain a favorable judgment, and then seek to enforce such judgment. She could alternately obtain a stipulation agreement signed by her and her tenant regarding payment of past due rent and thus try to avoid litigation. In some parts of the country and under some leases, a party may be entitled to double or treble damages resulting from certain actions or inactions of the other party. Check the lease and applicable landlord-tenant laws for clarification.

RESOLVING ONGOING DISPUTES

Sometimes a landlord and tenant will be involved in a dispute with no apparent simple solution. Written into many leases is a clause that allows the party who prevails in court to recover attorney's fees and costs. It is important to read the terms of your lease before deciding to pursue litigation. Due to the uncertainty of the outcome of litigation within our current corrupt judicial system, it might be best and may be required under the terms of your lease to exhaust all administrative remedies before filing suit. One author mediated and successfully settled a lengthy landlord-tenant dispute in favor of the tenant in order to correct a landlord's egregious behavior.

Common disputes between landlords and tenants concern security deposits—particularly a landlord keeping all or part of one. In most jurisdictions, a landlord must return a tenant's security deposit within a certain amount of time usually designated by statute. In order to justify the amount of the security deposit withheld, the landlord must normally provide an itemized accounting of repair costs. Receipts may help her prove necessary repairs were actually completed.

One prevalent case type seen in small claims court tends to be related to landlord-tenant security deposits. Small claims court is one way to resolve such a dispute. Chapter nine covered small claims cases in detail.

If you find yourself engaged in battle with your landlord in court because she contends you damaged the leased property during your tenancy and refuses to return your security deposit, you should come prepared with all evidence to disprove her allegations. This is why documenting everything, taking photographs at move-in and move-out, and requesting a move-out inspection with your landlord at the conclusion of the lease are of the utmost importance when you are trying to recoup your security deposit. Preparation of this sort should prove beneficial. It should help deflect any of your landlord's claims and bolster any of your claims.

Chapter 15: Probate, Wills, and Related Law

Nobody wants to read about the honest lawyer down the street who does real estate loans and wills. If you want to sell books, you have to write about the interesting lawyers—the guys who steal all the money and take off. That's the fun stuff. — **John Grisham**

Chapter Sections

- Background
- Probate
- The probate process
- Probate considerations
- Benefits of mediation
- Challenging a will in court
- Titling assets is part of estate planning
- Other considerations

BACKGROUND

The area of law discussed in this chapter bears a resemblance to divorce and other areas of family law. Certainly, the only two areas of law that pit family members against one another are probate law and family law. Another similarity between them is that emotions of litigants generally run high in both. Because they are so closely related, some jurisdictions have courts that aptly contain "Probate and Family Court" in their names and that handle all things family and probate related, such as divorce, child support, and issues pertaining to wills and estates.

Corruption in any court, probate included, is not out of the realm of possibilities. Perhaps because probate and related law comprise a smaller segment of the legal business than family law, corruption does not seem to be as prevalent in probate court in jurisdictions that have separate courts for each as it is where such courts are combined. Nonetheless, corruption might be more difficult to discern in any of these courts since emotions tend to run higher than in other courts and may blind a person to it. Note that some states call courts that handle probate "surrogate's court."

Many people initially encounter probate after a family member dies. Probate can be an expensive and oppressively lengthy process that a decedent's family must sometimes endure and can get messy amongst family members squabbling over money or precious family heirlooms. The emergence of modern American probate statutory codes was intended to make probate more efficient. Additionally, the evolution of the living trust as a substitute for a will provides an alternative to probate. Trusts such as these transfer wealth placed in them during their creator's lifetime to his beneficiaries once he is gone.

If your estate is relatively small, it may not need to be probated at all. Every state and Washington, D.C., have at least one alternative to regular probate for relatively small estates. "Small estate" is defined differently across the country. Many estates worth several hundred thousand dollars or less are eligible for special transfer procedures that hasten property ownership to inheritors. The exact amount varies greatly nationwide.

There are two main probate shortcuts. One is claiming property by using a short document stating the right of ownership to it under a will or law. This document, typically signed under oath, is called an "affidavit" (see appendix). If your estate qualifies, an inheritor can prepare one and provide it to certain establishments for this purpose. For example, when a financial institution holding an account of a decedent receives a copy of his death certificate and such an affidavit, it releases his money or other property under its control to the inheritor.

A second shortcut, a simpler and quicker version of probate, may be available. The probate court is still involved with this option, but it exercises much less control over the process. In many places, this expedited course of action is straightforward enough to handle without an attorney, so you can save time and money. To determine if a probate shortcut is applicable and any dollar limit of an estate that will qualify for it, check relevant probate statutes.

It should also be mentioned that most jurisdictions have ethical rules against an attorney taking any financial interest in the estate of a client for whom he prepares an estate plan. If you are ever in a situation wherein an attorney tries to take advantage of you by asking to be the recipient of something valuable in your will or trust, this should immediately raise a red flag and the attorney should be reported for unethical behavior. As explained many times previously, it is unlikely the overseeing board will do anything punitive, but there is a slim chance. Noting such an immoral lawyer's attempted procurement on one or more of the lawyer rating websites listed in the appendix may at least provide some public warning.

PROBATE

The term "probate" is used in different ways. Probate can refer to the act of presenting a will to a court officer for filing, as in "probating a will." But in a more general sense, probate refers to the method by which someone's estate is administered and processed through the court system after he dies. One of its intended functions is to ensure that title to his assets is validly transferred to the inheritors of his estate.[1]

Many people believe probate applies only if they have a will, but this is not correct. Your estate will likely be probated whether you have a will or not. But, as explained in the BACKGROUND section of this chapter, having a living trust or relatively small estate are two ways to avoid probate. If you have a valid will, then it determines how your estate is transferred during probate and to whom. If you die intestate, or without a valid will, or if you die partially intestate wherein only part of your estate is covered by a valid will, then intestate laws where you were living before your death determine how your uncovered property is distributed except for out-of-state real property. Such property is probated where it is located.

THE PROBATE PROCESS

Probate is a process controlled by the courts for the transmission of wealth. It is intended to ensure that a decedent's will is valid—if he left one, that his debts are paid, and that the rest of his probate estate is properly distributed to his inheritors. The process is supposed to assist with transferring an estate in an orderly and a supervised fashion. An estate must be dispersed in a certain way, such as paying debts and taxes before any inheritors receive their inheritance. Probate can be viewed as the "script" that guides the transfer of an estate according to law.

Probate normally takes about a year to complete, in part because creditors are typically given several months to file any claims against an estate. During that time, property is valued and inventoried, and the decedent's bills are paid. Tax returns are filed and perhaps audited. Property may be sold to pay taxes or debts, with any remainder being distributed among beneficiaries or heirs. Accounting reports are also prepared and filed with the court.[2] Associated fees usually consist of attorney's fees and a personal representative's commission, which collectively range approximately between 1 and 10 percent of the estate where set by law. In the majority of states and Washington, D.C., however, they are not. Fees set by law tend to be the more expensive fee option and may be best to avoid.

Even though you will not be alive if and when your estate goes through probate, it is important for you to understand how the process works for the benefit of the people you leave behind. At the most basic level, it involves two steps. The first is paying your debts, and the second is transferring any remaining assets to your inheritors.

In many parts of the nation, probate courts oversee the affair. Because they are not federal courts, the processes they follow vary across the country. Yet those processes all revolve around these fundamental steps despite any differences:

1. inaugurating your personal representative
2. notifying creditors, inheritors, and the public
3. inventorying your property
4. distributing your estate

Inaugurating Your Personal Representative

If you left a will that is upheld by the court, it should be the document designating the personal representative for your estate. However, the court can also designate your representative under these or other circumstances:

- You left a will but did not specify a personal representative.
- The person you selected has died or cannot or will not serve for some reason, and you did not name a replacement.
- A family member, your spouse or an adult child, for instance, has asked the court to appoint him. Generally, a compelling argument needs to be made for not honoring your wishes, aside from any corruption.
- You died intestate, and the court must appoint an administrator or administratrix—the counterpart of an executor or executrix named in a will.

Regardless of who is ultimately selected, the court gives your personal representative official rights to handle your estate's affairs, which thus becomes the duty of this person. As evidence that this person has authority to act on behalf of your estate, the court gives him a certified document, the letters of administration or letters testamentary. Typically, the former would apply in an intestate case, the latter when there is a will.

A personal representative has to be formally appointed by the probate court before officially taking the position. He may need to take an oath of office and complete a few additional steps after which he will then receive the aforementioned official documentation conveying his status. Someone who is not named as personal representative might fabricate documents or convince the court that he is supposed to serve this function. People you leave behind should beware of this possibility. If it happens, the person you designated as your personal representative has to come forward with evidence to prove to the court that a mistake has been made or fraud has been committed.

It should be noted that the personal representative can act in accordance with the decedent's wishes regarding distribution of assets to beneficiaries and other duties described in the will and pay taxes and debts without approval of the court. He would keep the court informed of his progress by filing all required documents. If an interested person thinks the personal representative is not doing a good job, that person can raise his concerns to the court, ask the court to begin supervised administration, or formally petition the court to remove the personal representative. Supervised administration involves the highest level of court oversight. A request for it is usually granted when there are serious concerns about the actions of the person performing this function.

To initiate the probate process, your personal representative files a document referred to as a "petition for probate of will and appointment of personal representative," or something similarly named, with the court. If you left a will, the court should issue an order admitting it into probate. Basically, the court would be presuming whatever was submitted is your will and is valid.

Notifying Creditors, Inheritors, and the Public

Some jurisdictions require your personal representative to publish a death notice in their local newspaper. However, it is best to consult applicable laws as to the permitted methods of publication due to the rapid changes in technology and physical newspapers becoming extinct. The death notice serves to inform the public of your estate's probate proceeding and enables people who think they have an interest in your estate, such as creditors, to file a claim against it. Notifying people in this way about matters regarding your estate is part of the public record and overall process. The exposure of your private estate matters to the public is seen by some as one of probate's disadvantages. For this reason, many people opt for creating a living trust, which avoids probate and making a person's estate and his financial situation a public matter.

After someone dies, his personal representative needs to inform inheritors and creditors of the death and close the deceased's credit accounts according to court rules. He can use a standardized form to notify banks, mortgage companies, credit card issuers, and other businesses with which the deceased had an account. He can check with the lawyer handling the proceedings, or if he is *pro se*, he can ask the probate clerk at the courthouse about the rules to make sure he is in compliance.

Inventorying Your Property

Your personal representative must inventory the property, both real and personal, that defines your estate so its value can be determined. Taking inventory is important for a couple of reasons. One is to make sure you left enough assets to cover your debts and allow any remainder to be distributed among beneficiaries. Certain debts, such as private student loans, can survive death. So, if a person dies with private student loans, the responsibility to pay them back may be passed onto others. If your estate does not meet the monetary obligations to your creditors and the intended bequests to your beneficiaries, it is subject to abatement, meaning that one or more beneficiaries may receive less than you had wanted or perhaps nothing at all.

Another reason taking inventory is important is to ensure that all property has been catalogued. Your personal representative is in charge of this in order to make sure that all of it is available for distribution at probate completion. Your beneficiaries will naturally want to know what assets are in your estate. If property is missing or not in your estate at the time of your death, it is said to have been adeemed by extinction. Nonademption statutes determine if another asset or a monetary equivalent should be substituted for that property, which could have been sold or destroyed but was designated for one or more of your beneficiaries. Ademption also applies if the specific bequest has substantially changed over time.

You should know the approximate value of your estate so you can make wise choices for your estate plan. Obviously, your personal representative needs to know too. Make sure he has easy access to the list itemizing your estate and valuating your assets. Even a slightly outdated list can serve as a starting point so that he does not have to create one from scratch. Any significant life-changing event—moving, getting married, buying a home, or having a child—should prompt a person to revisit his estate plan. A good estate planning attorney will ask about changes annually in order to keep your plan current.

Distributing Your Estate

The final step in the probate process is distributing your estate. Ideally, everyone, both your creditors and those you leave behind, gets what is coming to him. Whatever is left after your creditors receive their money, and taxes and fees are paid, gets distributed to your heirs or the beneficiaries you named in your will. If probate proceeds according to law and all notices and communications are properly handled, your personal representative is usually protected against personal liability from any subsequent late-arriving claims. He should be safe from your creditors after some specified period. If he does not proceed with caution, things can go wrong. That is why it might be best for a personal representative to seek the advice of counsel or educate himself properly about the procedures of the probate court and relevant laws where the estate will be administered.

PROBATE CONSIDERATIONS

Some probate proceedings can be relatively straightforward, while others can be particularly complicated, depending upon the complexity of an estate. The following subsections describe some important probate considerations that your beneficiaries or heirs may need to understand.

Probate Jurisdiction

All states and the District of Columbia have probate, and the property that comprises your estate, both real and personal, may be part of its probate. Tangible and intangible personal property, such as your collectibles and stock portfolio, respectively, are probated where you live, but your real property is probated where it is physically located. So, if you live on and own a ranch by yourself in Texas and are the individual owner of a vacation condominium in Arizona, probate will likely be necessary in both states. Avoiding it would be possible, however, if your estate is relatively small, if you secured a living trust as stated in this chapter's BACKGROUND section, or if you had instead jointly owned both properties. In addition, it should be noted that your personal representative will have to perform the process in another country, which will have its own rules and laws regarding how an estate is administered, if you own property there at the time of your death. It may be best for him to consult with a lawyer in each country where you had assets at the time of your passing in order to ascertain the best way to handle your affairs.

Advantages and Disadvantages of Probate

Avoiding probate can be advantageous, but doing so may not necessarily eliminate all headaches that accompany the distribution of a decedent's property. One cannot easily escape from estate income taxes or the professional fees incurred during the creation and administration of a trust, for instance. Furthermore, the distribution of assets might not be quickened by avoiding probate either since estate tax returns may need to be filed and paid prior to any remaining assets being distributed.

Certain advantages are associated with probate and should be considered. Probate has the tendency to shield estate assets from creditors' late claims. Claims against a decedent's probate estate usually have to be filed by creditors within months after the date of his death; otherwise, they may be rejected. The requisite time frame varies greatly across the country and can be three months, twelve months, or something in between and can possibly be shorter or longer.

The Probate Estate and Property Excluded from It

A common misconception is that probate applies to all your estate. Actually, probate governs the processing of all assets in your probate estate, which comprises all property that is distributed through probate. The remaining property is called "non-probate property."

In a general sense, your probate estate is composed of assets you own alone. Non-probate property is composed of assets you own with others, like a joint bank account. Such property should automatically pass to co-owners upon your death. Non-probate assets also include those that pass to a named beneficiary—proceeds from a life insurance policy, for example. Other non-probate assets include bank, retirement, and pension accounts with designated beneficiaries. Because they should pass to someone automatically, there should be no need for probate.

Payable-on-death (POD) accounts, also called "Totten trusts" and other things, and transfer-on-death (TOD) accounts are supposed to transfer to their beneficiaries upon death of their owners. Like jointly-owned property, these types of accounts should bypass probate. The banks and institutions where the decedent held such accounts should be provided with a copy of his death certificate. They will then contact any beneficiaries directly. If you are a beneficiary, they will likely ask you to complete forms in order to transfer the accounts into your name.

Real property titled "joint tenants with right of survivorship" should pass by operation of law to the surviving co-owners and would thus not be included in the decedent's probate estate. Another way to avoid distribution of some assets through probate is to give people during your lifetime the gifts you would otherwise leave them. This is a common sense approach many people overlook that can avoid problems after they have died.

Avoiding Probate Does Not Always Avoid Tax Liabilities

Probate fees and related taxes each serve vastly different purposes. While certain fees, such as court fees, attorney fees, and a personal representative's commission, can vary according to the size of a probate estate, they tend to be minimal for many estates.

Inheritance and estate taxes are mandated by law. These taxes are levied on a rather broad range of a decedent's assets, not just his probate assets, to impede avoidance. The government has strong interests to ensure that tax avoidance is not as simple as probate avoidance. Accordingly, property will sometimes be subject to estate and inheritance taxes, but exclusions, including irrevocable trusts and some jointly owned property, do exist.

Nature of Probate Disputes

Disputes arise during probate for a variety of reasons. Conflict may occur over the distribution of a decedent's property because beneficiaries are unhappy with his estate plan. Grief associated with the death sometimes creates tension, and lawsuits may ensue from misdirected anger as a result.

Quarrels could arise because family members have opposing views with respect to fair distribution of their loved one's property. For example, a child of a decedent may view equal distribution among all his siblings as equitable, while another sibling may think he should receive more because of special care he gave the parent prior to death. A disagreement could also manifest itself between children of a former marriage and the surviving spouse. The decedent's children might consider his property to be theirs, but the surviving spouse may see it as hers.

Probate court can address guardianship and conservatorship proceedings, proceedings for minors and older or incapacitated adults, respectively. If the minor, the adult, or any family members disagree with the care, quarrels may arise during these proceedings. Disagreements can also develop between family members and a care facility and frequently involve emotional issues.

Additionally, while settling any probate matter, disputes can occur between the fiduciary and inheritors. The inheritors might not agree over who should act as fiduciary, or they might voice concerns relevant to investment decisions or property management issues under his control. They may perceive conflicts of interest or inequities, real or imagined, if the fiduciary also happens to be an heir or a beneficiary.

BENEFITS OF MEDIATION

Surprisingly in probate, an area of law in which family issues dominate, mediation is still not widely used. Although mediation will not be appropriate for all probate disputes, it may allow parties to reach agreements preferable to a court's decision and may promote healing of strained family relationships in many cases.[3]

Sometimes disputes among family members can be resolved without the need to seek assistance outside the family unit. Even after one contacts an attorney, a negotiated settlement without legal assistance may still be possible. However, some families may require a more structured dispute resolution process. Some benefits of mediation over litigation are of particular interest to dispute resolution in probate. Mediation may not always be desirable or attainable, but the personal and familial aspects of probate make it particularly conducive to mediation. See chapter eight for more discussion about the subject.

CHALLENGING A WILL IN COURT

There are several legal reasons for challenging a will. It can be difficult and costly to contest a will. Nevertheless, below are some common legal grounds for contesting the validity of a will.[4]

The Will Was Not Signed in Compliance with Applicable Laws

Each state and the District of Columbia have specific laws dictating how a last will and testament must be signed and formalized. Consequently, failing to sign a will according to relevant law is a primary reason why a will is challenged and the most common reason why one is found invalid. Jurisdictions that allow a typed version of a will require that it be dated and signed by the testator, the will's creator, in the presence of at least two adult witnesses.

Most jurisdictions require that witnesses not be beneficiaries in the witnessed will. If, in such a jurisdiction, they are, their apportioned gifts could be voided but the rest of the will should not. Under various conditions, many jurisdictions permit handwritten, unwitnessed wills, "holographic wills" as they are called, which must be written and signed entirely by the testator. They must also be dated in some parts of the country. In principle, holographic wills should be the easiest to challenge since they are not witnessed by anyone. For a holographic will to be validated, the court, absent any corruption, must be convinced that the document was completely handwritten by the testator and that its intended purpose was to serve as his will.

The Testator Lacked Testamentary Capacity to Sign a Will

Testamentary capacity requires the testator to understand the nature and value of his assets, the people who should logically inherit them, and the legal effect of signing a will. Laws govern whether a testator lacks testamentary capacity. Usually, the threshold that must be overcome to prove he lacks such capacity is fairly high. In Florida, for instance, someone can show signs of dementia yet still be deemed to have testamentary capacity to sign his will. Therefore, testimony of witnesses to the signing of the will can be important. Absent a doctor's substantiating findings or an adjudication of incapacity within days of the will signing, lack of testamentary capacity is difficult to prove.

The Testator Was Unduly Influenced into Signing a Will

People become physically and mentally weaker as they age and therefore more susceptible to persuasion. In the context of a will contest, the key to undue influence is the question of whether the alleged influencer exerted enough pressure to put the testator under severe duress. If he caused the testator to lose free will and succumb to his will, the court will likely deem this to be undue influence. It is important to understand that threats, mere nagging, and verbal abuse are usually not enough. It takes much more to rise to the level of undue influence. Some examples include controlling access to the will, isolating the testator from family and friends, and having someone other than the testator choose and pay for an attorney to create a will, perhaps radically different from the previous one, thereby creating a conflict of interest. Similar to lack of testamentary capacity, undue influence is difficult to prove.

The Will Was Procured by Fraud

A will is procured by fraud when its testator is deceived into signing it. If a testator is presented a will that he thinks is something else, a deed or health care proxy, for instance, and signs it, then the will was procured by fraud. Since the primary witness, the testator, will almost certainly no longer be available to testify when charges of fraud are brought, the witnesses need to be asked about the details of the signing. Absent corroborating testimony, the will might be deemed invalid because it was improperly executed, not necessarily because it was fraudulently procured.

A Newer Will Supersedes the One Being Executed

An executor or executrix may be trying to fulfill the provisions of an outdated will, either knowingly or not. Therefore, to minimize this possibility, it is generally a good idea to destroy or void any will that becomes outdated once it is updated. Sometimes a person even declares in his newer will that it is intended to supersede his previous one. If a valid legal will emerges that is more recently dated than the one being executed, the court should recognize the newer version. This is why dating a will can be important. Laws vary as to what constitutes voided and updated wills, so be sure to check your local laws.

TITLING ASSETS IS PART OF ESTATE PLANNING

One type of co-ownership, tenants by the entirety, also called "tenancy by the entirety," (TBE) may provide worthwhile real property protection and can be a valuable tool in estate planning. TBE is a special type of co-ownership sometimes available to married couples or domestic partners, or simply to more than one person in some parts of the nation. This type of co-ownership is not available everywhere in America. Some states permit TBE ownership either by statutory or case law, but others may not allow it whatsoever. Additionally, it may not be allowed for all real property where it is otherwise available. You should consult relevant statutory and case law since there are differences in TBE laws. As an example, a few states limit TBE ownership strictly to primary residences. Yet some and Washington, D.C., also allow rental real estate to be held as TBE by statute; still others may allow it by case law.

In order for TBE co-ownership to be valid, it must also meet joint tenancy requirements. Normally, ownership will become tenants in common, also called "tenancy in common," for couples who decide to divorce and who own TBE property, or it will become joint tenancy. Unlike tenants in common in which shares can be unequal in size, joint tenant owners share equal rights to own and dispose of a property and have the right of survivorship. TBE offers right-of-survivorship benefits just as joint tenancy does, but it might also protect the asset from a creditor in some instances, provided at least one owner does not fall under attack of the creditor.

The reason it may provide this protection is that TBE property cannot normally be transferred or otherwise alienated without the consent of the other owners. Moreover, each owner does not own a fractional share of the property. Instead, each one claims an entire ownership interest in it, but such ownership interests are subject to each owner maintaining full right to the property. Because their respective ownership interests are indivisible and cannot generally be transferred without the others' consent, a creditor usually needs to pursue all owners of TBE property in order to place a lien on it.

TBE ownership has successfully shielded property on many occasions. However, one cannot assume that this form of ownership can be depended upon as an impenetrable creditor defense. On a positive note, it is rather straightforward for people to title assets as TBE in places that allow it. It is a way to add a layer of asset protection in such places. For instance, in a state where TBE ownership for some businesses is permissible, it may be a good idea to title the ownership of them as TBE. Simply stating property is held as TBE is not enough. The title documents of the asset should specifically declare that it is held as TBE.

OTHER CONSIDERATIONS

Many people think estate planning is only for the rich. Although not true, it is understandable why people might feel they cannot afford to have an attorney prepare necessary estate planning documents. There are certainly other options for people who want to do it themselves and save money. Legalzoom.com is one of the most popular online resources where someone can prepare an estate plan. Whether you own a home or have valuable assets to pass onto others, it is imperative to have a plan in place and to have your affairs in order before you die. If you have anything that you would like to bequeath to those you leave behind, a well-crafted estate plan should help distribute things the way you want. If no plan is made, you are letting the government choose how to distribute your assets, which is not the best option. Having no plan is not a good plan.

At the very least, you should have a will prepared and executed in accordance with law. In addition, having a healthcare power of attorney and a durable financial power of attorney is vital to maintaining your affairs if you are no longer physically or mentally capable of doing so yourself. A healthcare power of attorney allows another person to make your healthcare decisions. It is important because you can state in one when you create it whether you want to be kept alive on life support or not to be resuscitated should the issue arise. A durable financial power of attorney ensures that another person can make your monetary decisions. It is also a good idea to have designated beneficiaries of your choosing on bank accounts and retirement plans or any other related financial vehicles so that any such assets may be exempted from probate and can be given upon your death to the people you want to receive them.

Although the topic of estate planning and preparing for your own death can be morbid, depressing, and something you do not want to embrace, it is an important one. While this subject can be difficult to discuss with loved ones and thereafter execute, it is imperative that you properly plan for your own demise so that your affairs are administered according to your wishes once you are gone.

Chapter 16: Areas of Law Not Covered in Detail

There is no crueler tyranny than that which is perpetuated under the shield of law and in the name of justice. — **Charles de Montesquieu**

Chapter Sections
- Background
- Patent law
- Class actions
- Personal injury
- Workers' compensation
- Jurisdictional issues
- Identity theft
- Restraining orders
- Other areas of law not mentioned
- Conclusion

BACKGROUND

Obviously, no single legal resource can possibly cover in detail all areas of law within our bloated U.S. judicial bureaucracy. For that reason and because most areas of law discussed in this chapter are likely to affect a much smaller segment of the U.S. population, they are covered tersely and in rapid succession. Further research in other resources is suggested in order to glean more information on these topics. Our basic intent is simply to mention them, enlighten you about anything pertinent but not readily available elsewhere, and provide a starting point for additional investigation.

PATENT LAW

As stated during the discussion of original and exclusive jurisdiction in chapter eight's FEDERAL COURTS section, U.S. district courts have original jurisdiction over patent law. This does not mean the procedure to obtain a patent begins in these courts. Rather, claims regarding patent infringements should be filed in U.S. district courts, but claims regarding non-infringement patent issues can also be filed in courts other than these.

To obtain a patent, an inventor submits her idea to the U.S. Patent and Trademark Office (USPTO) via its application process. A patent search is then performed to ensure no other invention exactly like hers already exists. The inventor also pays fees of various amounts to the USPTO and generally, after a year or more, is given the patent to her invention if the application has passed scrutiny.

What makes this area of law rather distinct, at least its application process anyway, is that it is mostly pressure-free compared to divorce, criminal matters, small claims, and other areas of adversarial law. There are no court appearances to make or unreasonable deadlines to meet in order to get said patent. And the result is almost always a happy ending provided the patent is not rejected because the same thing already exists. All it takes, however, is one or two subtle substantive differences from an existing invention to establish a new invention as patent-worthy.

As of this writing, USPTO processing fees are generally in the $1,000 to $2,000 range for a do-it-yourselfer.[1] Hiring counsel can easily triple or quadruple that figure. The USPTO should offer some guidance to unrepresented individuals navigating the patent application process, negating the need for an attorney. Businesses and governmental agencies often have lawyers on staff specifically to do the leg work for their employee-inventors, but of all legal endeavors, this may be one of the simplest to go it alone for an individual with above average intelligence. After all, if someone has an invention, she probably is at least slightly above the intellectual average and should not have much difficulty acquiring her patent single-handedly.

Domestic patents expire after a maximum of twenty years.[2] Domestic patents, as the name implies, are exclusive to America. If an inventor wants to protect her invention outside U.S. borders, patents must be obtained in foreign countries, which is an entirely different process. Once a patent has become official and its corresponding invention gets produced, the inventor should not expect anyone to check for patent infringements anywhere in the world. The onus is on her to determine this and send a cease and desist letter to the violator or, in a U.S. district court, bring any domestic infringement claims against the violator. International infringement claims are more complicated, and legal action may need to be undertaken in one or more foreign courts and possibly in a U.S. district court in limited instances.

CLASS ACTIONS

By definition, the term "class action" denotes a group of people, the class, involved in a legal action. Thus, such lawsuits involve more than one plaintiff and usually encompass hundreds, if not thousands or millions, of people nationwide. If there is such a thing as "easy" in the U.S. court system from the plaintiff's perspective, this type of suit is probably it. Very few members of the class are directly involved in the case. Other than the lead, or named, plaintiff or plaintiffs whose names appear on the complaint, the other plaintiffs, or the rest of the class, can sit back, relax, and hope for a positive settlement or judgment in the matter. As just implied, there may be one or more lead plaintiffs in the lawsuit.

These causes of action usually stem from faulty consumer products, harmful side effects from pharmaceuticals, or any service, event, or act that affects or may affect many people. Since there are usually a vast number of individuals (potentially) affected and because they can live in various parts of the country, the damages sought are quite often in the millions of dollars, with the case frequently being filed in a U.S. district court. Some class actions might be limited to residents in a specific area of a certain state, such as those seeking damages because they have been negatively impacted by a local factory's contaminants. Other localized instances may also include, for example, those pertaining to people attempting to prevent construction of a major discount store that would inevitably create traffic issues near their residences. These smaller types of actions might be predominantly filed in state court.

As mentioned in chapter nine's THE PROCESS section, some small claims cases can resemble a full-blown class action suit. One difference between them, however, is that all plaintiffs in small claims cases can represent themselves and are mostly active participants. In a true class action, outside counsel is required. Furthermore, some members of the class may not even be aware of the litigation or live too far away to be actively involved in the matter and therefore have a default type of representation.

Major class actions sometimes originate from law firms seeking to start a case, but they need more information from a consumer or an afflicted party in order to compose their complaint to the court and thus contact prospective lead plaintiffs first. Once the leads have been selected, lawyers from the firm might ask them many questions while composing the complaint. For consumer products, they may ask questions that are technical or related to time-of-product failure, that are associated with out-of-pocket expenses paid to date, or about anything else that will help validate the complaint and move the case forward. The lead plaintiffs may be deposed, may be asked to provide affidavits, or may perform any functions common to other civil matters. Because lead plaintiffs do more legwork and spend more time on the case than other plaintiffs, their compensation in actions seeking damages is usually higher in the event of settlement or judgment in favor of the class.

Since both the law firm beginning the case and the defendant are normally relatively large, recognized, powerful players in the game, the impact of corruption may be minimized because of the canceling-out effect. The most prevalent source of corruption may come from the law firm representing the plaintiffs. It could try to gouge the very people it represents—in terms of exorbitant legal fees, which may translate into indulging in an extra large slice of any recovery pie. Amazingly, recent litigation has limited the amount that can be siphoned from the award pot to pay for such fees. See *Parker v. Time Warner Entertainment Co., L.P.* wherein part of the judicial opinion was, "As a matter of public policy, it would be unseemly for the rewards to Class Counsel to exceed those to Class Members, the ones for whom the litigation is ostensibly contested."[3]

Even if there is corruption external to the firm representing the class, each plaintiff is far more insulated from it. In a mutual fund, when individual stocks go up or down in value, the fund as a whole is less affected. So it is with a class action suit. The class as a whole is less affected by corruption than any individual would otherwise be in an ordinary civil lawsuit. Class actions frequently settle before trial anyway, mitigating any potential impact from corruption.

One of the niceties about many class actions is that the plaintiffs pay no fees to the attorneys or firm representing them. Since attorneys almost exclusively litigate monetary-based class actions for one thing, and one thing only—a sizable portion of the recovery—rest assured they will eagerly try to win such a case. Certainly, their fees are quite often exorbitant, but technically this typically comes out of the defendant's pocket and not the plaintiff's.

Besides the lead plaintiffs, other class members need not be present at any of the relevant proceedings nor provide any input to the case in general. For monetary-based class actions, all prospective members of the class are normally given the option of remaining part of the suit or not. Should a case of this type settle favorably for the class or a judgment be issued and be similarly favorable, those members who have opted to remain will claim a share of the settlement proceeds or award. Sometimes this is something other than money, such as free or discounted flights on an airline, free product from a manufacturer, or other similar (and sometimes useless) compensation.

Contacting all prospective class members is not always easy. When such members are involved in a financial securities transaction or are passengers on an aircraft or a sailing vessel, it is easier to determine who they are since the paper trail is quite clear. People who pay cash for a consumer product that later becomes the subject of a class action are nearly impossible to reach directly.

Sometimes the benefit of individually suing a corporation or another formidable party for relatively small damages is not cost-effective when many other people have similarly been injured. The likely return on investment is minimal for the average individual who proceeds as a lone, represented plaintiff in a claim that could otherwise proceed as a class action. This is because of the potentially high litigation costs required to fight a generally large and powerful entity with skilled attorneys. Pooling legal resources into one single claim against such an entity makes the best use of them.

A class action that engages a high-powered law firm that specializes in handling this type of litigation would normally be the preferred option and maximizes such resources. In fact, it is unlikely a class action with any of the plaintiffs representing the entire class will survive in court. The ruling all but eliminating this kind of representation was opined by the court in *Noah v. AOL Time Warner Inc.* as follows: "As the Fourth Circuit noted in this regard, 'the competence of a layman representing himself' is 'clearly too limited' to allow him to 'risk the rights of others' by representing a class of plaintiffs. *Oxendine v. Williams*, 509 F.2d 1405, 1407 (4th Cir. 1975)."[4]

Furthermore, most jurisdictions have laws, some of them criminal, about practicing law without a license, for which representing others in a class action could definitely be construed. If your potential adversary has any political clout, which is quite probable, criminal charges against you may come down the pike for such an undertaking. Because of their very nature, class actions might be the only type of case within U.S. borders wherein an individual is disallowed from proceeding without attorney representation.

PERSONAL INJURY

Of all areas of law, personal injury is possibly the most notorious in terms of attorney disrepute. The term "ambulance chaser" derives from this area of law and illustrates that point. Lawsuits of this type are usually big-ticket claims against deep-pocket insurance companies or large corporations. Most personal injury attorneys work on a contingent fee basis, typically receiving 33 to 40 percent of the recovery, and stand to collect large amounts of money.

Personal injury is one of many areas of tort law and involves a wide spectrum: vehicular accidents, slip and falls, defective products, medical and other professional malpractice, animal bites, food poisoning, defamation, intentional acts of violence, and more. While it is possible to tackle such a case *pro se*, keep in mind that as the amount of damages sought increases, the level of opposition from a powerful, responsible defendant will also likely increase. Along with this, any potentially influential personnel with whom the defendant has political ties may try to use their clout to influence the matter's outcome behind the scenes. Corruption may be more prevalent in this area of law than some others for this reason and due to the vulnerability of many personal injury victims and may have a greater chance manifesting itself as the sum at stake increases.

Some personal injury cases may be considered a "slam dunk," for example, when a medical professional leaves surgical tools inside someone after surgery or amputates the wrong limb. These might be relatively easy cases to win without litigation, but the fair settlement dollar amount is a big question mark. Who puts the price tag on an improperly lost limb or potentially lasting side effects from medical instruments left inside someone's body after surgery? Searching online or elsewhere in order to determine the settlements in these or other similar cases might help answer this question. It is unlikely the responsible party would risk a trial under such circumstances. Therefore, determining the dollar value of prior comparable cases may prove helpful when settling out of court whether proceeding *pro se* or with the assistance of counsel.

Particularly with medical malpractice, some jurisdictions have laws that, under certain conditions, limit damages plaintiffs can receive. From a purely numbers-based approach, you may want to consider any applicable limit for damages when deciding if it is worthwhile pursuing a case *pro se*. Suppose you are certain that your claim meets specific criteria and would only qualify you to receive a maximum of $X as compensation, the limit in the respective jurisdiction. If the offender is willing to settle for 90 percent of $X, then you may want to consider tackling the case yourself. However, if the proposed settlement is only 50 percent of $X, then the mere threat of hiring an attorney could get you much closer to a fair dollar amount. Comparing the numbers with personal injury attorneys who work on a 33 percent contingent fee basis, recovering a net of 70 percent or more of $X without counsel might be considered a victory. This same reasoning should hold true for any personal injury claims that have dollar amounts capped by law.

Other less decisive cases, some being legal malpractice and vehicular accidents, may be more difficult to win because they are not always clear-cut. It may take more leg work to recruit expert witnesses, review the evidence, and build the case in general. Also, as with most legal claims, keep in mind any statute of limitations when bringing a personal injury case to court. There is nothing to preclude negotiating with a party after filing the lawsuit. In fact, if the case is not filed soon after the injury, the would-be defendant may try to prolong negotiations until the statute of limitations expires, which will then leave you high and dry. Lastly, alternative dispute resolution (ADR) should also be considered for resolving personal injury matters. ADR was covered in chapter eight.

WORKERS' COMPENSATION

In a similar vein to personal injury laws, workers' compensation laws for both state and federal employees generally limit the dollar amount awardable in such claims. Limits for non-governmental employees are less clear and vary widely across the country. Several laws have been enacted that provide workers' compensation coverage for the overwhelming majority of U.S. workers. Various laws—the Federal Employees' Compensation Act, the Federal Employers' Liability Act, the Jones Act, the Longshore and Harbor Workers' Compensation Act, the Black Lung Benefits Act—purportedly protect different groups. These groups are nonmilitary federal employees, railroad employees, seamen, specific private maritime employees, and miners, respectively.[5]

While there have been many sources of abuse in this system, workers' compensation laws were put in place so that injured employees can recover lost wages, medical expenses, and other associated costs. Workers' compensation is basically a glorified insurance policy overseen by the government and is yet another liberal tool that flattens the playing field. As a tradeoff for its smaller monetary awards, the process is supposed to be shorter and easier for claimants to receive payment. Workers' compensation also blocks lawsuits from workers against their employers or coworkers for negligence, with the major exception being when harm has been inflicted intentionally. However, third parties, such as contractors who may have caused the worker's injury directly or indirectly or manufacturers of machinery used in the workplace and that contributed to the injury, are not immune from suit.

The "trust nobody" mantra, our familiar theme, is relevant in two distinct ways regarding workers' compensation. One of which involves our friends, big business and insurance companies. A report has found that people most deserving of benefits are having to fight long and hard to see any financial reimbursement for their losses. The report also shows that big business and insurance companies have lobbied for smaller payouts, prompting state after state to gut the compensation system with devastating impact to deserving workers. These changes are being made under the disguise of costs being portrayed as out of control, but the report revealed that employers are paying the lowest rates for the program since the 1970s.[6]

The other way the mantra is relevant concerns doctor's visits about an injury related to a workers' compensation claim. The typical doctor-patient confidentiality agreement is considered void during these examinations, so an employer can use any related information against its worker. Of course, there are appeal processes in place should the case not resolve favorably for the injured worker. If the case becomes more complicated and is headed towards or reaches the courts, consider ADR. Both parties must agree, but it is another avenue on which to proceed.

JURISDICTIONAL ISSUES

If there is such a thing as "fun" in the legal system from a litigant's perspective, catching court officiators acting outside their jurisdiction is probably as close to the definition as you can get. Recall from chapter eight in the JURISDICTION section that "jurisdiction" is defined as subject matter jurisdiction, or power to rule over the content of a dispute, and personal jurisdiction, or power to rule over the person or party. The court must have both in order to have official jurisdiction.

So, fun can enter the picture when either a judge or another officiator rules over a case in which she lacks jurisdiction. The United States Court of Appeals for the Ninth Circuit ruled in *Rankin v. Howard*, "When a judge knows that he lacks jurisdiction, or acts in the face of clearly valid statutes or case law expressly depriving him of jurisdiction, judicial immunity is lost."[7] Quoting

Bradley v. Fisher, the U.S. Supreme Court ruled in *Stump v. Sparkman*, "A judge will not be deprived of immunity because the action he took was in error, was done maliciously, or was in excess of his authority, but, rather, he will be subject to liability only when he has acted in the 'clear absence of all jurisdiction'."[8] As twisted as it may be, a judge is protected for malicious behavior, whereas absence of jurisdiction does not insulate her from suit.

In these earlier rulings and simply put, immunity was lost when jurisdiction was absent. More recently, however, some U.S. appellate courts have narrowed the scope for loss of immunity by ruling that judges must also *know* they lack *personal jurisdiction* in order to lose immunity—lack of personal jurisdiction alone is simply not enough.[9] The implication of losing immunity is that these individuals can now legitimately be sued for damages because of their misdeeds just like any other ordinary citizen. Relatively newer decisions by the appellate courts therefore mean that you should do your homework in advance and bring lack of personal jurisdiction to the judge's attention at the commencement of a case in order to increase your odds of a successful civil suit later. As explained in the IMMUNITY AND OTHER CONSIDERATIONS section of chapter three, immunity can also be lost when a judge's acts are not judicial in nature, but since that half of the two-prong test is not covered here, we encourage you to research it.

If you have caught a judge red-handed acting without requisite jurisdiction or performing acts that are not judicial in nature and plan to file suit against her, have confidence that you possess the intellectual capacity to pursue such a case *pro se*. You will likely need to proceed alone anyway since it is highly unlikely any lawyer will accept the case unless she has plans in the near future to retire or relocate as stated in the Proceeding on Your Own subsection of chapter two. Counsel would be selling out one of her own if she represented you in a lawsuit against a judge—not too good for future business.

One of the authors has had experience with a judge not abiding by *stare decisis* concerning jurisdiction of the court. Lack of personal jurisdiction was made perfectly clear to Judge Peter B. Regan during a traffic matter in Middletown, Rhode Island. He ignored oral and written arguments, including fully cited relevant state supreme court case law. Because of the judge's corruption in that lowest-level court, the coauthor initially lost the case but won it upon appeal to the Rhode Island Traffic Tribunal. The unanimous tribunal decision was later affirmed by a higher court after the tribunal's ruling was appealed by the plaintiff, the town of Middletown, Rhode Island.

The case was only appealed once the plaintiff learned that the coauthor-defendant was moving the court to collect attorney's fees and costs as allowed by law for prevailing defendants. See Rhode Island statutes § 9-22-4, § 9-22-5, § 9-22-9, § 9-22-16, § 9-29-21, and § 42-92-1. Also see judicial opinions about the case from both the Rhode Island Traffic Tribunal and the Rhode Island Sixth District Court.[10] [11]

Making money by suing a judge who has lost immunity or being reimbursed for fees and costs from a case such as this is theoretically quite possible, but the coauthor's case is ongoing at this time. Therefore, his personal statement conclusively proving either is unavailable. Certainly, to be successful with such claims, the relevant prerequisites are: keeping track of costs and attorney fees meticulously, observing timelines for filing, scrutinizing for veracity whatever any opposing attorney says or submits, and, of course, being thorough and persistent. If there are any local or state laws in the pertinent jurisdiction that allow a prevailing defendant in a civil lawsuit to be compensated by the plaintiff for legal expenses, keep in mind that it is quite possible you could be so compensated in an ordinary traffic case, a civil suit in many jurisdictions. The town or city most likely will not go down without a fight, but either can be defeated.

IDENTITY THEFT

While corruption in and detrimental effects of the judiciary are not directly related to identity theft, they certainly can be indirectly related. Identity theft is undoubtedly becoming more common because of the technological age and most definitely could spawn an array of legal battles. Someone who becomes a victim of this form of theft may soon become a victim of the legal system as well, further adding insult to injury. The system, once again, picks the low-hanging fruit and punishes the unfortunate for being unlucky. The ramifications of identity theft could be a civil or criminal case looming on the horizon without a person's knowledge. Once someone becomes entangled in the civil or criminal system, she becomes vulnerable to all the adversity described in previous chapters.

The odds of someone's identity being stolen to commit financial fraud are close to zero when she owns absolutely nothing and lives as a pauper. Even if it is stolen in such an instance, stealing from zero yields zero. But as income and wealth increase, so do the odds of having an identity stolen for financial gain. Of course, a credit report is one of the first indications of this crime having taken place. Unfortunately, most people do not see their credit report every day but typically become aware of their credit score only when purchasing a home or vehicle or when applying for rental living accommodations. Significant damage could be done prior to that point.

Know, however, that you can own nearly nothing but still have your identity stolen for purposes other than financial gain. A case in the People's Republic of Massachusetts is a horrifying example of such a theft.[12] Someone now named in the court records as S.M.F. had her identity stolen by another woman who then went on an apparent crime spree and identified herself as S.M.F. to the authorities. The real S.M.F. had to go to great lengths to extricate herself from the abyss otherwise known as the Massachusetts judiciary. Although the case was justifiably expunged by a district court judge, the state later appealed in order to have the expungement reversed. This is a clear example of the legal system punishing the unfortunate for being unlucky by forcing a hapless victim through its meat grinder while wringing money from her—an injustice in addition to the one already suffered at the hands of the *first* thief. There are ample resources that explain how to guard against and recover from identity theft, which will not be repeated here.[13] [14] [15]

Nowadays, the internet likely enables the stealing of personal information for the overwhelming majority of identity thefts. With so much of our daily lives involving commerce over the internet, it is not uncommon for an average person to have upwards of 100 or more different online accounts—eBay, email, utilities, banks, credit cards, and just about everything else imaginable—and passwords for each one. Remembering every single password is nearly impossible. Plainly writing passwords on paper or storing them on electronic media is an excellent way to prevent forgetting them but also an excellent way for a thief to gain easier access to them.

One author uses a preventative mechanism to lower the likelihood that stolen information will allow a hacker account access. A root password is selected, "catdog," for example, for all passwords, and then the word "standard" is used to represent it in written or electronic form, perhaps even being written backwards to add an extra level of security. The word "standard" is used merely as a reminder that it is a placeholder to be substituted with the real root password to reconstruct the actual password. Then, a prefix or suffix can be added to the placeholder as mandated by particular account requirements or as the account holder desires by using numbers, letters, or special characters.

A fully "encrypted password" may look like: !standard123. The real password would be the word you chose for its root, catdog, plus any prefix or suffix: !catdog123 in this example. If the word you choose as a root is nothing someone else can easily guess, you can store your "passwords" anywhere at home on paper or electronically or on the internet with confidence that they should be safe. If, however, you pick something easily guessable, your entire list of "passwords," such as standard, !standard123, and standard_!@#, could be compromised. Choose wisely.

The same author takes another preventative step when dictating his social security number or other personally identifiable information over the phone in public areas. When it is necessary to dictate data because it is not possible to use the keypad to enter it, talking not only as softly as practicable but also remaining in motion, if feasible, is important. Doing so will provide only a partial sequence of your sensitive information to a select group of people while within earshot of them. Continue to move until you have finished providing the data.

Be aware of your surroundings and that you are not being shadowed or overheard while relaying sensitive information. The preferred means of entering data is via the phone's keypad. When permitted, use this method, but be sure to turn off the audio tones for the keys while in the presence of others so that they cannot secretly record the audio sequence for later account hacking.

RESTRAINING ORDERS

Sometimes called "protective orders" or "abuse prevention orders," restraining orders may be divided into classes not discussed here. They are court orders intended to "protect" an individual or group of individuals. A more apt term for them would be "constraining orders" because they do not restrain a person in any way but actually constrain someone to do or stop doing a certain thing. This technicality aside, restraining orders are frequently given like candy by the courts.

The distinction is generally subtle between the three common names of these orders, but the consequences of violating them are usually not. Understand that there may be an explicit or implicit no-contact stipulation as part of a restraining order. If you have an attorney representing you in a case that precipitated such an order, she may or may not provide you with a small piece of important information indicating that contact may not be allowed in an indirect fashion either, that is, through a third party. The system will not care if this knowledge was not imparted to you or was lost in translation. Once such an order has been violated, your day could be ruined since the penalty can be quite severe.

Whenever the court is about to issue a restraining order against you, do not assume it is following its own rules in the process. Rules of procedure or statutory law may indicate that restraining orders are to be given only in cases of domestic violence or related matters, but the court can and does ignore rules and law and issue these orders for reasons of its own choosing. The best scenario is not to allow a restraining order to be issued against you in the first place, particularly if you know the system is breaking its own rules or laws while happily attempting to hand you one.

Frequently, restraining orders are automatically given in standard divorce proceedings. No domestic violence of any kind need have occurred to warrant their issuance. The most likely reason they are so prolific is the fees associated with filing them. Since divorce is one of the system's primary moneymakers, lumping additional and relatively smaller fees onto standard legal fees that ordinarily exceed four figures tends to go unnoticed in the grand scheme of things.

In some jurisdictions, the courts absolve the person seeking the order from paying its corresponding fee and instead levy it upon the alleged offender. This reasoning is similar to billing someone for being incarcerated against her will. Based upon our experience, quite often no real reason exists justifying issuance of a restraining order—just the word of the "victim" is sufficient. Without any sanity check, these orders are a great source of consistent revenue for the courts.

OTHER AREAS OF LAW NOT MENTIONED

There is an overabundance of laws in our country. While we have covered common areas of law elsewhere in this book and mentioned a few other areas in this chapter, there are still plenty that were not discussed. Remember that there are many different legal resources to consult—some more reputable than others. However, not even the reputable ones are always 100 percent accurate. We found errors in some writings by a popular legal self-help publisher and with data reported on some governmental websites. As we said in the introduction, performing thorough research, finding crucial answers, and making solid arguments are 99 percent of good lawyering.

Much of the content of this book can be applied to almost any legal battle. Consider not only the material we have provided in its body but also in its appendix. Additionally, check other resources, and consider hiring a lawyer when appropriate. There is much to know about the law, but certainly, it is far more important to know about the legal system and how it truly operates than about the law itself—a message we have tried to convey to you throughout this book. Law can generally be referenced whenever the need arises. Moreover, it frequently changes; therefore, future research of it will most likely be necessary. Most importantly, it is often ignored by our glorified, sometimes unelected, lawyers in black gowns anyway.

Tackle anything not covered in part III of this book with the same preparedness, thoroughness, and resolve, keeping in mind all information discussed in parts I and II and being constantly vigilant for ubiquitous corruption. Chances are good that you will fare just as well in unexplored areas of law as you would in areas we mentioned in this chapter or covered in more detail in prior chapters when conditions are characteristically similar.

CONCLUSION

In conclusion, this book may have been a startling revelation to people who have not yet been victimized by the legal system. For those who have personally had exposure to the very bowels of it, the material we have presented concerning its ugly corruption and repulsive operation may have been review. However, many of the methodologies propounded to help Americans prepare for, defend against, and attack a legal problem are probably new even to the individuals who have had firsthand experience with our malevolent system. We hope we have supplied you with the knowledge, insight, and weaponry crucial to fighting all legal battles that lie ahead and have helped you *stack the legal odds in your favor*!

Appendix

An individual who breaks a law that conscience tells him is unjust, and who willingly accepts the penalty of imprisonment in order to arouse the conscience of the community over its injustice, is in reality expressing the highest respect for the law. — **Martin Luther King, Jr**.

AFFIDAVIT TEMPLATE

[COURT NAME]

{[COUNTY]}   {[COURT DIVISION]}

[name(s) of plaintiff(s)], Plaintiff{s}	))))
v.	)))
[name(s) of defendant(s)], Defendant{s}	))))

Docket No. [case number]
*("Docket No." may be
"Case No." or otherwise)*

AFFIDAVIT OF [NAME OF PERSON STATING THE FOLLOWING]

I, [same name as in title directly above], declare {under oath} as follows:

1. [first fact relevant to the case, for example, "I was, at one time, doing business as XYZ Consulting in the state of Texas."]

2. [second fact relevant to the case, for example, "XYZ Consulting was licensed to conduct business in the state of Texas."]

3. [third fact relevant to the case, for example, "XYZ Consulting did, in fact, perform work for Defendant, ABC Disposal, in Dallas, Texas, during an eight-day span from August 22, 2012, through August 29, 2012."]

4. [fourth fact relevant to the case, for example, "The work consisted of approximately fifty (50) hours of troubleshooting and repairing ABC Disposal's company software."]

5. [Keep adding one fact per number until complete.]

I, [name of person stated for AFFIDAVIT OF above], declare {under penalty of perjury} {under the laws of the state of [state] [, city, county,]} {under the laws of the United States of America} {under the laws of the District of Columbia} that the foregoing is true and correct. *(At most, you will use either "under the laws of the state of...," "under the laws of the United States of America," or "under the laws of the District of Columbia." The latter two would be used for federal affidavits and those filed in the nation's capital, respectively.)*

Executed this [day, e.g., "1st"] day of [month], [year]   [signature of person directly above]
                                                                    [name of person directly above]

{[notary public's sworn statement and signature]}

AFFIDAVIT TEMPLATE

Everything in "[ ]" is to be replaced with information specific to your case. Everything in "{ }" may or may not be part of your affidavit and depends upon court protocol and other factors. *Italicized* text in "( )" is commentary for informational purposes only and is not to be included in your affidavit.

Affidavits are used by litigants, witnesses, and others to state facts on the court record. In general, they can be used to provide a form of testimony if a witness is unavailable for trial, but one of their most common uses is for litigants themselves to make statements about a case. Affidavits are used to support motions, claims, counterclaims, answers, and other such legal documents. In all known U.S. courts below the appellate level, the plaintiff is listed before the defendant in the heading on the first page just like any other adversarial legal document filed in those courts.

The format of affidavits can vary widely, but the one shown here is representative of some commonly seen in many U.S. legal matters. The general protocol for an affidavit is to number each distinct statement sequentially beginning with the number one. If two distinct statements are made, they should be numbered separately. Usually, just one or two sentences comprise each numbered item. You may have noticed the seemingly redundant phrase "fifty (50) hours of troubleshooting and repairing" in item four. The practice of using "number (X)" in legal writing is traditionally done to prevent error or forgery and to make the intent as obvious as possible. For example, it would be much more difficult to change a "3" to an "8" if it is written "three (3)."

For any expert witnesses, be sure their affidavits include the dates (and times, if applicable) any observations were made, whatever was done to justify their opinion given, the conclusion based on the observations or opinion, and any estimate of cost to repair, replace, or redo as appropriate. Attach a resume, list of credentials, or relevant qualifications summary for doctors, engineers, and other experts if possible. For ordinary witnesses, a simpler format can be followed wherein just the dates/times of relevant facts and observations are included along with the facts and observations themselves.

Keep in mind affidavits are sometimes worth no more than the paper on which they are written. One of the authors has found them to be complete falsifications by adversaries in legal proceedings—who include ordinary people, lawyers, and police officers alike. The problem arises when trying to disprove them. Doing so may not be easy. Nonetheless, despite affidavits usually being made under oath and signed under penalty of perjury, the court is unlikely to take any action against a perjuring person who also happens to be a public official or lawyer even if you do manage to prove his affidavit false.

Note that there are times when "Petitioner" can replace "Plaintiff" or "Defendant" and "Respondent" can replace the other in the affidavit heading. Affidavits such as those associated with a petition for interlocutory relief would typically use a "Petitioner v. Respondent" format. In certain types of matters, including some criminal proceedings, "Petitioner" may also be substituted for "Defendant" and "Respondent" might then replace "Plaintiff."

For affidavits submitted to an appellate court, the first party listed in the heading will sometimes be "Appellant" instead of "Plaintiff." The second party listed would then be "Appellee" or "Respondent" instead of "Defendant," just like most other case-related documents submitted to the particular court. To confuse matters more, sometimes the terms "Plaintiff-Appellee," "Plaintiff-Appellant," "Defendant-Appellant," or "Defendant-Appellee" are used, with any term referencing Appellant generally being listed first. The substitution of any of the foregoing is either a matter of personal preference or is the protocol for the court in question, so you will need to check whether this nomenclature is a requirement of the court. Additional variations regarding heading terminology and structure are possible.

DEMAND LETTER TEMPLATE

FINAL DEMAND LETTER

[date]

[name of party to whom you are making the demand]
[street address of party]
[city, state, zip code of party] *(Of course, "state" will not be used in the nation's capital.)*

(The following is an actual demand letter sent to an attorney asking for the return of a retainer in a legal matter in which he did no work for one of the authors. The actions outlined below describing what will be done if he does not fulfill his obligations might be misconstrued as extortion, but note that the letter does not physically threaten or force him in any way, and the money sought does not belong to him. Keep in mind this is an attorney we are talking about. Short of these legal threats, he would not have returned the deposit. However, the retainer was returned in full after this letter was sent. Understand that this is just a template. The content of your letter will likely vary significantly.)

Re: [Client Fee Agreement between you and name of complainant or short description of whatever matter is at hand] *(If the letter is written by a third party, such as a lawyer, this and everything that follows would then be in the third person.)*

Dear [Mr. or Ms.] [last name of responsible person]:

Let me inform you that there is no agreement between us (orally or in writing) that states you would keep any unused portion of the retainer if you withdrew from the case. Furthermore, I have no signed agreement whatsoever from you as a client, which is in clear violation of the RULES OF PROFESSIONAL CONDUCT—one of a plethora you have violated.

I understand you may have reviewed correspondence from Attorney Cohen, which probably took a total of ten (10) minutes. Why you decided to review correspondence from Attorney Biagiotti, a person completely unrelated to the case, is beyond me and on your own time.

The verbiage in your recent letter to me makes it perfectly clear that you never had any intention of faithfully representing me and that you were biased in the defendant's favor all along. When you make statements like, "and have conferred with Attorney Michaud regarding your behavior toward Ms. Parent," and, "I spoke with Attorney Michaud, and if there were any issues in this case, it was because of you," you leave no doubt that you put forth zero effort to resolve the case in my favor and that you did not have my best interests at heart.

Add to this your request for an additional retainer of $1,000 to continue "representing" me in a case wherein you stated, "I do not believe that you have a case in your favor," and it's clear that your intent was unmistakably dubious. The foregoing and your previous letters are exactly the fuel I need in a complaint against you with the Office of the Bar Counsel, and I thank you kindly for this. Perhaps now you understand why I like my correspondence in writing. *(The attorney had insisted on talking by phone, which the coauthor-plaintiff refused for this very reason.)*

In light of your legal record not only in my case but in others, you should be grateful I am merely asking for a refund and not punitive damages when your inaction nearly cost me this case. If I do not have a check for the FULL amount of my deposit IN HAND within thirty (30) days of the date of this letter

1. I will contact the local media and inform them about the details of this matter.
2. I will contact the Better Business Bureau and file a complaint.
3. A complaint will be filed against you with the Office of the Bar Counsel. With the one filed against you earlier in March of this year resulting in a reprimand, you will likely be suspended. *(Any complaint filed against him with the overseeing board had nearly no chance of resulting in discipline, as is frequently the case with such complaints nationwide, but he miraculously had received a reprimand already in an unrelated matter. The threat of being disciplined again could have been perceived as being quite real.)*
4. I will sue you. You WILL lose and owe court costs in addition to my original deposit.
5. Very accurate (and very negative) reviews will be recorded about you and your firm on these and other websites:

   * http://www.avvo.com
   * http://www.lawyers.com
   * http://www.yelp.com
   * http://www.lawyerratingz.com

Keep in mind this is not an exhaustive list of remedies.

Thank you once again for your immediate attention to this matter,

[your signature]
[your name]
[your address]
{[your phone number]}
{[your email address]}

DEMAND LETTER TEMPLATE

Everything in "[ ]" is to be replaced with information specific to your dispute. Everything in "{ }" may or may not be part of your letter and depends upon your preference. *Italicized* text in "( )" is commentary for informational purposes only and is not to be included in your letter.

There are many kinds of demand letters, which should be tailored to fit the circumstances surrounding a dispute. The content in yours will likely vary significantly from the template. Such letters should outline the problem, specify the solution, and define the ramifications if demands are not met. Generally, most demand letters include the number of days in which the addressee is expected to act; otherwise, repercussions defined in the letter will ensue. Allowing only one or two days for a response is unrealistic, but thirty, sixty, or ninety days should be adequate.

Ensure that the letter arrives at its destination by using a mail service that requires a signature from the receiver or by delivering it via some other verifiable means. If demands made in the letter are unsuccessful and legal processes must follow, having record of affirmative reception of the letter by its intended recipient should solidify your position with respect to any demand letter prerequisites of law prior to filing suit.

MOTION TEMPLATE

[COURT NAME]

{[COUNTY]}   {[COURT DIVISION]}

[name(s) of plaintiff(s)],) Plaintiff{s})	Docket No. [case number] *("Docket No." may be* *"Case No." or otherwise)*
)) v.))	{[judge's name]} {[date and time of hearing]}
[name(s) of defendant(s)],) Defendant{s})	{[department]}

{EX PARTE} MOTION [TO CONTINUE | TO DISMISS | TO CHANGE VENUE | TO COMPEL | TO STRIKE | FOR SANCTIONS | FOR ATTORNEY'S FEES AND COSTS]

{Facts and Travel}

(If using the Facts and Travel section in your motion, be sure to list only facts in the case, not legal arguments. Number each item. Facts would be such things as dates of court appearances, dates of events related to the case that are not in dispute, and information available from a court record that has not been "fixed." Travel pertains to the various courts where the case has been heard and describes the overall lifecycle of it. This section orients the reader, which may be necessary since the official who reads the motion may not be familiar with the case nor know where it stands.)

1. The case associated with this motion was filed on [date] in [name of court].

2. [Plaintiff | Defendant] has made [number of appearances to date] appearances to date in an attempt to resolve the matter.

3. [fact, such as "Defendant failed to appear at the last hearing on May 1, 2015."]

4. [Keep adding one fact or unique travel information per number until complete.]

{Jurisdiction of the Court}

(Sometimes this section is needed when the court must be made aware that it has jurisdiction to hear the motion. Your adversary may argue that the court does not. By including this section and citing applicable statutes and relevant case law that give the court jurisdiction, the opposing party will have a difficult time disputing it.)

The court has jurisdiction to hear this motion according to [cited statutory law or other authority]. Additionally, the following cases with identical motions were heard in this court; therefore, the principle of *stare decisis* should apply in the instant motion: *(The purpose of citing cases is to draw a comparison between the ones cited and your own, further supporting the argument that your motion should be heard by the particular court.)*

MOTION TEMPLATE

[name and explanatory details of first case]

[name and explanatory details of second case]

•

•

•

[name and explanatory details of last case]

{Legal Argument}

(Oftentimes it is necessary to make a legal argument in support of your motion. Do that in this section to demonstrate why your motion should be granted. If more than one argument is relevant, list some or all that are. If one fails, another may not. All it takes is one of several to hold legal merit in order for your motion to be granted by a non-corrupt officiator. Be precise and thorough.)

{Conclusion}

(If this section is included in your motion, which it frequently should be, it will be the last section and should be relatively brief. Summarize the argument(s) you made previously, and mention any salient topics, particularly anything that clearly establishes your position as being correct. Be sure to reiterate whatever you are asking the court to do. If you are asking for attorney's fees and costs in the amount of $2,000 but you have cited statutory or case law that allows for treble amounts, list the total sum of $6,000 or $8,000 here. The value chosen is determined by law. Treble figures that are strictly multiplicative would include the former; those that are multiplicative and additive would include the latter. It is better to ask for too much than not enough. Chances are slim that the court will award you everything you are requesting. Personal experience has shown that courts do not do this.)

Date: [date sent to plaintiff(s) or defendant(s) and court]   [your signature]

[your name]

[your address]

{[your phone number]}

{[your email address]}

(If you intend to file a motion, understand that you would normally have to be a plaintiff or defendant in an existing case. Motions in U.S. courts can only be filed when a case exists, that is, it is already in the system. In rare instances, you might want to file a motion yourself even if you have an attorney representing you. On such occasions, you would write your name and sign the motion, not your attorney, just as you would in the pro se *instance above.)*

MOTION TEMPLATE

[CERTIFICATE | PROOF | AFFIDAVIT] OF SERVICE {OF PROCESS | BY MAIL}

The undersigned hereby certifies that a true copy of the within {EX PARTE} MOTION [TO CONTINUE | TO DISMISS | TO CHANGE VENUE | TO COMPEL | TO STRIKE | FOR SANCTIONS | FOR ATTORNEY'S FEES AND COSTS] was this day served upon the [plaintiff(s) | defendant(s)], [name(s) of plaintiff(s) | name(s) of defendant(s)], {via [his | her | their] attorney(s)} at [address(es) of plaintiff(s) | address(es) of defendant(s) | address(es) of attorney(s)], [by U.S. mail | in hand | by third party name | by electronic mail | by other court-approved method].

I, [your name], declare {under penalty of perjury} {under the laws of the state of [state] [, city, county,]} {under the laws of the United States of America} {under the laws of the District of Columbia} that the foregoing is true and correct. *(At most, you will use either "under the laws of the state of…," "under the laws of the United States of America," or "under the laws of the District of Columbia." The latter two would be used for federal motions and those filed in the nation's capital, respectively.)*

Executed this [day, e.g., "1st"] day of [month], [year] [your signature] _____
[your name]

[your address]

{[your phone number]}

{[your email address]}

MOTION TEMPLATE

Everything in "[ ]" is to be replaced with information specific to your case. The "|" symbol is used to denote that one of the options within "[ ]" is to be selected from the template—and perhaps modified—for use in your motion. Everything in "{ }" may or may not be part of your motion and depends upon motion type, court protocol, and other factors. *Italicized* text in "( )" is commentary for informational purposes only and is not to be included in your motion.

In all known U.S. courts below the appellate level, the plaintiff is listed before the defendant in the heading on the first page just like any other adversarial legal document filed in those courts. There are many kinds of motions that can be filed in court, but the ones that we list in the template's tentative title are the ones we find to be the most common.

Whatever you write in the body of your motion is based upon whatever you are asking the court to do. For example, a motion to continue could explain that you have a scheduled medical procedure that precludes you from attending court on your assigned date. The words "(emphasis added)" are used at the end of a sentence when underlining, bolding, or otherwise emphasizing a portion of cited case law, quoted statute, or any other direct legal reference.

If you are filing a pretrial motion, it can be filed anytime before trial up to and including the day of trial itself if allowed by court rules of procedure. Some courts also allow verbal motions, so you could read your written version aloud to the court in addition to handing the judge a copy. If, for some reason, you know your motion will first be presented on trial day and not beforehand, there is no need to mail it to anyone. However, making three copies may be a good idea for motions made at trial or in court at any other time. This way, you can give one to your adversary, give one to the judge, and keep one as a reference copy so you can field any questions from the judge.

Whenever a matter will be heard in court at a later date and you need to play defense by composing a written motion in order to counter an adversary's previous oral or written argument, a good strategy might be to address and counter only the argument made by your opponent. By "defense," we mean that the opposing party has submitted a document or made a statement to the court to which you need to respond and attempt to disprove. If you discover additional facts or counterpoints that can be included to bolster your position while composing your motion, you might consider simply making notes and presenting that information orally in court when the time comes.

In other words, you may only want to provide in your written motion whatever is needed to negate the other side's position and not give them anything more than necessary by introducing new argumentative subject matter. This way, they will not get wind of the new evidence, case law, or whatnot once you have provided a copy of your motion to them as typically required by court rules of procedure. Therefore, you will have a better chance of catching them off guard since they will only learn about your new findings in court. They will have to think quickly on their feet without having had the opportunity to research a rebuttal. Their spontaneous response to your new material will not be supported by any written case law and thus may not be sufficient to counter it.

Note that there are times when "Petitioner" can replace "Plaintiff" or "Defendant" and "Respondent" can replace the other in the motion heading. Motions such as those associated with a petition for interlocutory relief would typically use a "Petitioner v. Respondent" format. In certain types of matters, including some criminal proceedings, "Petitioner" may also be substituted for "Defendant" and "Respondent" might then replace "Plaintiff."

For motions submitted to an appellate court, the first party listed in the heading will sometimes be "Appellant" instead of "Plaintiff." The second party listed would then be "Appellee" or "Respondent" instead of "Defendant," just like most other case-related documents submitted to the particular court. To confuse matters more, sometimes the terms "Plaintiff-Appellee," "Plaintiff-

MOTION TEMPLATE

Appellant," "Defendant-Appellant," or "Defendant-Appellee" are used, with any term referencing Appellant generally being listed first. The substitution of any of the foregoing is either a matter of personal preference or is the protocol for the court in question, so you will need to check whether this nomenclature is a requirement of the court. Additional variations regarding heading terminology and structure are possible.

The opposing party must usually be provided with a copy of the motion as stated three paragraphs prior. If not submitted at trial or during a hearing, it should be sent to the opposing party by U.S. mail or, in any event, some court-approved method. In small claims court, pre-printed forms are often used in lieu of handmade motions.

An accompanying CERTIFICATE (or PROOF or AFFIDAVIT) OF SERVICE is also required by many courts upon filing a motion or anything else with them regarding adversarial matters. Lawyers in some jurisdictions need not provide this certificate but simply can use "cc: [attorney or opposing party name]" on anything they submit to the court because it is assumed they will serve the opposition. However, you are not presumed to know the rules of court as a self-represented litigant; therefore, a written statement indicating that you have served your adversary is generally a prerequisite to the court accepting such filings.

The exact wording for the title of the written certification can vary greatly. It was not feasible to put all combinations in the tentative title. Conventional or other kinds of U.S. mail are sometimes allowed when serving the opposing party. Personal service may also be permissible. Email and alternative forms of service are acceptable or mandated in some jurisdictions. Any of these and more may be incorporated into the title wording. It may be best to research the applicable customs or requirements in order to determine the proper heading for your certifying document.

SMALL CLAIMS COMPLAINT TEMPLATE

GIVEN COURT NAME

_____)
) Docket No. _(court assigns number)_
[your name {, other plaintiff name(s)}],) _("Docket No." may be "Case No." or_
Plaintiff{s}   ) _otherwise)_
)
            v.   )
)
[name(s) of part(y/ies) you are suing],)
Defendant{s}   )
_____)

SMALL CLAIMS COMPLAINT

1. I/We, _____ [your name {, other plaintiff name(s)} | designee] _____, am/are the plaintiff(s) (or an authorized representative of the plaintiff(s)).
   (Type or print plaintiff or authorized representative name(s) in the blank space.)

2. The defendant(s) is/are _____ [name(s) of person(s) and/or compan(y/ies) you are suing] _____.
   (Type or print defendant name(s) in the blank space.)

3. The defendant owes me/us exactly $ _____ [amount for which you are suing] _____.
   (Type or print the exact amount in the blank space. This figure must be _(some maximum dollar amount established by the court)_ or less in order for you to proceed in small claims court.)

4. The reason the defendant owes me/us this sum is:
   (Select only ONE reason listed below that describes the facts of your case.)

❏ Defendant agreed in a written contract to pay me/us this money but has not paid me/us even though I/we have demanded payment. (You need to attach a copy of the written contract to this complaint or attach a sworn statement explaining why you are not able to attach a copy.)

Date(s) this happened: _____ [date(s)] _____

❏ Defendant wrongfully took, destroyed, or damaged my/our personal property.

Date(s) this happened: _____ [date(s)] _____

Describe what happened: _____ [description in your own words] _____
_____
_____

❏ Defendant verbally agreed to pay me/us this money but has not paid me/us even though I/we have demanded payment.

Date(s) this happened: _____ [date(s)] _____

❏ Defendant agreed to do certain work for me/us but has not done it properly even though I/we paid for the work.

SMALL CLAIMS COMPLAINT TEMPLATE

Date(s) this happened: _____ [date(s)] _____

Describe what happened: _____ [description in your own words] _____

_____

_____

_____

❐ Defendant injured me/us.

Date(s) this happened: _____ [date(s)] _____

Describe your injury: _____ [description in your own words] _____

_____

_____

_____

Describe what happened: _____ [description in your own words] _____

_____

_____

_____

❐ Some other reason (If none of the reasons above apply, describe here why the defendant owes you the money you claim.)

_____ [description in your own words] _____

_____

_____

_____

_____

Date(s) this happened: _____ [date(s)] _____

VERIFICATION

Under penalty of perjury under *(State will be specified here.)* state law, the undersigned certifies that the statements set forth in this instrument are true and correct, except as to matters herein stated to be on information and belief, and as to such matters, the undersigned certifies as aforesaid that the undersigned verily believes the same to be true.

Date: _____ [date] _____   _____ [your signature | designee's] _____
                                           Plaintiff's Signature

Plaintiff's Address: Defendant's Address:

_____ [your name | designee's] _____   _____ [name(s) of part(y/ies) you are suing] _____

_____ [your address | designee's] _____ _____ [address(es) of part(y/ies) you are suing] _____

Phone: [your number | designee's]   Phone: [number(s) of part(y/ies) being sued]

SMALL CLAIMS COMPLAINT TEMPLATE

Everything in "[ ]" is to be replaced with information specific to your case. The "|" symbol is used to denote that one of the options within "[ ]" is to be selected from the template—and modified—for use in your complaint. Everything in "{ }" may or may not be part of your complaint and depends upon the number of plaintiffs and defendants. *Italicized* text in "( )" is commentary for informational purposes only and is not to be included in your complaint.

Like other small claims forms, this is one of few court filings that are not entirely self-generated by a party to a legal action. The overall format is somewhat comparable to most complaints filed with any other U.S. court—relatively standardized header, complaint body, sometimes also containing numbered items, and signature, occasionally under penalty of perjury. But all known jurisdictions use pre-printed forms that are completed by the plaintiff or a designee, that are one or two pages long, and that may or may not look like this one.

The proper form for the particular small claims court relevant to your matter is to be completed and sent to that court with the appropriate filing fee. This one will not likely be used and is for reference only. Once the original complaint is returned to you with the docket/case number and a trial day assigned by the court, it can be served to the defendant by various means as defined in the particular jurisdiction. Texas has a slightly different process that begins with the issuance of a "citation" as mentioned in the SERVING THE COMPLAINT section of chapter nine. Others states could as well; therefore, the complaint itself may not be served in such instances.

SMALL CLAIMS ANSWER AND COUNTERCLAIM TEMPLATE

GIVEN COURT NAME

[name(s) of part(y/ies) suing you], Plaintiff{s}	))))	Docket No. [case number] *("Docket No." may be "Case No." or otherwise)*
v.	)))	
[your name {, other defendant name(s)}], Defendant{s}	))))	

SMALL CLAIMS ANSWER AND COUNTERCLAIM

1. I/We, _____ [your name {, other defendant name(s)} | designee] _____, am/are the defendant(s) (or an authorized representative of the defendant(s)). (Type or print defendant or authorized representative name(s) in the blank space.)

2. ❑ This matter **IS NOT** contested. I/We agree with the plaintiff's claim. Judgment may be taken as requested in the complaint plus costs and interest as allowed by law.

-OR-

3. ❑ This matter **IS** contested. I/We do not agree with the plaintiff's claim. This matter should be scheduled so that the parties may present their evidence. The reason(s) why the matter is contested is/are as follows:

[description in your own words]

_____
_____
_____
_____
_____
_____
_____
_____

❑ See attached for additional information.

Do not complete counterclaim section below unless you have a claim of your own against the plaintiff(s).

❑ I/We do have a claim against the plaintiff(s).

Defendant's demand:

I/We demand judgment against the plaintiff(s) for $ [amount] plus interest, costs, attorney fees, if any, and such other relief as the court deems proper.

221

SMALL CLAIMS ANSWER AND COUNTERCLAIM TEMPLATE

Brief statement of dates and facts: _____ [description in your own words] _____

_____

_____

_____

_____

_____

_____

_____

_____

❐ See attached for additional information.

Defendant(s) certif(y/ies) that a copy of this answer and counterclaim has been or will be delivered to the plaintiff(s) or plaintiff's attorney, if any, by *(Court-approved method(s) will be specified here.).*

VERIFICATION

Under penalty of perjury under *(State will be specified here.)* state law, the undersigned certifies that the statements set forth in this instrument are true and correct, except as to matters herein stated to be on information and belief, and as to such matters, the undersigned certifies as aforesaid that the undersigned verily believes the same to be true.

Date: _____ [date] _____   _____ [your signature | designee's] _____
                                          Defendant's Signature

Plaintiff's Address: Defendant's Address:

   [name(s) of part(y/ies) suing you]   _____ [your name | designee's] _____

   [address(es) of part(y/ies) suing you]   _____ [your address | designee's] _____

Phone: [number(s) of part(y/ies) suing you]   Phone: _ [your number | designee's] _

SMALL CLAIMS ANSWER AND COUNTERCLAIM TEMPLATE

Everything in "[ ]" is to be replaced with information specific to your case. The "|" symbol is used to denote that one of the options within "[ ]" is to be selected from the template—and modified—for use in your answer and counterclaim. Everything in "{ }" may or may not be part of your answer and counterclaim and depends upon the number of plaintiffs and defendants. *Italicized* text in "( )" is commentary for informational purposes only and is not to be included in your answer and counterclaim.

Like other small claims forms, this is one of few court filings that are not entirely self-generated by a party to a legal action. The overall format is somewhat comparable to most answers and counterclaims filed with any other U.S. court—relatively standardized header, answer and counterclaim bodies, sometimes also containing numbered items, and signature, occasionally under penalty of perjury. But all known jurisdictions use pre-printed forms that are completed by the defendant or a designee, that are one or two pages long, and that may or may not look like this one.

Remember that a counterclaim can be filed by a defendant in a civil suit when the party suing him has injured him physically, financially, or in some other way. This also holds true for small claims cases. If you have a claim arising from the underlying events of an action filed against you by the plaintiff, you as the defendant could file a counterclaim against the plaintiff in that same action in addition to filing your answer to the plaintiff's claim. Sometimes, instead of filing a counterclaim in the current case, a separate claim can be filed later in an entirely different action with you as the plaintiff and the current plaintiff as the defendant, but the rules about this vary nationwide and by type of claim.

The proper form is to be completed and sent to the court with any applicable filing fee. This one will not likely be used and is for reference only. Although many courts require a fee to file a small claims counterclaim, fewer impose one to file an answer. Courts in Arizona and Colorado are some that do. The counterclaim—and sometimes an answer filed without a counterclaim—must be served to the plaintiff by various means as defined in pertinent rules of civil procedure.

Note that in addition to the overall format of a small claims answer and counterclaim mentioned above, it is much the same as in any other civil case with respect to the answer being given first followed by the counterclaim, if any. Time limits also apply to filing an answer (and a counterclaim, if applicable) and should be consulted in the appropriate rules of procedure. Some jurisdictions also separate the answer and counterclaim into two different forms.

STATE COURT PETITION FOR INTERLOCUTORY RELIEF TEMPLATE

No._____

IN THE [SUPREME COURT | OTHER COURT] OF [STATE]

[your name],

Petitioner

v.

[name(s) of judge(s) or court personnel or applicable part(y/ies)], {individually,

[lower court name(s) where any individuals identified above work,] et al.,}

Respondent{s}

Ongoing case in the [lower court name]

Case No. [number of ongoing case in the lower court]

PETITION FOR INTERLOCUTORY RELIEF

[your name]

[your address]

{[your phone number]}

{[your email address]}

[date sent to respondents and supreme or other court in title above]

STATE COURT PETITION FOR INTERLOCUTORY RELIEF TEMPLATE

(The following is a portion of an actual petition filed against Judge Kevan Cunningham and others in the Taunton District Court in Massachusetts for, among other improprieties, the state and federal crimes they committed during one author's case.)

TABLE OF CONTENTS

STATEMENT OF ISSUES PRESENTED ....[page]
JURISDICTION ....[page]
STATEMENT OF THE CASE ....[page]
LEGAL DISCUSSION...[page]
CONCLUSION..[page]
APPENDIX A *(Appendices are not shown in this template.)*...................[page]
APPENDIX B *(Add lines for additional appendices as necessary.)*...........[page]

STATEMENT OF ISSUES PRESENTED

(The questions below can be written instead as declarative sentences. Your questions (or statements) may contain some or none of the below as appropriate.)

1. Do{es} the respondent{s} have the right to violate [state] rules of civil procedure?
2. Do{es} the respondent{s} have the right to violate [state] statutory law?
3. Do{es} the respondent{s} have the right to violate the civil liberties of the petitioner?
4. Do{es} the respondent{s} have the right to violate the U.S. Constitution?
5. [other questions (or declarations) of law]

JURISDICTION

The jurisdiction of this court is invoked under [Cite statutory law or other authority giving the court jurisdiction, for example, "M.G.L. ch. 211, sec. 3."].

STATEMENT OF THE CASE

(The statements below should be reflective of criminal matters, if appropriate.)

1. A civil case was commenced by the petitioner, [your name], in the [court name] on [date]. This case has been recorded in the docket as case no. [number of ongoing case in the lower court] (hereinafter, "the civil case").
2. Respondents have allowed Defendant's spurious answer in the civil case to be filed well beyond the twenty-day (20-day) requirement of MA R. Civ. P. 12(a)(1) and, in doing so, have violated such rule of procedure. To wit, Defendant's answer was filed nearly nine (9) years late.
3. Respondents have allowed Defendant's illegitimate permissive counterclaim in the civil case to be filed well beyond the twenty-day (20-day) requirement of MA R. Civ. P. 12(a)(1) and, in doing so, have violated such rule of procedure. To wit, Defendant's counterclaim was also filed nearly nine (9) years late.
4. [Continue to make other statements relevant to your case.]

LEGAL DISCUSSION

(The following example partial discussion/argument is based upon Massachusetts general law chapter 211, section 3, and should be modified as applicable to your case. The actual content in your petition will likely vary significantly.)

...The word "prevent" is clearly used in the statute. The only way prevention can be achieved, by definition, is to act ***before*** any event, or ruling, occurs—one synonym for the word is, in fact, "to deal with beforehand."[1] Upon closer examination, the first sentence of the statute seems to be an apparent contradiction. The phrase "prevent errors and abuses" implies preventative action must be taken by the high court *before* all remedial actions have been exhausted, thereby meaning that a final appeal or appeal of any kind need not be undertaken in any court in order for the high court to intervene. The succeeding phrase "if no other remedy is expressly provided" seemingly conflicts with the prior phrase and indicates that a petition can only be heard as a last-ditch effort by the petitioner. This thinking is also supported by case law—law that focuses strictly on remedial actions and not on preventative actions.

However, neither phrase is given particular weight over the other in statute. Delving further into the construction of the first sentence, this apparent disagreement of phrases might not necessarily exist if the ambiguous wording was instead written "if no other remedy is expressly *and currently* provided." If it was, the contradictory nature of the first sentence would be nullified, and the statute, or at least the first paragraph, would be logically sound under any rigorous analysis in all circumstances. In the alternative, if "and prevent" was stricken from the sentence, then all existing case law elucidating the high court's role as a last-resort correction mechanism would be fully supportive of that new wording. But all case law arguments completely overlook the usage and meaning of these two words.

Moreover, there is also no case law mentioning the fact of there being two somewhat opposing phrases in the opening sentence of the statute and that the second somehow should overshadow the first in any way. Because of this and the fact that neither phrase has superiority over the other according to statute, the high court must act now before the conclusion of the civil case. Doing so would correct the significant errors already made, repair the corresponding damage done, and prevent further errors that might be made by the respondents before case disposition.

This petition is being submitted because the state has abolished a remedy formerly available to the petitioner, the writ of *mandamus*, under MA R. Civ. P. 81(b). The petitioner also filed a complaint against Kevan J. Cunningham with the Massachusetts Commission on Judicial Conduct (CJC) on July 14, 2015 (see appendix A). As with all complaints filed with the CJC and Office of the Bar Counsel by persons of little political power, the complaint was summarily dismissed shortly thereafter without investigation.

In fact, of the six (6) or seven (7) complaints filed by the petitioner in two different states against both transgressing attorneys and corrupt judges, exactly zero have been meaningfully addressed by oversight boards in either state. However, the offenders have

---

[1] http://www.merriam-webster.com

violated a cumulative total of more than thirty (30) rules and canons. With the "fox effectively in charge of the henhouse" regarding most of these governing boards that are composed primarily of lawyers and judges nationwide, the average litigant has hardly a prayer in just and rightful disposition of such complaints.

Therefore, the only form of redress at the state level remaining for the petitioner at this time is a petition to the Supreme Judicial Court of Massachusetts. Thereafter, the petitioner will be forced to file a complaint with the Federal Bureau of Investigation (FBI) against the respondents (and possibly others) for acting under the "color of law" in flagrant violation of 18 U.S. Code § 242.

Regarding case management, the district court has not been straightforward with its duties. Email correspondence from it on September 8, 2014, confirms a default judgment in favor of the petitioner/plaintiff being vacated:

> "Please be advised that, after further review and consultation with the Clerk Magistrate, the judgement [*sic*] that issued has been vacated and will be scheduled for a motion hearing on 10/29/2014 @ 10:00 AM. You, or an Attorney on your behalf, will need to be present."

An entry in the convoluted court record on September 15, 2014, however, shows the defendant's motion to vacate being filed on September 9, 2014, a day later than the above email message, and states, "Judgment entered on 08/27/2014 vacated; issued in error; parties notifed [*sic*]" (see appendix B). Although there is no entry on the docket for such motion being heard on October 29, 2014, there is a paradoxical ruling by Judge Cunningham on November 09, 2014, allowing the motion to vacate an already vacated judgment.

On September 10, 2014, Petitioner received an additional email from the court clerk:

> "Based upon our file, your motion for default judgement [*sic*] must be heard and allowed by a Judge. Therefore, since the judgement [*sic*] was entered in error it has been vacated. The Defendant has also filed a Motion to Dismiss, Motion to Vacate Default Judgement [*sic*], and Opposition to Plaintiff's Motion for Default Judgement [*sic*]. All 4 motions will be heard at the same time on **10-29-14**."

The implication of any error in entry is incorrect since civil procedure rule 55(b)(1) clearly states:

> "(b) Judgment. Judgment by default may be entered as follows:
> (1) By the Clerk. When the plaintiff's claim against a defendant is for a sum certain or for a sum which can by computation be made certain, the clerk upon request of the plaintiff and upon affidavit of the amount due and affidavit that the defendant is not an infant or incompetent person or an incapacitated person as defined in G.L. c.190B, shall enter judgment for that amount and costs against the defendant, if he has been defaulted for failure to appear."

The motion for default judgment was filed under this rule. Although the district court had stated in the above email that the default entry was in error, it was not. All requirements of the civil case were met perfectly according to rule 55(a) and (b)(1). Now, if rules 55(c), 60(a), and 60(b) are all studied carefully, it can be seen that the only way an error-free default judgment can be vacated is by motion under 60(b). The emails by court personnel and the confusing court record are all likely part of a smokescreen to mask a call by Joseph L. Michaud, defense counsel, (hereinafter "Michaud") to the court on or about September 8, 2014, in order to get the judgment orally vacated. At a time beginning shortly thereafter, the court then tried to cover its tracks with multiple docket entries to conceal the political favor.

The petitioner knows of this call because a package from Michaud was delivered by U.S. mail not long after September 8, 2014, to the mailing address the petitioner gave the clerk by email on August 28, 2014. The only way Michaud could have known of this address is by calling the court since this is not the residential address of the petitioner. It may not be against court rules of procedure to contrive the court record and perform political favors or against rules of professional conduct for a lawyer to ask for them, but it certainly violates the petitioner's right of due process under the Fourteenth Amendment.

The high court has ruled in *Commonwealth v. Bertini*, "We therefore allow interlocutory review under G.L. c. 211, § 3, only where 'there are <u>substantial claims alleging violation of the appellant's substantive rights</u>,' and the error complained of is 'irremediable so that an order for a new trial in the normal process of appeal will not put the defendant in statu quo'," quoting *Beckman v. Commonwealth* (emphasis added). Obviously, violating court rules of procedure and statutory law rise to the level of, if not eclipse, "violation of the appellant's substantive rights." Denying the petitioner his right of due process under the Fourteenth Amendment and possibly denying him other constitutional rights as well in the civil case likewise and quite easily exceed this standard. Also in *Bertini*, the high court stated it has "previously considered appeals...<u>pretrial</u>..." (emphasis added). Since the civil case is pretrial, the high court would not be setting precedent by granting this petition.

Because time is of the essence, the petitioner therefore requests that this court quickly direct its attention to mandating that the respondents remedy their violations of court rules of procedure and statutory law. He also asks this court to investigate the engineering of the court record, which was done in an attempt to conceal a politically motivated favor for Michaud, and to instruct the lower court to abide by the U.S. Constitution. Because of this direction from the high court, the respondents will have no choice but to disallow the defendant's untruthful answer in the civil case, dismiss the defendant's fictitious counterclaim, and strike all references to any mention of matters now under seal within the Commonwealth of Massachusetts.

Lastly, the petitioner requests the high court to provide additional corrective direction to the respondents while litigation is ongoing. The judges now acting on the civil case will undoubtedly be antagonized and likely biased because of this petition.

Therefore, the petitioner also requests that this court strongly encourage all relevantly named respondents to follow the protocol of recusal in order for justice to be served.

CONCLUSION

From the foregoing argument, it is clear the respondents do not have any of the rights enumerated in the STATEMENT OF ISSUES PRESENTED, and the high court therefore should grant this petition for interlocutory relief.

Date: [same date as on cover page]   [your signature] _____

                                                 [your name]

STATE COURT PETITION FOR INTERLOCUTORY RELIEF TEMPLATE

Other than for all instances of "[*sic*]," everything in "[ ]" is to be replaced with information specific to your case. The "|" symbol is used to denote that one of the options within "[ ]" is to be selected from the template—and perhaps modified—for use in your petition. Everything in "{ }" may or may not be part of your petition and depends upon the number of parties and other factors. *Italicized* text in "( )" is commentary for informational purposes only and is not to be included in your petition.

In all known U.S. jurisdictions, the petitioner is listed before the respondent on the first page. A petition on which the template is based was actually filed with the Massachusetts Supreme Judicial Court to address corruption in the Taunton District Court. For informational purposes, the original petition was left mostly intact to create the template. The actual content of your petition will likely vary significantly.

Because that state's highest court made no effort to provide the corrective relief sought, the coauthor was forced to file criminal complaints with the FBI and DOJ against government officials in the Massachusetts courts, including judges, because of the federal criminal offenses committed by them. Acting under the "color of law" was one of several such offenses. The possibility of having to file complaints with the FBI and DOJ was mentioned in chapters three and seven.

The general form of this type of petition is similar across the country; however, small formatting nuances may be requisite. Note that the words "(emphasis added)" are used when underlining, bolding, or otherwise emphasizing a portion of cited case law, quoted statute, or any other direct legal reference as shown in the template. Also note that the court may require confirmation that the petition was served. See the CERTIFICATE (or PROOF or AFFIDAVIT) OF SERVICE template at the end of the MOTION TEMPLATE and the relevant descriptive narrative text that follows. Service is sometimes made by U.S. mail directly to the offending court if a judge, a court officer, or other court personnel are the respondents.

TRAFFIC REQUEST FOR PRODUCTION OF DOCUMENTS TEMPLATE

[COURT NAME]

{[COUNTY]}   **{[COURT DIVISION]}**

)	Docket No. [citation number]
[city, town, state, or federal] Police {Dept.},)	*("Docket No." may be*
Plaintiff)	*"Case No." or otherwise)*
)	
v.)	
)	
[your name],)	
Defendant)	
)	

REQUEST FOR PRODUCTION OF DOCUMENTS

Pursuant to [Cite rule of civil or criminal procedure, whichever applies, related to producing documents, for example, "MA R. Civ. P. 34."], Defendant requests that, within [number of days specified in rule, for example, "thirty (30)"] days, Plaintiff produce for inspection and copying by Defendant all documents and things within the possession, custody, or control of Plaintiff as set forth below and requested herein and provide same to Defendant at address specified below.

1. the time officer [badge number] was recorded as being on duty on [date of citation]

2. a copy of the registration certificate, including VIN and license plate or other identifying number, for the vehicle used by officer [badge number] on [date of citation] *(This should be included for stops initiated by an officer on or in a motorized ground vehicle. See note below.*)*

3. explanation/clarification of the following from the original citation:

    a. [for example, "VIOLATION CODE S"]
    b. [for example, "ROAD CONDITION D"]
    c. [Keep adding entries for any such cryptic or questionable codes on citation.]

4. a copy of officer [badge number]'s notes, arrest log, statements, diagrams, and drawings made on any piece of paper, including the reverse of [his or her] copy of the citation, or other medium of information storage on [date of citation]

5. [DOT speed study or whatever it may be called in the relevant jurisdiction] of [road name(s) at location of the alleged violation] *(This should be included when fighting speeding violations and may have to be obtained from the local DPW or a local official.)*

6. an [engineering and traffic survey or whatever it may be called in the relevant jurisdiction] of [road name(s) at location of the alleged violation] *(This should be included when fighting speeding violations and may have to be obtained from the local DPW or a local official.)*

7. video footage from the dashboard camera or any other recording source in or on the vehicle identified in request number 2 and/or body camera worn by officer [badge number] from [fifteen minutes before the stop to three minutes after you or he or she left the scene] on [date of citation] *(This should be included for stops initiated by an officer on or in a motorized ground vehicle when he or she made his or her observations or when needed to defend the case in general. See note below.*)*

8. the make, model number, and serial number of the [radar, lidar, VASCAR, or other] device allegedly used by officer [badge number] on [date of citation] *(See note below.*)*

9. documentation indicating that the vehicle identified in request number 2 contained the [radar, lidar, VASCAR, or other] device named in request number 8 on [date of citation] *(See note below.*)*

10. documentation indicating the date that the vehicle identified in request number 2 was initially equipped with the [radar, lidar, VASCAR, or other] device named in request number 8 *(See note below.*)*

11. documentation indicating the times that the [radar, lidar, VASCAR, or other] device named in request number 8 was in operation on [date of citation] from [one half hour before to one half hour after the time of citation] *(See note below.*)*

12. officer [badge number]'s training certification and/or accreditation regarding [his or her] training for the [radar, lidar, VASCAR, or other] device named in request number 8 *(See note below.*)*

13. the calibration certificates or, if not available, a log of the calibration dates and times for the [radar, lidar, VASCAR, or other] device named in request number 8 from [one-year time span or a sufficient period that includes the calibration interval requirements of the manufacturer or statute, whichever is longest, immediately prior to the date and time of the citation] *(See note below.*)*

14. the manufacturer's operator's manual for the [radar, lidar, VASCAR, or other] device named in request number 8 *(See note below.*)*

15. if calibration for the [radar, lidar, VASCAR, or other] device named in request number 8 is done by tuning forks, the makes, model numbers, and serial numbers of the forks; otherwise, the names of the instruments used to calibrate the [radar, lidar, VASCAR, or other] device named in request number 8 along with the instruments' makes, model numbers, and serial numbers *(See note below.*)*

16. [town, city, state, or federal police] {Department} regulations and guidelines regarding the use of, operation of, and policies for speed detection equipment *(See note below.*)*

17. documentation indicating that the tuning forks or calibration devices identified in request number 15 have been tested and calibrated and the dates and times they have been tested and calibrated by a certified technician from [one-year time span or a sufficient period that includes the calibration interval requirements of the manufacturer or statute, whichever is longest, immediately prior to the date and time of the citation] *(See note below.*)*

18. documentation indicating that the tuning forks or calibration devices identified in request number 15 have been recalibrated after exposure to excessive heat *(See note below.*)*

19. documentation indicating that the tuning forks or calibration devices identified in request number 15 are not cracked, bent, or otherwise damaged *(See note below.*)*

20. documentation (including VIN) indicating when the speedometer for the vehicle identified in request number 2 was last calibrated prior to [the date and time of the citation] {according to [state or federal or District of Columbia] law § [cited statute requiring calibration, for example, "46.2-882"]} *(This should be included when fighting speeding violations that resulted from speed measurements attempted from a moving motorized ground vehicle and can be requested even with no supporting state, federal, or District of Columbia law. See note below.*)*

21. all timing, maintenance, and engineering records for the traffic control signal located at the intersection of [road names at the intersection of the traffic control signal allegedly disobeyed] *(This should be included when fighting all traffic light violations.)*

22. documentation indicating the installation date of the traffic light camera allegedly located at the intersection of [road names at the intersection of the traffic control signal allegedly disobeyed] *(This should be included only when fighting traffic light violations of which you have been notified by mail.)*

23. documentation indicating that the traffic light camera allegedly located at the intersection of [road names at the intersection of the traffic control signal allegedly disobeyed] was in operation on [date of citation] from [one half hour before to one half hour after the time of citation] *(This should be included only when fighting traffic light violations of which you have been notified by mail.)*

(*Numbers 2, 7, and 20 can also be included/adapted for aircraft or seacraft when relevant. For all other requests so asterisked, they should be included for speeding citations issued whenever the officer used a speed measuring device.)

Date: [date sent to police, plaintiff, and court]   [your signature] _____
                                                          [your name]
                                                          [your address]
                                                          {[your phone number]}
                                                          {[your email address]}

TRAFFIC REQUEST FOR PRODUCTION OF DOCUMENTS TEMPLATE

Everything in "[ ]" is to be replaced with information specific to your case. Everything in "{ }" may or may not be part of your request and depends upon several factors. *Italicized* text in "( )" is commentary for informational purposes only and is not to be included in your request.

In all known U.S. courts below the appellate level, the plaintiff is listed before the defendant in the heading on the first page just like any other adversarial legal document filed in that court. You typically send a copy of the request to each of: the court, the plaintiff/prosecutor, and the issuing police organization—with all being sent by U.S. mail or, in any event, a court-approved method. The police organization and plaintiff/prosecutor's office may be one and the same; they may not. Also, you may want to ensure receipt via certified mail or otherwise.

Pore over all information returned from the plaintiff, which could be an inch thick or more if they respond fully for a speeding charge, and look for any conflicting information. For example, look for VINs that do not match on any combination of: the registration certificate, the documentation identifying the vehicle in or on which the speed measuring device was installed, the speed measuring device's calibration certificate, or the vehicle's speedometer calibration certificate. Any such conflicts should disqualify the citation. At most, the plaintiff likely will only partially respond to your request.

One of the critical pieces of information is the license plate number of the officer's vehicle, which you should have wisely photographed or otherwise recorded during the stop. This is the key to get the ball rolling when disputing many speeding violations, but the plate number can also be important for disputing other violations. With this piece of information, you can check that the license plate number you recorded matches the one on the copy of the vehicle's registration certificate supplied to you. The VIN or plate number on that document then can be used to validate (or invalidate) everything related to the speed detecting equipment allegedly installed and used on or in the officer's vehicle in addition to doing the same with its speedometer calibration certificate.

Make sure you understand why everything is needed and why the plaintiff may be required by law to provide you with the requested information if it falls under the Freedom of Information Act—a federal law also enacted at the state level. Nevertheless, discovery should allow it to be requested regardless of the act's requirements. The plaintiff is not always forthcoming with everything in the request, and the judge may try to eliminate from the case as much of the missing requested material as possible, given the chance. If you cannot justify the reason you need all of it, that opens the door widely to giving the judge exactly that opportunity.

Since some numbered items may not be included in your request, keep in mind that the numbering may have to change as might references to numbered items within it. Depending upon the date of your trial and rules of court, it might be better not to send the request the day after receiving a citation or soon thereafter. You can definitely begin to compose it well beforehand while everything is fresh in your mind, which will also give you plenty of time to recheck your work. But by waiting as long as reasonable before delivering your request, things will have a chance to get misplaced or forgotten by law enforcement. It will also put them under a tighter deadline to produce all the requested information—and possibly induce them not to respond whatsoever.

Finally, a request such as this *is not* necessarily a one-shot deal. Several requests can be made to the opposing party until the information needed to formulate a strong defense has been obtained. As long as whatever is requested is related to that purpose, it can be included. Personally identifiable information protected by privacy, such as a social security number and date of birth, is usually not allowed or is objectionable. Also note that the court may require confirmation that the request was served. See the CERTIFICATE (or PROOF or AFFIDAVIT) OF SERVICE template at the end of the MOTION TEMPLATE and the relevant descriptive narrative text that follows.

RESIDENTIAL RENTAL AGREEMENT AND/OR LEASE TEMPLATE

RENTAL AGREEMENT AND/OR LEASE

This rental agreement and/or lease, hereinafter referred to as "AGREEMENT," shall evidence the complete terms and conditions to which the parties whose signatures appear below have agreed. Landlord/lessor/agent, [given party's name], is hereinafter referred to as "LANDLORD," and tenant(s)/lessee(s), [tenant name(s)], is(are) hereinafter referred to as "TENANT." As consideration for this AGREEMENT, LANDLORD agrees to rent/lease to TENANT and TENANT agrees to rent/lease from LANDLORD for use solely as a private residence the premises located at [address].

1. TERM:
This AGREEMENT shall begin on [date] and continue through [date] as a leasehold. If TENANT should move from the premises prior to expiration of this period, s/he shall be liable for all rent due until such time that the residence is occupied by a LANDLORD-approved paying resident or expiration of said period, whichever is shorter.

2. PAYMENTS:
TENANT agrees to pay rent in advance in the amount of $[amount] per [week or month or year] on the [day, e.g., "1st"] day of each [week or month or year]. Rent and other charges are to be paid by [desired method, for example, "direct deposit into a bank account provided by LANDLORD"]. The first and last [week or month or year]'s rent, $[amount] each, shall be paid upon execution of this AGREEMENT.

3. SECURITY DEPOSIT:
A security deposit of $[amount, the maximum of which may be set by statute—about half the states have no statutory limit, but others and the nation's capital do] shall secure compliance with the terms and conditions of this AGREEMENT. Said deposit shall be refunded to TENANT within [The maximum amount of time varies greatly nationwide, but other than only one known state with no statutory limit, "sixty (60) days" would be the maximum here.] after the premises have been completely vacated less any amount necessary to pay LANDLORD: a) unpaid rent, b) cleaning costs, c) key replacement costs, d) costs for repair of damage to premises and/or common areas above ordinary wear and tear, and e) any other amount legally allowable under the terms of this AGREEMENT. A written accounting of said charges shall be presented to TENANT within [length of time, e.g., "thirty (30) days"] of move-out. If deposit does not cover such costs, TENANT shall immediately pay said additional costs to LANDLORD. LANDLORD acknowledges receipt of the first and last [week or month or year]'s rent payment and the security deposit for a total payment of $[amount] upon execution of this AGREEMENT.

4. LATE RENT:
A late fee of $[amount, the maximum of which may be set by statute—several states and the District of Columbia have laws regarding the maximum fee that can be charged, time constraints that must be observed, and related criteria] shall be added and due for any payment of rent made after the [day, e.g., "1st"] day of the [week or month or year].

Replace everything in "[ ]" with information specific to your lease. Other changes may be needed.

5. UTILITIES:
TENANT agrees to pay all utilities/services (gas, electric, water, sewer) and can reimburse LANDLORD or transfer them into TENANT's name and pay them directly.

6. OCCUPANTS:
Guests staying more than [length of time, e.g., "fifteen (15) days"] without the written consent of LANDLORD shall be considered a breach of this AGREEMENT. ONLY the following individuals and animals AND NO OTHERS shall occupy the subject residence for more than [same length of time as above] unless the express written consent of LANDLORD is obtained in advance: [tenant/pet name(s)].

7. PETS:
No animal, fowl, fish, reptile, or pet of any kind, other than as listed in provision 6, shall be kept on or about the premises for any amount of time without obtaining the prior written consent of LANDLORD and meeting the requirements of LANDLORD ["and condominium association" can also be added if relevant]. Such consent, if granted, shall be revocable at LANDLORD's option upon giving TENANT a [length of time, e.g., "thirty-day (30-day)"] written notice. In the event laws are passed or permission is granted to have a(n additional) pet or an animal of any kind, an additional deposit in the amount of $[amount] will be required along with additional [weekly or monthly or yearly] rent of $[amount] and the signing (or updating in the case of another pet) of LANDLORD's Pet Agreement. TENANT also agrees to carry insurance deemed appropriate by LANDLORD to cover possible liability and damage that may be caused by such animals.

8. LIQUID FILLED FURNISHINGS:
No liquid-filled furniture or receptacle containing more than ten (10) gallons of liquid is permitted without prior written consent and meeting the requirements of LANDLORD. When permitted, TENANT also agrees to carry insurance deemed appropriate by LANDLORD to cover possible losses that may be caused by such items.

9. PARKING:
If and when TENANT is assigned a parking area/space on LANDLORD's property, the parking area/space shall be used exclusively for parking passenger automobiles and/or those approved vehicles listed on TENANT's application attached hereto. TENANT is hereby assigned the parking area/space immediately in front of the residence's garage. The garage can also be used for parking. The parking fee for assigned spaces (if applicable) is $[amount] [weekly or monthly or yearly]. Said spaces shall not be used for the painting or repairing of vehicles, other than simple routine maintenance. Major repairs are allowed in the garage but so as not to damage the concrete floor. No other parking space shall be used by TENANT or TENANT's guests except for the community parking spaces; however, these spaces may not be available during snow events. TENANT is responsible for oil leaks and other vehicle discharges for which TENANT shall be charged cleaning fees if deemed necessary by LANDLORD.

Replace everything in "[ ]" with information specific to your lease. Other changes may be needed.

10. NOISE:

TENANT agrees not to cause or allow any noise and/or activity on the premises that might disturb the peace and quiet of another resident and/or neighbor. Said noise and/or activity shall be a breach of this AGREEMENT.

11. DESTRUCTION OF PREMISES:

If the premises become totally or partially destroyed during the term of this AGREEMENT so that TENANT's use is seriously impaired, LANDLORD or TENANT may terminate this AGREEMENT immediately upon [length of time, e.g., "three-day (3-day)"] written notice to the other party.

12. CONDITION OF PREMISES:

TENANT acknowledges that s/he has examined the premises and that said premises; all furnishings, fixtures, furniture, plumbing, heating, and electrical facilities; all items listed on the attached Property Condition Checklist, if any; and/or all other items provided by LANDLORD are clean and in satisfactory condition except as may be indicated elsewhere in this AGREEMENT. TENANT agrees to keep the premises and all items in this provision in good order and good condition and to pay immediately for costs to repair or replace any portion of them damaged by TENANT, his or her guests, and/or his or her invitees, except as provided by law. At the termination of this AGREEMENT, all items in this provision shall be returned to LANDLORD in clean and good condition except for reasonable wear and tear, and the premises shall be free of all personal property and trash not belonging to LANDLORD. It is agreed that all dirt, holes, tears, burns, and stains of any size or amount in the carpets, drapes, or walls or any other part of the premises do not constitute reasonable wear and tear.

13. ALTERATIONS:

TENANT shall not paint; wallpaper; alter or redecorate; change or install locks; install screws, fastening devices, nails, adhesive materials, an antenna, or other equipment; or place signs, displays, or other exhibits on or in any portion of the premises without the written consent of LANDLORD except as may be provided by law.

14. PROPERTY MAINTENANCE:

TENANT shall deposit all garbage and waste in a clean and sanitary manner into the proper receptacles and shall cooperate in keeping the garbage area neat and clean. TENANT shall be responsible for disposing items of such size and nature that are not normally acceptable by the garbage hauler. TENANT shall be responsible for keeping the kitchen and bathroom drains free of things that may tend to cause clogging of the drains. TENANT shall pay for the cleaning out of any plumbing fixture that may need to be cleared of stoppage and for the repair of damage caused by stopping of waste pipes or overflow from bathtubs, wash basins, or sinks.

Replace everything in "[ ]" with information specific to your lease. Other changes may be needed.

15. RULES:

TENANT shall comply with all rules as stated on a separate addendum, the [House Rules or Condominium Rules and Regulations or Applicable Rules], but that are deemed part of this AGREEMENT, and a violation of any of the rules in the [House Rules or Condominium Rules and Regulations or Applicable Rules] is considered a breach of this AGREEMENT.

16. CHANGE OF TERMS:

The terms and conditions of this AGREEMENT are subject to future change by LANDLORD after expiration of the agreed lease period but upon giving TENANT a minimum [length of time, e.g., "sixty-day (60-day)"] written notice prior to the date whereupon such change becomes effective. Any changes are subject to laws in existence at the time of the notice of change of terms.

17. TERMINATION:

After expiration of the leasing period, this AGREEMENT is automatically renewed from [week-to-week or month-to-month or year-to-year] but may be terminated by either party giving to the other a minimum [length of time, e.g., "sixty-day (60-day)"] written notice of intention to terminate. Where laws require "just cause," such just cause shall be so stated on said notice. The premises shall be considered vacated only after all areas, including storage areas, are clear of all TENANT's belongings and keys and other property furnished for TENANT's use are returned to LANDLORD. Should TENANT hold over beyond the termination date or fail to vacate all possessions on or before the termination date, TENANT shall be liable for additional rent and damages, which may include damages due to LANDLORD's loss of prospective new renters.

18. POSSESSION:

If LANDLORD is unable to deliver possession of the residence to TENANT on the agreed date because of the loss or destruction of the residence or because of the failure of the prior residents to vacate or for any other reason, TENANT or LANDLORD may immediately cancel this AGREEMENT upon written notice to the other party at their last known address, whereupon neither party shall have liability to the other, and any sums paid under this AGREEMENT shall be refunded in full. If neither party cancels, this AGREEMENT shall be prorated and begin on the date of actual possession.

19. RIGHT OF ENTRY AND INSPECTION:

LANDLORD (or designated representative) may enter, inspect, and/or repair the premises at any time in case of emergency or suspected abandonment. LANDLORD shall give [length of time—minimum occasionally set by law, usually twenty-four or forty-eight hours] notice and may enter during normal business hours for smoke alarm inspections; for normal inspections and repairs; and/or for the purpose of showing the premises to prospective renters, buyers, and/or lenders. LANDLORD is permitted to make all alterations and repairs that, in LANDLORD's judgment, are necessary to be completed.

Replace everything in "[ ]" with information specific to your lease. Other changes may be needed.

20. INSURANCE:

TENANT acknowledges that LANDLORD's insurance does not cover personal property loss or damage caused by fire, theft, rain, war, acts of God, acts of others, and/or any other causes, nor shall LANDLORD be held liable for such losses. TENANT is hereby advised to obtain his or her own insurance policy to cover any personal losses.

21. ASSIGNMENT:

TENANT agrees not to transfer, assign, or sublet the premises or any part thereof.

22. PARTIAL INVALIDITY:

Nothing contained in this AGREEMENT shall be construed as waiving any of LANDLORD's or TENANT's rights under the law. If any provision of this AGREEMENT is in conflict with the law, that provision shall be void to the extent that it is in conflict, but it shall not invalidate this AGREEMENT, nor shall it affect the validity or enforceability of any other provision of this AGREEMENT.

23. NO WAIVER:

LANDLORD's acceptance of rent with knowledge of any default by TENANT or waiver by LANDLORD of any breach of any provision of this AGREEMENT shall not constitute a waiver of subsequent defaults or breaches. Failure to require compliance or to exercise any right shall not be constituted as a waiver by LANDLORD of said provision and/or right and shall not affect the validity or enforceability of any provision of this AGREEMENT.

24. FEES:

If any legal proceedings are brought by either party of this AGREEMENT against the other, the prevailing party shall be reimbursed by the losing party for all reasonable attorney's fees and costs in addition to damages awarded. For any fees/fines associated with TENANT's actions but assigned to LANDLORD, TENANT will immediately reimburse LANDLORD such costs.

25. NOTICES:

All notices to TENANT shall be served at the premises, and all notices to LANDLORD shall be served at [address].

26. REPORT TO CREDIT/TENANT AGENCIES:

You are hereby notified that a nonpayment, late payment, or breach of any of the provisions of this AGREEMENT may be submitted/reported to a credit and/or tenant reporting agency and may create a negative entry on your credit report.

27. INVENTORY:

The premises contain LANDLORD's items (to be determined) that TENANT may use. TENANT hereby agrees to accept all risk for usage of said items and releases LANDLORD from all liability.

Replace everything in "[ ]" with information specific to your lease. Other changes may be needed.

28. REPAIRS:

Repairs to the premises can be made by TENANT with LANDLORD's permission. Costs will be split equally between LANDLORD and TENANT whether repairs are made by TENANT or a third party. However, costs will be borne exclusively by TENANT for items damaged by him or her, his or her guests, and/or his or her invitees as stated in provision 12, except as provided by law.

29. KEYS AND ADDENDUMS:

TENANT acknowledges receipt of the following, which shall be deemed part of this AGREEMENT: (Please check)

____ Keys: number and purposes_____

____ [House Rules or Condominium Rules and Regulations or Applicable Rules]

____ Pet Agreement

____ Property Condition Checklist

30. JOINTLY AND SEVERALLY:

The undersigned TENANTs are jointly and severally responsible and liable for all obligations under this AGREEMENT.

31. RECEIPT OF AGREEMENT:

The undersigned TENANTs have read and understand this AGREEMENT and hereby acknowledge receipt of a copy of this AGREEMENT.

TENANT's Signature _____ Date _____

TENANT's Signature _____ Date _____

LANDLORD's Signature _____ Date _____

Replace everything in "[ ]" with information specific to your lease. Other changes may be needed.

HELPFUL WEBSITES

BANKS IN CAYMAN ISLANDS

http://www.cimoney.com.ky/WorkArea/DownloadAsset.aspx?id=610

https://thebanks.eu/banks-by-country/Cayman-Islands

COUNTRIES WITH EXTRADITION AGREEMENTS WITH THE U.S.

http://www.law.cornell.edu/uscode/text/18/3181 (see "Notes" tab for list of countries)

FEDERAL LAW

Statutes:	http://www.law.cornell.edu/uscode/text
Search:	http://uscode.house.gov/search/criteria.shtml
Courts:	http://www.uscourts.gov/about-federal-courts
Rules of civil procedure:	http://www.uscourts.gov/file/rules-civil-procedure
Rules of criminal procedure:	http://www.uscourts.gov/file/document/rules-criminal-procedure

STATE/D.C. LAW

If any state or District of Columbia links below become invalid, there are other websites that can be accessed in order to gather identical information, such as lexisnexis.com, various university sites, and more. Note that as of this writing, some states do not maintain their own databases or search engines for statutes or court rules of procedure but instead redirect to other websites. Lexisnexis.com, westlaw.com, and google.com are some such sites. Note also that laws and rules of procedure change from time to time, and the ones located at the relevant websites indicated below may be out-of-date. The ideal place to search for them is the law library or court, which should have the latest versions.

Remember—many states have "spin-off" rules of procedure for family court, traffic court, or other courts that are to be used in conjunction with, but supersede, the underlying general rules of civil or criminal procedure applicable to any given civil or criminal case as appropriate. However, some states, Delaware being one, have no basic underlying civil or criminal rules but instead maintain separate, coequal rules for each court type. When a single webpage does not list all applicable rule sets in those instances, just the link for one set of rules is shown below.

ROCivP = rules of civil procedure

ROCrP = rules of criminal procedure

Alabama

Statutes:	http://alisondb.legislature.state.al.us/alison/codeofalabama/1975/coatoc.htm
Search:	http://alisondb.legislature.state.al.us/alison/CoASearchContent.aspx
Courts:	http://judicial.alabama.gov
ROCivP:	http://judicial.alabama.gov/library/rules_civ_procedure.cfm
ROCrP:	http://judicial.alabama.gov/library/rules_crim_procedure.cfm

Alaska

Statutes:	http://www.legis.state.ak.us/basis/statutes.asp
Search:	http://www.legis.state.ak.us/basis/statutes.asp
Courts:	http://courts.alaska.gov
ROCivP:	http://courts.alaska.gov/rules/civ2.htm
ROCrP:	http://courts.alaska.gov/rules/crpro.htm

HELPFUL WEBSITES

Arizona

Statutes: http://www.azleg.gov/ArizonaRevisedStatutes.asp

Search: http://www.azleg.gov/ArizonaRevisedStatutes.asp

Courts: http://www.azcourts.gov

ROCivP: https://govt.westlaw.com/azrules/Browse/Home/Arizona/ArizonaCourtRules/ArizonaStatutesCourtRules?guid=ND4E6D1300BBC11E2B693E1305F461EC5&transitionType=CategoryPageItem&contextData=(sc.Default)&bhcp=1

ROCrP: https://govt.westlaw.com/azrules/Browse/Home/Arizona/ArizonaCourtRules/ArizonaStatutesCourtRules?guid=NCB1EB43070CB11DAA16E8D4AC7636430&transitionType=CategoryPageItem&contextData=(sc.Default)

Arkansas

Statutes: http://www.lexisnexis.com/hottopics/arcode/Default.asp

Search: http://www.lexisnexis.com/hottopics/arcode/Default.asp

Courts: https://courts.arkansas.gov

ROCivP: https://courts.arkansas.gov/rules-and-administrative-orders/rules-of-civil-procedure

ROCrP: https://courts.arkansas.gov/rules-and-administrative-orders/rules-of-criminal-procedure

California

Statutes: http://leginfo.legislature.ca.gov/faces/codes.xhtml

Search: http://leginfo.legislature.ca.gov/faces/codes.xhtml

Courts: http://www.courts.ca.gov

ROCivP: http://www.courts.ca.gov/rules.htm

ROCrP: http://www.courts.ca.gov/rules.htm

Colorado

Statutes: http://www.lexisnexis.com/hottopics/colorado/

Search: http://www.lexisnexis.com/hottopics/colorado/

Courts: http://www.courts.state.co.us

ROCivP: http://www.lexisnexis.com/hottopics/colorado/

ROCrP: http://www.lexisnexis.com/hottopics/colorado/

Connecticut

Statutes: http://www.cga.ct.gov/current/pub/titles.htm

Search: http://search.cga.state.ct.us/dtsearch_pub_statutes.html

Courts: http://www.jud.ct.gov/courts.htm

ROCivP: http://www.jud.ct.gov/Publications/PracticeBook/PB.pdf

ROCrP: http://www.jud.ct.gov/Publications/PracticeBook/PB.pdf

Delaware

Statutes: http://delcode.delaware.gov

Search: http://delcode.delaware.gov

Courts: http://courts.delaware.gov

ROCivP: http://courts.delaware.gov/rules/index.stm

HELPFUL WEBSITES

ROCrP: http://courts.delaware.gov/rules/index.stm

Florida
Statutes: http://www.flsenate.gov/Laws/Statutes
Search: http://www.flsenate.gov/Laws/Statutes
Courts: http://www.flcourts.org
ROCivP: http://www.leg.state.fl.us/Statutes/index.cfm?App_mode=Display_Index&Title_Request=VI#TitleVI
ROCrP: http://www.leg.state.fl.us/Statutes/index.cfm?App_mode=Display_Index&Title_Request=XLVII#TitleXLVII

Georgia
Statutes: http://law.justia.com/codes/georgia/2010/
Search: http://law.justia.com/codes/georgia/2010/
Courts: http://www.georgiacourts.gov
ROCivP: http://www.gasupreme.us/rules/
ROCrP: http://www.gasupreme.us/rules/

Hawaii
Statutes: http://www.capitol.hawaii.gov/docs/HRS.htm
Search: http://www.capitol.hawaii.gov
Courts: http://www.courts.state.hi.us
ROCivP: http://www.courts.state.hi.us/docs/court_rules/rules/hrcp.htm
ROCrP: http://www.courts.state.hi.us/docs/court_rules/rules/hrpp.htm

Idaho
Statutes: http://legislature.idaho.gov/idstat/TOC/IDStatutesTOC.htm
Search: http://legislature.idaho.gov/idstat/idstat.htm
Courts: http://www.isc.idaho.gov
ROCivP: http://www.isc.idaho.gov/ircp
ROCrP: http://www.isc.idaho.gov/icr

Illinois
Statutes: http://www.ilga.gov/legislation/ilcs/ilcs.asp
Search: http://www.ilga.gov/search/iga_search.asp?scope=ilcs
Courts: http://www.state.il.us/court/
ROCivP: http://www.state.il.us/court/SupremeCourt/Rules/Art_II/default.asp
ROCrP: http://www.state.il.us/court/SupremeCourt/Rules/Art_IV/default.asp

Indiana
Statutes: https://iga.in.gov/legislative/laws/2014/ic/
Search: https://iga.in.gov/legislative/laws/2014/ic/
Courts: http://www.in.gov/judiciary/
ROCivP: http://www.in.gov/judiciary/rules/trial_proc/
ROCrP: http://www.in.gov/judiciary/rules/criminal/index.html

HELPFUL WEBSITES

Iowa
Statutes: https://www.legis.iowa.gov/law/iowaCode
Search: https://www.legis.iowa.gov/publications/search
Courts: http://www.iowacourts.gov
ROCivP: https://www.legis.iowa.gov/docs/ACO/CourtRulesChapter/01-30-2015.1.pdf
ROCrP: https://www.legis.iowa.gov/docs/ACO/CourtRulesChapter/01-30-2015.2.pdf

Kansas
Statutes: http://www.kslegislature.org/li/b2015_16/statute/
Search: http://www.kslegislature.org/li/b2015_16/statute/
Courts: http://www.kscourts.org/kansas-courts/general-information/
ROCivP: http://www.kslegislature.org/li/b2015_16/statute/060_000_0000_chapter/060_002_0000_article/
ROCrP: http://www.kslegislature.org/li/b2015_16/statute/022_000_0000_chapter/

Kentucky
Statutes: http://www.lrc.ky.gov/statutes/index.aspx
Search: http://www.lrc.ky.gov/statutes/search.aspx
Courts: http://courts.ky.gov/Pages/default.aspx
ROCivP: https://govt.westlaw.com/kyrules/Browse/Home/Kentucky/KentuckyCourtRules/KentuckyStatutesCourtRules?guid=N2C3C8B00A79211DAAB1DC31F8EB14563&transitionType=CategoryPageItem&contextData=(sc.Default)
ROCrP: https://govt.westlaw.com/kyrules/Browse/Home/Kentucky/KentuckyCourtRules/KentuckyStatutesCourtRules?guid=N5D4D9400A79211DAAB1DC31F8EB14563&transitionType=CategoryPageItem&contextData=(sc.Default)

Louisiana
Statutes: http://legis.la.gov/Legis/Laws_Toc.aspx?folder=75&level=Parent
Search: http://www.legis.la.gov/legis/LawSearch.aspx
Courts: http://louisiana.gov/Government/Judicial_Branch/
ROCivP: http://legis.la.gov/Legis/Laws_Toc.aspx?folder=68&level=Parent
ROCrP: http://legis.la.gov/Legis/Laws_Toc.aspx?folder=69&level=Parent

Maine
Statutes: http://legislature.maine.gov/statutes/
Search: http://legislature.maine.gov/statutes/search.htm
Courts: http://www.courts.maine.gov
ROCivP: http://www.courts.maine.gov/rules_adminorders/rules/text/mr_civ_p_2015-9-1.pdf
ROCrP: http://www.courts.maine.gov/rules_adminorders/rules/text/mru_crim_p_only_2015-11-1.pdf

Maryland
Statutes: http://mgaleg.maryland.gov/webmga/frmStatutes.aspx?pid=statpage&tab=subject5
Search: http://mgaleg.maryland.gov/webmga/frmStatutes.aspx?pid=statpage&tab=subject5
Courts: http://www.mdcourts.gov/courtsdirectory/

HELPFUL WEBSITES

ROCivP: https://govt.westlaw.com/mdc/Browse/Home/Maryland/MarylandCodeCourtRules?guid
=NDFFF2D009CCE11DB9BCF9DAC28345A2A&originationContext=documenttoc&transitionType=
Default&contextData=(sc.Default)

ROCrP: https://govt.westlaw.com/mdc/Browse/Home/Maryland/MarylandCodeCourtRules?guid
=N705D7A409B6811DB9BCF9DAC28345A2A&originationContext=documenttoc&transitionType=
Default&contextData=(sc.Default)

Massachusetts

Statutes: https://malegislature.gov/laws/generallaws/search

Search: https://malegislature.gov/laws/generallaws/search

Courts: http://www.mass.gov/courts/

ROCivP: http://www.mass.gov/courts/case-legal-res/rules-of-court/civil-procedure/

ROCrP: http://www.mass.gov/courts/case-legal-res/rules-of-court/criminal-procedure/

Michigan

Statutes: http://www.legislature.mi.gov/(S(mlp2zjub4llft2rg35p0w0mp))/mileg.aspx?page=Chapt
erIndex

Search: http://www.legislature.mi.gov/(S(l4acrun2swf5klrmxngtncyc))/mileg.aspx?page=MCLBa
sicSearch

Courts: http://courts.mi.gov/Pages/default.aspx

ROCivP: http://courts.mi.gov/Courts/MichiganSupremeCourt/rules/Documents/CHAPTER
202.%20CIVIL%20PROCEDURE%20(entire%20chapter).pdf

ROCrP: http://courts.mi.gov/Courts/MichiganSupremeCourt/rules/Documents/CHAPTER%206.
%20CRIMINAL%20PROCEDURE%20(entire%20chapter).pdf

Minnesota

Statutes: https://www.rcvisor.mn.gov/statutes/

Search: https://www.revisor.mn.gov/statutes/

Courts: http://www.mncourts.gov

ROCivP: http://www.mncourts.gov/Documents/0/Public/Rules/Civil_Rules_effective_7-1-
2013.pdf

ROCrP: http://www.mncourts.gov/Documents/0/Public/Rules/Crim_Rules_as_amended_eff_0
3-01-2015.pdf

Mississippi

Statutes: http://law.justia.com/codes/mississippi/2013/

Search: http://law.justia.com/codes/mississippi/2013/

Courts: https://courts.ms.gov

ROCivP: https://courts.ms.gov/rules/msrulesofcourt/rules_of_civil_procedure.pdf

ROCrP: https://courts.ms.gov/rules/msrulesofcourt/urccc.pdf

Missouri

Statutes: http://www.moga.mo.gov/mostatutes/statutesAna.html

Search: http://www.moga.mo.gov/htmlpages2/Statuteconstitutionsearch.aspx

Courts: http://www.courts.mo.gov

ROCivP: http://www.courts.mo.gov/page.jsp?id=676
ROCrP: http://www.courts.mo.gov/page.jsp?id=671

Montana

Statutes: http://leg.mt.gov/bills/mca_toc/index.htm
Search: http://leg.mt.gov/bills/mca_toc/index.htm
Courts: http://courts.mt.gov/default.mcpx
ROCivP: http://leg.mt.gov/bills/mca_toc/25_20.htm
ROCrP: http://leg.mt.gov/bills/mca_toc/46.htm

Nebraska

Statutes: http://nebraskalegislature.gov/laws/browse-statutes.php
Search: http://nebraskalegislature.gov/laws/laws.php
Courts: http://www.nebraska.gov/featured/courts-legal.html
ROCivP: http://nebraskalegislature.gov/laws/browse-chapters.php?chapter=25
ROCrP: http://nebraskalegislature.gov/laws/browse-chapters.php?chapter=29

Nevada

Statutes: http://www.leg.state.nv.us/Division/Legal/LawLibrary/NRS/index.cfm
Search: http://search.leg.state.nv.us/NRS/NRS.html
Courts: http://www.nevadajudiciary.us
ROCivP: http://www.leg.state.nv.us/courtrules/nrcp.html
ROCrP: http://www.leg.state.nv.us/courtrules/SecondDCR_Crim.html

New Hampshire

Statutes: http://www.gencourt.state.nh.us/rsa/html/nhtoc.htm
Search: http://www.gencourt.state.nh.us/rsa/html/indexes/search.html
Courts: http://www.courts.state.nh.us
ROCivP: http://www.courts.state.nh.us/rules/supercr-new/index-new.htm
ROCrP: http://www.courts.state.nh.us/rules/criminal-rules/

New Jersey

Statutes: http://lis.njleg.state.nj.us/cgi-bin/om_isapi.dll?clientID=36670774&depth=2&expandheadings=off&headingswithhits=on&infobase=statutes.nfo&softpage=TOC_Frame_Pg42
Search: http://lis.njleg.state.nj.us/cgi-bin/om_isapi.dll?clientID=36670774&depth=2&expandheadings=off&headingswithhits=on&infobase=statutes.nfo&softpage=TOC_Frame_Pg42
Courts: http://www.judiciary.state.nj.us
ROCivP: http://www.judiciary.state.nj.us/rules/part4toc.htm
ROCrP: http://www.judiciary.state.nj.us/rules/part3toc.htm

New Mexico

Statutes: http://public.nmcompcomm.us/nmpublic/gateway.dll/?f=templates&fn=default.htm
Search: http://public.nmcompcomm.us/nmpublic/gateway.dll/?f=templates&fn=default.htm

HELPFUL WEBSITES

Courts: http://www.nmcourts.gov/index.php
ROCivP: https://www.nmcourts.gov/newface/new/dmanual/pdf/05CVProcedures.pdf
ROCrP: https://www.nmcourts.gov/newface/new/dmanual/pdf/06CRCriminalProcedures.pdf

New York

Statutes: http://public.leginfo.state.ny.us/lawssrch.cgi?NVLWO (Select "Laws of New York" from the "Laws" drop down list.)
Search: http://public.leginfo.state.ny.us/lawssrch.cgi?NVLWO (Select "Laws of New York" from the "Laws" drop down list.)
Courts: http://www.nycourts.gov
ROCivP: http://www.nycourts.gov/rules/trialcourts/index.shtml
ROCrP: http://www.nycourts.gov/rules/trialcourts/index.shtml

North Carolina

Statutes: http://www.ncga.state.nc.us/gascripts/statutes/statutestoc.pl
Search: http://www.ncga.state.nc.us/gascripts/statutes/statutestoc.pl
Courts: http://www.nccourts.org
ROCivP: http://www.ncga.state.nc.us/gascripts/statutes/statutestoc.pl?Chapter=0001A
ROCrP: http://www.ncga.state.nc.us/gascripts/statutes/StatutesTOC.pl?Chapter=0015a

North Dakota

Statutes: http://www.legis.nd.gov/general-information/north-dakota-century-code
Search: http://www.legis.nd.gov/general-information/north-dakota-century-code
Courts: http://www.ndcourts.gov/court/courts.htm
ROCivP: http://www.ndcourts.gov/rules/civil/frameset.htm
ROCrP: http://www.ndcourts.gov/rules/criminal/frameset.htm

Ohio

Statutes: http://codes.ohio.gov/orc/
Search: http://codes.ohio.gov/orc/
Courts: http://www.supremecourt.ohio.gov
ROCivP: http://www.supremecourt.ohio.gov/LegalResources/Rules/civil/CivilProcedure.pdf
ROCrP: http://www.supremecourt.ohio.gov/LegalResources/Rules/criminal/CriminalProcedure.pdf

Oklahoma

Statutes: http://www.oklegislature.gov/tsrs_os_oc.aspx (Select "Oklahoma Statutes - Titles 1-85A.")
Search: http://www.oklegislature.gov/tsrs_os_oc.aspx
Courts: http://www.oscn.net/applications/oscn/start.asp?viewType=COURTS
ROCivP: http://webserver1.lsb.state.ok.us/OK_Statutes/CompleteTitles/os12.rtf
ROCrP: http://webserver1.lsb.state.ok.us/OK_Statutes/CompleteTitles/os22.rtf

Oregon

Statutes: https://www.oregonlegislature.gov/bills_laws/Pages/ORS.aspx

HELPFUL WEBSITES

Search: https://www.oregonlegislature.gov/bills_laws/Pages/ORS.aspx

Courts: http://courts.oregon.gov/OJD/courts/pages/index.aspx

ROCivP: https://www.oregonlegislature.gov/bills_laws/Pages/orcp.aspx

ROCrP: https://www.oregonlegislature.gov/bills_laws/lawsstatutes/2013ors131.html

Pennsylvania

Statutes: http://www.legis.state.pa.us/cfdocs/legis/LI/Public/cons_index.cfm

Search: http://www.legis.state.pa.us/cfdocs/legis/LI/Public/cons_index.cfm

Courts: http://www.pacourts.us

ROCivP: https://ujsportal.pacourts.us/localrules/ruleselection.aspx (Select "Civil Procedure" from "Rule Type" drop-down, then "Search.")

ROCrP: https://ujsportal.pacourts.us/localrules/ruleselection.aspx (Select "Criminal Procedure" from "Rule Type" drop-down, then "Search.")

Rhode Island

Statutes: http://webserver.rilin.state.ri.us/Statutes/

Search: http://webserver.rilin.state.ri.us/search/search.asp?SearchWhere=/Statutes/

Courts: https://www.courts.ri.gov/Pages/default.aspx

ROCivP: http://webserver.rilin.state.ri.us/Statutes/title9/index.htm

ROCrP: http://webserver.rilin.state.ri.us/Statutes/title12/index.htm

South Carolina

Statutes: http://www.scstatehouse.gov/code/statmast.php

Search: http://www.scstatehouse.gov/query.php?search=FIRST&searchtext=&category=CODEOFLAWS

Courts: http://www.judicial.state.sc.us

ROCivP: http://www.judicial.state.sc.us/courtreg/indexADR.cfm (Select "Civil" tab.)

ROCrP: http://www.judicial.state.sc.us/courtreg/indexADR.cfm (Select "Criminal" tab.)

South Dakota

Statutes: http://legis.sd.gov/Statutes/Codified_Laws/default.aspx

Search: http://legis.sd.gov/statutes/Codified_Laws/TextSearch.aspx?cookieCheck=true

Courts: http://www.ujs.sd.gov

ROCivP: http://legis.sd.gov/Statutes/DisplayStatute.aspx?Type=Statute&Statute=15

ROCrP: http://legis.sd.gov/Statutes/DisplayStatute.aspx?Type=Statute&Statute=23A

Tennessee

Statutes: http://law.justia.com/codes/tennessee/2010

Search: http://law.justia.com/codes/tennessee/2010

Courts: http://www.tsc.state.tn.us

ROCivP: http://www.tsc.state.tn.us/courts/supreme-court/rules/rules-civil-procedure

ROCrP: http://www.tsc.state.tn.us/courts/court-rules/rules-criminal-procedure

Texas

Statutes: http://www.statutes.legis.state.tx.us/?link=TN

HELPFUL WEBSITES

Search: http://www.statutes.legis.state.tx.us/Search.aspx
Courts: http://www.txcourts.gov
ROCivP: http://www.txcourts.gov/media/1084233/Texas-Rules-of-Civil-Procedure.pdf
ROCrP: http://www.statutes.legis.state.tx.us/?link=CR

Utah
Statutes: http://le.utah.gov/xcode/code.html
Search: http://le.utah.gov/xcode/code.html
Courts: http://www.utcourts.gov/index.html
ROCivP: http://www.utcourts.gov/resources/rules/urcp/
ROCrP: http://www.utcourts.gov/resources/rules/urcrp/

Vermont
Statutes: http://legislature.vermont.gov/statutes/
Search: http://legislature.vermont.gov/statutes/search
Courts: https://www.vermontjudiciary.org/default.aspx
ROCivP: http://www.lexisnexis.com/hottopics/vtstatutesconstctrules/ (Open/expand the "RULES OF CIVIL PROCEDURE" heading.)
ROCrP: http://www.lexisnexis.com/hottopics/vtstatutesconstctrules/ (Open/expand the "RULES OF CRIMINAL PROCEDURE" heading.)

Virginia
Statutes: https://lis.virginia.gov/cgi-bin/legp604.exe?000+cod+TOC
Search: https://lis.virginia.gov/000/src.htm
Courts: http://www.courts.state.va.us/courts/home.html
ROCivP: http://law.lis.virginia.gov/vacode/title8.01/
ROCrP: http://law.lis.virginia.gov/vacode/titlc19.2/

Washington
Statutes: http://apps.leg.wa.gov/rcw/
Search: http://search.leg.wa.gov/search.aspx#document&searchQuery=&searchBase=RCW
Courts: http://www.courts.wa.gov
ROCivP: https://www.courts.wa.gov/court_rules/?fa=court_rules.list&group=clj&set=CRLJ
ROCrP: https://www.courts.wa.gov/court_rules/?fa=court_rules.list&group=clj&set=CrRLJ

West Virginia
Statutes: http://www.legis.state.wv.us/WVCODE/Code.cfm
Search: http://www.legis.state.wv.us/WVCODE/Code.cfm
Courts: http://www.courtswv.gov
ROCivP: http://www.courtswv.gov/legal-community/court-rules/civil-procedure/contents.html
ROCrP: http://www.courtswv.gov/legal-community/court-rules/criminal-procedure/contents.html

Wisconsin
Statutes: http://docs.legis.wisconsin.gov/statutes/prefaces/toc

HELPFUL WEBSITES

Search: http://docs.legis.wisconsin.gov/statutes/prefaces/toc
Courts: https://www.wicourts.gov
ROCivP: http://docs.legis.wisconsin.gov/statutes/statutes (chapters 801-807)
ROCrP: http://docs.legis.wisconsin.gov/statutes/statutes (chapters 967-974)

Wyoming
Statutes: http://legisweb.state.wy.us/NXT/gateway.dll?f=templates&fn=default.htm
Search: http://legisweb.state.wy.us/NXT/gateway.dll?f=templates&fn=default.htm
Courts: http://www.courts.state.wy.us
ROCivP: http://www.courts.state.wy.us/WSC/CourtRule?RuleNumber=48
ROCrP: http://www.courts.state.wy.us/WSC/CourtRule?RuleNumber=31

District of Columbia
Statutes: http://dccode.elaws.us/code
Search: http://dccode.elaws.us
Courts: http://www.dccourts.gov/internet/
ROCivP: http://www.dccourts.gov/internet/legal/dcscrules.jsf
ROCrP: http://www.dccourts.gov/internet/legal/dcscrules.jsf

HELPFUL WEBSITES

SOURCES FOR LEGAL DEFINITIONS

*Black's Law Dictionary**

http://thelawdictionary.org

http://www.nationallibertyalliance.org/files/docs/Books/Black's%20Law%204th%20edition,%201891.pdf

*Bouvier's Law Dictionary**

http://www.republicsg.info/dictionaries/1856_bouvier_6.pdf

http://www.supremelaw.org/ref/dict/

*Note that editions at the websites indicated above may not be the latest ones.

LAWYER REVIEWS AND RATINGS WEBSITES

https://lawyers.law.cornell.edu

https://www.avvo.com

https://www.bbb.org

http://www.lawyerratingz.com

http://www.lawyers.com

http://www.legaladvice.com

https://www.martindale.com

http://www.ripoffreport.com

https://www.yelp.com

JUDGE REVIEWS AND RATINGS WEBSITES

http://www.robeprobe.com

http://www.therobingroom.com

http://www.uglyjudge.com

OTHER RESOURCES

https://www.bbb.org/en/us	(Better Business Bureau)
https://www.consumerfinance.gov	(Consumer Financial Prot. Bureau)
https://www.fbi.gov	(Federal Bureau of Investigation)
https://www.ftc.gov	(Federal Trade Commission)
https://www.justia.com	(Legal help website)
https://www.justice.gov	(U.S. Department of Justice)
https://www.lawguru.com	(Legal help website)
https://www.legalzoom.com	(Legal help website)
http://www.naag.org/naag/attorneys-general/whos-my-ag.php	(Attorneys general nationwide)
https://www.probono.net	(Legal help website)
https://www.rocketlawyer.com	(Legal help website)
https://www.usa.gov/state-consumer	(Consumer protection agencies)

References

Chapter 1

[1] Ex-Texas prosecutor first in history to be jailed for …http://www.nbcnews.com/news/other/ex-texas-prosecutor-first-history-be-jailed-withholding-evidence-f8C11566289.

[2] Maclin, T. 2012. Tracey Maclin Boston University School of Law Jennifer … http://www.bu.edu/law/faculty/scholarship/workingpapers/documents/SSRN-id2025970rev.pdf.

[3] What We've Lost Since 9/11 | Peter Van Buren - Huffington …http://www.huffingtonpost.com/peter-van-buren/what-weve-lost-since-911_b_5497673.html.

[4] 14th Amendment | Constitution | U.S. Law | LII / Legal … http://www.law.cornell.edu/constitution/amendmentxiv.

[5] General Laws: PART IV. https://malegislature.gov/laws/generallaws/partiv.

[6] New Jersey Legislature. http://www.njleg.state.nj.us/.

[7] 2014 Minnesota Statutes - Office of the Revisor of Statutes. https://www.revisor.mn.gov/statutes/.

[8] Legislative Research Commission - KRS Search - Kentucky … http://www.lrc.ky.gov/statutes/search.aspx.

[9] Washington State Legislature - External Legislative Search. http://search.leg.wa.gov/.

[10] New Search - Illinois General Assembly. http://www.ilga.gov/search/iga_search.asp?scope=ilcs.

[11] List of United States federal legislation - Wikipedia, the free … http://en.wikipedia.org/wiki/List_of_United_States_federal_legislation.

[12] Who Moves? Who Stays Put? Where's Home? | Pew … http://www.pewsocialtrends.org/2008/12/17/who-moves-who-stays-put-wheres-home/.

[13] U.S. and World Population Clock - Census.gov. http://www.census.gov/popclock/.

[14] Highest to Lowest - Prison Population Rate | International … http://www.prisonstudies.org/highest-to-lowest/prison-population-total?field_region_taxonomy_tid=All.

[15] FAQs:How many innocent people are there in prison?. http://www.innocenceproject.org/Content/How_many_innocent_people_are_there_in_prison.php.

[16] Glaze, LE. 2014. Correctional Populations in the United States, 2013. http://www.bjs.gov/content/pub/pdf/cpus13.pdf.

[17] "Low-Crime Taxes" Guarantee Profits for Private Prison … http://www.inthepublicinterest.org/criminal-how-lockup-quotas-and-low-crime-taxes-guarantee-profits-for-private-prison-corporations/.

[18] Federal prisoners stealing our business - CNN Money. http://money.cnn.com/2012/08/14/smallbusiness/federal-prison-business/.

[19] How US prison labour pads corporate profits at taxpayers …http://www.theguardian.com/commentisfree/2012/jul/06/prison-labor-pads-corporate-profits-taxpayers-expense.

[20] Criminal justice: The kings of the courtroom | The Economist. http://www.economist.com/news/united-states/21621799-how-prosecutors-came-dominate-criminal-justice-system-kings-courtroom.

[21] The National Registry of Exonerations - Exoneration Registry. https://www.law.umich.edu/special/exoneration/Pages/about.aspx.

[22] Comments of Disciplinary Panel's Chairman - The New York …http://www.nytimes.com/2007/06/17/us/17duke-text.html?_r=1&oref=slogin.

[23] Court Rules for Cleaners In $54 Million Pants Suit. http://www.washingtonpost.com/wp-dyn/content/article/2007/06/25/AR2007062500443.html.

[24] examining the work of state courts - Court Statistics Project. http://www.courtstatistics.org/~/media/microsites/files/csp/ncsc_ewsc_web_nov_25_14.ashx.

[25] State Court Organization, 1998: Part 6. http://www.bjs.gov/content/pub/pdf/sco9806.pdf.

[26] "Fifth Amendment | Wex Legal Dictionary / Encyclopedia | LII …" 2011. 1 Nov. 2014 http://www.law.cornell.edu/wex/fifth_amendment

[27] Hurtado v. California - Legal Information Institute - Cornell …http://www.law.cornell.edu/supremecourt/text/110/516.

Chapter 2

[1] Who Goes to Jail? Matt Taibbi on American Injustice Gap … http://www.democracynow.org/2014/4/15/who_goes_to_jail_matt_taibbi.

[2] Matt Taibbi JPMorgan Whistleblower Story - Business Insider. http://www.businessinsider.com/matt-tabbi-jp-morgan-whistleblower-story-2014-11.

[3] Kids for cash scandal - Wikipedia, the free encyclopedia. http://en.wikipedia.org/wiki/Kids_for_cash_scandal.

[4] Judge Tosses Retaliation Lawsuit by Fired NY Fed Examiner. http://www.propublica.org/article/judge-tosses-retaliation-lawsuit-by-fired-n.y.-fed-examiner.

[5] FL Highway Patrol Trooper, Scott Kuntsmann, arrested for … http://archive.wtsp.com/rss/article/281738/8/Highway-Patrol-arrested-for-fabricating-arrest-reports.

[6] Prosecutors modify plea deal with ex-FHP trooper … http://www.heraldtribune.com/article/20131021/ARTICLE/131029947.

[7] United States Attorneys' Annual Statistical Report - US … http://www.justice.gov/sites/default/files/usao/legacy/2011/09/01/10statrpt.pdf.

[8] "Nine Philadelphia judges arrested on charges of corruption …" 2013. 4 May. 2015 http://www.sott.net/article/257560-Nine-Philadelphia-judges-arrested-on-charges-of-corruption

[9] N.C. FLUNKS LAWYER COMPLAINT, DISCIPLINE TEST … http://www.fayobserver.com/news/local/n-c-flunks-lawyer-complaint-discipline-test/article_92b1d388-913c-5abe-b5d6-3587bd49df36.html.

[10] Rule 1.5: Fees - American Bar Association. http://www.americanbar.org/groups/professional_responsibility/publications/model_rules_of_professional_conduct/rule_1_5_fees.html.

[11] 422 U.S. 806 - FindLaw. http://caselaw.findlaw.com/us-supreme-court/422/806.html.

[12] Table S-4. U.S. Courts of Appeals—Sources of Pro Se … http://www.uscourts.gov/file/12157/download.

[13] Download Table B-19—U.S. Courts of Appeals Judicial … http://www.uscourts.gov/file/14289/download.

[14] Pro Se: Meeting the challenge of self-represented litigants. https://www.wicourts.gov/publications/reports/docs/prosereport.pdf.

[15] pdf - American Bar Association. http://www.americanbar.org/content/dam/aba/migrated/marketresearch/PublicDocuments/public_perception_of_lawyers_2002.pdf.

[16] Citing Workload, More Public Defenders Are Refusing New … http://www.nytimes.com/2008/11/09/us/09defender.html.

[17] As Court Fees Rise, The Poor Are Paying The Price : NPR. http://www.npr.org/2014/05/19/312158516/increasing-court-fees-punish-the-poor.

[18] Parents in Prison and Their Minor Children - Bureau of … http://www.bjs.gov/content/pub/pdf/pptmc.pdf.

[19] About the Supreme Court - U.S. Courts. http://www.uscourts.gov/educational-resources/get-informed/supreme-court/about-supreme-court.aspx.

Chapter 3

[1] Ex-Detroit court clerk, man accused of taking bribes. http://www.detroitnews.com/story/news/local/detroit-city/2015/12/01/ex-detroit-court-clerk-man-accused-taking-bribes/76598764/.

[2] Fallout mounting from cop's alleged theft of drug evidence … http://www.wptz.com/news/fallout-mounting-from-cops-alleged-theft-of-drug-evidence/30063198.

[3] Lt. Thomas Foye Accused Of Pocketing Drugs From Police … http://www.huffingtonpost.com/2013/08/16/thomas-foye_n_3768601.html.

[4] U.S. GAO - Seized Drugs and Weapons: DEA Needs to … http://www.gao.gov/products/GAO/AIMD-00-17.

[5] 'rat' for protesting stop-and-frisk quotas - New York Daily News. http://www.nydailynews.com/new-york/testifies-called-rat-protesting-stop-and-frisk-quotas-article-1.1294612.

[6] 31-27-25. http://www.rilin.state.ri.us/statutes/title31/31-27/31-27-25.HTM.

[7] "Bite the Bullet – We've Got Too Many Agencies With Armed …" 2012. 9 Nov. 2014 http://www.theblaze.com/contributions/bite-the-bullet-weve-got-too-many-agencies-with-armed-agents/

[8] Customary IHL - Practice Relating to Rule 75. Riot Control … https://www.icrc.org/customary-ihl/eng/docs/v2_rul_rule75.

[9] "Police defend use of surplus military weapons - Washington …" 2014. 9 Nov. 2014 http://www.washingtontimes.com/news/2014/sep/14/police-defend-use-of-surplus-military-weapons/?page=all

[10] Ex-judge pleads guilty in bribery case - San Antonio … http://www.expressnews.com/news/local/article/Ex-judge-pleads-guilty-in-bribery-case-6197707.php.

[11] "Chicago Police Department - Wikipedia, the free encyclopedia." 2004. 10 Nov. 2014 http://en.wikipedia.org/wiki/Chicago_Police_Department

[12] "City of Chicago :: Current Employee Names, Salaries, and …" 2011. 10 Nov. 2014 http://www.cityofchicago.org/city/en/depts/dhr/dataset/current_employeenamessalariesandpositiontitles.html

[13] "police board - City of Chicago." 2014. 10 Nov. 2014 http://www.cityofchicago.org/content/dam/city/depts/cpb/AnnualReports/CPBAnnualReport2013.pdf

[14] Civil Procedure Rule 81: Applicability of Rules - Mass.Gov. http://www.mass.gov/courts/case-legal-res/rules-of-court/civil-procedure/mrcp81.html.

[15] General Laws: CHAPTER 211, Section 3 - MAlegislature.gov. https://malegislature.gov/Laws/GeneralLaws/PartIII/TitleI/Chapter211/Section3.

[16] General Laws: CHAPTER 231A, Section 2 - MAlegislature.gov. https://malegislature.gov/Laws/GeneralLaws/PartIII/TitleII/Chapter231A/Section2.

[17] FBI — Color of Law. https://www.fbi.gov/about-us/investigate/civilrights/color_of_law.

[18] 09-571 Connick v. Thompson (03/29/2011) - Supreme Court. http://www.supremecourt.gov/opinions/10pdf/09-571.pdf.

[19] "The Untouchables: America's Misbehaving Prosecutors …" 2013. 10 Nov. 2014 http://www.huffingtonpost.com/2013/08/01/prosecutorial-misconduct-new-orleans-louisiana_n_3529891.html

[20] United States Court of Appeals - U.S. Government Printing … http://www.gpo.gov/fdsys/pkg/USCOURTS-ca7-13-01195/pdf/USCOURTS-ca7-13-01195-0.pdf.

Chapter 4

[1] 11 U.S. Code § 523 - Exceptions to discharge | LII / Legal … http://www.law.cornell.edu/uscode/text/11/523.

[2] File:Wikipediamapfinal3.pdf - WIKI 2. Wikipedia Republished. https://upload.wikimedia.org/wikipedia/commons/b/bf/Adverse_possession_US.pdf.

[3] Federal Land Ownership: Overview and Data - Federation of … https://fas.org/sgp/crs/misc/R42346.pdf.

[4] Fifth Amendment | Constitution | US Law | LII / Legal … http://www.law.cornell.edu/constitution/fifth_amendment.

[5] Kelo v. City of New London, Connecticut (04-108) - Legal … http://www.law.cornell.edu/supct/cert/04-108.

[6] Eminent domain - Wikipedia, the free encyclopedia. http://en.wikipedia.org/wiki/Eminent_domain.

[7] Bell, A, and A Bell. 2006. Taking Compensation Private - Penn Law: Legal … http://scholarship.law.upenn.edu/cgi/viewcontent.cgi?article=1546&context=faculty_scholarship.

[8] City of Norwood v. Horney - Wikipedia, the free encyclopedia. http://en.wikipedia.org/wiki/City_of_Norwood_v._Horney.

[9] 18 US Code § 981 - Civil forfeiture - Legal Information Institute. http://www.law.cornell.edu/uscode/text/18/981.

[10] This Federal Program Lets Cops Seize Cash … - Forbes. http://www.forbes.com/sites/instituteforjustice/2014/09/29/highway-cash-seizures-civil-forfeiture/.

[11] Civil forfeiture in the United States - Wikipedia, the free … http://en.wikipedia.org/wiki/Civil_forfeiture_in_the_United_States.

[12] The IRS Can Seize Your Cash Through Forfeiture … http://www.businessinsider.com/the-irs-can-seize-your-cash-through-forfeiture-2014-10.

[13] Law Lets I.R.S. Seize Accounts on Suspicion, No Crime … http://www.nytimes.com/2014/10/26/us/law-lets-irs-seize-accounts-on-suspicion-no-crime-required.html.

[14] Asset forfeiture both an effective tool, civil-liberties nightmare. http://www.chron.com/news/nation-world/article/Asset-forfeiture-both-an-effective-tool-4546043.php.

Chapter 5

[1] Federal Rules of Civil Procedure - Legal Information Institute. http://www.law.cornell.edu/rules/frcp.

[2] Federal Rules of Criminal Procedure - Legal Information ... http://www.law.cornell.edu/rules/frcrmp.

[3] Iraq War Veteran Scott Olsen Reaches $4.5M Settlement in ... http://www.nbcbayarea.com/news/local/Iraq-War-Veteran-Scott-Olsen-Win-45M-Settlement-in-Occupy-Oakland-Beag-Bag-Case-251438961.html.

[4] Woman Found Guilty of Assaulting Officer at an Occupy Wall ... http://www.nytimes.com/2014/05/06/nyregion/occupy-wall-street-protester-is-found-guilty-of-assaulting-officer.html.

[5] Houston, We've Got A First Amendment Problem - Forbes. http://www.forbes.com/sites/daviddavenport/2014/10/15/houston-weve-got-a-first-amendment-problem/.

[6] 12-246 Salinas v. Texas (06/17/13) - Supreme Court. http://www.supremecourt.gov/opinions/12pdf/12-246_7l48.pdf.

[7] USA: Close Guantánamo and end human rights hypocrisy ... http://www.amnesty.org/en/news/usa-close-guant-namo-and-end-human-rights-hypocrisy-2014-01-22.

[8] SUPREME COURT OF WISCONSIN - Wisconsin Court System. https://www.wicourts.gov/sc/opinion/DisplayDocument.pdf?content=pdf&seqNo=28227.

[9] MICHIGAN v. BRYANT - Legal Information Institute - Cornell ... http://www.law.cornell.edu/supct/html/09-150.ZS.html.

[10] Traffic Tribunal - Rhode Island Judiciary. https://www.courts.ri.gov/courts/rhodeislandtraffictribunal/pdf/knowyourrights.pdf.

[11] ARTICLE VI. JUDICIAL CONDUCT - Rhode Island Judiciary. https://www.courts.ri.gov/PublicResources/JudicialTenureandDiscipline/PDFs/JudicialTenureJudicialConduct.pdf.

[12] "Code of Conduct for United States Judges | United States Courts." https://www.uscourts.gov/judges-judgeships/code-conduct-united-states-judges.

[13] Law-Breaking Judges Took Cases That Could Make Them ... http://www.thedailybeast.com/articles/2014/04/28/law-breaking-judges-took-cases-that-could-make-them-even-richer.html.

[14] Federal judges plead guilty | Center for Public Integrity. http://www.publicintegrity.org/2014/04/28/14630/federal-judges-plead-guilty.

[15] Non-Lawyers Find It Hard Avoid Breaking Bar's Vague Rules. http://www.forbes.com/sites/danielfisher/2011/07/25/non-lawyers-find-it-hard-avoid-breaking-bars-vague-rules/.

Chapter 6

[1] 42-92-1. http://www.rilin.state.ri.us/statutes/title42/42-92/42-92-1.HTM.

[2] General Laws: CHAPTER 89, Section 9 - MAlegislature.gov. https://malegislature.gov/Laws/GeneralLaws/Chapter89/Section9.

[3] General Laws: CHAPTER 85, Section 2 - MAlegislature.gov. https://malegislature.gov/Laws/GeneralLaws/PartI/TitleXIV/Chapter85/Section2.

[4] Criminal Procedure Rule 30: Postconviction Relief - Mass.Gov. http://www.mass.gov/courts/case-legal-res/rules-of-court/criminal-procedure/crim30.html.

[5] News Archives > Filing a Complaint Against a Federal Judge. http://www.uscourts.gov/file/document/2010/03/filing-complaint-judicial-misconduct-or-judicial-disability-against-federal.

[6] "Filing a Complaint | cjdt." https://cjdt.dc.gov/service/filing-complaint.

[7] 42 U.S.C. 1983 - Legal Information Institute - Cornell ... http://www.law.cornell.edu/uscode/text/42/1983.

[8] Monroe v. Pape - Legal Information Institute - Cornell ... http://www.law.cornell.edu/supremecourt/text/365/167.

[9] Bivens v. Six Unknown Named Agents - Wikipedia, the free ... http://en.wikipedia.org/wiki/Bivens_v._Six_Unknown_Named_Agents.

Chapter 7

[1] Table 5.4 U.S. District Courts—Criminal Defendants ...http://www.uscourts.gov/uscourts/Statistics/JudicialFactsAndFigures/2013/Table504.pdf.

[2] Trial Court Statistics. http://trialstats.flcourts.org/.

[3] 2013 Court Statistics Report - California Courts. http://www.courts.ca.gov/documents/2013-Court-Statistics-Report.pdf.

[4] Stronger Hand for Judges After Rulings on Plea Deals - The ... http://www.nytimes.com/2012/03/23/us/stronger-hand-for-judges-after-rulings-on-plea-deals.html.

[5] Why grand jury indictments in police shootings are so rare ... http://www.cbsnews.com/news/why-grand-jury-indictments-in-police-shootings-are-so-rare/.

[6] EXCLUSIVE: Detective is NYPD's most-sued cop with 28 ... http://www.nydailynews.com/new-york/lawsuits-nypd-double-decade-costing-taxpayers-1b-article-1.1615919.

[7] Ancillary Service Endorsements - Postal Explorer. http://pe.usps.com/text/qsg300/Q507.htm.

[8] Land Court Dockets (link is external) - MassCourts.org. http://www.masscourts.org/eservices/home.page.2.

Chapter 8

[1] Court Role and Structure | United States Courts - U.S. Courts. http://www.uscourts.gov/about-federal-courts/court-role-and-structure.

[2] Comparing Federal & State Courts - U.S. Courts. http://www.uscourts.gov/about-federal-courts/court-role-and-structure/comparing-federal-state-courts.

[3] 28 U.S. Code Chapter 85 - DISTRICT COURTS ... http://www.law.cornell.edu/uscode/28/pIVch85.html.

[4] 28 U.S. Code § 1362 - Indian tribes | US Law | LII / Legal ... http://www.law.cornell.edu/uscode/28/usc_sec_28_00001362----000-.html.

[5] 28 U.S. Code § 1346 - United States as defendant | US Law ... http://www.law.cornell.edu/uscode/text/28/1346.

[6] Vaccine Claims/Office of Special Masters | US Court of ... http://www.uscfc.uscourts.gov/vaccine-program-readmore.

[7] United States Court of International Trade. http://www.cit.uscourts.gov/.

[8] United States Tax Court: About the Court - U.S. Tax Court. https://www.ustaxcourt.gov/about.htm.

[9] Population of Interest: Municipalities & Townships - Census ... https://www.census.gov/govs/go/municipal_township_govs.html.

[10] rhodeislandtraffictribunal - Rhode Island Judiciary. https://www.courts.ri.gov/Courts/rhodeislandtraffictribunal/Pages/default.aspx.

[11] County Courts - Florida Courts. http://www.flcourts.org/florida-courts/trial-courts-county.stml.

[12] 28 U.S.C. § 1332(a) - Legal Information Institute - Cornell ... http://www.law.cornell.edu/uscode/text/28/1332.

[13] General Laws: CHAPTER 249, Section 4 - MAlegislature.gov. https://malegislature.gov/Laws/GeneralLaws/PartIII/TitleIV/Chapter249/Section4.

[14] Family Court Rules - Hawaii State Judiciary. http://www.courts.state.hi.us/docs/court_rules/rules/hfcr.htm.

Chapter 9

[1] Statute of Limitations - California Courts. http://www.courts.ca.gov/9618.htm.

[2] Statute of Limitations - Fair Debt Collection. http://www.fair-debt-collection.com/sol-by-state.html.

[3] Tips to help consumers with disputes on credit card charges ... http://usatoday30.usatoday.com/money/perfi/credit/2009-01-25-consumer-credit-card-charge-disputes_N.htm.

[4] City and County of San Francisco v. Small Claims Court ... http://law.justia.com/cases/california/court-of-appeal/3d/141/470.html.

[5] What Is Small Claims Court? - Department of Consumer Affairs. http://www.dca.ca.gov/publications/small_claims/basic_info.shtml.

[6] Your Guide to Small Claims & Commercial Small Claims in ...
http://www.nycourts.gov/courts/10jd/suffolk/dist/pdf/ucs_small_claims_booklet.pdf.

[7] Civil Code section 1719 - California Legislative Information.
http://leginfo.legislature.ca.gov/faces/codes_displaySection.xhtml?lawCode=CIV&sectionNum=1719..

[8] Ancillary Service Endorsements - Postal Explorer. http://pe.usps.com/text/qsg300/Q507.htm.

[9] United States Postal Service § 265.6 - U.S. Government ... http://www.gpo.gov/fdsys/pkg/CFR-2011-title39-vol1/pdf/CFR-2011-title39-vol1-sec265-6.pdf.

[10] Trial Courts - County - Florida Courts. http://www.flcourts.org/florida-courts/trial-courts-county.stml.

[11] Small Claims Court - King County. https://www.kingcounty.gov/courts/district-court/small-claims/how-to.aspx.

[12] Supreme Court Rule 138 - Illinois Courts. http://www.illinoiscourts.gov/supremecourt/rules/art_ii/artii.htm.

[13] Request for Dismissal - Small Claims - Superior Court, San ...
http://www.sdcourt.ca.gov/pls/portal/docs/PAGE/SDCOURT/GENERALINFORMATION/FORMS/SMALLCLAIMSFORMS/SC044.PDF.

[14] Small Claims Motion to Dismiss and Order. http://www.slcdocs.com/courts/small_claims/forms/MotiontoDismiss&Order.pdf.

[15] Glossary of Terms - Department of Consumer Affairs - State ... http://www.dca.ca.gov/publications/small_claims/glossary.shtml.

[16] Small Claims Booklet - Vermont Judiciary.
https://www.vermontjudiciary.org/GTC/Civildivision/DocumentLibrary/Small%20Claims%20Booklet.pdf

[17] Small Claims Court Procedures (English) - Fairfax County ... http://www.fairfaxcounty.gov/courts/gdc/publications/small-claims-court-procedures-english.pdf.

[18] Rule 2.816 - Title Two Rules - rules_of_court. http://www.courts.ca.gov/cms/rules/index.cfm?title=two&linkid=rule2_816.

[19] Small Claims Court - Know My Rights. http://www.knowmyrights.org/index.php?option=com_content&view=article&id=42:small-claims-court&catid=18&Itemid=123&showall=&limitstart=6.

[20] small claims court limits - Connecticut General Assembly. http://www.cga.ct.gov/2013/rpt/2013-R-0070.htm.

[21] 26 U.S. Code § 6334 - Property exempt from levy | LII / Legal ... http://www.law.cornell.edu/uscode/text/26/6334.

Chapter 10

[1] Bureau of Justice Statistics (BJS) - Traffic Stops. http://www.bjs.gov/index.cfm?ty=tp&tid=702.

[2] As Court Fees Rise, The Poor Are Paying The Price : NPR. http://www.npr.org/2014/05/19/312158516/increasing-court-fees-punish-the-poor.

[3] Traffic Fines for State Court - City of Albany, Georgia. http://www.albany.ga.us/filestorage/1800/2887/2979/Traffic_fines_for_State_Court.pdf.

[4] Reckless Driving - Virginia State Crime Commission. http://vscc.virginia.gov/documents/Reckless%20Driving.pdf.

[5] LIS > Code of Virginia > 18.2-11. https://leg1.state.va.us/cgi-bin/legp504.exe?000+cod+18.2-11.

[6] Fees, Penalties Nearly Quadruple Traffic Ticket Costs For ... http://losangeles.cbslocal.com/2013/09/26/fees-penalties-nearly-quadruple-traffic-ticket-costs-for-calif-drivers/.

[7] California drives up traffic fines with fees earmarked for ... http://cironline.org/reports/california-drives-traffic-fines-fees-earmarked-projects-5223.

[8] Gray v. State :: 1980 :: Court of Appeals of Georgia ... - Justia. http://law.justia.com/cases/georgia/court-of-appeals/1980/60322.html.

[9] In Pictures: 10 States With The Toughest Tickets - Forbes. http://www.forbes.com/2007/12/18/highways-automobiles-virginia-biz-logistics-cx_tvr_1218speeding_slide_3.html.

[10] ZYKOWSKI v. GARDNER | Leagle.com. http://www.leagle.com/decision/199222321992MassAppDiv240_12128.

[11] General Laws: CHAPTER 89, Section 9 - Massachusetts. https://malegislature.gov/Laws/GeneralLaws/PartI/TitleXIV/Chapter89/Section9.

[12] Crawford, M. 2014. CPI Detailed Report: Data for January 2014 - Bureau of ... http://www.bls.gov/cpi/cpid1401.pdf.

[13] The Great Parking Ticket Boom : Citations Are Harder Than ... http://articles.latimes.com/1988-05-19/news/vw-4799_1_parking-ticket.

[14] No more $63 tickets - Los Angeles Times. http://www.latimes.com/opinion/opinion-la/la-ol-parking-ticket-reform-los-angeles-blowback-20140703-story.html.

[15] Illegally Parked Cars Receive a Mark of Shame - NYTimes ... http://www.nytimes.com/1988/09/04/nyregion/illegally-parked-cars-receive-a-mark-of-shame.html.

[16] Violation Codes, Fines, Rules & Regulations - NYC.gov. http://www1.nyc.gov/site/finance/vehicles/services-violation-codes.page.

[17] Judge Calls Summons In Nassau 'Defective' - NYTimes.com. http://www.nytimes.com/1993/08/19/nyregion/judge-calls-summons-in-nassau-defective.html.

[18] Parking Violations | Nassau County, NY - Official Website. https://www.nassaucountyny.gov/1932/Fine-Assessment.

[19] "Metro Matters; Now Hear This! Or Is the Honking Too Loud? - The New ...." 19 Jan. 1989, https://www.nytimes.com/1989/01/19/nyregion/metro-matters-now-hear-this-or-is-the-honking-too-loud.html.

[20] "The $350 Honk - The New York Times." 30 Oct. 2011, https://www.nytimes.com/2011/10/31/opinion/the-350-honk.html.

[21] Has Obamacare Fixed U.S. Healthcare Inflation? - Forbes. http://www.forbes.com/sites/theapothecary/2015/03/09/has-obamacare-fixed-u-s-healthcare-inflation/

[22] College Costs Out Of Control - Forbes. http://www.forbes.com/sites/steveodland/2012/03/24/college-costs-are-soaring/.

[23] How To Get Out Of A Speeding Ticket - Business Insider. http://www.businessinsider.com/how-to-get-out-of-a-speeding-ticket-2013-7.

[24] Ticket Takers | News and Features | Style Weekly ... http://www.styleweekly.com/richmond/ticket-takers/Content?oid=2044419.

[25] Civil Motor Vehicle Infractions FAQ - Mass.Gov. http://www.mass.gov/courts/selfhelp/tickets/cmvi-faq.html.

[26] General Laws: CHAPTER 90C, Section 3 - Massachusetts. https://malegislature.gov/Laws/GeneralLaws/PartI/TitleXIV/Chapter90C/Section3.

[27] 58% Of People Who Fought Traffic Tickets In Washington ... http://blog.motorists.org/58-percent-win-traffic-tickets-washington-dc/.

[28] Ticket Takers | News and Features | Style Weekly ... http://www.styleweekly.com/richmond/ticket-takers/Content?oid=2044419.

[29] Video shows trooper shooting unarmed man ... - CNN.com. http://www.cnn.com/2014/09/25/justice/south-carolina-trooper-shooting/.

[30] CA Codes (veh:40500-40522). http://www.leginfo.ca.gov/cgi-bin/displaycode?section=veh&group=40001-41000&file=40500-40522.

[31] Officer's Unaided Visual Estimation of a Vehicle's Speed ... http://www.supremecourt.ohio.gov/PIO/summaries/2010/0602/091069.asp.

[32] Summary of State Speed Laws - EMS.gov. http://www.ems.gov/pdf/HS810826.pdf.

[33] Envirotran Single-Phase Overhead Transformers. http://www.cooperindustries.com/content/public/en/power_systems/products/transformers_andcomponents/singlephase_overhead/envirotran-ef-transformer.html.

[34] Envirotran Three-Phase Pad-Mounted Transformers. http://www.cooperindustries.com/content/public/en/power_systems/products/transformers_andcomponents/three-phase_pad-mounted/envirotran_ef_three-phasepad-mountedtransformers.html.

[35] Police Radar - PB Electronics. http://www.pbelectronics.com/police_radar.htm.

[36] Police Radar - PB Electronics. http://www.pbelectronics.com/police_radar.htm.

[37] How does weather affect lasers? - Physics Van - University ... https://van.physics.illinois.edu/qa/listing.php?id=23968.

[38] Hall v. State, 264 S.W.3d 346 - CourtListener.com. https://www.courtlistener.com/opinion/1629663/hall-v-state/.

[39] Title 29-A, §2057: Traffic-control devices - Maine Legislature. http://www.mainelegislature.org/legis/statutes/29-a/title29-Asec2057.html.

[40] Title 29-A, §101: Definitions - Maine Legislature. http://legislature.maine.gov/statutes/29-A/title29-Asec101.html.

[41] 31-13-6. http://www.rilin.state.ri.us/statutes/title31/31-13/31-13-6.htm.

[42] 338 Limitation of colored lights used in traffic-control signals. http://www.lrc.ky.gov/statutes/statute.aspx?id=44640.

[43] RED LIGHT CAMERA ENFORCEMENT CASES. http://cga.ct.gov/2011/rpt/2011-R-0113.htm.

[44] RED LIGHT CAMERA ENFORCEMENT CASES. http://cga.ct.gov/2011/rpt/2011-R-0113.htm.

[45] 'Whitey' Bulger Appears in Boston Courthouse - ABC News. http://abcnews.go.com/US/james-whitey-bulger-appears-boston-courthouse-run-mid/story?id=13921244.

[46] State Speed and Red Light Camera Laws. http://www.ghsa.org/html/stateinfo/laws/auto_enforce.html.

[47] examining the work o f state courts - Court Statistics Project. http://www.courtstatistics.org/~/media/microsites/files/csp/ncsc_ewsc_web_nov_25_14.ashx.

[48] CA Codes (pen:1381-1388). http://leginfo.legislature.ca.gov/faces/codes_displaySection.xhtml?sectionNum=1382.&lawCode=PEN.

[49] 316.0083 - Statutes & Constitution :View Statutes : Online ... http://www.leg.state.fl.us/statutes/index.cfm?App_mode=Display_Statute&URL=0300-0399/0316/Sections/0316.0083.html.

[50] LOCAL RULES - CENTRAL DISTRICT OF CALIFORNIA ... https://www.cacd.uscourts.gov/sites/default/files/documents/LRs-Effective-2013-June-1-Chapter-1_0.pdf.

[51] GLIK v. CUNNIFFE | FindLaw. http://caselaw.findlaw.com/us-1st-circuit/1578557.html.

[52] Christopher Drew, artist who fought Illinois eavesdropping ... http://articles.chicagotribune.com/2012-05-10/news/ct-met-drew-obit-20120510_1_eavesdropping-case-eavesdropping-law-separate-case.

[53] Woman who recorded cops acquitted of felony ... http://articles.chicagotribune.com/2011-08-25/news/ct-met-eavesdropping-trial-0825-20110825_1_eavesdropping-law-police-officers-law-enforcement.

[54] Fees curb urge to appeal traffic tickets - Boston.com. http://www.boston.com/news/local/massachusetts/articles/2011/03/07/controversial_ticket_appeal_fees_to_have_sjc_hearing/.

[55] BOSTON POLICE DEPT. v. MOUGHALIAN, None ... - Casetext. https://casetext.com/case/boston-police-dept-v-moughalian.

[56] 42-92-1. http://www.rilin.state.ri.us/statutes/title42/42-92/42-92-1.HTM.

Chapter 11

[1] General Laws: CHAPTER 208, Section 1B - MAlegislature.gov. https://malegislature.gov/Laws/GeneralLaws/PartII/TitleIII/Chapter208/Section1B.

[2] FastStats - Marriage and Divorce. http://www.cdc.gov/nchs/nvss/marriage_divorce_tables.htm

[3] Cities Where Getting Divorce Will Cost You - Business Insider. http://www.businessinsider.com/cities-where-getting-divorce-will-cost-you-2013-11.

[4] Miller, DP. 2012. Falling Further Behind? Child Support Arrears and Fathers ... http://www.ncbi.nlm.nih.gov/pmc/articles/PMC3737002/.

[5] Cost of raising children not as high as government would ... http://www.caller.com/business/local/cost-of-raising-children-not-as-high-as-would.

[6] Costs of Raising Children: Texas | CFRP Child and Family ... http://childandfamilyresearch.org/research/corc/.

[7] Basics on Child Support - Minnesota Judicial Branch. http://www.mncourts.gov/selfhelp/?page=1171.

[8] Brinig, MF. 2000. Why Most Divorce Filers Are Women - The University of ...
http://www.unc.edu/courses/2010fall/econ/586/001/Readings/Brinig.pdf.

[9] Grall, TS. 2009. Custodial Mothers and Fathers and Their Child Support: 2007. https://www.census.gov/prod/2009pubs/p60-237.pdf.

[10] Chart: Grounds for Divorce and Residency Requirements ...
http://www.americanbar.org/content/dam/aba/publications/family_law_quarterly/vol45/4win12_chart4_divorce.authcheckdam.pdf.

[11] General Laws: CHAPTER 208, Section 34 - MAlegislature.gov. https://malegislature.gov/Laws/GeneralLaws/PartII/TitleIII/Chapter208/Section34.

[12] How DNA Testing Is Changing Fatherhood - NYTimes.com. http://www.nytimes.com/2009/11/22/magazine/22Paternity-t.html?pagewanted=all.

[13] Man Forced To Pay Child Support For 13 Years For Girl That ... http://houston.cbslocal.com/2015/03/25/man-forced-to-pay-child-support-for-13-years-for-girl-that-dna-proves-isnt-his/.

[14] 'The Divorce Process' - CBS News. http://www.cbsnews.com/news/the-divorce-process/.

[15] The Four Divorce Alternatives - Forbes. http://www.forbes.com/sites/jefflanders/2012/04/24/the-four-divorce-alternatives/.

[16] A jury in a divorce case? Yes, in Georgia | www.ajc.com. http://www.ajc.com/news/news/local/a-jury-in-a-divorce-case-yes-in-georgia/nQHdj/.

[17] family code chapter 6. suit for dissolution of marriage. http://www.statutes.legis.state.tx.us/Docs/FA/htm/FA.6.htm.

[18] General Laws: CHAPTER 208, Section 30 - MAlegislature.gov. https://malegislature.gov/Laws/GeneralLaws/PartII/TitleIII/Chapter208/Section30.

Chapter 12

[1] U.S. and World Population Clock - Census.gov. http://www.census.gov/popclock/.

[2] examining the work of state courts - Court Statistics Project.
http://www.courtstatistics.org/~/media/microsites/files/csp/ncsc_ewsc_web_nov_25_14.ashx.

[3] examining the work of state courts - Court Statistics Project.
http://www.courtstatistics.org/~/media/microsites/files/csp/ncsc_ewsc_web_nov_25_14.ashx.

[4] FBI — Clearances. http://www.fbi.gov/about-us/cjis/ucr/crime-in-the-u.s/2012/crime-in-the-u.s.-2012/offenses-known-to-law-enforcement/clearances.

[5] The Station nightclub fire - Wikipedia, the free encyclopedia. http://en.wikipedia.org/wiki/The_Station_nightclub_fire.

[6] FY 2012 Overview of Federal Criminal Cases | July 2013. http://www.ussc.gov/sites/default/files/pdf/research-and-publications/research-publications/2013/FY12_Overview_Federal_Criminal_Cases.pdf.

[7] Justice Deferred - Slate.
http://www.slate.com/articles/news_and_politics/jurisprudence/2015/03/cameron_todd_willingham_prosecutor_john_jackson_charges_corrupt_prosecution.html.

[8] NACDL - News Release ~ 05/05/2010. https://www.nacdl.org/NewsReleases.aspx?id=19556.

[9] reining in overcriminalization: assessing the problem ... http://www.gpo.gov/fdsys/pkg/CHRG-111hhrg58476/html/CHRG-111hhrg58476.htm.

[10] Title 11 - Delaware Code - State of Delaware. http://www.delcode.delaware.gov/title11/c005/sc07/index.shtml.

[11] SCREWS et al. v. UNITED STATES. | US Law | LII / Legal ... http://www.law.cornell.edu/supremecourt/text/325/91.

[12] 18 U.S. Code § 3559 - Sentencing classification of offenses ... http://www.law.cornell.edu/uscode/text/18/3559.

[13] CLASS 1 FELONIES - Arizona State Legislature. http://www.azleg.gov/alisPDFs/council/Felonies.pdf.

[14] Michigan Legislature - Section 750.30.
https://www.legislature.mi.gov/(S(3qjaut23kefbqm45u4g44q2p))/mileg.aspx?page=getobject&objectName=mcl-750-30.

[15] 11-30-113. Unlawful cutting of ears of sheep. - Justia. http://law.justia.com/codes/wyoming/2012/title11/chapter30/section11-30-113.

[16] All charges dropped against Rochester Hills man accused ... http://www.theoaklandpress.com/general-news/20120719/all-charges-dropped-against-rochester-hills-man-accused-of-reading-wifes-email-without-permission.

[17] Desk Doodling Arrest - Huffington Post. http://www.huffingtonpost.com/2010/02/05/desk-doodling-arrest-alex_n_450859.html.

[18] Boy, 13, arrested for passing gas | Bradenton Herald. http://www.bradenton.com/news/article34062843.html.

[19] Boy booked for opening Christmas present - wistv.com ... http://www.wistv.com/story/5774586/boy-booked-for-opening-christmas-present.

[20] 18 U.S. Code § 19 - Petty offense defined https://www.law.cornell.edu/uscode/text/18/19

[21] Lewis v. United States :: 518 US 322 (1996) - Justia US ... https://supreme.justia.com/cases/federal/us/518/322/case.html.

[22] Local Feeding the homeless: Act of charity or a crime?. http://www.floridatoday.com/story/news/local/2014/11/05/feeding-homeless-act-charity-crime/18562839/.

[23] Vegetable Garden Brings Criminal Charges in Oak Park ... http://abcnews.go.com/US/vegetable-garden-brings-criminal-charges-oak-park-michigan/story?id=14047214.

[24] Welty, J. 2014. Overcriminalization in North Carolina - North Carolina Law ... http://www.nclawreview.org/2014/08/overcriminalization-in-north-carolina/.

[25] 361 US 147 - Justia US Supreme Court Center. https://supreme.justia.com/cases/federal/us/361/147/case.html.

[26] United States v. Wulff, 758 F.2d 1121 | Casetext. https://casetext.com/case/united-states-v-wulff.

[27] James Duane (professor) - Wikipedia, the free encyclopedia. http://en.wikipedia.org/wiki/James_Duane_(professor).

[28] Innocent or guilty, what should you do if a Police officer says ... http://www.avvo.com/legal-guides/ugc/innocent-or-guilty-what-should-you-do-if-a-police-officer-says-she-would-like-to-talk-to-you.

[29] Supreme Court. 2010. BERGHUIS v. THOMPKINS - Legal Information Institute. http://www.law.cornell.edu/supct/html/08-1470.ZO.html.

[30] Information - Legal Dictionary - The Free Dictionary. http://legal-dictionary.thefreedictionary.com/information.

[31] State Court Organization, 1998: Part 6. http://www.bjs.gov/content/pub/pdf/sco9806.pdf.

[32] Grand Juries State Links | NCSC.org. http://www.ncsc.org/Topics/Jury/Grand-Juries/State-Links.aspx.

[33] State Court Organization 2004 - Bureau of Justice Statistics. http://www.bjs.gov/content/pub/pdf/sco04.pdf.

[34] Overview of Criminal Justice in Ohio - Bureau of Justice .... https://www.bjs.gov/content/pub/pdf/ocjo-obts.pdf.

[35] New York State Felony Processing Report Indictment ... http://www.criminaljustice.ny.gov/crimnet/ojsa/nys-felony-process-report2013.pdf.

[36] The single chart that shows that federal grand juries indict ... http://www.washingtonpost.com/blogs/wonkblog/wp/2014/11/24/the-single-chart-that-shows-that-grand-juries-indict-99-99-percent-of-the-time/.

[37] Criminal | USAO-WDVA | Department of Justice. http://www.justice.gov/usao-wdva/criminal.

[38] Criminal Cases | United States Courts - U.S. Courts. http://www.uscourts.gov/about-federal-courts/types-cases/criminal-cases.

[39] STATE v. MARTINEAU | FindLaw. http://caselaw.findlaw.com/nh-supreme-court/1454325.html.

[40] Rule 11. Pleas - Legal Information Institute - Cornell University. http://www.law.cornell.edu/rules/frcrmp/rule_11.

[41] Alschuler, A. 1979. Plea Bargaining and Its History - Chicago Unbound. http://chicagounbound.uchicago.edu/cgi/viewcontent.cgi?article=2005&context=journal_articles.

[42] Tens Of Thousands Of Innocent People Plead Guilty: Judge. http://www.huffingtonpost.com/2014/05/29/thousands-innocent-pled-guilty_n_5412494.html.

[43] Why Innocent People Plead Guilty by Jed S. Rakoff | The ... http://www.nybooks.com/articles/archives/2014/nov/20/why-innocent-people-plead-guilty/.

[44] Go to Trial: Crash the Justice System - NYTimes.com. http://www.nytimes.com/2012/03/11/opinion/sunday/go-to-trial-crash-the-justice-system.html.

[45] 404 US 257 - Justia US Supreme Court Center. https://supreme.justia.com/cases/federal/us/404/257/case.html.

[46] Houston DA resigns over e-mail scandal - USATODAY.com. http://usatoday30.usatoday.com/news/nation/2008-02-15-4147676836_x.htm.

[47] Ex-Casey Anthony prosecutor confirms Ashley Madison ... http://www.nydailynews.com/news/national/fla-attorney-jeffrey-ashton-confirms-ashley-madison-account-article-1.2334976.

[48] RSA 570-A:2 - NH General Court. http://www.gencourt.state.nh.us/rsa/html/lviii/570-a/570-a-2.htm.

[49] 12 U.S. Code § 3102 - Establishment of Federal branches ... http://www.law.cornell.edu/uscode/12/3102.html.

[50] NRS: CHAPTER 695D - PLANS FOR DENTAL CARE. https://www.leg.state.nv.us/NRS/NRS-695D.html.

[51] 18 US Code § 2511 - Interception and disclosure of wire, oral. https://www.law.cornell.edu/uscode/text/18/2511.

[52] NSA Spy Target Challenges Warrantless Wiretapping Law ... https://www.aclu.org/blog/nsa-spy-target-challenges-warrantless-wiretapping-law.

[53] On NSA Spying: A Letter to Congress by Ronald Dworkin ... http://www.nybooks.com/articles/archives/2006/feb/09/on-nsa-spying-a-letter-to-congress/.

[54] United States v. Beckton, No. 13-4037 - South Carolina Law ... http://sclawreview.org/united-states-v-beckton-13-4037/.

[55] Rule 611 - Legal Information Institute - Cornell University. http://www.law.cornell.edu/rules/fre/rule_611.

[56] 18 U.S. Code § 3553 - Imposition of a sentence | US Law ... http://www.law.cornell.edu/uscode/text/18/3553.

[57] 18 U.S. Code § 3624 - Release of a prisoner | LII / Legal ... http://www.law.cornell.edu/uscode/text/18/3624.

[58] 2012 Federal Sentencing Guidelines Manual - United States ... http://www.ussc.gov/sites/default/files/pdf/guidelines-manual/2012/manual-pdf/2012_Guidelines_Manual_Full.pdf.

[59] Rossman, D, and D Rossman. 1990. Were There no Appeal - Scholarly Commons - Northwestern ... http://scholarlycommons.law.northwestern.edu/cgi/viewcontent.cgi?article=6667&context=jclc.

[60] Massachusetts Criminal Procedure Rule 29 - Mass.Gov. http://www.mass.gov/courts/case-legal-res/rules-of-court/criminal-procedure/crim29.html.

[61] Massachusetts Criminal Procedure Rule 30 - Mass.Gov. http://www.mass.gov/courts/case-legal-res/rules-of-court/criminal-procedure/crim30.html.

[62] FBI — Arrest Disposition Submission. http://www.fbi.gov/about-us/cjis/fingerprints_biometrics/arrest-disposition-submission.

[63] Title 11 - Delaware Code - State of Delaware. http://www.delcode.delaware.gov/title11/c043/sc07/index.shtml.

[64] Commonwealth - Pardons. https://commonwealth.virginia.gov/judicial-system/pardons/.

[65] Clemency - Florida Commission on Offender Review. https://www.fcor.state.fl.us/clemencyOverview.shtml.

[66] General Laws: CHAPTER 276, Section 100A - Massachusetts. https://malegislature.gov/Laws/GeneralLaws/Chapter276/Section100A.

[67] Not guilty, but stuck with big bills, damaged career - USA ... http://usatoday30.usatoday.com/news/washington/judicial/2010-09-27-hyde-federal-prosecutors_N.htm.

Chapter 13

[1] International Guide - Debt Collection in The United States. http://www.alqlist.com/internationalguide.html.

[2] The secret world of government debt collection - CNN Money. http://money.cnn.com/interactive/pf/debt-collector/government-agencies/.

[3] Fair Debt Collection Practices Act - Wikipedia, the free ... https://en.wikipedia.org/wiki/Fair_Debt_Collection_Practices_Act.

[4] 15 U.S. Code § 1692a - Definitions | US Law | LII / Legal ... http://www.law.cornell.edu/uscode/15/1692a.html.

[5] "HOLMES v. TELECREDIT SERVICE CORP. | Leagle.com." 10 Aug. 2015 http://www.leagle.com/decision/19902025736FSupp1289_11832.xml/HOLMES%20v.%20TELECREDIT%20SERVICE%20CORP.

[6] Fair Debt Collection Practices Act - Wikipedia, the free ... https://en.wikipedia.org/wiki/Fair_Debt_Collection_Practices_Act.

[7] Submit a complaint > Consumer Financial Protection Bureau. http://www.consumerfinance.gov/complaint/.

[8] NAAG | Who's My AG? - National Association of Attorneys ... http://www.naag.org/naag/attorneys-general/whos-my-ag.php.

[9] Time-Barred Debts | Consumer Information. http://www.consumer.ftc.gov/articles/0117-time-barred-debts.

[10] "Text - H.R.2419 - 110th Congress (2007-2008): Food ... - Congress.gov." https://www.congress.gov/bill/110th-congress/house-bill/2419/text.

[11] If I dispute a debt that is being collected, can a debt collector ... http://www.consumerfinance.gov/askcfpb/338/if-i-dispute-a-debt-that-is-being-collected-can-a-debt-collector-still-try-to-collect-debt-from-me.html.

Chapter 14

[1] Millennials: Forever Renters? - The Atlantic. http://www.theatlantic.com/business/archive/2015/10/millennials-forever-renters/412165/.

[2] Dealing With Problems - Department of Consumer Affairs. http://www.dca.ca.gov/publications/landlordbook/problems.shtml.

[3] JAVINS V. FIRST NATIONAL REALTY CORPORATION, 428 ... https://casetext.com/case/javins-v-first-national-realty-corporation.

[4] CA Codes (civ:1940-1954.1). http://www.leginfo.ca.gov/cgi-bin/displaycode?section=civ&group=01001-02000&file=1940-1954.1.

[5] CA Codes (hsc:17920-17928). http://www.leginfo.ca.gov/cgi-bin/displaycode?section=hsc&group=17001-18000&file=17920-17928.

[6] "Hinson v. Delis (1972) :: :: California Court of Appeal ... - Justia Law." https://law.justia.com/cases/california/court-of-appeal/3d/26/62.html.
[7] EDWARDS V. HABIB, 397 F.2d 687 (D.C. Cir. 1968) | Casetext. https://casetext.com/case/edwards-v-habib.
[8] Unfair Rental Practices details - DATCP.Wisconsin.gov. http://datcp.wi.gov/uploads/Consumer/pdf/UnfairRentalPracticesDetails.pdf.
[9] "§ 18-16-101 - Failure to pay rent -- Refusal to vacate upon ... - Justia Law." https://law.justia.com/codes/arkansas/2010/title-18/subtitle-2/chapter-16/subchapter-1/18-16-101.

Chapter 15

[1] Probing Probate: What You Should Know - For Dummies. http://www.dummies.com/how-to/content/probing-probate-what-you-should-know.html.
[2] Taxation: The Probate Process | Semmes Estate Planning ... http://www.semmes.com/practice_areas/estates-probates-trust/probate-process.asp.
[3] probate dispute - American Bar Association.
http://www.americanbar.org/newsletter/publications/law_trends_news_practice_area_e_newsletter_home/0506_estate_probate.html.
[4] Reasons to Challenge a Will - FindLaw - Estate Planning. http://estate.findlaw.com/wills/reasons-to-challenge-a-will.html.

Chapter 16

[1] USPTO Fee Schedule | USPTO. http://www.uspto.gov/learning-and-resources/fees-and-payment/uspto-fee-schedule.
[2] 2701- - United States Patent and Trademark Office. http://www.uspto.gov/web/offices/pac/mpep/s2701.html.
[3] PARKER v. TIME WARNER ENTERTAINMENT CO., L.P. ...
http://www.leagle.com/decision/In%20FDCO%2020090707765.xml/PARKER%20v.%20TIME%20WARNER%20ENTERTAINMENT%20CO.,%20L.P..
[4] Noah v. AOL Time Warner, Inc., 261 F. Supp. 2d 532 ... - Justia. http://law.justia.com/cases/federal/district-courts/FSupp2/261/532/2515648/.
[5] Workers compensation | Wex Legal Dictionary ... http://www.law.cornell.edu/wex/workers_compensation.
[6] The Demolition of Workers' Compensation - ProPublica. https://www.propublica.org/article/the-demolition-of-workers-compensation.
[7] RANKIN v. HOWARD | Leagle.com. http://www.leagle.com/decision/19801477633F2d844_11364.xml/RANKIN%20v.%20HOWARD.
[8] 435 US 349 - Justia US Supreme Court Center. https://supreme.justia.com/cases/federal/us/435/349/case.html.
[9] "GROSS v. RELL, 585 F.3d 72 (2d Cir. 2009) | Casetext." https://casetext.com/case/gross-v-rell.
[10] M12-0011 - Rhode Island Judiciary. https://www.courts.ri.gov/Courts/rhodeislandtraffictribunal/Decisions/M12-0011.pdf.
[11] 13-26 - Rhode Island Judiciary. https://www.courts.ri.gov/Courts/districtcourt/appeals/decisions/13-26.pdf.
[12] 40 Mass. App. Ct. 42 - Mass Cases. http://masscases.com/cases/app/40/40massappct42.html.
[13] Identity Theft | Consumer Information. https://www.consumer.ftc.gov/topics/identity-theft.
[14] Identity Theft | CRIMINAL-FRAUD | Department of Justice. http://www.justice.gov/criminal-fraud/identity-theft/identity-theft-and-identity-fraud.
[15] FBI — Identity Theft - Federal Bureau of Investigation. https://www.fbi.gov/about-us/investigate/cyber/identity_theft.

one humanity, one justice — **Mark Knopfler of Dire Straits, stated during the concert celebrating Nelson Mandela's 70th birthday at Wembley Stadium 1988**

Printed in Great Britain
by Amazon